NELSON'S
BIG BOOK
OF LAUGHTER

150 Illustrations and
Thousands of Smiles
from A to Z

LOWELL D. STREIKER

NELSON

Published in Nashville, Tennessee, by Thomas Nelson, Inc.

ART CREDITS: Illustrations in this collection are from the following sources, and are used by permission: Corel Corp., BCM Graphics, and Grin Graphics. (BCM Graphics and Grin Graphics are distributed by Lowell Streiker, 3309 El Camino Dr., Cottonwood, CA 96022.)

ISBN 0-7852-4514-6

Printed in the United States of America

Acknowledgments

THANKS TO:

Eric Petritsch, Access guru extraordinaire, for database guidance.

Ron Dentinger. One of the great aphorists of our time, Ron Dentinger is a corporate comedian. From his home in Dodgeville, Wisconsin, he travels coast-to-coast on the banquet circuit. Various jokes in this book are from his book, *Down Time,* published by Kendall/Hunt, and are used with his permission or from his columns (also titled, "Down Time") in *The Dodgeville* [Wisconsin] *Chronicle.* Ron may be reached by phone at (606) 935-2417.

James "Doc" Blakely, CSP, CPAE, professional humorist/speaker for permission to use material from the book, *How the Platform Professionals Keep 'em Laughin'.* Doc may be contacted at 3404 Fairway Drive, Wharton, TX 77488.

Mel Gibbon and Make 'em Laugh, Ltd. for permission to use selections from their 1000-cartoon collection. They may be contacted by calling (800) 874-3668 or by e-mail at ussales@makemlaugh.com.

Gabe Martin for his *Borderline* cartoons.

Max Hengeveld and Gospel Communications for permission to use Rev. Fun cartoons. Max may be reached at max@gospelcom.net, (616) 773-3361, ext. 247, P.O. Box 455, Muskegon, MI 49443; http://www.gospelcom.net/~max.

Agnes Stogdell. My wife's "Aunt Aggie" helped in the selection of material from many, many sources. She proofread and offered advice (as well as lemon meringue and pecan pies).

Connie Streiker—my wife, who laughed and/or moaned and groaned as I tried out anecdotes on her, often interrupting her reading or TV viewing. No one could have been more supportive!

Charles T. Miles of Grin Graphics and Gary Cooper for their clever artwork.

And my thanks to Teri Wilhelms, Editorial Director, and Ramona Richards, CD-rom Editor, at Thomas Nelson, for their attention to detail and their sense of humor. And thanks to John Adams and Jennifer Zimmerman of ProtoType Graphics, Nashville, Tennessee, for their diligence in turning my files into this readable book.

He Who Laughs, Lasts!

An essay on humor by Lowell D. Streiker

Mark Twain observed that humans are the only animals that blush—or need to. And Samuel Butler notes, "Man is the only animal that laughs and has a state legislature." We laugh because we sense the contradiction between the way things are and the way they ought to be. The same impulse that makes us religious also makes us humorous. As a minister, I have found humor a valuable resource as I have sought to communicate spiritual truths to church audiences on Sunday mornings. Sometimes the truth contained in a humorous story or quip gains attention while the same truth in its usual prosaic form is ignored or taken for granted.

Sometimes, to quote actor Woody Harrelson, "the only way to get a serious message across is through comedy." Also the humorous illustrations in a talk, a lecture, or a sermon are remembered long after the other content of the address is forgotten. As Isaac Asimov, author of hundreds of books and lifetime collector of humorous anecdotes, once related, "Jokes of the proper kind, properly told, can do more to enlighten questions of politics, philosophy, and literature than any number of dull arguments." Actor-comedian John Cleese maintains, "If I can get you to laugh with me, you like me better, which makes you more open to my ideas. And if I can persuade you to laugh at the particular point I make, by laughing at it you acknowledge its truth." And Joel Goodman remarks, "Mirth can be a major tool for insight, changing 'ha-ha' to 'aha.'"

This is a collection of some of my all-time favorite anecdotes, jokes, quips, and witty comments. I trust that they will be of value to you as you meet and communicate with others—whatever your vocation may be. Laughter is a powerful force and it is yours to use whether you are a public speaker, a minister, a teacher, a salesman, an office worker, a psychologist, or a plumber!

The laughter encouraged by this collection is supportive of human dignity. It is life-affirming and life-giving. And it is, to borrow a word from religion, prophetic. It comforts the afflicted and afflicts the comfortable. It ennobles our spirits and extends our love to others.

I believe that God is a fantastic humorist and we are all his jokes. God fills each of our lives with more irony and coincidence than a Shakespearean comedy or an afternoon soap opera.

Did you know that Jesus was a fabulous comedian? It is hard to read his parables without laughing. They are filled with irony, wit, and surprise endings. His teachings are replete with hyperbole and exaggeration: "If your eye offends you, pluck it out . . . Don't be so concerned about the speck in your brother's eye. Take care of the rafter in your own." He puts the pretentious and pompous in their place. He celebrates the triumph of little people. If only we could see the smile on his face, we might understand him much better. If I had to summarize his teachings in a single sentence, that sentence would be: "The first shall be last and the laughs shall be first."

Many observers claim that a sense of humor is essential to mental well-being and good physical health. When struggling to overcome a painful and debilitating disease, Norman Cousins discovered, "Ten minutes of genuine belly laughter had an anesthetic effect and would give me at least two hours of pain-free sleep." As Anne Wilson Schaef recognizes, "A chuckle a day may not keep the doctor away, but it sure does make those times in life's waiting room a little more bearable." Mahatma Gandhi confessed, "If I had no sense of humor, I should long ago have committed suicide."

"Laughter," says an anonymous commentator, "is like changing a baby's diaper—it doesn't permanently solve any problems, but it makes things more acceptable for a while." Psychologist Rollo May explains, "Humor is the healthy way of feeling 'distance' between one's self and the problem, a way of standing off and looking at one's problems with perspective." And to quote Anne Wilson Schaef again, "I realize that humor isn't for everyone. It's only for people who want to have fun, enjoy life, and feel alive."

I have read that Saint Theresa of Ávila "always looked for novices who knew how to laugh, eat, and sleep. She was sure that if they ate heartily they were healthy, if they slept well they were more likely free of serious sin, and if they laughed they had the necessary disposition to survive a difficult life."

As serious a person as Billy Graham recognizes the value of humor. He writes: "A keen sense of humor helps us to overlook the unbecoming, understand the unconventional, tolerate the unpleasant, overcome the unexpected, and outlast the unbearable."

Laughter, of course, can be helpful or harmful. It can be derisive. It can ridicule whatever and whomever we fear, we misunderstand, we resent. Hence, there are racial and ethnic jokes, in-law jokes, sexist jokes, etc. Archie Bunker is never far away in American humor.

In this collection, I have sought to avoid being unnecessarily offensive—which means that at times I may have been a bit rough on someone in order to make a point. Remember what I said about "afflicting the comfortable." Pompous, self-important, insensitive people are always fair game to the humorist. Even so, I have attempted not to be mean-spirited. All humor walks this fine line.

And I have selected "good, clean" anecdotes and jokes. If I could not tell a story from the pulpit or when speaking on television, it is not in this collection.

But let me do more than tell you about this collection and how it can be of value to you. Let me show you exactly what the laughter evoked by a good story can do. (All of the following anecdotes are taken from the body of this collection.)

Laughter sets things in their proper perspective. I am reminded of the college student who wrote to her parents as follows:

"Dear Mom and Dad, I'm sorry to be so long in writing, but all my writing paper was lost the night the dormitory burned down. I'm out of the hospital now, and the doctor says my eyesight should be back to normal sooner or later. The wonderful boy, Bill, who rescued me from the fire, kindly offered to share his little apartment with me until the dorm is rebuilt. He comes from a good family, so you won't be surprised when I tell you we are going to be married. In fact you always wanted a grandchild, so you will be glad to know you will be grandparents early next year." Then she added this postscript: "Please disregard the above practice in English composition. There was no fire. I haven't been in the hospital. I'm not pregnant. And I don't have a steady boyfriend. But I did get a 'D' in French and an 'F' in chemistry, and I wanted to be sure you received the news in proper perspective. Love, Mary."

Laughter is the great leveler:

Three burly fellows on huge motorcycles pulled up to a highway cafe where a truck driver, just a little guy, was perched on a stool quietly eating his lunch. As the three fellows came in, they spotted him, grabbed his food away from him and laughed in his face. The truck driver said nothing. He got up, paid for his food and walked out. One of the three cyclists, unhappy that they hadn't succeeded in provoking the little [guy] into a fight commented to the waitress: "Boy, he sure wasn't much of a man, was he?" The waitress replied, "Well, I guess not." Then looking out the window, she added, "I guess he's not much of a truck driver, either. He just ran over three motorcycles."

Laughter keeps us from taking ourselves too seriously:

I was once invited to speak at a local Rotary club. I felt flattered by the invitation until the master of ceremonies rose to introduce me. "Unfortunately," he said, "our original choice to be today's speaker is unable to attend." Then, in a clumsy attempt at humor, he pointed to a broken window pane which had been covered over with a piece of cardboard. "Our speaker," he said, "is like that piece of cardboard in the window. He's a substitute." Being somewhat taken aback by the ungraceful introduction, I decided to show them: Substitute or not I would knock their socks off. And I did! When I finished the speech, I received a standing ovation. But when the emcee returned to the lectern, his attempt to thank me was even more awkward than his introduction. "Reverend," he said, "we want you to know that you were not at all like a cardboard substitute. You were a real pane!"

That humiliation was nothing compared to what happened later. After the meeting, the club president gave me a check for $100. I gave it back and told him to use it for his club's favorite charity. He said, "Oh, good, we can put it in our 'special fund,' the one we use to pay for really good speakers!"

Actually neither incident really happened to me. They are anecdotes which I applied to myself so that my audience could have a laugh at my expense. And since I am in a profession that is notorious for taking itself too seriously, such self-deflating humor is of enormous value.

Lenoard I. Sweet, President of United Theological Seminary in Dayton, Ohio, gives a vivid illustration from his own career.

It was my first "stewardship campaign." I had been appointed by the bishop to the missionary church in a small-college community in New York's Genessee Valley. The first year had been a nervous one for both me, a young, not-dry-behind-the-ears pastor and wetback Ph.D., and the congregation which was comprised of an odd and unconsummated coupling of rural folk and "academic types." But there was significant enough progress to warrant the belief that we could double the budget after my first year there. If only we had a slogan . . . some catchy motto or jingle around which to design our development campaign.

Or so I thought. The weekend before the "Stewardship Sunday" kick-off, I sought some solitary confinement in Toronto, Canada. There I hit first on a slogan and then an idea: Why not have T-shirts made up for those "every-member canvassers" who could then call on parishioners emblazoned with my newly brainstormed stewardship theme: It seemed the perfect plan.

During the "Community Concerns" time of the morning worship the next Sunday, the chair of the campaign, Doug Klapper, did an outstanding job of making the committee's case for our controversial financial leap forward. As soon as he finished, I bolted to the front, prevented him from returning to his seat, and presented him with a "surprise gift" that I announced confidently would give our campaign focus and force.

The color of Doug's face when he unwrapped his "surprise gift" should have alerted me to what was to come. His embarrassed refusal ("You do it," he giggled) to hold up the T-shirt for the congregation to see was another missed warning signal. But it was not until the moment that I held up that T-shirt and announced that there were enough of these "surprise gifts" for every one of our canvassers to wear that I realized exactly what I had done. Our stewardship slogan would be, I proudly read,

I Upped My Pledge.
Up Yours

I had lost it. At first a trickling tickle, then a torrent of laughter. I tried to preach. But convulsions of laughter drowned out my sermon at unpredictable moments, ebbing and flowing like a moonshine tide. But that moment of my greatest embarrassment and mistake, a moment from which that worship service never fully recovered, was the moment of my ministry's recovery in that community. For suddenly this upstart preacher and hotshot Ph.D. became human, and could do something so outrageously stupid and foolish that it redeemed all his jarring strangeness. From that Sunday on, I became their pastor and was bonded to them for life. And for the next seven years, as I walked the streets of the village, I would find myself greeted with the query, "Are you the 'up-yours' preacher?"

As a pastor, Dr. Sweet was no longer affected by that debilating disease of preachers, terminal seriousness. In the eyes of his congregation, he was no longer a stranger, he was a human being who—just like them—could "do something . . . outrageously stupid and foolish." As humor writer Larry Wilde proclaims, "If you are willing to make yourself the butt of a joke, you become one of the guys, a human being, and people are more willing to listen to what you have to say."

A story that punctures the pomposity of experts in general and ministers in particular is told about:

. . . an engineer, a psychologist, and a theologian [who] were hunting in the wilds of northern Canada. [Suddenly, the temperature dropped and a snowstorm descended, lashing them with its fury. As they trudged on, they] . . . came across an isolated cabin, far removed from any town. Because friendly hospitality is a virtue practiced by those who live in the wilderness, the hunters knocked on the door to ask permission to rest.

No one answered their knocks, but, discovering the cabin was unlocked, they entered. It was a simple place—two rooms with a minimum of furniture and household equipment. Nothing was surprising about the cabin except the stove. It was large, potbellied, and made of cast iron. What was unusual was its location: it was suspended in midair by wires attached to the ceiling beams.

"Fascinating," said the psychologist [, stroking his beard]. "It is obvious that this lonely trapper, isolated from humanity, has elevated his stove so he can curl up under it and vicariously experience a return to the womb."

"Nonsense!" replied the engineer [as he scratched some calculations in the dust on the cabin floor]. "The man is practicing the laws of thermodynamics. By elevating his stove, he has discovered a way to distribute heat more evenly throughout the cabin."

"With all due respect," interrupted the theologian, [folding his hands in a gesture of piety,] "I'm sure that hanging his stove from the ceiling has religious meaning. Fire LIFTED UP has been a religious symbol for centuries."

The three debated the point for several hours without resolving the issue. When the trapper finally returned, they immediately asked him why he had hung his heavy potbellied stove from the ceiling.

His answer was succinct: "Had plenty of wire, not much stove pipe!"

Humor, notes Southern folklorist Loyal Jones, "helps us keep objective, reminds us that we are fallible, that we are not the center of the unvierse, and that there is a whole lot that we do not know and still more that we don't understand. Humor puts us in our place just as the teachings of Jesus do. Humor reiterates what he said: The one who exalts himself shall be humbled and the one who humbles himself shall be exalted.

But humor does more than encourage humility.

Laughter makes pain palatable:

A group of high school students went to New York for their senior trip. They had reserved rooms in one of the finest hotels. When they arrived in the city they went to the hotel and registered. A bellhop led them to their rooms, which were on the 30th floor. After getting settled in their rooms they went out to see the sights. They went to Rockefeller Center, the United Nations Plaza, the Guggenheim Museum, the Empire State Building, the Statue of Liberty, etc. Finally they came back to their hotel, utterly exhausted. They went to the desk and asked for the keys to their rooms.

The clerk said, "I am sorry, the elevators are not running. You will have to walk up or wait until the elevators are repaired."

They were so weary that all they could think of were the comfortable beds in their rooms. Tired as they were, they decided they would climb the thirty flights of stairs. One of them had an idea. He said, "On the way up, each of us will tell the funniest story we know." The others agreed and they started the climb. When they reached the tenth floor they were still going strong.

When they reached the twentieth floor their legs were like lead and they were panting for breath. The steps got longer and longer but they trudged on. The one whose turn it was to tell the next funny story said, "I'm sorry, I'm just too exhausted to laugh."

They trudged on in silence. When they reached the 29th floor, one of them began to laugh. He sat down on the steps and almost had hysterics. Finally, he said, "I have just thought of one of the funniest things I have ever heard of in my life."

The others said, "What is it? Tell us!"

He said, "Our room keys—we left them in the lobby!"

Laughter is therapeutic.

It can mend anything from a broken heart to the crack of dawn. From Alison Crane, executive director of the American Association for Therapeutic Humor, comes a story originally told to her by a middle-aged pastor:

I had a very serious accident a few years ago; it was amazing I survived. And, of course, I was in the hospital for a very long time recuperating.

Because I was there for so long, I became rather nonchalant with the nurses about the procedures they subjected me to—you can't keep decorum up for very long with no clothes on. I was also having trouble finding a relatively painless spot to put yet another injection of pain medication.

One time I rang for the nurse, and when she came on the intercom, I told her I needed another pain shot. I knew it would take just about as long for her to draw up the medication as it would for me to gather the strength to roll over and find a spot for her to inject it. I had succeeded in rolling over, facing away from the door, when I heard her come in. "I think this area here isn't too bad," I said, pointing to an exposed area of my rear. But there was an awful silence after I said that. My face paled as I rolled over slowly to see who had actually come in—it was one of my twenty-two-year-old parishioners. I apologized and tried to chat with her, but she left shortly thereafter, horribly embarrassed.

Well, about thirty seconds after she left, the impact of the situation hit me and I started to laugh. It hurt like you can't imagine, but I laughed and laughed. Tears were rolling down my face and I was gasping when my nurse finally came in. She asked what had happened. I tried to tell her, but couldn't say more than a word or two before convulsing into laughing fits again. Amused, she told me she would give me a few minutes to calm down and she'd be back to give me my shot.

I had just started to regain my composure when my nurse reappeared and asked again what had happened. I started to tell her, but got to laughing again, and she started to laugh just from watching me, which made it worse. Finally, she left again, promising to try back in fifteen more minutes. This scenario repeated itself a couple of more times, and by the time I could tell her what had happened, I felt absolutely no pain. None. I didn't need medication for three more hours. And I know it was an emotional turning point in my recovery.

As an editorial writer for the *Chicago Tribune* declared about the therapeutic power of humor:

> Jokes are no laughing matter to the brain. They are a type of release valve that enables us to think the unthinkable, accept the unacceptable, discover new relationships, adjust better and maintain our mental health. They are also funny. Without them we probably would be a dull, dimwitted society, trapped in a harsh world too serious to bear.

And finally,

Laughter reminds us how poorly we communicate with others and how readily we misunderstand those who communicate with us:

> There was a nice lady, a minister's widow, who was a little old-fashioned. She was planning a week's vacation in California at Skylake Yosemite campground (Bass Lake, to the uninitiated), but she wanted to make sure of the accommodations first. Uppermost in her mind were bathroom facilities, but she couldn't bring herself to write "toilet" in a letter. After considerable deliberation, she settled on "bathroom commode," but when she wrote that down, it still sounded too forward, so, after the first page of her letter, she referred to the bathroom commode as "BC." "Does the cabin where I will be staying have its own 'BC'? If not, where is the 'BC' located?" is what she actually wrote.
>
> The campground owner took the first page of the letter and the lady's check and gave it to his secretary. He put the remainder of the letter on the desk of the senior member of his staff without noticing that the staffer would have no way of knowing what "BC" meant. Then the owner went off to town to run some errands.
>
> The staff member came in after lunch, found the letter, and was baffled by the euphemism, so he showed the letter around to several counselors, but they couldn't decipher it either. The staff member's wife, who knew that the lady was the widow of a famous Baptist preacher, was sure that it must be a question about the local Baptist Church. "Of course," the first staffer exclaimed, " 'BC' stands for 'Baptist Church.' " And he sat down and wrote:
>
> *Dear Madam,*
>
> *I regret very much the delay in answering your letter, but I now take the pleasure in informing you that the BC is located nine miles north of the campground and is capable of seating 250 people at one time. I*

admit it is quite a distance away if you are in the habit of going regularly, but no doubt you will be pleased to know that a great number of people take their lunches along and make a day of it. They usually arrive early and stay late.

The last time my wife and I went was six years ago, and it was so crowded we had to stand up the whole time we were there. It may interest you to know that right now there is a supper planned to raise money to buy more seats. They are going to hold it in the basement of the ''BC.''

I would like to say that it pains me very much not to be able to go more regularly, but it is surely not lack of desire on my part. As we grow older, it seems to be more of an effort, particularly in cold weather.

If you decide to come down to our campground, perhaps I could go with you the first time, sit with you, and introduce you to all the folks. Remember, this is a friendly community.

Well, the particular local church each of us attends is also a friendly community, and a community that knows there is a time for laughter. We know that God cares, that he takes away our sorrows and turns them into delight. We know that God weeps with us when we weep and laughs with us when we laugh.

So here is Dr. Lowell's prescription for being happy and spreading happiness: take two jokes before you go to bed and call in the morning—or whenever you have a laugh to spare. And the next time you see someone on the street who appears to have no happiness in him, not even a smile to share, give him one of yours.

Finally, always remember: laughter is an expression of confidence—in God, in yourself, in the future. Laugh and you will endure. Laugh and you will triumph. Laugh and you will overcome adversity. In simplest terms: He who laughs, LASTS!

ACCIDENTS

A kindhearted farmer came upon a young boy who had just lost a load of hay along the side of the road, and suggested that the boy come home with him and have dinner before reloading the wagon. The boy said he didn't think his father would like that, but the farmer persisted, and finally the boy agreed. After eating dinner and relaxing a bit, the farmer drove the boy back to the scene of the accident, and started to help him put the hay back on the wagon. "By the way," the farmer said, "you're awfully young to be pitching this hay yourself. Where's your father?" "He's under this hay," the boy replied.

—How the Platform Professionals Keep 'em Laughin'

In filling out an application for a factory job, a man was puzzled for a long time over this question: "Person to notify in case of accident." Finally he wrote: "Anybody in sight."

For 27 years, Uncle Irv had never been late for work. However, one morning instead of checking in at 9:00, he arrived at 10:00. His face was crisscrossed with adhesive tape, and his right arm was in a sling. His neck was in a brace. Mr. Benson, his boss, demanded to know why he was late. Irv explained, "I leaned out a window after breakfast and fell three stories." His boss just shrugged and said, "What, that takes an hour?"

A man was hit by a car, and as he lay in the street waiting for an ambulance, an onlooker covered him with a jacket and propped his head on a pillow. "Are you comfortable?" the helper asked. The injured man replied, "I make a living."

ACTORS

Dustin Farnum, a talented but conceited actor, once droned on to his dinner host, writer Oliver Herford, about a play he was doing at the time. "Why, yesterday," boasted Farnum, "I had the audience glued to their seats." To which Herford replied, "How clever of you to think of it!"

My old drama coach used to say, "Don't just do something, stand there."

—Clint Eastwood

A Broadway producer hired a talented young actor whose ego became more inflated with each hit. After another successful opening night, the actor strutted haughtily off the stage. Just as he disappeared into the wings, there was a loud explosion in the street. "By golly," the producer gasped, "his head's burst."

—Joe Martinez

~

The hero of the small-town theatrical performance was to jump into a river. As he leaped offstage, the sound-effects girl was supposed to make appropriate splashing sounds in a tub of water. One night, however, she missed her cue, and the actor hit the floor with a mighty thud, but no splash. There was a moment of dead silence. Then, out of the wings, came the feeble voice of the actor: "My goodness! The river is completely frozen over!"   —Gene Brower

~

A young actor was cast in a performance of *Julius Caesar*. One evening, at the height of the dramatic scene portraying Caesar's brutal stabbing, an offstage phone suddenly rang. Without missing a beat, the actor lifted his head and said, "What do we tell them if it's for Caesar?" —Terrence Currier, WETA-FM

~

An actress was belittling the late Marie Dressler's comedy. "What dignity is there in making people laugh?" she squeaked. "I make them cry." Miss Dressler retorted: "Any onion can do that. Show me a vegetable that can make people laugh."

ADS

A New Zealand publication carried an intriguing advertisement of a tested and proven method for cutting household bills in half. It offered prospective customers the opportunity to get in on the secret for only $3. How could the promoters guarantee such fantastic results? That was what the police wanted to know. They found that the advertisers planned to send each customer a cheap pair of scissors.   —King Duncan

~

A TV commercial I saw while staying in Seattle had an interesting claim near the end: "Pepsi products now contain 25 percent recycled plastic." I wonder if Coke paid for the ad?

~

An ad in a British newspaper: Circumstances force me to sell 1979 Volvo 144, good condition, will accept smaller car in part exchange for wife.

~

Personal ad in local paper: "David G. Contact me soon! Bring three rings: Engagement, wedding and teething. Have news.—Debbie."

I, my wife and children regret to announce the opening of my office all day Saturday for the convenience of working mothers and fathers who have found it impossible to accommodate my previous office hours. Please don't invite me to any more Friday night parties.

> —Notice from a dentist in the Ocean County, N.J., *Times-Observer*

Hauling—You holler and I'll hauler.   —Lancaster-Fairfield, Ohio, *Advertiser*

I find some amazing things in the newspapers. These are actual classified ads:

- From the Saginaw, Michigan, *News:* For Sale—Eight puppies from a German Shepherd and an Alaskan Hussy.
- From the Roanoke, Illinois, *Review:* Hope chest—brand new, half price, long story.
- From the Help Wanted ads in a Michigan paper: Adult or mature teenager to baby-sit. One dollar an hour—plus fridge benefits.
- From the Los Altos, California, *Town Crier:* Lost: Gray and white female cat. Answers to electric can opener.
- Midwest newspaper ad: Idaho bachelor wants wife. Must be interested in farming and own tractor. Please enclose picture of tractor.
- From the *New York Times:* Young man, Democrat, would like to meet young lady, Republican. Object: third party.
- Notice: to the person or persons who took the large pumpkin on Highway 87 near Southridge storage: please return the pumpkin and be checked. Pumpkin may be radioactive. All other plants in vicinity are dead.
- Tired of working for only $9.75 per hour? We offer profit sharing and flexible hours. Starting pay: $7–$9 per hour.
- Help Wanted: Busy lawyer seeks alert young woman to serve as deceptionist.
- For Rent: One-bedroom apt. Adults, no pets. Well, maybe a cat.
- Help wanted: Saleslady for cosmetic counter in department store. Must like people part or full time.
- Help wanted: Secretary wants job; no bad habits; willing to learn.
- From a display ad for an automotive dealership in Cleveland, Tenn.: "Why go anywhere else and get cheated when you can come here!"
- The Orange Street Food Farm ran an ad in the Missoula, Mont., *Missoulian* for "Golden, Ripe, Boneless Bananas, 39 cents a pound."
- Help wanted: From the York, Pa., *Daily Record:* Attention: Good hours, excellent pay, fun place to work, paid training, mean boss. Oh well, four out of five isn't bad.

FOR SALE:

- 1 man, 7 woman hot tub—$850/offer
- Snow blower . . . only used on snowy days.
- Free puppies . . . part German Shepherd—part dog
- 2 wire mesh butchering gloves: 1 5-finger, 1 3-finger, pair: $15
- '83 Toyota hunchback—$2000

- Star Wars job of the hut—$15
- Free puppies: ½ Cocker Spaniel—½ sneaky neighbor's dog
- Free Yorkshire Terrier. 8 years old. Unpleasant little dog.
- German Shepherd 85 lbs. Neutered. Speaks German. Free.
- Free 1 can of pork and beans with purchase of 3 br 2 bath home.
- For sale: Lee Majors (6 Million Dollar Man)—$50
- Nordic Track $300 hardly used. Call Chubbie
- Shakespeare's Pizza—free chopsticks
- Hummels—largest selection ever. If it's in stock, we have it!
- Harrisburg postal employees gun club
- Georgia peaches—California grown—89 cents lb.
- Nice parachute: never opened—used once—slightly stained
- Free: farm kittens. Ready to eat.
- American flag—60 stars—pole included $100
- Exercise equipment: queen size mattress and box springs—$175.
- Joining nudist colony! Must sell washer and dryer $300.
- Ground beast: 99 cents lb.
- Open house—Body Shapers Toning Salon—free coffee and donuts.
- Fully cooked boneless smoked man—$2.09 lb.
- Puppies for sale. Mother registered AKC St. Bernard. Father, a VERY REMARK-ABLE beagle.
- 100-year-old brass bed. Perfect for antique lovers.
- Amana washer $100. Owned by clean bachelor who seldom washed.
- Complete set of *Encyclopedia Britannica*. 45 volumes. Excellent condition. $1,000.00 or best offer. No longer needed. Got married last weekend. Wife knows everything.
- Monster! John Deere, 38″, front-end, snow blower. Hurls snow from your drive well onto neighbor's property. (I did, he got mad, that's why I'm selling.)
- We put up the loot; daughter won't toot. First $175 takes the flute.
- Free Tasmanian devil. Currently disguised as small puppy. Good watchdog.
- Van—'94 Dodge Grand Caravan. One owner, lady driver, loaded
- Fiberglass boat, 2 sets of sails & spinnaker, trailer. Must sell, crew pregnant.

ADULTS

Adults are obsolete children.

—Dr. Seuss

When childhood dies, its corpses are called adults.

—Brian Aldiss

Here I am, fifty-eight, and I still don't know what I want to be when I grow up.

—Peter Drucker

Adults are always asking kids what they want to be when they grow up because they are looking for ideas.

—Paula Poundstone

ADVERTISING

There is truth in advertising. I saw that junker car I used to drive. It's on the dealer's lot, and it has a great big sign on it that reads: "TODAY ONLY—$499—THIS ONE WON'T LAST LONG."   —Ron Dentinger

~

Many a small thing has been made large by the right kind of advertising.
                                                                 —Mark Twain

~

Running a business without advertising is like winking at a girl in the dark. You know what you're doing, but she doesn't.

~

In the late 1600's the finest musical instruments came from three rural families whose workshops were side by side in the Italian village of Cremona. Outside the shop of the Arnatis hung a sign which read, "The Best Violins In All Italy." Not to be outdone, their next-door neighbors, the Guarnieris, hung a sign proclaiming "The Best Violins In All The World!" At the end of the street was the workshop of Anton Stradivarius, and on his front door was a simple notice which read, "The Best Violins On The Block."

~

One advertising-agency copywriter to another: "Hi! What's new and improved?"   —Tony Zarro

ADVICE

A woman called the utility company and complained that her electricity was out. What should she do? The voice on the other end advised, "Open your freezer and eat the ice cream."

~

Always stay in with the outs.   —David Halberstam

~

Be yourself is about the worst advice you can give some people.
                                                                 —Jeff Marder

~

General Mark Clark was asked what was the best advice he ever had. The general thought for awhile then replied, "Well, the best advice I ever had was to marry the girl I did." And then the young officer that asked Mark Clark that question said, "Well, sir, who gave you that advice?" And General Clark replied, "She did."

Two quick ways to disaster:
1) Take nobody's advice.
2) Take everybody's advice. —Ralph Cansler

~

The trouble with most sound advice is that it's 99 percent sound and one percent advice. —Peter F. Cullip

~

Accept good advice gracefully—as long as it doesn't interfere with what you intended to do in the first place.

AFTERLIFE (*See also* HEAVEN)

Harvey Fenway, the great jazz pianist, dies and is ushered into heaven. Waiting for him there is his friend Bob Gilpin, the bassist with whom he had played for many years. "Bob, Bob, is it really you?" says the ecstatic Fenway. "Yes, indeed, it is," replies the equally joyous Gilpin. "Hey," says Fenway, "what kind of place is this heaven anyway?" "Well," says Gilpin, "I gotta tell you, I'm jamming up here every day. I'm playing with Bird and Trane, and Count Basie just got in a little while ago! Man, it is smoking!" "Oh, wow!" says Fenway. "That sounds terrific! Tell me more, tell me more!" "Well, let me put it to you this way," says Gilpin. "There's good news and there's bad news. The good news is that these guys are in top form. I mean, I have never heard them sounding better. They are really wailing up here." "Yes," says Fenway, "so what's the bad news?" Gilpin answers, "The bad news is that God has this girlfriend who sings . . ."

~

I don't want to go to hell, but considering the luck I've had with my travel agent lately . . .

~

Aunt Aggie says, "I believe in reincarnation. I've had other lives, I know. I've had clues. First of all, I'm exhausted."

~

When the new preacher moved into town, one of the first people he met said, "I certainly hope that you're not one of these narrow-minded ministers who think that only the members of their congregation are going to heaven." "I'm even more narrow-minded than that," replied the preacher. "I'm pretty sure that some of the members of my congregation aren't going to make it."

—Msgr. Arthur Tonne

When Sherlock Holmes, the great detective, arrived in heaven, St. Peter said to him: "Can you help us solve a mystery? You see, Adam and Eve have been missing for the past several thousand years. Can you find them for us?" Sherlock began his investigation, and after several days, he returned and told St. Peter: "You will find Adam and Eve over there beyond the gate." He pointed them out. "How did you find them?" St. Peter asked. "Elementary, my dear St. Peter," Sherlock replied. "They are the only two up here who have no navels."   —Rev. Dennis R. Fakes

George dies and goes to hell. He notices one sign that says Capitalist Hell, and another that says Socialist Hell. There's a long line of souls waiting for socialist hell, but no one waiting to get into capitalist hell. George asks the guard, "What do they do to you in socialist hell?" "They boil you in oil, whip you and then put you on the rack," says the guard. "And what do they do to you in capitalist hell?" George asks. "Same thing," replies the guard. "Then why is everybody in line for socialist hell?" "Because in socialist hell," the guard explains, "they're always out of oil, whips and racks."

Three friends die in a car accident and they go to an orientation in heaven. They are all asked, "When you are in your casket and friends and family are mourning you, what would you like to hear them say about you? The first guy says, "I would like to hear them say that I was a great doctor of my time, and a great family man." The second guy says, "I would like to hear that I was a wonderful husband and school teacher who made a huge difference in our children of tomorrow." The last guy replies, "I would like to hear them say . . . 'Look, he's moving!'"

AGE

Two women in their 20s on a lunch break at the City Market, were chatting about a new boyfriend, a man in his 50s. "Well, he's very nice," said one, "but he is a bit old for you, don't you think?" To which the young woman with the new boyfriend replied: "Well, he may be a bit old, but he's very immature."

—Quote

I was interviewing a woman who was applying for a church staff position, read her application and said, "I see your birthday is April 12. What year?" Her simple reply was, "Every year."

—Msgr. Arthur Tonne, *Jokes Priests Can Tell,* vol. 6

Thirty is the ideal age for a woman—especially if she's forty.

A very wealthy 72-year-old man who married a shapely 21-year-old blonde was asked, How did a 72-year-old codger like you manage to marry such a young, beautiful woman? "I told her I was 90," he replied.

It's not that she's too old. But she's got beautiful antique jewelry . . . and she bought it when it was new.

An elderly gentleman was overheard complaining to a friend: "You know the worst thing about getting old? I'll tell you—it's having to listen to advice from your children."

I'm beginning to think my wife lied to me about her age. Who do you know has a recipe for curds and whey?

—Robert Orben, *2500 Jokes To Start 'Em Laughing*

AGING

During his presidency, Ronald Reagan told the following story at a White House reception. "It seems that an 80-year-old man's golf game was hampered by poor eyesight. He could hit the ball well but he couldn't see where it went. So his doctor teamed him up with a 90-year-old man who had perfect eyesight and was willing to go along to serve as a spotter. The 80-year-old man hit the first ball and asked his companion if he saw where it landed. 'Yep,' said the 90-year-old. 'Where did it go?' the 80-year-old demanded. The 90-year-old replied, 'I don't remember.' "

~

Old people shouldn't eat health foods. They need all the preservatives they can get.   —Robert Orben

~

You know you're getting older when the only thing you want for your birthday is not to be reminded of it.   —Jeff Rovin

~

They're not making mirrors the way they used to. The ones I buy now are full of wrinkles.   —Phyllis Diller

~

Uncle Leo reports: "When the doctor asked what I did for exercise, I said pushing ninety is exercise enough!"

~

I found out the hard way: By the time a man can afford to buy one of those exotic little sports cars, he's too fat to get into it.

~

Sad but true: By the time some men learn to watch their step, they are too old to go anywhere.

~

Louise Adams recently reached her one hundredth birthday. She was honored at a lavish catered birthday celebration arranged for her by her four daughters. She was asked if she felt that old. She perused the crowd for a moment and then gave her answer. "I really don't feel this old, except that I look around the room and see these white-haired ladies and realize they are all my daughters!"

~

"I'm doing what I can," the doctor explained, "but I can't make you any younger, you know." "The heck with that," said the patient. "I'm not interested in getting younger, I just want to get older."   —Joey Adams

It's an awful thing to grow old alone. My wife hasn't had a birthday in six years.

～

What's the best thing about turning sixty-five? No more calls from life insurance salesmen.

～

At age 75, Uncle Sid flattered himself that he was still a ladies' man, and decided to flirt with the comely waitress. "So tell me, sweetheart, where have you been all my life?" he crooned. "Actually, sir," she pointed out sweetly, "for the first fifty years of it, I wasn't even around."

～

Years ago, my grandfather was talking to an old friend, our honorary Uncle Morty, who at the age of 89 was still a bachelor. Grandfather was kidding him and jokingly asked, "Morty, you old codger, can you remember the first girl you ever kissed?" Morty gave a hollow laugh. "Meyer," he remarked dryly, "I can't even remember the last one."

～

You're getting older when it takes you more time to recover than it did to tire you out.
—Milton Berle

～

My dad says, "Every morning when I get up, I read the obituary page. If my name's not there, I shave and dress."

～

You know you're getting older when you try to blow out the candles on your birthday cake and the heat drives you back.

～

You know you're getting older when by the time you've lit the last candle on your cake, the first one has burned out.
—Jeff Rovin

～

My parents live in Cape Coral, Florida, a haven for the elderly. My folks are a mere 84-years-old each. Once my dad went to a local service club meeting. I asked him the age of the members. "They were old," he commented. "In fact," he added after a moment's thought, "I would say that their average age was deceased."

～

The older I grow the more I distrust the familiar doctrine that age brings wisdom.
—H. L. Mencken

The secret of staying young is to live honestly, eat slowly, and lie about your age. —Lucille Ball

If a man has to get old, he might as well get as old as he can.

—Ansel Adams

At age fifty, every man has the face he deserves.   —George Orwell

It's not your age that matters, it's how your matter ages.

—Martin A. Ragaway

My wife's Aunt Aggie claims: "There are four advantages to getting old and forgetful: One, you meet new friends every day; two, every joke you hear is new; three, you can hide your own Easter eggs; and I forget the fourth thing."

WISDOM FROM SENIOR CITIZENS

- I started with nothing. I still have most of it.
- When did my wild oats turn to prunes and All Bran?
- I finally got my head together, now my body is falling apart.
- Funny, I don't remember being absent-minded.
- All reports are in. Life is now officially unfair.
- If all is not lost, where is it?
- It is easier to get older than it is to get wiser.
- If at first you do succeed, try not to look astonished.
- The first rule of holes: if you are in one, stop digging.
- I tried to get a life once, but they told me they were out of stock.
- I went to school to become a wit, only got halfway though.
- It was so different before everything changed.
- It's not hard to meet expenses; they are everywhere.
- Nostalgia isn't what it used to be.
- Health is merely the slowest possible rate at which one can die.
- A day without sunshine is like a day in Seattle.
- I wish the buck stopped here! I could use a few.
- A closed mouth gathers no feet.
- It's not the pace of life that concerns me, it's the sudden stop at the end.
- It's hard to make a comeback when you haven't been anywhere.
- Living on Earth is expensive, but it does include a trip around the sun.
- The only time the world beats a path to your door is if you're in the bathroom.
- If God wanted me to touch my toes, He would have put them on my knees.
- Never knock on death's door, ring the bell and run (he hates that).

- Lead me not into temptation (I can find the way myself).
- When you are finally holding all the cards, why does everyone else decide to play chess?
- If you are living on the edge, make sure you're wearing your seatbelt.
- There are two kinds of pedestrians. The quick and the dead.
- An unbreakable toy is useful for breaking other toys.
- The only difference between a rut and a grave is the depth.

Several years ago, a retrospective showing of Pablo Picasso's works was held at the Museum of Modern Art in New York City. Nearly a thousand of Picasso's works were displayed in chronological order, beginning when he was a very young boy. The early works were traditional landscapes and still-lifes. Then, as the artist advanced in age, brilliant colors began to emerge, and the still-lifes were no longer very still. Finally, of course, the works turned into the kind of bold, zesty abstractions for which Picasso is best known. One art critic who saw the show recalled that once, when Picasso was eighty-five, he was asked the reason why his earlier works were so solemn and his later works so ecstatic and exciting. "How do you explain it?" asked the interviewer. "Easily," Picasso responded, his eyes sparkling. "It takes a long time to become young!"

In America, the young are always ready to give to those who are older than themselves the full benefit of their inexperience.   —Oscar Wilde

When I was younger I could remember anything, whether it had happened or not; but my faculties are decaying now and soon I shall be so I cannot remember any but the things that never happened. It is sad to go to pieces like this but we all have to do it.   —Mark Twain

An elderly woman in a nursing home declined her pastor's suggestion that she get a hearing aid. "At 91, I've heard enough," she said.   —Catherine Hall

When people praise you for your leadership qualities, it means you are starting to resemble George Washington.

Time may be an excellent healer, but as a beautician, it's not so hot.

Retirement is the time when you never do all those things you said you wanted to do if you only had the time.

Old age is a time when you complain that your grown-up children don't visit enough; but when they do visit, you can't wait for them to leave.

~

Ron Cichowicz observes, "When you're over the hill, you tend to repeat yourself. When you're over the hill, you tend to repeat yourself."

~

Betsy Maxwell Cronkite, on husband, Walter: "Errol Flynn died on a 70-foot boat with a 17-year-old girl. Walter has always wanted to go that way, but he's going to settle for a 17-footer with a 70-year-old."

~

Forty is the old age of youth; fifty is the youth of old age.   —Victor Hugo

~

The error of youth is to believe that intelligence is a substitute for experience, while the error of age is to believe that experience is a substitute for intelligence.   —Lyman Bryson

~

I'm too young to be old and too old to be young.
                                        —Fanny Flagg, *Fried Green Tomatoes*

~

Maturity is the stage of life when you don't see eye to eye but can walk arm in arm.   —Claude McDonald

~

My grandmother has always led a very busy life. Recently, she celebrated her 90th birthday. "Granny," I said, "it's remarkable how young you look. How do you do it?" "It takes time to grow old, Robert," she answered, "and I've never had any."   —Msgr. Arthur Tonne, *Jokes Priests Can Tell,* vol. 7

~

Old-timer to neighbor: "I've reached the age where the happy hour is a nap."

~

Award-winning novelist Penelope Fitzgerald was asked in an interview whether there is any one character in fiction with whom she identifies. Fitzgerald answered, "It changes so much as you get older. I used to weep for Romeo and Juliet, but now I think, *Their poor parents!*"
                                        —Lucinda Evans in *Telegraph Sunday Magazine,* London

It's paradoxical that the idea of living a long life appeals to everyone, but the idea of getting old doesn't appeal to anyone. —Andy Rooney

Why is it when you're seven, today is forever and tomorrow never; but when you're 70, tomorrow's yesterday before you knew it was today?
—Sue Jane Purcell

It take about ten years to get used to how old you are.

My minister told me that at my age I should be giving some thought to what he called "the hereafter." I told him that I think about it many times a day. "That's very wise," he said. I explained that it's not a matter of wisdom. It's when I open a drawer or a closet and ask myself, "What am I here after?"

Nothing makes you feel older than the discovery that your children are studying in history class what you studied in current events.
—*The Toastmaster's Treasure Chest,*
edited by Herbert V. Prochnow & Herbert V. Prochnow, Jr.

AIR TRAVEL

An airplane took off and headed for Paris. The plane's intercom was open by mistake, and the passengers could hear the pilot's every word as he chatted with the co-pilot: "Well, now that we've taken off, first I'm going to have a cup of coffee, and then I'm going to find that gorgeous new stewardess and kiss her like she's never been kissed before!" The stewardess heard the pilot's voice coming from the loud speaker, so she hurried to tell him that the intercom was open. When she passed the second row, an elderly lady seated by the aisle stopped her and whispered, "Wait, dear—let him finish his coffee first."

An old-timer who had never flown was taking out some insurance prior to a flight across Lake Michigan. On the application, one of the questions was: "Who should we notify in case of emergency?" The old gent put down: "The Coast Guard." —Ron Dentinger

Two-year-old Stephen was having a terrific time on his first plane trip. He pushed every button in sight, ran through the aisles at top speed and finally crashed into the flight attendant as she was serving a tray of coffee. Barely able to keep her balance, she handed the tray to another flight attendant, grabbed Stephen by the arm, forced a smile and cooed as gently as she could, "Little boy, why don't you go outside and play?"

YOU KNOW IT'S A NO-FRILLS AIRLINE WHEN . . .

- They don't sell tickets, they sell chances.
- All the insurance machines in the terminal are sold out.
- Before the flight, the passengers get together and elect a pilot.
- If you kiss the wing for luck before boarding, it kisses you back.
- You cannot board the plane unless you have the exact change.
- Before you take off, the stewardess tells you to fasten your Velcro.
- The Captain asks all the passengers to chip in a little for gas.
- When they pull the steps away, the plane starts rocking.
- The Captain yells at the ground crew to get the cows off the runway.
- You ask the Captain how often their planes crash and he replies, "Just once."
- No movie. Don't need one. Your life keeps flashing before your eyes.
- You see a man with a gun, but he's demanding to be let off the plane.
- All the planes have both a bathroom and a chapel.

Tower: "Flight 1234, for noise abatement turn right 45 degrees." Pilot: "Roger, but we are at 35,000 feet. How much noise can we make up here?" Tower: "Sir, have you ever heard the noise a 707 makes when it hits a 727?"

While cruising at 40,000 feet, the airplane shuddered and Mr. Benson looked out the window. "Good Lord!" he screamed. "One of the engines just blew up!" Other passengers left their seats and came running over; suddenly the aircraft was rocked by a second blast as yet another engine exploded on the other side. The passengers were in a panic now, and even the stewardesses couldn't maintain order. Just then, standing tall and smiling confidently, the pilot strode from the cockpit and assured everyone that there was nothing to worry about. His words and his demeanor seemed to make most of the passengers feel better, and they sat down as the pilot calmly walked to the door of the aircraft. There, he grabbed several packages from under the seats and began handing them to the flight attendants. Each crew member attached the package to their backs. "Say," spoke up an alert passenger, "aren't those parachutes?" The pilot said they were. The passenger went on, "But I thought you said there was nothing to worry about?" "There isn't," replied the pilot as a third engine exploded. "We're going to get help."

~

Question: How can you tell when an airplane is about to experience turbulence? Answer: The flight attendant is serving coffee.　　　—Joey Adams

AIRPLANES

You know you're in trouble when you go to the airline desk to complain about losing your luggage and the guy behind the counter is wearing your clothes.

~

Pastor Harold saw a member of the flock off at the airport yesterday: "May God and your luggage go with you."

~

Pilot to passengers on a commuter flight: I've got some good news and bad news. The bad news is that we're lost. But the good news is that we've got a strong tail wind.

~

Uncle Sid walked up to the airline counter and set three pieces of luggage before the clerk. "I want the brown bag to go to Dallas, the black one goes to Milwaukee, and I want you to send the other to Orlando." The clerk said, "I'm sorry, but we're not a parcel post, sir! We can't do that." In a slightly raised voice, Uncle Sid said, "Why not? That's what you did with my bags the last time!"

~

Everybody's cutting back. Instead of movies, one airline asks passengers to just pass around pictures of their children.

~

In South America, scientists have found strange, ancient lost airstrips. They've also found strange, ancient lost luggage.

ALIMONY

I know a couple that got remarried. He missed two alimony payments and she repossessed him.　　　—Bill Barner

~

Paying alimony is like having the TV on after you have fallen asleep.

　　　—Doc Blakely

Banks have long printed checks in a wide spectrum of colors; some have offered checks with floral or scenic backgrounds. The modest-sized Bank of Marin in Marin County, California, has gone one step further. A customer can simply bring in a personal photograph or drawing and have it printed onto a standard check form. Undeterred by the higher cost, more than five hundred customers signed for the illustrated checks. But perhaps the most imaginative and vindictive customer is the one who ordered special checks to be used solely for making his alimony payments. They show him kissing his new—and beautiful—wife.

Alimony is an arrangement in which two people make a mistake, but only one pays for it.
                                                                    —Jeff Rovin

AMERICA

You know what they're doing with your taxes? They're spending your money, hundreds of billions of dollars, on defense. To defend us from the Russians, the Nicaraguans, the Libyans, the Iranians. When was the last time a Russian broke into your car and stole your stereo? I'm not worried about Russians, I'm worried about Americans! If you're going to defend me, defend me from Americans! Get me back from Burger King alive!   —Blake Clark

I went to the movies last night. Incredible! Cars crashing, buildings burning, people fighting with guns and knives. And that was just on my way home.

Autumn is a wonderful time of the year even in Los Angeles. You can sit for hours in the smog and watch the birds change colors and fall out of the trees.

Americans love healthy, outdoor sports—especially if they are played indoors.

America is the land where half our salary goes to buy food and the other half to lose weight.

My farmer neighbor says he has one rooster so lazy that when the other roosters crow, he just nods his head.

You can lead a horse to water—but if you can get him to float on his back—well, then you've got something.

The boss complains his dog isn't very smart. "I bought one of those dog whistles," he said, "and he won't use it."

Talking to the suntanned New Mexican about the weather in Albuquerque, the tourist asked, "Doesn't it ever rain here?" The native replied, "Mister, do you remember the story of Noah and the Ark, and how it rained forty days and forty nights?" "Of course I do," the man answered. "Well," drawled the south-westerner, "we got half an inch that time."

Our daughter came from New York to visit us in the small town of Douglas, Ariz., about a hundred miles southeast of Tucson on the Mexican border. As we drove home from the airport, there were lone stretches where nothing could be seen but cactus and cattle. I asked what she thought of Arizona scenery. "I'm impressed; I've never seen so much of nothing so well-fenced."
—Francis C. Gaudet in *Arizona Highways*

Never criticize Americans. They have the best taste that money can buy.
—Miles Kington

Of course, America had often been discovered before Columbus, but it had always been hushed up.   —Oscar Wilde

Americans always try to do the right thing—after they've tried everything else.
—Winston Churchill

ANCESTORS/ANCESTRY

The Smiths were proud of their family tradition. Their ancestors had come to America on the Mayflower. They had included senators and Wall Street wizards. They decided to compile a family history, a legacy for their children and grandchildren. They hired a fine author. Only one problem arose—how to handle great-uncle George, who was executed in the electric chair. The author said he could handle the story tactfully. The book appeared. It said, "Great-uncle George occupied a chair of applied electronics at an important govern-ment institution, was attached to his position by the strongest of ties, and his death came as a great shock."

"Yes," said the boastful young man, "my family can trace its ancestry back to William the Conqueror." "I suppose," remarked his friend, "you'll be telling

us that your ancestors were in the Ark with Noah?" "Certainly not," said the other. "My people had a boat of their own." —*Retired Teachers Journal*

ANIMALS

Phil Johnson, the Evangelical Covenant missionary to a newly independent African nation, encountered a ferocious looking, man-eating lion as he was walking from one mission station to another. Johnson fell to his knees and buried his face in his hands. Nothing seemed to be happening; the lion was silent. The missionary peeked through his fingers and saw the lion on its knees, its face buried in its paws. The missionary said in a trembling (but relieved) voice, "I'm thanking God for delivering me from the jaws of death. But what on earth are you doing?" The lion growled, "I'm saying grace."

In Minnesota three pastors got together for coffee one day and found all their churches had bat-infestation problems. "I got so mad," said Pastor Johnson, "I took a shotgun and fired at them. It made holes in the ceiling, but did nothing to the bats." "I tried trapping them alive," said Pastor Linquist. "Then I drove 50 miles before releasing them, but they returned." "I haven't had any more problems," said Pastor Stephens. "What did you do?" asked the others amazed. "I simply baptized and confirmed them," he replied. "I haven't seen them since."

"Did I ever tell you about the time I came face to face with a lion?" asked Steve. "No, what happened?" responded Dave. "There I stood without a gun. The lion growled ferociously and crept closer and closer . . ." "What did you do?" "I moved to the next cage." —*Quote*

A man had a gopher in his yard. He wanted to get rid of it, and asked an exterminator for his opinion. "I suggest the four-day process," the exterminator said. "How does it work?" "Simple," the exterminator said. "For three mornings you drop an apple and a cookie down the gopher's hole. On the fourth morning you drop in an apple. Then you wait 10 minutes." "And?" "And," the exterminator explained, "when the gopher pokes his head up and says, 'Where's the cookie?' you clobber him." —*Capper's Weekly*

When the country temporarily goes to the dogs, cats must learn to be circumspect, walk on fences, sleep in trees, and have faith that all this woofing is not the last word. —Garrison Keillor

An antelope and a lion entered a diner and took a booth near the window. When the waiter approached, the antelope said, "I'll have a bowl of hay and a side order of radishes." "And what will your friend have?" "Nothing," replied the antelope. The waiter persisted. "Isn't he hungry?" "Hey, if he were hungry," said the antelope, "would I be sitting here?"

~

The good Lord didn't create anything without a purpose, but the fly comes close. —Mark Twain

~

Penguins mate for life. That doesn't surprise me much, because they all look alike. It's not like they're going to meet a better-looking penguin someday. —Ellen Degeneres

~

"That's marvelous, having a lion and a monkey in the same cage," said the visitor to a small zoo. "How do they get along?" "Okay, usually," answered the zookeeper. "Occasionally they have a disagreement, and we have to get a new monkey." —Ohio Motorist

~

These two rabbits are enjoying a peaceful snack on some grass in the country when, out of the surrounding forest, bursts two wolves. The rabbits take off like a shot, hopping and bounding away like the devil was on their tails. They're running frantically with the wolves gaining ground every second. But out of nowhere a ditch appears, and the rabbits dash into the culvert. One of the wolves hops over the road and blocks their exit, and the first takes up a position at the end they ran into. So the rabbits are trapped in the culvert, the wolves have each end guarded but cannot get in as they are too big. One of the rabbits is frantic. "What are we going to do! We're trapped! What can we do to get out of this?" Then he breaks down and starts sobbing. "Don't worry friend," the other rabbit says. The first rabbit dries its eyes and a puzzled look appears on his face. "But, what are we going to do?" The other rabbit replied, "Simple, we'll wait here until we outnumber them."

~

A panda walks into a restaurant, sits down and orders a sandwich. He eats the sandwich, pulls out a gun and shoots the waiter dead. As the panda stands up to go, the manager shouts, "Hey! Where are you going? You just shot my waiter and you didn't pay for your sandwich!" The panda yells back at the manager, "Hey man, I'm a PANDA! Look it up!" The manager opens his dictionary and sees the following definition for panda: "A tree dwelling marsupial of Asian origin, characterized by distinct black and white coloring. Eats shoots and leaves."

⁓

Did you know that dolphins are so intelligent that within only a few weeks of captivity, they can train Americans to stand at the very edge of the pool and throw them fish?

⁓

I live in a semi-rural area. We recently had a new neighbor call the local township administrative office to request the removal of the Deer Crossing sign on our road. The reason: Many deer were being hit by cars and he no longer wanted them to cross there.

⁓

It's a sunny morning in the Big Forest and the Bear family are just waking up. Baby Bear goes downstairs and sits in his small chair at the table. He looks

The
BORDERLINE ™
By Gabe Martin
borderln@cts.com

© 1996 GABE MARTIN

http://www.the-borderline.com/

"Oh, boy . . . tube socks."

into his small bowl and it's empty! "Who's been eating my porridge?" he squeaks. Daddy Bear arrives at the table and sits in his big chair. He looks into his big bowl and it is also empty! "Who's been eating my porridge!?" he roars. Mommy Bear puts her head through the serving hatch from the kitchen and screams, "For crying out loud, how many times do we have to go through this?! I haven't made the porridge yet!"

My Uncle Jack, a grain salesman, is driving to his next appointment when he looks out his car window and sees a three-legged chicken running parallel to his car. The car is going forty miles per hour, but somehow the chicken is keeping up. When the salesman speeds up to fifty, the chicken speeds up with him. Absolutely amazed by what he see, Jack starts going sixty, but there's the chicken, still beside him, and not even breathing hard. Uncle Jack is about to speed up yet again when the chicken suddenly takes off and disappears in a cloud of dust. Dazed with astonishment, Uncle Jack immediately slows down and pulls over to the side. He finds the farmer and says, "You won't believe what happened to me. I was doing sixty on this road and a three-legged chicken passed me like I was standing still!" "Oh, yeah, I know all about it," says the farmer. "That chicken belongs to me. You see, there's three of us— myself, my wife, and little Davy, and whenever Louise serves chicken for

REVEREND FUN WWW.REVERENDFUN.COM

©COPYRIGHT 1999 GOSPEL FILMS, INC.

"I don't understand why all of us animals have to go, too . . . shoot, I don't even LIKE apples."

dinner, we all want a drumstick. The only solution we could think of was to start raising three-legged chickens." "That's remarkable," says Uncle Jack. "How do they taste?" "I don't really know," says the farmer. "We've never been able to catch one."

ANTIQUES

Antiques have become so popular, right now there are 15 million Americans who have things that are old, funny-looking, don't work, and are only kept around for sentimental purposes. Some of these are called antiques—and the rest are called husbands.

—Robert Orben, *2500 Jokes To Start 'Em Laughing*

APATHY

Ronald Reagan was speaking in Seattle of those people who continued to criticize his efforts. He said, "They sort of remind me of the fellow who was asked which was worse, ignorance or apathy, and he said, 'I don't know and I don't care.'"

~

I've been feeling really apathetic lately. Like today—Jimmy cracked corn, but I don't care.   —Howie Mandell

APPEARANCE

Mike McClurg, a newly minted lawyer, watched the very first person enter his office. He decides to impress his visitor by looking busy, so he picks up the phone and starts talking: "Look, Belli, about that syndication deal. I think I better run over to CBS and handle it personally. Yes. No. No, I don't think three million will swing it. We better have Silverman from Dean Witter meet us there. OK. Call you back later." He looks up at the visitor and says, "Good morning, how may I help you?" And the visitor says, "You can't help me at all. I'm just here to hook up your phone."

~

Aunt Mildred and Uncle Joe were driving through south Chicago one summer afternoon. The weather was hot and humid but the windows were rolled up. "Honey," Mildred said, "please open the windows." "Are you crazy!" Joe exclaimed. "And let our neighbors driving in the next lane know our car isn't air-conditioned?"

~

If I were two-faced, would I be wearing this one?   —Abraham Lincoln

A four-hundred-dollar suit on him would look like socks on a rooster.

—Earl Long

He must have had a magnificent build before his stomach went in for a career of its own. —Margaret Halsey

His face was filled with broken commandments. —John Masefield

She got her good looks from her father. He's a plastic surgeon.

—Groucho Marx

She was what we used to call a suicide blonde—dyed by her own hand.

—Saul Bellow

She wears her clothes as if they were thrown on with a pitchfork.

—Jonathan Swift

APPROVAL

We can secure other people's approval, if we do right and try hard but our own is worth a hundred of it, and no way has been found of securing that.

—Mark Twain

ART/ARTISTS

The artist is nothing without the gift, but the gift is nothing without work. —Emile Zola

Abstract art? A product of the untalented, sold by the unprincipled to the utterly bewildered. —Al Capp

At an art museum: "There was a time when the artist had to suffer—now it's the viewer."

—Bernhardt in *Mature Living*

When Grant Wood painted scenes of his native Iowa, he would depict the villages and fields the way he wished they looked, rather than as they were. Once, after completing a picture of a neighbor's farm, he showed the work to the farmer, who remarked: "Yep, looks just like it. And thanks for cutting the weeds." —*Sunshine* Magazine

ATHEISTS

They have Dial-a-Prayer for atheists now. You can call up and it rings and rings but nobody answers.

❧

Most people past college age are not atheists. It's too hard to be one in our society, for one thing . . . you don't get any days off. And if you're an agnostic you don't know whether you get them off or not. —Mort Sahl

AUTOMOBILES

What a horrible car accident. I had the right of way, but the other guy had the truck.

❧

I like driving around with my two dogs, especially on the freeway. I make them wear little hats so I can use the car pool lanes. —Monica Piper

❧

Nothing depreciates your car so fast as a new model in your neighbor's garage.

❧

Mortimer Lee, a young real estate salesman, was so proud of his new red Cadillac that he just had to show it off, so he cruised through the bad part of town. At a stoplight a giant-sized older man hauled him out of the driver's seat, drew a circle around him in the road, and told him not to step out of the circle unless he wanted to get the stuffing beat out of him. The older man started to demolish the Caddie, beginning with the headlights and windows, when he heard the young man laughing. He moved on to the body and engine, but in between crashes he couldn't help hearing the young man's hysterical giggles. Finally, the older man came over with his crowbar and said, "What are you laughin' at? Your fancy car's never gonna run again." Snickering, the young man replied, "So? Ever since you've been tearing up my car, I've been stepping in and out of this circle."

❧

When he was in high school, our son Matt loved fast cars and was thrilled to land a summer job with the local Alfa-Romeo service center. "Gee, Mr. Vespucci," he gushed, grabbing a wrench, "I can't wait to learn all the ins and outs of fixing up these babies." So he was startled when Mr. Vespucci told him to put down his tools and listen up. "The first thing you gotta learn how to do," he instructed the kid, "is to open the hood, stand back, and shake your head very, very sadly."

After hearing about gasohol, a sports fan tried mixing gasoline with Gatorade. Now he says his car will only run a sideline pattern.

An automobile fancier who claims they don't build 'em like they used to says: "We finally got the perfect second car—a tow truck."

The sports-car owner was taking his friend for his first ride in his new low-slung car. The friend appeared to be puzzled, so the driver asked him what was wrong. "I can't figure out where we are. What's that long wall we've been passing?" "That's no wall," snapped the driver. "That's the curb."

—How the Platform Professionals Keep 'em Laughin'

Man with car trouble on a country road: "How far is it to the next town?" Farmer: "Two miles as the crow flies." Man: "How far is it if the crow has to walk and roll a flat tire?"

A teenager had an old car he wanted to sell and put this sign on it: "FOR SALE: $4,000. Rebate: $3,500!"

Uncle Sid's wife bawled him out for taking so long to choose a new car. "You married me only one week after you met me," she yelled. "Yeah," he replied defensively, "but buying a new car is serious."

Some sports-car buffs were talking about cars. "You know," said one, "my brother is the greatest mechanic you ever saw. He made his own car by using the wheels from a Ford, a radiator from a Chrysler, an engine from a Cadillac, a transmission from a Chevy and a body from a Buick." "That sounds like a great machine," replied another. "But with all those parts from different cars, what did he finally end up with?" "Five years."   —Winston K. Pendleton

Auto repairman to customer: "If you want, we can freeze your car until future mechanics discover a way to repair it."   —Stan Fine in *Medical Economics*

When an auto mechanic tells you the repair job will run a certain amount—give or take a few dollars—you know right then who will give and who will take.   —Arnold H. Glasow

Detroit's most pressing problem is to design a car small enough to conserve gas and large enough not to disappear into a pothole.
—Aaron Gold in *Chicago Tribune*

One winter morning, the man heard his neighbor trying unsuccessfully to start her car. He went outside and asked: "Did you try choking it?" "No," she said, gritting her teeth, "but I sure felt like it."   —*Catholic Workman*

A motorist brought his car in for its 1,500 mile inspection. "Is there anything the matter with it?" the service manager asked. "Well, there's only one part of it that doesn't make a noise," the customer replied, "and that's the horn."
—*Grit*

-------------------------------------- **B** --------------------------------------

BABIES

My parents put us to sleep by tossing us up in the air. Of course, you have to have low ceilings for this method to work.

A baby is an inestimable blessing and bother.   —Mark Twain

A mother had just brought her newborn triplets home from the hospital. Her older boy, a four-year-old, took his first doubtful look at the new babies and said, "We'd better start calling folks. They're going to be a lot harder to get rid of than kittens."

Second grader Stepaniee came home from school and said to her mother, "Mom, guess what? We learned how to make babies today." The mother, more than a little surprised, tried to keep her cool. "That's interesting," she said. "How do you make babies?" "It's simple, replied the girl. "You just change 'y' to 'i' and add 'es.'"

Taking care of your baby is easy, as long as you don't have anything else to do.

All a newborn baby really needs is food, warmth and love. Pretty much like a hamster, only with fewer signs of intelligence. —Dave Barry

A man finds out what is meant by a spitting image when he tries to feed cereal to his infant. —Imogene Fey

Babies are nature's way of showing people what the world looks like at 2 A.M.
—*Parts Pups*

A FEW INSTRUCTIONS FOR FIRST-TIME FATHERS

- Given the choice, it's always better to use a bib than to Scotch Guard your baby.
- Many babies look alike. Marking yours with a colorful sticker will keep it from being mixed up in a group.
- A bouncing baby boy doesn't actually mean it bounces.
- You may not return your baby—even if you still have the receipt.
- Bouncing a well-fed baby may be hazardous to your clothes.
- A cat carrier should never be substituted for a car seat.
- Baby-sitting does not involve actually sitting on the baby.
- Baby formula, when properly mixed, does not produce a new baby.
- Godzilla is not basically the same as Barney.
- Generally, a hunk of cheese is not a good pacifier.
- Newspapers are not basically the same as diapers.
- Avoid dusting your baby with a vacuum cleaner.
- Never leave your baby where it may be stepped on by a cow.

Arriving for a visit, Joan Ludwig asked her small granddaughter, "Angela, how do you like your new baby brother?" "Oh, he's all right," the child shrugged. "But there were a lot of things we needed worse."

BABYSITTERS

We used to terrorize our babysitters when we were little, except for my great-grandfather, because he used to read to us—from his will. —Brian Kiley

Babysitter: A teenager who must behave like an adult so that the adults who are out can behave like teenagers. —John R. Fox

Babysitter to parents: "By the way, I promised Amy that if she'd go to bed without any fuss, you'd buy her a pony in the morning."

BACHELORS

A bachelor is a man who never makes the same mistake once.   —Ed Wynn

~

A confirmed bachelor is a guy who believes in wine, women, and so long.

~

Bachelors know more about women than married men. If they didn't, they would be married too.   —H. L. Mencken

~

Bachelors should be heavily taxed. It's not fair that some men should be happier than others.   —Oscar Wilde

~

I belong to Bridegrooms Anonymous. Whenever I feel like getting married, they send over a lady in a housecoat and hair curlers to burn my toast for me.
                                                    —Dick Martin

~

She was another one of his near Mrs.   —Alfred McFote

~

My Uncle Ted, who has never married, claims that a bachelor is a person who believes in life, liberty, and the happiness of pursuit.

BAD NEWS

Never buy a portable TV set on the sidewalk from a man who's out of breath.

~

Bad news travels fast. Good news takes the scenic route.

BANKS

The newly rich real estate developer splurged on a Rolls Royce Silver Shadow and couldn't wait to show it off. So after a meeting with the manager of his bank, he offered him a ride home. "Whaddaya think?" he couldn't resist asking his passenger after a mile or two. "Pretty snappy, eh? I bet you've never ridden in one of these before." "Actually I have," replied the banker graciously, "but this is my first time in the front seat."

A bank is a place that will lend you money if you can prove that you don't need it.
—Bob Hope

~

Overheard at the bank: "The reason we need a loan is we're expecting a baby. Incidentally, our need for it is rather urgent. Matter of fact, we're on our way to the hospital now."

~

Ever notice . . . that we trust banks with our money, but they don't trust us with their pens?
—*Current Comedy*

~

I should have known the bank was in trouble. The calendar they gave me only went up to March.

~

My neighbor works in the operations department in the central office of a large bank. Employees in the field call him when they have problems with their computers. One night he got a call from a woman in one of the branch banks who had this question, "I've got smoke coming from the back of my terminal. Do you guys have a fire downtown?"

~

Customer to bank official: "I'd like to apply for a credit card. I'm tired of my checks bouncing all over the place."
—Bob Thaves

BARBERS

"Your hair needs cutting badly," remarked the barber. "It does not," exclaimed the customer, sitting down in the chair. "It needs cutting nicely. You cut it badly last time."
—*Grit*

BASEBALL

Gerry Girard of WPIX News in New York had a great baseball quote in reference to the then losing-streak-haunted Baltimore Orioles. It went something like this: "And the Orioles are still without a win. But despite losing their 10th straight, attendance is up . . . all the players showed up tonight."

~

St. Peter and Satan were having an argument one day about baseball. With a beguiling leer, Satan proposed a game (to be played on neutral grounds) between a select team from the heavenly host and his own hand-picked Hades boys. "Very well," the gatekeeper of the Celestial City agreed. "But you realize,

I hope, that we have all the good players and the best coaches, too." "I know," said Satan calmly, "but we have all the umpires!"

—How the Platform Professionals Keep 'em Laughin'

"While I was playing with the Pirates," writes Joe Garagiola, "I gave a speech to the Pittsburgh Junior Chamber of Commerce. Trying to make the best of a terrible season, I said, 'We may not be high in the standings, and we don't win many ballgames, but you've got to admit we play some interesting baseball.' A voice from the back of the room yelled, 'Why don't you play some dull games and win a few?'"

Baseball is too much of a sport to be a business and too much of a business to be a sport.   —Philip K. Wrigley

"Each year I don't play I get better!" said Joe Garagiola. "The first year on the banquet trail I was a former ballplayer, the second year I was great, the third year one of baseball's stars, and just last year I was introduced as one of baseball's immortals. The older I get, the more I realize that the worst break I had was playing."   *—Quote*

Don, a minor-league umpire, is used to being heckled by fans. But imagine his surprise when he was rushing to umpire an exhibition game at Coors Field in Denver. After a long search for a place to change clothes, Don finally located a room with a neatly lettered sign: "Dressing Room, Umpires Only." As he was about to go in, however, he inspected the sign more closely. Below the printed legend was the same message . . . written in Braille.

Two buddies, Frank and Steve, were two of the biggest baseball fans in America. For their entire adult lives, Frank and Steve discussed baseball history in the winter and they pored over every box score during the season. They went to 60 games a year. They even agreed that whoever died first would try to come back and tell the other if there was baseball in heaven. One summer night, Frank passed away in his sleep after watching the Yankee victory earlier in the evening. He died happy. A few nights later, his buddy Steve awoke to the sound of Frank's voice from beyond. "Frank is that you?" Steve asked. "Of course it's me," Frank replied. "This is unbelievable!" Steve exclaimed. "So tell me, is there baseball in heaven?" "Well I have some good news and some bad news for you. Which do you want to hear first?" "Tell me the good news first." "Well, the good news is that, yes, there is baseball in heaven, Steve." "Oh, that is wonderful! So what could possibly be the bad news?" "You're pitching tomorrow night."

~

A rookie pitcher was struggling at the mound, so the catcher walked up to have a talk with him. "I've figured out your problem," he told the young southpaw. "You always lose control at the same point in every game." "When is that?" "Right after the National Anthem." —Jeff MacNelly

~

A few years back, a reporter asked Mickey Mantle how much he thought he'd be making if he were playing baseball now. "Oh, about $500,000," Mantle said. "But, Mick," replied the surprised reporter, "guys these days are making $7 million." "Yeah," Mantle answered, "but I'm 60 years old."

~

Rex (Hurricane) Hudler, on being released by the San Francisco Giants after batting .238 in spring training: "I was downgraded from a hurricane to a tropical depression."

BASKETBALL

Old basketball players never die. They just sit in front of you at the movies.

~

One longtime basketball coach is thinking of becoming a track coach. "It's the easiest job of all," he says. "All you have to do is tell them to turn left and get back as quick as they can."

~

My neighbor says he'll be hearing any day now whether his son made the starting basketball team at State University, or if the coach intends to play favorites again this year.

~

The coach of our local community college basketball team, explaining why the team did not pray before games this year: "We've got so many things to pray for, we'd be penalized for delay of game."

~

No basketball coach cares about the height of the players as long as their ears pop then they stand up. —Dick Vitale

B

A basketball coach reportedly told some friends about a dream he had. "I was walking down the street," he said, "when this Rolls Royce pulled up beside me. Inside, there was a beautiful young woman—blonde, maybe 24 or 25 years old. She asked me to get in. She took me to a fantastic restaurant where we ate and drank and she paid the bill. Then she asked me if I wanted to go home with her. And I said yes. And we did." "Then what happened?" a listener urged. "The best part of all!" the coach drooled. "She introduced me to her four brothers, and all of them were over 7 feet tall!"

BIBLE

Question: Do you know what would have happened if it had been Three Wise Women who came to the stable instead of Three Wise Men?

Answer: They would have asked for directions, arrived on time, helped deliver the baby, cleaned the stable, made a casserole, and brought practical gifts!

～

The Bible is a very ancient book, yet it is always relevant to our lives. People in it have the same problems we do. Think of Noah . . . it took him forty days to find a place to park.

REVEREND FUN WWW.REVERENDFUN.COM

©COPYRIGHT 1999 GOSPEL FILMS, INC.

"Dear God, if you let me make this foul shot, I promise to stop skipping church to play ball."

At Bayside Baptist, Sandra Alexander, the pastor's wife, asked her Sunday school class, "What do we learn from the story of Jonah and the whale?" Ten-year-old Samantha volunteered: "People make whales sick."

~

Harriett Feneman, the new Sunday school teacher, asked her class, "What do we learn from the story of Jonah?" Robert Ashley, an eight-year-old, put up his hand. "Travel by air," he said.

~

When I was pastor of the Little Brown Church, I went to visit a family. Before leaving I asked if they would like for me to read from the Bible. The lady of the house said to one of the boys, "Go bring the Big Book we read out of so much!" The boy brought the Sears catalog.

~

Seven-year-old Keith found an old family Bible and began to look through it. As he was turning the pages, a pressed tree leaf fell out. "Hey," he exclaimed, "this must be where Adam and Eve left their clothes!"

~

Five-year-old Stephanie asked her seven-year-old brother Paul, "Why does grandmother read her Bible so much?" Replied Paul with all the wisdom of his additional two years, "I guess she must be cramming for her finals."

~

My daughter-in-law Dalacie was mailing the old family Bible to her brother in a distant city. The postal clerk examined the heavy package carefully and inquired if it contained anything breakable. "Nothing but the Ten Commandments," was her quick reply.

~

It is illegal to read the Bible in the public schools of Illinois, but a law requires the STATE to provide a Bible for every convict! Don't worry kids, if you can't read the Bible in school, you'll be able to when you get to prison. —*Illinois Baptist Beacon*

~

A little girl returned home from Sunday School. Her mother asked her if she remembered her Bible lesson for the day. The little girl replied, "I sure do! I can even remember the Zip Code—Luke 19:40." —*Capper's Weekly*

After a week of Bible school, our four-year-old son, Erik, decided one day to give us his version of the Noah's Ark story:

"A long, long time ago, there was a good man named Noah and a whole bunch of bad people. God decided to wash away the bad people with a big rain. But He liked Noah and He didn't want Noah to get wet. So He told Noah to build a giant boat and call it an ark. He told Noah to take a bunch of different animals on the Ark, too. Noah did what God told him; he built the Ark and went to get the animals. Then he helped his wife pack a great big cooler so they wouldn't have to go to the grocery store in the rain."   —*Family Digest*

Over at Fortitude Holiness Tabernacle, Dexter Rice, the Sunday School teacher, was telling his class the story of the Prodigal Son. Wishing to emphasize the resentful attitude of the elder brother, he laid stress on this part of the parable. After describing the rejoicing of the household over the return of the wayward son, Dexter spoke of one who, in the midst of the festivities, failed to share in the jubilant spirit of the occasion. "Can anybody in the class," he asked, "tell me who this was?" Nine-year-old Olivia Crombie had been listening sympathetically to the story. She waved her hand in the air. "I know!" she said beamingly. "It was the fatted calf."

THE TOP TEN THINGS SAID BY NOAH

    10. Strange! We haven't seen another boat for weeks.
     9. If only I'd brought along more rhino litter!
     8. How many times around this place makes a mile?
     7. I never want to sleep in a waterbed again.
     6. I wonder what my friends are doing right now.
     5. An outboard motor would have made this more exciting!
     4. Fish for supper—again?
     3. Does anyone have more Dramamine?
     2. What? You don't have film to photograph the rainbow?
     1. I should have killed those darn mosquitoes when I had the chance!

Pastor Paul W. Kummer, Grace Lutheran Church, Destin, Florida

Teacher to Pupil: Who were the Pharisees?
Pupil: They were horses.
Teacher: Why do you think they were horses?
Pupil: Because in the Bible, Jesus said, "Whoa" to the Pharisees.
                                                                    —*Family Digest*

BIGAMY

A bigamist is a man who marries a beautiful woman and a good cook.

~

"I find you not guilty of the charge of bigamy," said the judge. "You can go home to your wife now." "Thank you, your honor," said the grateful man. "But to which one?"

~

There once was an old man of Lyme
Who married three wives at a time.
When asked, "Why a third?"
He replied, "One's absurd!
And bigamy, sir, is a crime."
                                        —William Cosmo Monkhouse

BIRDS

Little Jessica was visiting her grandparents' farm. Investigating the chicken lot, she came upon their peacock. She ran quickly to the house, shouting, "Granny, come quick! One of your chickens is in bloom!"

~

Uncle Irv bought a parrot at an auction after some very spirited bidding. "Now you're sure this bird talks?" he asked the auctioneer. "Talk?" replied the auctioneer. "He's been bidding against you for the past 10 minutes."

BIRTH

This sounds a lot like an urban myth, but my brother-in-law tells me that this happened to the wife of someone he works with. I must admit that I'm a bit skeptical but its certainly worth a chuckle. It seems that this lady didn't quite make it to hospital for the birth of her child, in fact, the baby was born on the lawn just outside the main entrance. The poor woman was dreadfully embarrassed and was being consoled by one of the nurses, who said, "Don't worry about it. It could have been worse. Why, two years ago we had a woman who gave birth in the elevator." The woman cried, "That was me!" And she burst into tears."

~

Somewhere on this globe, every ten seconds, there is a woman giving birth to a child. She must be found and stopped.   —Sam Levenson

~

In the back woods of Scotland, Ian's wife went into labor in the middle of the night, and the doctor was called out to assist in the delivery. To keep the

B

nervous father-to-be busy, the doctor handed him a lantern and said: "Here, you hold this high so I can see what I'm doing." Soon, a wee baby boy was brought into the world. "Whoa, there, Ian!" said the doctor. "Don't be in a rush to put the lantern down . . . I think there's yet another wee one to come yet." Sure enough, within minutes he had delivered a bonnie lass. "No, no, don't be in a great hurry to be putting down that lantern, lad . . . It seems there's yet another one besides!" cried the doctor. Then Ian scratched his head in bewilderment, and asked the doctor: "Do ye think it's the light that's attractin' them?"

➤

A proud father phoned the newspaper and reported the birth of his twins. The girl at the desk didn't quite catch the message. "Will you repeat that?" she asked. "Not if I can help it," he replied.   —*Quote*

➤

I don't know how old I am because the goat ate the Bible that had my birth certificate in it. The goat lived to be twenty-seven.   —Satchel Paige

BIRTH CONTROL

One of the best responses I've ever heard to a talk show host who tried to nail a guest came when Dick Cavett asked Father Theodore Hesburgh, president of

Adam's Midlife Crisis

Notre Dame, if he believed birth control was a sin. "I hope not," replied the savvy padre. "I've been practicing it for years."   —Bruce Haney

BLAME

Aunt Edna toured Europe by car with a woman friend. She posed for a souvenir snapshot before the fallen pillars of a historic ruin in Greece. "Don't get the car in the picture," she said, "or my husband will swear I ran into the place!"

~

There's a new computer out that's so human—when it makes a mistake it blames it on another machine.   —Mickey Freeman in *Parade*

~

To err is human; to blame it on somebody else is even more human.

    —John Nadeau

BOOKS

Never judge a book by its movie.   —W. J. Eagan

~

I drive my stepson Todd crazy. I always read the last chapter of mystery novels first. I know who did it, but I have no idea what they did.

~

This isn't generally known, but Webster is supposed to have written the first dictionary because of a nagging wife. That's right. Every time he opened his mouth, she'd say, "And what's that supposed to mean?"

~

A man who was very much interested in old books ran into an unbookish acquaintance of his who'd just thrown away an old Bible which had been

packed away in the attic of his ancestral home for generations. He happened to mention it. "Who printed it, do you know?" asked the book lover. "Somebody named Gutensomething," replied the man with an effort. "Not Gutenberg?" gasped the booklover. "You idiot, you've thrown away one of the first books ever printed. A copy sold at auction recently for over $400,000!" The other man was unmoved. "My copy wouldn't have brought a dime," he announced firmly. "Some fellow named Martin Luther had scribbled all over it."   —*How the Platform Professionals Keep 'em Laughin'*

B

Mark Twain warned, "Be careful about reading health books. You may die of a misprint."

~

I know of no sentence that can induce such immediate and brazen lying as the one that begins "Have you read . . . ?"   —Wilson Mizner

BORES

There was a man at the party who seemed a self-appointed authority on every subject. One of the guests approached the host of the party and told the host, "He certainly is outspoken, isn't he?" The host disagreed, "Not by anyone I know."

~

It is the dull man who is always sure, and the sure man who is always dull.
                                                              —H. L. Mencken

~

The trouble with people who don't have much to say is that you have to listen so long to find out.   —Quoted by Ann Landers

~

British actress Mrs. Patrick Campbell made short work of bores. At a dinner party her professorial companion subjected her to a tiresome defense of the ant world: "They are wonderful little creatures; they have their own police force and their own army." Leaning forward with a show of absorbed interest, she breathlessly asked, "No navy, I suppose?"
            —Margot Peters, *Mrs. Pat: The Life of Mrs. Patrick Campbell*

~

Some are born great; some achieve greatness; and some just grate upon you.

~

Bore: Someone who, when you ask him how he is, tells you!

~

She plunged into a sea of platitudes, and with the powerful breast stroke of a channel swimmer, made her confident way towards the white cliffs of the obvious.   —W. Somerset Maugham

~

She's so boring you fall asleep halfway through her name.   —Alan Bennett

~

The trouble with her is that she lacks the power of conversation but not the power of speech.   —George Bernard Shaw

Some people can stay longer in an hour than others can in a week.
>—William Dean Howells

BORING

She's so boring, she can't even entertain a doubt.
>—William R. Evans III and Andrew Frothingham

❧

A wingtip personality in a Reebok world.   —Al McGill

❧

He is not only dull himself, he is the cause of dullness in others.
>—Samuel Johnson

BOSSES

Herb and his sales manager stood before a map on which colored pins indicated the representative in each area. "I'm not going to fire you, Uttley," the manager said, "but just to emphasize the insecurity of your position, I'm loosening your pin a little."

❧

It wasn't exactly what the boss expected when he asked his employees to put suggestions in a box as to how the business could be improved. "When I come in each morning, I like to see everyone in his or her place and started on the day's work. Anyone have any suggestions?" The next day he found only one suggestion in the box. It read, "Wear squeaky shoes."

❧

Overheard in a meeting: Please don't think of me as your boss. Think of me as your friend who is never wrong.   —Ron Dentinger

❧

Boss to new employee: "I want you to know that my door is always open. Please walk by quietly."

❧

When he got fired from his last place of employment, the boss told him: "You've been like a son to me—insolent, rude, and ungrateful."

❧

Employee to boss: "The reason I didn't laugh at your joke, Mr. Walters, is because it wasn't funny, it was in bad taste and I'm retiring tomorrow."
>—Zahn in *The Wall Street Journal*

B

Boss to employee: "We've decided, Sherman, to give you more responsibility. From now on, you'll be responsible for everything that goes wrong."
—Marty Lowe in The Wall Street Journal

The manager of a brokerage firm called in a sales representative. "Bomfield," he said, "you've had a tremendous impact on our bottom line since joining us a year ago." "Why, thank you," Bomfield said, beaming. "Yes," the manager continued, "now we'll be able to file as a nonprofit organization."
—John Pizzuto, The Great Wall Street Joke Book

"How long have you been working here?" "Since the boss threatened to fire me."
—Shelby Friedman

Pete was telling a friend that he had just lost his job. "Why did the foreman fire you?" the friend asked in surprise. "Oh," Pete said, "you know how foremen are. They stand around with their hands in their pockets watching everybody else work." "We all know that," replied his friend. "But why did he let you go?" "Jealousy," answered Pete. "All the other workers thought I was the foreman."   —Sunshine Magazine

For a real quick energy boost, nothing beats having the boss walk in.
—Robert Orben, 2500 Jokes To
Start 'Em Laughing

BOXING

Conan O'Brien on George Foreman knocking out Michael Moorer and regaining the heavyweight championship a few years back: "It's amazing that a guy in his mid-forties, who can't stop eating cheeseburgers, is that powerful. I mean, besides President Clinton."

The prizefighter staggered back to his corner after taking a terrific one-sided beating for 7 rounds. "Don't give up now, boy," his manager whispered in his ear. "You've got a no-hitter going!"   —Quote

George Foreman, champion boxer and grandfather, has this to say about his endurance: "A long time after I die, they're going to dig up my body and search for stuff to explain how I could do what I did. When they examine my DNA, they're going to find a substance called 'cheese' and another substance called 'burger.'"

～

The sport of boxing has had more than its share of scandals and scoundrels, but this one takes the cake. Two boxers were scheduled to fight each other and each placed a hefty bet against himself, betting he would lose the fight. When the fight started they both danced around the ring, each of them throwing harmless little air-jabs. Neither fighter wanted to land a punch. And then, one of the fighters accidentally brushed the other with his glove. The other fighter saw his chance, and hit the floor. The ref started to count. Realizing he had to do something or he'd win the fight, the fighter who was standing ran over, kicked the fighter on the ground, and was disqualified.

BROTHERS

When I was ten years old, my two-year-old brother Scott and I were out playing in the snow. Suddenly I ran to the front door of the nearest house and yelled to the startled neighbor, "Mrs. Giacomo, Help! Give me a shovel, quick. My brother is stuck in the snow up to his boot tops!" Mrs. Giacomo calmly asked, "Why doesn't he walk out?" My earnest reply, "Because he's in head first."

～

My brother Scott was great at playing hide-and-seek. He was so good at it, we haven't seen him since 1967!

～

Two fellows grew up in the mountains, and when they were grown, one of them said he was going up North to seek his fortune. The other one said he'd stay home and look after the farm and their parents. The one up North became a salesman, soon was sales manager, and then vice president and president of the company. Before long, his business was bought out by a big company out West. In a little while, he became president of the parent company. One day he got a call from his brother on the farm, who said, "Daddy died, and the funeral is Friday." He said, "Oh, my goodness. I have to leave Thursday for a big merger meeting in Japan. I just can't come, but I want you to give Daddy the best funeral you can get and send the bill to me. It's the least I can do." Well, the brother did that, and in a few weeks, the successful brother received a bill for $6,000, and he paid it. The following month, a bill for $100 came. Thinking they had forgotten something, he paid it. The next month, another bill for $100 came, and he paid that one, too. When another $100 bill arrived the third month, he called his brother and asked if he knew why he was getting these bills. "Oh, yes," the brother said, "I think I do. See, when we got Daddy all dressed up in his old serge suit in that new casket with that polished wood and satin lining, he just didn't look right, and since you said you wanted the best, we rented him a tuxedo."

> —J. Richard Carleton in *Hometown Humor, U.S.A.,*
> edited by Loyal Jones and Billy Edd Wheeler

BUREAUCRATS

My friend Ed was a sheep rancher in Idaho. One day a stranger walked up to him and asked, "If I can guess how many sheep you have may I have one?" Thinking this impossible, Ed agreed. The stranger declared, "You have 1,795 sheep." "Now how did he figure that out?" Ed wondered as the man selected an animal, slung it over his shoulder and turned to leave. "Wait," called the Ed. "If I can guess your occupation can I have that animal back?" "Sure," said the man. "You're a government bureaucrat," said Ed with a grin stretching from ear to ear. "How did you figure that out?" asked the stunned man. "Well," said Ed, "put my dog down and I will tell you."

If you're going to sin, sin against God, not the bureaucracy. God will forgive you. But the bureaucracy won't.   —Hyman Rickover

You may be a bureaucrat if:
   You've counted the pencils in your desk drawer.
   You know your exact retirement date even though it's more than five years
      away.
   You believe that the more employee rules there are, the fewer employee
      problems.
   Co-workers set their watches by your morning trip to the restroom.

> —Dale Dauten, King Features

Paperwork is the embalming fluid of bureaucracy, maintaining an appearance of life where none exists.   —Robert J. Meltzer

An Affirmative Action official of the State of Pennsylvania wrote to a business officer of a company whose policies were being investigated: "Please send to this office a list of all your employees broken down by sex." Some time later, this reply was received: "As far as we can tell, none of our employees is broken down by sex."

A zoning board had just been set up in a new community. A householder went to the office to request permission to build a small toolshed in his backyard.

"Have you a plan?" asked the director. "Oh, yes," said the householder, who showed him a map of his neighborhood, the dimension of his yard, and a sketch of the shed. "That looks fine," said the director. He pulled out a piece of paper, wrote a few words on it, xeroxed it, and said, "Here's your permission." A month later, a neighbor in almost exactly the same situation also wanted permission for a shed in her yard. She went to the director, got as far as a secretary, and made her request. "Thank you, Mrs. Smith," said the secretary, taking the documents. "Telephone me in two weeks and I'll let you know what the director's decision is, or what further steps are necessary." "But," groaned Mrs. Smith, "a month ago my neighbor got permission right away." "Oh, yes," said the secretary, "but that was before we got organized."

—Eric W. Johnson, *A Treasury of Humor*

BUSINESS

The chief executive officer of an electronics company called in his public relations director. "Listen, Wilson. Someone is trying to buy us out. It's your job to get the price of our stock up so it'll be too expensive for them. I don't care how you do it, just do it!" And he did. When asked how, he replied, "I started a rumor Wall Street obviously liked." "What was that?" "I told them you were resigning."

The shopkeeper was dismayed when a brand new business much like his own opened up next door and erected a huge sign that read: "BEST DEALS." He was horrified when another competitor opened up on his right, and announced its arrival with an even larger sign, reading, "LOWEST PRICES." The shopkeeper was panicked, until he got an idea. He put the biggest sign of all over his own shop—it read, "MAIN ENTRANCE."

The two biggest problems in corporate America are making ends meet and making meetings end.

The following corporate mergers were announced today, and the new companies will be called . . .

- Fairchild Electronics and Honeywell Computers: New company will be called Fairwell Honeychild
- Polygram Records, Warner Brothers and Keebler: Poly-Warne Cracker
- 3M and Goodyear: MMM Good,
- John Deere and Abitibi-Price: Deere Abi
- Honeywell, Imasco and Home Oil: Honey, I'm Home,
- Denison Mines, Alliance, and Metal Mining: Mine, All Mine,
- 3M, J. C. Penney, and Canadian Opera Company: 3 Penney Opera,
- Knott's Berry Farm and National Organization of Women: Knott NOW!
- Zippo Manufacturing, Audi, Dofasco, NS Dakota Mining: Zip Audi Do-Da.

One woman to another at a stockholder's meeting: "We might as well go. Whenever they load their speeches with funny little stories, there isn't going to be a dividend."   —Franklin Folger

At a business seminar: "I like the meatloaf kind of convention. Half the time you meet—half the time you loaf."   —*Wildlife Harvest*

C

CALIFORNIA

I've been married to the same woman for fourteen years. Which is like eighty-something in LA years.   —Robert G. Lee

Motto seen on the sweatshirt of a young woman exiting the physical sciences building at California State University, Los Angeles: "St. Andreas, Protect Us from Our Faults."

Nothing is wrong with California that a rise in the ocean level wouldn't cure.
                                                —Ross MacDonald

In California, they don't throw their garbage away—they make it into TV shows.   —Woody Allen

CALVIN COOLIDGE

I wish that we had more presidents like Calvin Coolidge. Coolidge, frustrated with the idea of paying $25,000 for an entire squadron of aircraft, is said to have asked, "Why can't we just buy one airplane and let the aviators take turns flying it?"

~

When Calvin Coolidge was Governor of Massachusetts, a lady asked him at dinner whether he had participated in athletic events as a student at Amherst. "Yes," he answered, munching a nut. "I held the stakes," and lapsed into silence.

~

Will Rogers recalled: "President Calvin Coolidge was pretty tight-lipped and never smiled much. Somebody bet me that I couldn't make the President laugh. Well, when we were introduced I said to him: 'I'm sorry. I didn't get the name.' And by golly, Coolidge laughed."

~

While he was Vice President, Coolidge was visited by Channing Cox, his successor as Governor of Massachusetts. Cox inquired how Coolidge had been able to see so many visitors a day and still leave the office at 5 P.M., whereas he himself often left as late as 9 P.M. "Why the difference?" Cox asked. "You talk back," said Coolidge.   —Paul F. Boller, Jr., *Presidential Anecdotes,* B

~

Artist Howard Chandler Christy was commissioned to do a portrait of First Lady Grace Coolidge, who wanted to pose with a white collie. Christy suggested that she wear a red gown for contrast. When the President, who valued thriftiness, heard that a new dress might be involved, he suggested, "Why not wear white and paint the dog red?"

—Frank Cormier, *Presidents Are People, Too*

CATHOLICISM

During a children's sermon, a priest asked the youngsters, "Does anyone know what a bishop does?" A young lad raised his hand. "Moves diagonally."

~

Father Vazken Movsesian, a Bay area Catholic priest, recalls: "Uplifted by the Papal Mass at San Francisco's Candlestick Park a few years back, I gave my congregation a detailed account of how I was escorted to the 49ers' locker room, where I met with representatives of other Christian churches. I expressed the feeling of warmth that was radiating from the 70,000 faithful that day. Finally, I summarized the inspirational message of Pope John Paul II. At the conclusion of my remarks, I asked for questions. A young voice piped up eagerly, 'Father, did you get to see Joe Montana's locker?'"

CATS

Our new coffee table was hand-carved . . . by the cat.　　　—Ron Dentinger

～

Once upon a time, a woman had a wonderful, faithful cat. One day, a man ran over the cat accidentally with his car. So, the man went to the old woman and said, "I'm terribly sorry about your cat. I'd like to replace him." "That so nice of you!" said the old woman, deeply touched. "So how good are you at catching mice?"

～

Woman: "What's your cat's name, little boy?"
Boy: "Ben Hur."
Woman: "That's a funny name for a cat. How did you happen to pick up such a name for it?"
Boy: "Well, we just called him Ben until he had kittens."　　—*Quote*

～

Herman: "Well, Jack, I read in the paper that your rich aunt just died."
Jack: "Yeah, I spent the last five years pretending that I loved her cats so she'd remember me in her will."
Herman: "Really? And what did she leave you?"
Jack: "The cats!"　　—Msgr. Arthur Tonne, *Jokes Priests Can Tell,* vol. 6

～

Cats don't caress us—they caress themselves on us.　　—Rivarol

～

The real measure of a day's heat is the length of a sleeping cat.
—Charles J. Brady in *Home Life*

～

The problem with cats is that they get the exact same look on their faces whether they see a moth or an ax murderer.　　—Paula Poundstone

～

If Darwin's theory of evolution was correct, cats would be able to operate a can opener by now.　　—Larry Wright

A 12-year-old girl once wrote to a TV network about a commercial that claimed a rodent poison was more effective than anything else at killing mice. She asked if cats had been included in the research.

     —Virginia Satkowski in White Plains, N.Y., *Reporter Dispatch*

An antiques collector was passing a small shop when he noticed a cat on the sidewalk out front, licking milk from a saucer. The man immediately realized the saucer was very old and valuable. He stepped into the shop with an uninterested look and asked to buy the cat. "I'm sorry," the shop owner said, "but the cat is not for sale." "Please," the collector urged, "I need a cat around my house to catch mice." "I'll give you 20 dollars." "The cat is yours," the proprietor said, taking the money. "Listen," the collector added, "I wonder if you could throw in that old saucer as well. The cat seems to like it, and I'd hate to have him give it up." "Sorry," the shop owner answered , "but that saucer brings me luck. Why, just this week I've sold 68 cats!" —Soupy Sales

CELEBRITIES

Brooke Shields, on why she wanted to become spokesperson for a federal anti-smoking campaigns: "Smoking kills. If you're killed, you've lost a very important part of your life."

With profits from his food company, Paul Newman helped build a camp for critically ill children. It's called the Hole in the Wall Gang Camp, from Newman's film *Butch Cassidy and the Sundance Kid*. Newman was sitting at a table one day with a camper who asked him who he was. The actor reached for a carton of Newman's Own lemonade and showed the boy his likeness on the container. "This is me," Newman said. Wide-eyed, the camper asked, "Are you lost or something?"   —Quoted in *Yale-New Haven Hospital Magazine*

Unfailingly courteous to fans, Jay Leno always signs autographs, poses for pictures and somehow finds time to call many of the people who write to him. "I called one woman," says Jay, "and I asked, 'Is Susan there?'" "No, who's this?" "This is Jay Leno." "Well, this is her mother. Whaddya want?" "She wrote me a letter," I replied. "Oh, well," she answered. "She writes to every crackpot on television!"   —Russell Miller

The nice thing about being a celebrity is that when you bore people they think it's their fault.   —Henry Kissinger

CHANGES

Often we change jobs, friends, and spouses instead of ourselves.

—Akbarali H. Jetha

CHARACTER

Many a man's reputation would not know his character if they met on the street. —Elbert Hubbard

You take the lies out of him, and he'll shrink to the size of your hat; you take the malice out of him, and he'll disappear. —Mark Twain

CHARITY

A solicitor from an established charity made a financial appeal to W. C. Fields. Fields responded that he would have to confer with his lawyer. "And what will you do if your lawyer says yes?" the solicitor inquired. "Get another lawyer," replied Fields.

CHARM

The wit and charm of Adlai E. Stevenson II made him a constant target for autograph seekers. Once, as he left the United Nations Building in New York City and was as usual surrounded by admirers, a small, elderly woman in the crowd finally succeeded in approaching him. "Please, Mr. Ambassador," she said, holding out a piece of paper, "your autograph for a very, very old lady." "Delighted!" Stevenson replied with a smile. "But where is she?"

CHESS

Chess is a game that requires intense concentration and absolute silence. During one game, a player sneezed and his opponent said, "Gesundheit." The first player said, "Did you come here to play or talk?"

—Robert Orben, *2500 Jokes To Start 'Em Laughing*

CHICAGO

Former heavyweight boxer James "Quick" Tillis was a cowboy from Oklahoma who fought out of Chicago in the early 1980s. Years later, he still remembers his first day in the Windy City after his arrival from Tulsa. "I got off the bus with two cardboard suitcases under my arms in downtown Chicago and stopped in front of the Sears Tower. I put my suitcases down and I looked up at the Tower and I said to myself, 'I'm going to conquer Chicago.' When I looked down, the suitcases were gone."

Norman Ross, who had won many swimming titles, was in the habit of swimming in Lake Michigan early every morning before reporting for his job on the sports desk of a Chicago newspaper. Ross sometimes would spot a solitary person walking along the lakeside. He would then swim to the shore and call out, "What town is this?" "Chicago," the startled pedestrian would reply. "Oh, I want Milwaukee," Ross would call out, and then plunge back into the water and swim away. —*Modern Handbook of Humor*

CHILDHOOD

Some childhood! My dad hired another kid to play me in our home movies.
—Ron Dentinger

~

We had a quicksand box in our backyard. I was an only child, eventually.
—Steven Wright

~

Until I was twelve, my family and I lived in a Chicago neighborhood near Garfield Park. My best friend and constant playmate was a boy my own age named Harry Joseph. When we moved we lost contact. Now Harry and I were both stamp collectors and were always engaged in swaps, each of us believing that he had gotten the better of the other. Many years later, I remember telling my wife that I often felt guilty about some of our deals. Perhaps I had taken advantage of Harry. When I was in my early fifties, I was attending a conference in Indianapolis and called home to hear from my wife that someone named Harry Joseph was trying to contact me. After forty years, I asked myself, could he still be angry about the stamps? I phoned him at his Manhattan number, and we had a marvelous conversation. He had seen me on television and tracked me down. He told me that his parents had died and that while cleaning out their basement, he had found some stamps I had sold him. These reminded him of our childhood friendship and had prompted his call. I expected him to ask for a refund. Instead he asked my mailing address, and, in a few days, the stamps arrived at my home as a gift from Harry.

~

The imaginary friends I had as a kid dropped me because their friends thought I didn't exist. —Aaron Machado

~

"What a childhood I had," says Rodney Dangerfield. "My parents sent me to a child psychiatrist. The kid was no help at all!"

CHILDREN

Here are some tip-offs that your child may have some flaws . . . even though you may think he or she is perfect:

Your child gets extra credit for being absent.

Neighbors always have their cement poured while you are on vacation.

You find the phone off the hook and the mailbox in his room.

You are shopping with your child and a clerk gives you a flyer from the store across the street.

❧

Jack: "My wife used to play the piano a lot, but since the kids came she doesn't have time."

Mack: "Kids are a comfort, aren't they?"

Kids say the darndest things. Some grade school teachers must agree with that, because they keep journals of amusing things their students have written in papers. Here are a few examples:

- The future tense of I give is I take.
- The parts of speech are lungs and air.
- The inhabitants of Moscow are called Mosquitoes.
- A census taker is man who goes from house to house increasing the population.
- Water is composed of two gins. Oxygin and hydrogin. Oxygin is pure gin. Hydrogin is gin and water.
- (Define H_2O and CO_2.) H_2O is hot water and CO_2 is cold water.
- A virgin forest is a forest where the hand of man has never set foot.
- The general direction of the Alps is straight up.
- A city purifies its water supply by filtering the water then forcing it through an aviator.
- Most of the houses in France are made of plaster of Paris.
- The people who followed the Lord were called the 12 o'possums.
- The spinal column is a long bunch of bones. The head sits on the top and you sit on the bottom.
- We do not raise silk worms in the United States, because we get our silk from rayon. He is a larger worm and gives more silk.
- One of the main causes of dust is janitors.
- A scout obeys all to whom obedience is due and respects all duly constipated authorities.
- One by-product of raising cattle is calves.
- To prevent head colds, use an agonizer to spray into the nose until it drips into the throat.
- The four seasons are salt, pepper, mustard and vinegar.
- The climate is hottest next to the Creator.
- Oliver Cromwell had a large red nose, but under it were deeply religious feelings.

- The word trousers is an uncommon noun because it is singular at the top and plural at the bottom.
- Syntax is all the money collected at the church from sinners.
- The blood circulates through the body by flowing down one leg and up the other.
- In spring, the salmon swim upstream to spoon.
- Iron was discovered because someone smelt it.
- In the middle of the 18th century, all the morons moved to Utah.
- A person should take a bath once in the summer, not so often in the winter.

In his book, *How to Use Humor for Business Success,* Malcolm Kushner reports that there are three ways to get things done: 1) Do it yourself. 2) Ask someone else to do it. 3) Ask your kids not to do it.

After the family sang some carols, four-year-old Kevin Kneeland commented, "Wasn't it good of the shepherds to put on clean clothes when they went to see baby Jesus?" His mother asked, "What do you mean?" Johnny explained, "We just sang, 'While Shepherds Washed Their Socks by Night.'"

The wife of an army colonel had made an all-night flight to meet her husband at his latest military assignment in Germany. She arrived weary at Rhein-Main Air Base in Germany with her nine children, all under age eleven. Collecting their many suitcases, the ten of them entered the cramped customs area. A young customs official watched them in disbelief. "Ma'am," he said, "do all these children and all this luggage belong to you?" "Yes, sir," she said with a sigh. "They're all mine." The customs agent began his interrogation: "Ma'am, do you have any weapons, contraband, or illegal drugs in your possessions?" "Sir," she calmly answered, "if I'd had any of those items, I would have used them by now!" She was allowed to pass without having to open a single suitcase.

Helen Wilton, a Sunday school teacher at the Cottonwood Methodist Church, asked her class of preschoolers if they knew where God lives. Stephen Mason, a precocious six-year-old, raised his hand, and the teacher called on him." God lives in my bathroom," the boy confidently answered. "Why do you say that God lives in your bathroom?" inquired the teacher. "Because every morning my dad pounds on the bathroom door and says, 'Good Lord, are you still in there?'"

Ten-year-old Keith Uttley came into the house covered with mud after finishing a rough day at play. "Mom," he shouted at the top of his voice, "if I fell out of a tree, would you rather I broke a leg or tore my pants?" "What a silly question," his mother answered from the next room. "I'd rather you tore your pants!" "Well, I got good news for you then," the boy replied triumphantly. "That's exactly what happened!"

C

~

As a kid I used to have a lemonade stand. The sign said, "All you can drink for a dime." So some kid would come up, plunk down the dime, drink a glass, and then say, "Refill it." I'd say, "That'll be another dime." "How come? Your sign says, 'All you can drink for a dime.' " "Well, you had a glass, didn't you?" "Yeah." "Well, that's all you can drink for a dime."   —Flip Wilson

~

The kindergarten class went on a field trip to the local police station where a kindly patrolman showed them around. Stopping in front of a Ten Most Wanted poster, he explained how citizens often help bring about arrests. "Are those pictures of the bad guys?" asked one six year old. The policeman soberly informed him they were indeed. "Well," pursued the kid, "why didn't you hold onto him after you took his picture?"

—H. Aaron Cohl, *The Friars Club Encyclopedia of Jokes*

~

You know what's a humbling experience? Whenever I would help the kids with their homework, their grades would go down.   —Ron Dentinger

BATH MAT: A little rug that wet children like to stand next to.

—Ron Dentinger

~

Little Milly had gone to bed, and her father was downstairs reading the paper. A terrible thunderstorm came up, with lightning and fierce noises. Milly shouted down to her father: "Daddy, I'm scared. Come up and help me." Milly's father, engrossed in the paper, shouted back, "Don't worry, Milly, you'll be all right. You know God loves you." "I know God loves me," cried Milly, "but I need something with skin on."

—Eric W. Johnson, *A Treasury of Humor* II

~

"I'm really worried," said one teenager to another. "Dad slaves away at his job so I'll never want for anything and so I can go to college. Mom spends every day washing and ironing and cleaning up after me, and she takes care of me when I'm sick." "So what are you worried about?" "I'm afraid they might try to escape!"

—Jack Moore, Universal Press Syndicate

~

Once when I was babysitting, my six-year-old grandson refused to eat anything set before him. In exasperation, I asked, "Jonathan, you tell me you don't like

meat, you don't like chicken, you don't like fish, you don't like fruit, you don't like vegetables, you don't like milk, you don't like juice. Tell me, what do you like?" Turning his innocent blue eyes on me, he answered, "Why, I like you, Grampa!"

~

Mother's little darling returns from his first day of school. "Oh, I hope you didn't cry," his mother says reassuringly. "I didn't," he says, "but, boy, the teacher sure did."

—King Duncan

~

When my son was in first grade, I learned an important lesson. You can always tell a six-year-old, but you have to tell him more than once.

~

When I was a graduate student, I took my daughter's Montessori school class to a farm near Princeton, New Jersey. Five-year-old Claudia, my daughter's best friend, visiting a farm for the first time, was looking at a fat sow lying in a pen. Said the farmer, "She's mighty big, isn't she?" "She sure is," said Claudia. "I just saw six little piggies blowing her up a few minutes ago."

We had a new teacher and she wanted to know if I had any brothers and sisters, and I told her I was an only child. "What did she say?" my mother asked. She said "Thank goodness!"   —King Duncan

~

Steve: "What is your son going to be when he graduates?"
Matt: "An old man."

~

Bill Cell and Ed Woodward, two professors of theology, were walking across the campus of United Theological Seminary when Bill asked Ed, "Do you believe in Original Sin?" Ed answered, "Yes, I do. We have a child." "Do you believe in Total Depravity?" asked Bill. "No, I don't. That is an excess of Calvinistic theology," replied Ed. Bill rejoined, "Just wait until you have two children!"

~

Some cute modern variants on ancient proverbs uttered by fourth grade students at St. George's Episcopal Day School in Clarksdale, Mississippi.:

    A penny saved . . . buys one piece of gum. (Heather Franklin)
    Where there's a will . . . there's a greedy son. (Amanda Daho)
    If you can't stand the heat . . . hop in the pool. (Tucker Dearman)
    People who live in glass houses . . . don't take baths. (Charles Flower)

~

Two of my grandsons were playing marbles when a pretty little girl walked by. "I'll tell you," said Jake to JD, "when I stop hating girls, that's the one I'm going to stop hating first."

~

Tommy, one of my neighbor's grandsons, walked into the convenience store and asked the clerk for a box of Tide so that he could wash his dog, Petey. The clerk was appalled and told the boy, "Son, you can't use Tide on a dog. It might hurt him. Are you sure you want Tide?" "Oh, yes," Tommy insisted. So the clerk sold the boy a box of Tide. The next day, Tommy skulked into the store with a very sad look on his face. "What's the matter, Tommy," the clerk asks. "My dog died," the boy blurted out, tears rolling down his cheeks. "That's terrible," said the clerk. "But remember, I told you that Tide might hurt your dog." The boy responded, "I don't think it was the Tide. I think it was the spin cycle."

On children: The best way to keep children home is to make the home atmosphere pleasant—and let the air out of the tires.   —Dorothy Parker

❧

Children are a great comfort in one's old age—which one wouldn't reach so quickly if one didn't have children.

❧

Ask your child what he wants for dinner only if he's buying.

—Fran Lebowitz

❧

I take my children everywhere, but they always find their way back home.

—Robert Orben

❧

Never lend your car to anyone to whom you have given birth.

—Erma Bombeck

❧

Tomorrow's kids will probably have to make up something they had to do without.   —Martin A. Ragaway

❧

If God had wanted sex to be fun, He wouldn't have included children as punishment.   —Ed Bluestone

❧

If you want to recapture your youth, cut off his allowance.   —Al Bernstein

❧

My eight-year-old grandson Jonathan was waiting in line at an ice cream stand and hanging on to the hand of his three-year-old cousin Mark. Mark kept yelling impatiently, "I want vanilla!" The stand was out of vanilla, but the older boy handled the situation with all the skill of a child psychologist. He bought two strawberry cones and handed one to his cousin, saying, "Here you are— pink vanilla!"

❧

Aunt Frieda asked her five-year-old daughter Heather, "Why can't you behave like Tracy next door?" "Because she's a doctor's kid," Heather protested. "What's that got to do with it?" her mother demanded. "The doctor always keeps the best babies for himself," Heather replied.

In 1962, my five-year-old came home from a birthday party and told his mother, "I'm never going to believe another word you say. I was the only kid at the party who didn't know that babies are brought by the stork."

⌒

When my son Stephen was a first-grader, he demonstrated how practical children can really be. He slipped in the hall at school and skinned his knee. A gym teacher attempted psychological first aid with, "Remember, big boys don't cry, sonny." Steve replied, "I'm not going to cry—I'm gonna sue!"

⌒

When my daughter Susan was in kindergarten, the teacher displayed several flags. "What flag is this?" asked the teacher. "This is the flag of our country," answered Susie. "And what is the name of our country?" asked the teacher. Susie's quick reply: "'Tis of thee!"

⌒

Little boy to his mother, "Can I go outside and help Daddy put snow chains on the car? I know all the words."

⌒

Another tale told by my neighbor, Rosemary Pulaski: "We set out our crèche for the holidays, and my five-year-old daughter, Laura, was watching me put all of the figurines in it—especially baby Jesus. I explained what a manger was—that they didn't have a crib for him, so they had to lay a blanket on the hay and put him there. She thought about that for a minute, and then she looked at me and said, 'Mom, did they have to use a manger for his car seat, too?'"

⌒

My boss' son is five years old. He attended his first funeral with his family. I saw him on Sunday and asked him what he thought of it. His answer, "She was already dead when we got there."

⌒

A three-year-old went with his dad to see a litter of kittens. On returning home, he breathlessly informed his mother there were 2 boy kittens and 2 girl kittens. "How did you know?" his mother asked. "Daddy picked them up and looked underneath," he replied. "I think it's printed on the bottom."

⌒

Another three-year-old put his shoes on by himself. His mother noticed the left shoe was on the right foot. She said, "Son, your shoes are on the wrong feet." He looked up at her with a raised brow and said, "Don't kid me, Mom, I KNOW they're my feet."

～

On the first day of school, the kindergarten teacher said, "If anyone has to go to the bathroom, hold up two fingers." A little voice from the back of the room asked, "How will that help?"

～

A mother and her young son returned from the grocery store and began putting away the groceries. The boy opened the box of animal crackers and spread them all over the table. "What are you doing?" his mother asked. "The box says you can't eat them if the seal is broken," the boy explained. "I'm looking for the seal."

～

Teacher: "Can people predict the future with cards?"
Pupil: "My mother can."
Teacher: "Really?"
Pupil: "Yes, she takes one look at my report card and tells me what will happen when my father gets home."

～

A four-year-old girl was learning to say the Lord's Prayer. She was reciting it all by herself without help from her mother. She said, "And lead us not into temptation, but deliver us some e-mail. AMEN."

～

A four-year-old was at the pediatrician for a check up. As the doctor looked down her ears with an otoscope, he asked, "Do you think I'll find Big Bird in here?" The little girl stayed silent. Next, the doctor took a tongue depressor and looked down her throat. He asked, "Do you think I'll find the Cookie Monster down there?" Again, the little girl was silent. Then the doctor put a stethoscope to her chest. As he listened to her heart beat, he asked, "Do you think I'll hear Barney in there?" "Oh, no!" the little girl replied. "Jesus is in my heart. Barney's on my underpants."

～

During a dinner party at my sister's home, her two little children entered the dining room totally naked and walked slowly around the table. Sis and her husband were so embarrassed that they pretended nothing was happening and kept the conversation going. The guests cooperated and also continued as if nothing extraordinary was happening. After going all the way around the room, the children left, and there was a moment of silence at the table, during which one child was heard to say, "You see, it IS vanishing cream!"

C

～

A wife invited some people to dinner. At the table, she turned to their six-year-old daughter and said, "Would you like to say the blessing?" "I wouldn't know what to say," the girl replied. "Just say what you hear Mommy say," the wife answered. The daughter bowed her head and said, "Lord, why on earth did I invite all these people to dinner?"

～

One day at work, while I was waiting on a customer, my colleague asked the customer's little boy how old he was. "I can't tell you," the child replied. "I have my mittens on."   —*Catholic Digest*

～

A mother put carrots on her daughter's plate, knowing she didn't like them. She told her to eat them anyway since they were good for her eyes and would help her see in the dark. The little girl pushed the carrots onto her mother's plate and said, "You eat them, Mommy. I'll just use a flashlight."   —*Capper's Weekly*

～

Mort was laying on the discipline and my teenager shot back, "Did I ask to be born?" Mort said, "If you had, the answer would have been no!"

～

I've got two boys, both of 'em training to be astronauts by correspondence. They're at home taking up space.

～

One student's definition of a grandmother: "That's someone who comes to visit and keeps your mother from spanking you."

～

My son keeps a hamster in his room. At first the smell was terrible . . . but the hamster got used to it.

～

Walking down the street, a man passes a house and notices a child trying to reach the doorbell. No matter how much the little guy stretches, he can't make it. The man calls out, "Let me get that for you," and he bounds onto the porch to ring the bell. "Thanks, mister," says the kid. "Now let's run."

~

A four-year-old boy accompanied his pregnant mother to the gynecologist's office. When mother heaved a sigh and clutched her stomach, her son looked alarmed. "Mommy, what is it?" he asked. "The baby brother you're going to have is kicking," his mother explained. "He's probably getting restless," the youngster decided. "Why don't you swallow a toy?"

~

The mother of three notoriously unruly youngsters was asked whether or not she'd have children if she had it to do over again. "Sure," she replied, "but not the same ones."

~

Even though children are deductible, they can also be very taxing.

~

I don't want to sound like an old fuddy-duddy, but I know children get confused when we layer the holiest of seasons with fantasy. (No, I don't want to get rid of Santa Claus.) However, I can appreciate the frustration of the Sunday school teacher who was working with her primary group. "Do you know who Matthew was?" she asked. When she received no answer she asked, "Do any of you know who Mark was?" Still no answer. "I'm sure that somebody knows who Peter was," she said. "Can anyone tell me please, who was Peter?" A little boy raised his hand and said, "I think he was a wabbit."

—King Duncan

A pastor adjusted his height and knelt in front of a group of church preschoolers at a special service. He talked to the children about being good and going to heaven. At the end of his talk, the pastor asked, "Where do you want to go?" The little voices shouted out, "Heaven!" "And what must you be to get to heaven?" the pastor asked. "Dead!" a loud chorus yelled.

—Msgr. Arthur Tonne

Benjamin Leese, fifteen, who teaches Sunday school class for the third-graders at Trinity Lutheran Church, East Berlin, Pennsylvania, asked his students: "What is a prophet?" One young boy quickly replied, "When someone makes a good investment."

After telling her class the story of God's promise to give His people a land flowing with milk and honey, a Sunday school teacher asked her little ones: "What do you think a land flowing with milk and honey would be like?" "I think it would be pretty sticky," Eric replied.   —Msgr. Arthur Tonne

Human beings are the only creatures that allow their children to come home.

—Bill Cosby

After Cardinal James Hickey's visit to a parochial school in Maryland, a puzzled youngster asked his teacher, "Why did they keep calling him 'His M&M's'?"

—Albert I. Murphy

Ever notice . . . that you can't get your kids to sit still when you want to take their picture, but when you use a video camera, you can't get them to move?

—Jay Trachman

The best time to put children to bed is whenever they'll go.   —Dave Preston

Although there were only enough cookies for each child to have three at a party for little folks, young Bobby took four. "You're supposed to get only three cookies, Bobby," said the hostess. "You ought to put the fourth one back." "Can't," exclaimed Bobby. "I ate that one first."

THE WISDOM OF CHILDREN

- "Never trust a dog to watch your food." Patrick, age 10
- "When your dad is mad and asks you, 'Do I look stupid?' don't answer." Hannah, 9
- "Never tell your mom her diet's not working." Michael, 14
- "Stay away from prunes." Randy, 9
- "Don't squat with your spurs on." Noronha, 13
- "When your mom is mad at your dad, don't let her brush your hair." Taylia, 11
- "Never allow your three-year-old brother in the same room as your school assignment." Traci, 14
- "Don't sneeze in front of mum when you're eating crackers." Mitchell, 12
- "Puppies still have bad breath even after eating a Tic-Tac." Andrew, 9
- "Never hold a Dust Buster and a cat at the same time." Kyoyo, 9
- "You can't hide a piece of broccoli in a glass of milk." Armir, 9
- "Don't wear polka-dot underwear under white shorts." Kellie, 11
- "If you want a kitten, start out by asking for a horse." Naomi, 15
- "Felt markers are not good to use as lipstick." Lauren, 9
- "Don't pick on your sister when she's holding a baseball bat." Joel, 10
- "When you get a bad grade in school, show it to your mom when she's on the phone." Alyesha, 13
- "Never try to baptize a cat." Eileen, 8

A kindergarten teacher asked, "What is the shape of the earth?" One girl spoke up: "According to my Daddy—terrible!"

Trying to come to the aid of his father, who was stopped by an officer for speeding, the lil' tyke piped up, "Yeah? Well, if we were speeding, so were you!"

Two kids were trying to figure out what game to play. One said, "Let's play doctor." "Good idea," said the other. "You operate, and I'll sue."

Upon eating a snack of some munchies or other my Grandson asked what vitamins they had in them. I told him I doubted there were any at all. He replied wide-eyed, "You mean these are just for fun?"

A small boy is sent to bed by his father . . . [Five minutes later] "Da-ad . . ."
"What?" "I'm thirsty. Can you bring me a drink of water?" "No. You had
your chance. Lights out." [Five minutes later] "Da-aaaad . . ." "WHAT?" "I'm
THIRSTY . . . Can I have a drink of water??" "I told you NO! If you ask again
I'll have to spank you!!" [Five minutes later] "Daaaa-aaaAAAAD . . ." "WHAT??!!"
"When you come in to spank me, can you bring me a drink of water?"

~

Pastor Heather Anderson informs me: "I was casting kids in our church for
our annual Christmas play, and I was giving out choices, such as Shepherd,
Lamb, Villager. One 5-year-old couldn't decide, so I said, 'Luke, you can be a
Villager.' He said, 'OK,' and ran over to his parents. Very excited, he said to
them, 'Guess what! I get to be a mini-van!' "

~

One Sunday, I heard two brothers, ages 8 and 4, discussing Adam and Eve.
The eight-year-old asked: "How did Adam and Eve die?" And the four-year-old
said: "They ate bad fruit."

~

It is frequently said that children don't know the value of money. This is only
partially true. They don't know the value of your money. Their money, they
know the value of.
                    —Judy Markey, *You Only Get Married For the First Time Once*

~

It is not easy to be crafty and winsome at the same time, and few accomplish
it after the age of six.   —John W. Gardner and Francesca Gardner Reese,
                                        in *Know or Listen to Those Who Know*

~

Children certainly brighten up a home. Whoever saw a child under 12 turn
off an electric light?   *—Farm Journal*

~

Parents spend the first two years of a child's life getting him to walk and talk
and the next ten getting him to sit down and shut up.

~

The five-year-old had apparently trained her younger sister. For, as the congregation recited the Lord's Prayer at Mass, there came in clear—and loud—young
voices from the pew behind me, ". . . And forgive us our trash passes as we
forgive those who pass trash against us."   *—Family Digest*

CHOCOLATE

THE LAWS OF CHOCOLATE

- If you get melted chocolate all over your hands, you're eating it too slowly.
- Chocolate-covered raisins, cherries, orange slices and strawberries all count as fruit, so eat as many as you want.
- Problem: How to get two pounds of chocolate home from the store in a hot car. Solution: Eat it in the parking lot.
- Diet tip: Eat a chocolate bar before each meal. It'll take the edge off your appetite and you'll eat less.
- A nice box of chocolates provides your total daily intake of calories in one place. Isn't that handy?
- If you can't eat all your chocolate, it will keep in the freezer. But if you can't eat all your chocolate, it may be a sign of a deeper problem.
- If calories are an issue, store your chocolate on top of the fridge. Calories are afraid of heights, and they will jump out of the chocolate to protect themselves.
- Equal amounts of dark chocolate and white chocolate are a balanced diet.
- Two phrases: Money talks. Chocolate sings.
- The preservatives in chocolate make you look younger.
- Question: Why is there no such organization as Chocoholics Anonymous? Answer: Because no one wants to quit.
- If not for chocolate, there would be no need for control-top pantyhose. An entire garment industry would be devastated.
- Put "eat chocolate" at the top of your list of things to do today. That way, at least you'll get one thing done.

CHRISTMAS

I was sitting in my office on the first Saturday of December. Outside in the courtyard of our church the men of the church were in the process of building the stage for a live nativity scene. Since my door was open, I heard two children discussing the process. One asked of the other, "What is this going to be?" Answered the other, "Oh, they're building a live fertility scene."

—Walter Lauster

The stores love it when the bells we hear at Christmas are from a cash register.

—Gene Perret

We got the kids something nice for Christmas—their own apartments.

"Last night," a wife told her husband, "I dreamed you gave me $200 to spend on a Christmas wardrobe. Surely, you wouldn't do anything to spoil a dream like that, would you?" "Of course not," he replied. "You may keep the $200."
—*Capper's Weekly*

C

"Thanks for the harmonica you gave me for Christmas," little Joshua said to his uncle the first time he saw him after the holidays. "It's the best Christmas present I ever got." "That's great," said his uncle. "Do you know how to play it?" "Oh, I don't play it," the little fellow said. "My mother gives me a dime a day not to play it during the day and my father gives me fifty cents a week not to play it at night."

The children of our parish in Tokyo had been practicing their Christmas play for days and knew all their lines. Right on cue, the innkeeper said, "There is no room. You cannot stay here." No one was prepared, however, for Joseph when he turned to Mary and said, "I told you to make reservations!"   —William Grimm, M.M., *Maryknoll Magazine*

Could I get my husband to address the Christmas cards? I wondered. The family was coming. There was shopping yet to do, gifts to wrap, the tree to decorate, cooking, cleaning. I arranged the cards, stamps, and address book on the table, then hopefully pulled up a chair and said, "Come on, Dear, let's get these out of the way." He glanced at the array on the table, turned away, and went into the den, while I looked daggers at his back. I heard a drawer jerk open and bang shut. He returned with a high stack of cards, stamped, sealed, and addressed. "They're last year's," he said. "I forgot to mail them. Now let's go out to dinner and relax. You've been working too hard."   —*Catholic Digest*

Our youngest daughter, Nancy, was almost four. My wife and I and our four older children had tried to prepare Nancy for Christmas by talking with her about the real meaning of Christmas and why the family celebrated it. Nancy had a wonderful Christmas with a lot of presents and toys. A few days later, she was talking with her older sister about what a great Christmas she had, and said, "I sure hope Joseph and Mary have another baby."

—Donald W. Dugan

The first-grade class presented a nativity play shortly before Christmas. When Joseph came to the inn and asked if there was room at the inn, the little boy playing the innkeeper replied, "You're lucky. We just had a cancellation."

—George Goldtrap

During the children's sermon, on the third Sunday in Advent at First Baptist Church in Gainesville, Florida, the youth minister remarked: "Bethlehem was

a real small town. In fact, it was so small, I'll bet they didn't even have a Pizza Hut." One young lad quickly and seriously remarked, "Maybe they had a Little Caesar's!"   —Lynwood Walters

Small boy giving his Christmas gift wish lists to his parents: "Fax this list to Santa Claus, e-mail this one to God, and I want to talk direct to Grandma."

Christmas is the season when people run out of money before they run out of friends.   —Larry Wilde

Christmas is a strange time of year. That's when people celebrate the birth of the Prince of Peace by buying toy rockets, submarines, artillery, and hand grenades for their children.

It's a good idea to send the kids to bed early on Christmas Eve. It gives fathers a few more hours to play with their toys.

The cheapest place to meet for the holidays is Grandma's house—unless you're Grandpa.

Banks never seem to get totally into the holiday spirit. My bank sent me a card that said, "Have a Happy Holiday. If You Are Already Having A Happy Holiday, Please Disregard This Notice."

No matter how many Christmas cards you send out, the first one you get is
from someone you missed.   —*Capper's Weekly*

The nicest things in the world are a Christmas tree when it's first put up—and
the living room when you finally take the tree down.

—Lois Reed in *Farm Journal*

Every Christmas we get a visit from the jolly gent with the great big bag over
his shoulder. It's my son home from college and the great big bag is laundry.

—Robert Orben, *2500 Jokes To Start 'Em Laughing*

CHURCH BULLETINS

Announcement in a church bulletin: "The
annual church picnic will be held Saturday
afternoon. If it rains, it will be held in the
morning."

Newburg Church tries to assist in serving
a luncheon for the families of church
members who have died immediately following the funeral.

Notice in a Florida church bulletin, repri-
manding parents for driving too fast when
dropping children off at parish functions:
"We want everyone to know that safety is
one of our priorities. Driving slowly on
church property is a necessity or we may
have to install bums on the driveways."

From the bulletin of the Church of the Incarnation in Sarasota, Florida: "*The
Magic of Lassie,* a film for the whole family, will be shown Sunday at 5 P.M.
in the church hall. Free puppies given to all children not accompanied by
parents."

EXCERPTS FROM CHURCH BULLETINS:

- The ladies of the church have cast off clothes of every kind and they may be seen
  in the church basement on Friday afternoon.

- As the maintenance of the church yard is becoming increasingly costly, it would be appreciated if those who are willing would clip the grass around their own graves.
- A note from the pastor: I shall be away from the parish attending the Diocesan Clergy School from April 21–24. It will be convenient if parishioners will abstain from arranging to be buried, or from making other calls on me during this time.
- There is joy in the presence of the angels over one singer who repents.
- All the youth choirs of Our Redeemer have been disbanded for the summer with the thanks of the entire church.
- From the Holy Week bulletin of St. John's Anglican Church, Edmonton, Alberta: Maundy Thursday, April 8, 7 P.M. We will re-enact the Last Supper and journey to the Garden of Gethsemane. We will strip the altar and sanctuary of all color and symbol. Together, we will leave the church bare and in silence.
- From Lenten bulletin of Zion Lutheran Church, Garretson, South Dakota: 7:30 LENTEN SERVICE. The final Lenten Service theme is: 'Why Doesn't God Do Something?' with Pastor Meidinger.
- In the bulletin of the Westchester (Illinois) Community United Church of Christ: And we give you thanks, O God, for people of many cultures and nations; for the young and old and muddle-aged.
- On March 16th, the prayer group met at the home of Margaret Ressler, who is no longer able to attend church. What a blessing!
- ADULT FORUM. Beginning November 5, Pastor Hodges will lead a six-part series on the book of Genesis. Were Adam and Eve really naked in the Garden? Come and see for yourself.
- From the yearbook of Trinity Lutheran Church, Jeffers, Minnesota: The (correspondence) committee will assist with the mailing of the newsletter and stapling of the Annual Report to congregational members.

The Sunday bulletin of St. Teresa of Avila parish in Augusta, Ga., listed the sacraments available at the church, including: "Anointing of the Sick. If you are going to be hospitalized for an operation, contact the priest. Celebrated also for those who are seriously sick by request."

~

From a Sarasota, Florida, church bulletin: "Students will study Matthew 14:22–33, 'Jesus Walks on Walter.'"

~

From a Lewiston, Idaho, church bulletin: "We need models for our 'Satan and Lace Wedding Party.'"

~

"Offertory solo: 'O Holy Nighty.'"
>—Music listing in Kansas City, Mo., church bulletin

In an Ohio church bulletin: "The Church Board of Bartlett will meet for a few minutes after the school board."

CHURCHES

Conversation overheard at a Denny's shortly after the morning church service one Sunday:

Wife: Did you see the new hat Mrs. Smith wore to church this morning?
Husband: No!
Wife: A lot of good it does you to go to church!

～

Johnny Zezas, Wyoming's top wrangler, came up with this dash of whimsy: "Many people have nothing but praise for the church, especially when the collection plate is handed round."

～

At Mt. Ebal Baptist Church, Melanie Nelson was in charge of promoting the denominational magazine among the members of the congregation. At the Sunday morning service, Pastor Wall gave her a minute to make an appeal to the congregation. "Please, brothers and sisters, if all of us start our subscriptions at the same time, and mail them in before the end of the month, then we'll be able to expire together."

～

The church today is raising a whole generation of mules. They know how to sweat and to work hard, but they don't know how to reproduce themselves.

～

The Maywood Community Church once brought in a performing horse. They asked the horse how many Commandments, and he stamped ten times. Then they asked how many apostles, and he stamped twelve times. Some wise guy in the crowd asked, "How many hypocrites are there in this church?" The horse went into a tap-dance on all fours.

～

Oliver Mendell, Ph.D., the noted scientist, made a careful study of people who fell asleep in church. His conclusion was that if all the sleeping congregants were laid end to end, they would be a lot more comfortable.

～

There appears to be a hymn for virtually every profession:

Dentists: Crown Him with Many Crowns
Contractors: The Church's One Foundation
Obstetricians: Come, Labor On

Golfers: There Is a Green Hill Far Away
Politicians: Standing on the Promises
Gardeners: Lo, How a Rose E'er Blooming
Librarians: Let All Mortal Flesh Keep Silence
Lawyers: In the Hour of Trial
Accountants: Ten Thousand by Ten Thousand
Clothiers: Blessed Be the Tie
Students: Ask Ye What Great Things I Know
Dry Cleaners: O For a Faith That Will Not Shrink
Credit Card Purchasers: A Charge to Keep I Have
Weather Forecasters: From Every Stormy Wind That Blows
Orators: O Could I Speak the Matchless Word
Choir Directors: Sing Them Over and Over Again to Me
Traffic Engineers: Where Cross the Crowded Ways of Life
IRS: We Give Thee But Thine Own
Pastors: Be Not Dismayed
There's even a hymn for **Absent Church Members:** Jesus, I Am Resting.

❧

When it comes to church leadership, some members rise to the occasion, while others merely hit the ceiling.

REVEREND FUN WWW.REVERENDFUN.COM

©COPYRIGHT 1999 GOSPEL FILMS, INC.

"Your father has agreed to stay awake in church today since it is Mother's Day . . .
It would be nice if you would do the opposite for once."

My friend Father Miles, a Roman Catholic priest, described the hearing of the confessions of nuns as like being stoned to death with popcorn.

◆

Father Ralph, the local Episcopalian priest, was wearing his clerical collar while visiting his wife, who was in the hospital for minor surgery. He stopped in to see her and chatted with her for quite some while. Before leaving, he leaned down and gave his wife a great passionate kiss and left the room. The woman in the next bed over stared in disbelief. After the priest left, the stunned woman spoke to her roommate, "You know, I've been a faithful member of the United Methodist Church all my life, but my pastor has never even come close to treating me as well as yours does."

◆

First Baptist Church always has a coffee hour after the Sunday worship service. One Sunday, after Pastor Ed preached much longer than usual, he was enjoying a homemade cookie and the fellowship of his congregation after the service. He was conversing with the Bowmount family and he happened to ask Alex Bowmount, a seven-year-old, if he knew why they served the coffee. "I think," said the boy, "it's to get the people awake before they drive home."

◆

My grandson Justin returned from his first time in church and was asked how it went. He said, "The music was nice, but the commercial was too long."

◆

The women of St. Matthew's Church had a handsome, foot-tall papier maché stork, which was used frequently for baby showers. The last time they got it out for one of these occasions, however, they couldn't use it—someone had wrung the bird's neck.

◆

As she left church, Hilda Watson shook hands with the minister and said: "Thank you for your sermon. It was like water to a drowning man."

◆

An elderly couple was observed, Sunday after Sunday, sitting in church with the woman holding her husband's hands. It seemed just wonderful, being so in love after so many years. One day the woman was asked about it and she said, "It's not so much love. I'm just trying to keep him from cracking his knuckles."   *—Capper's Weekly*

The pastor of a large church was anxious to introduce some new hymnbooks to his congregation so he directed his assistant to make an announcement to that effect immediately after his sermon. But it happened that the assistant had an announcement of his own to make, as follows: "All those who have children they wish to be baptized, please hand in their names at once." The clergyman, who was rather deaf, then arose and said: "And I wish to say, for the benefit of those who haven't any, that they may be obtained from me any day between three and four o'clock. The ordinary little ones are a dollar fifty, and the special ones with red backs are two fifty each."

Mrs. Hansen had been a member of First Baptist church for 25 years. As she walked toward the pastor, who stood waiting at the sanctuary door after the service, it was obvious that she had something on her mind. "Reverend, if God were alive today, He would be shocked at the changes in this church!"

PASTOR QUITS SPORTS: TWELVE REASONS WHY A LOCAL CLERGYMAN STOPPED ATTENDING ATHLETIC CONTESTS

1. Every time I went, they asked me for money.
2. The people with whom I had to sit didn't seem very friendly.
3. The seats were too hard and not comfortable.
4. The coach never came to call on me.
5. The referee made a decision with which I could not agree.
6. I was sitting with some hypocrites—they came only to see what others were wearing.
7. Some games went into overtime, and I was late getting home.
8. The band played some numbers that I had never heard before.
9. The games are scheduled when I want to do other things.
10. My parents took me to too many games when I was growing up.
11. Since I read a book on sports, I feel that I know more than the coaches anyhow.
12. I don't want to take my children, because I want them to choose for themselves what sport they like best.

On the bottom of the page was this one line postscript: "With apologies to those who use these same excuses for not coming to church."—Moody Monthly

A man and his ten-year-old son were on a fishing trip miles from home. At the boy's insistence, they decided to attend the Sunday worship service at a small rural church. As they walked back to their car after the service, the father was filled with complaints. "The service was too long," he lamented. "The sermon was boring, and the singing was off key." Finally the boy said, "Daddy, I thought it was pretty good for a dime."

~

C

My home church welcomes all denominations, but really prefers tens and twenties.

~

After the church service, a pastor told a woman, "I noticed your husband walked out in the middle of my sermon. I hope I didn't say something that offended him." "Not at all," replied the wife. "My husband has been walking in his sleep for years."

~

A pastor was talking with a hard-working woman who was a devoted member, present at all services. He expressed his thanks for seeing her so attentive to the services every Sunday. "Yes," she said, "it is such a rest after a long, hard week's work to come to church, sit down on the soft cushions, and not think about anything."   —Tal Bonham

~

On vacation with her family in North Dakota, a mother drove her van past a church in a small town and pointing to it, told the children that it was St. John's Church. "It must be a franchise," her eight-year-old son said. "We've got one of those in our town too."

~

A preacher in Chilhowie, Virginia, was visiting a perennial church no-show in his home. "All right," the man finally said. "I'll come to church Easter Sunday if I'm alive." But he didn't show up. After the service, the preacher took a lily from the Easter altar, went to the man's home, and knocked on the door. When the man came to the door, the preacher held out the lily and said, "Where's the body?"   —Larry Eisenberg

~

My father used to say, "You must have a terrible conscience if you can't sleep in church."   —George Goldtrap

~

I don't know why some people change churches—what difference does it make which one you stay home from?   —Rev. Denny Brake

~

During a visit to the big island of Hawaii, my wife and I attended Sunday services at a small Congregational church known for its informality. One Sunday a deacon asked me if I would usher at the morning service. I protested that I was much too casually dressed. "At home," I explained, the deacons always look for a man wearing a tie when they needed an usher." "Over here," the deacon laughingly replied, "we look for someone wearing shoes."

~

At the Little Brown Church, our music director used to refer to the choir as the prison ensemble. When I asked her why, she explained, "because they're always behind a few bars and always looking for the key."

~

At the Little Brown Church, our Christmas Eve service included a candle-lighting ceremony in which each member of the congregation lit a candle from his neighbor's candle. At the conclusion of the ceremony, the congregation sat hushed, pondering the inspiring beauty of the moment. I rose to announce the concluding hymn and was taken completely by surprise when laughter broke out in response to my invitation: "Now that everyone is lit, let's sing 'Joy to the World.'"

~

My office at the Little Brown Church, had a full-length mirror. So, for my first wedding service, I let the bride use the office as her dressing room. To protect her privacy, I posted this sign on the door: "Caution—do not enter—bride under construction."

~

I was in my office at the church on day when the phone rang. "Is the Reverend there?" a man asked. I explained that I was a minister. The man wanted to know which Scripture verses applied to funeral services. I gave him several references, and he jotted them down. "What about the 'ashes to ashes, dust to dust' part?" he asked. I read it to him slowly. Then, intending to offer him some sympathy, I inquired, "And who is the deceased?" "My daughter's pet turtle," he replied.

~

The choir was practicing one Wednesday evening while I worked on my sermon in the church office, just a few feet away. The choir was rehearsing a

C

particularly difficult piece by Mozart when a ferocious thunderstorm burst overhead. Alarmed, I walked into the sanctuary and said to the choir director, "That sounds like hail." "Oh, no," she said reassuringly. "They weren't that bad."

~

Pity the poor pastor who was delivering his sermon when a gentlemen in the back pew turned his head to one side, put his hand to his ear, and said, "Louder." The preacher raised his voice somewhat and continued with his sermon, which was not too interesting. After a few minutes the man said again, "Louder!" The preacher strained even more and continued on, but by now the sermon had become quite boring. The man said again, "Louder!" At this point a man on the front row couldn't stand it any longer and yelled back to the man in the rear. "What's the matter, can't you hear?" "No," said the man in the back. "Well," said the man down front, "move over, I'm coming back to join you."

~

Six-year-old Angie and her four-year-old brother Joel were sitting together in church. Joel giggled, sang, and talked out loud. Finally, his big sister had

". . . All I wanted to know is what the weather is going to be tomorrow."

enough. "You're not supposed to talk out loud in church." "Why? Who's going to stop me?" Joel asked. Angie pointed to the back of the church and said, "See those two men standing by the door? They're hushers."

WHEN CHURCH SERVICES ARE LIKE FOOTBALL GAMES

- Church Football Quarterback Sneak—Church members quietly leaving during the sermon.
- Draw Play—What many children do with the bulletin during worship.
- Halftime—The period between Sunday school and worship when many choose to leave.
- Benchwarmer—Those who do not sing, pray, work, or apparently do anything but sit.
- Backfield-in-Motion—Making a trip to the back (restroom or water fountain) during the service.
- Staying in the Pocket—What happens to a lot of money that should be given to the Lord's work.
- Two-minute Warning—The point at which you realize the sermon is almost over and begin to gather up your children and belongings.
- Instant Replay—The preacher loses his notes and falls back on last week's illustrations.
- Sudden Death—What happens to the attention span of the congregation if the preacher goes "overtime."
- Trap—You're called on to pray and are asleep.
- End Run—Getting out of church quick, without speaking to any guest or fellow member.
- Flex Defense—The ability to allow absolutely nothing said during the sermon to affect your life.
- Halfback Option—The decision of 50% of the Easter Sunday congregation not to return for the following week's worship service.
- Blitz—The rush for the restaurants following the closing prayer.

Gladys attended church services one particular Sunday. The sermon seemed to go on forever, and many in the congregation fell asleep. After the service, to be social, she walked up to a very sleepy looking gentleman, in an attempt to revive him from his stupor, extended her hand in greeting, and said, "Hello, I'm Gladys Dunn." To this the gentleman replied, "You're not the only one!"

The church steeple in Port Gibson is very high, and was being painted on a rather hot day. The painter was about half-way down and, as the steeple was widening out, it was taking more and more paint. The painter felt that he might not have enough paint to finish. Since he was hot and tired, and did not care to make another trip to the ground, he decided to stretch the amount of paint by adding some paint thinner to it. When finished, he lowered himself to the ground and went about cleaning up. Then he looked up to see the results of his work and noted that the area with the thinned paint looked decidedly different. He was pondering about what to do about it when the sky turned dark and there was a lightning flash and loud thunderclap. Then in a loud, booming voice from the sky came the words, "REPAINT AND THIN NO MORE!"

~

As the pastor began his Sunday sermon, there was a loud clap of thunder, signaling the start of a downpour. "Isn't that just like the Lord?" he said. "Here we are sitting and relaxing, and He's out there washing our cars."

~

During the installation of new lighting inside Liverpool Cathedral, an electrician working in the roof space accidentally left the elevator door open, preventing anyone below from calling it.

Visitors were stunned to see the Clerk of Works standing in the middle of the cathedral, yelling heavenward, "Peter! Close the gates!"

—Sidesman in *The Church Times,* England

CLERGY (*See also* MINISTERS)

Wanda Watson had asked me to offer the blessing at the women's luncheon being held at her home. But I was delayed by an unforeseen parish emergency. (A snake had appeared in the midst of the preschool playground.) Mrs. Watson was disturbed. She waited as long as she could for me to appear. Finally, she asked her husband Henry to fill in. Henry hated to speak in public, let alone pray out loud. He was visibly shaken but stood and announced reverently: "As there is no clergyman present, let us thank God."

~

It happened during a parish supper in the church basement, celebrating the Confirmation ceremony. One of the amateur high school waitresses acciden-

tally bumped the arm of the pastor just as he was taking a sip of coffee. The brown fluid spilled all over his arm and shoulder and on to the tablecloth. With half a smile and half a frown the good padre exclaimed to the parishioners across the table: "Will one of you laymen please say something appropriate?"
—Msgr. Arthur Tonne, *Jokes Priests Can Tell,* vol. 6

The main course at the big civic dinner was baked ham with glazed sweet potatoes. Rabbi Cohen regretfully shook his head when the platter was passed to him. "When," scolded Father Kelly playfully, "are you going to forget that silly rule of yours and eat ham like the rest of us?" "At your wedding reception, Father Kelly," said Rabbi Cohen without skipping a beat.

How do you tell the Episcopal priest at an ecumenical ceremony? She's the one who sends back the wine.

The
BORDERLINE ™

By Gabe Martin
borderln@cts.com

© 1995 GABE MARTIN

http://www.the-borderline.com/

Daniel in the Lion's Living Room

General Ulysses S. Grant once asked Henry Ward Beecher: "Why does a little fault in a clergyman attract more notice than a great fault in a bad man?" Replied Beecher: "Perhaps it is for the same reason that a slight stain on a white garment is more readily noticed than a large stain on a colored one.

CLOTHING

I've got a shirt for every day of the week. It's blue.   —Ron Dentinger

The trouble with fitted shirts is that they were made to fit someone else's body.

Overheard in a women's fitting room: "They don't make large as big as they used to!"

HELPFUL HINT FOR THE HOMEMAKER: You can remove ink stains from a silk dress with ordinary scissors.   —Ron Dentinger

Distrust any enterprise that requires new clothes.   —Henry David Thoreau

Everything you buy today is imported. Look at this shirt. You know what the washing instructions were? "First—find a flat rock!"
—Robert Orben, *2500 Jokes To Start 'Em Laughing*

Our daughter is learning dressmaking. Last week she cut out a dress pattern on the floor. She wound up with two dresses. One silk and one broadloom.
—Robert Orben, *2500 Jokes To Start 'Em Laughing*

COFFEE

Overheard: "I was making $100,000.00 a year, had 75 people under me, a condo in Aspen and was being considered for the Senate—then I switched to decaf."   —Bob Thaves, Newspaper Enterprise Assn

COLLEGE

I learned law so well, the day I graduated I sued the college, won the case, and got my tuition back.   —Fred Allen

The reason that colleges have been described as a place for the accumulation of learning is that freshmen bring some in, and graduating seniors students take none out—so knowledge accumulates.

~

The father was very proud when his son went off to college. He came to tour the school on Parents' Day, and observed his son hard at work in the chemistry lab. "What are you working on?" he asked. "A universal solvent," explained the son, "a solvent that'll dissolve anything." The father whistled, clearly impressed, then wondered aloud, "What'll you keep it in?"

~

I just spoke to my friend Alex, who is an assistant professor at a major Catholic university, and he was in a tizzy. It seems that he is behind in his theological research and is rushing to publish a much needed paper, without which, there is a very good possibility that he will be reassigned as a priest to a congregation somewhere in the boondocks. He told me that this situation affected most of the Brothers at the school, at one time or another, just as it affects many professors at universities and colleges all over the world. That's right. Even at a religious college, it's either publish or parish.

~

A physics professor at a state university in Michigan was famous for his animated lectures. He was short and thin with wild white hair and an excited expression. In lecture he would throw himself from the top of desks and throw frisbees to students in the back row to illustrate various principles. One day in class he was spinning on an office chair holding weights in each hand when he lost his balance and tumbled into the first row. He apologized to his class for going off on a tangent.

~

"I hear you have a boy in college. Is he going to become a doctor, an engineer, or a lawyer, perhaps?" The slow, quizzical answer was, "That I do not know. Right now the big question is: Is he going to become a sophomore?"

—*Quote*

~

Overheard in a university classroom: "I don't believe in astrology. We Scorpios aren't taken in by those things."

A college education should equip one to entertain three things: a friend, an idea and oneself.   —Thomas Ehrlich, *The Courage to Inquire*

My philosophy instructor would have made a good parking lot attendant. He tries to tell you where to go, but you can never understand him.

COLLEGE SENIORS VS. FRESHMEN . . .

Freshmen: Are never in bed past noon.
Seniors: Are never out of bed before noon.

Freshmen: Read the syllabus to find out what classes they can cut.
Seniors: Read the syllabus to find out what classes they need to attend.

Freshmen: Brings a can of soda into a lecture hall.
Seniors: Brings a jumbo hoagie and six-pack of Mountain Dew into a recitation class.

Freshmen: Calls the professor "Professor."
Seniors: Calls the professor "Bob."

Freshmen: Would walk ten miles to get to class.
Seniors: Drives to class if it's farther than three blocks away.

Freshmen: Memorizes the course material to get a good grade.
Seniors: Memorizes the professor's habits to get a good grade.

Freshmen: Knows a book-full of useless trivia about the university.
Seniors: Knows where the next class is. Maybe . . .

Freshmen: Shows up at a morning exam clean, perky, and fed.
Seniors: Shows up at a morning exam in sweats with a cap on and a box of Pop Tarts in hand.

Freshmen: Have to ask where the computer labs are.
Seniors: Have 'own' personal workstations.

Freshmen: Use the campus buses to go everywhere.
Seniors: Use the campus buses to run block while crossing the street.

Freshmen: Worry about the last freshman composition essay.
Seniors: Worry about the last GRE essay.

Freshman: Lines up for an hour to buy his textbooks in the first week.
Senior: Starts to think about buying textbooks in October . . . maybe.

Freshman: Looks forward to first classes of the year.
Senior: Looks forward to first party of the year.

Freshman: Is proud of his A+ on Calculus I midterm.
Senior: Is proud of not quite failing his Complex Analysis midterm.

Freshman: Calls his girlfriend back home every other night.
Senior: Calls Domino's every other night.

Freshman: Is appalled at the class size and callousness of Profs.

Senior: Is appalled that the campus "Subway" burned down over the summer.

Freshman: Is excited about the world of possibilities that awaits him, the unlimited vista of educational opportunities, the chance to expand one's horizons and really make a contribution to society.

Senior: Is excited about new dryers in the laundry room.

Freshman: Takes meticulous four-color notes in class.

Senior: Occasionally stays awake for all of class.

A student reported for her university final examination which consisted of "yes/no" type questions. She took her seat in the examination hall, stared at the question paper for five minutes, and then in a fit of inspiration took out her purse, removed a coin, and started tossing the coin and marking the answer sheet—Yes for heads and No for tails. Within half an hour she had completed the exam while the rest of the class was feverishly continuing to work. During the last few minutes, she desperately began throwing the coin, swearing, and sweating. The instructor, alarmed, approached her and asked if there was a problem. "I finished the exam in half an hour," she replied. "Now, I am rechecking my answers."

~

Wife: "Donald, when was the last time we received a letter from our son?"
Husband: "Just a second, honey, I'll go look in the checkbook."

—Die Weltwoche, Switzerland

~

"Son," said his father sternly, "after four years of college you're nothing but a loafer, a bum, and nuisance. I can't think of one good thing it's done for you."
"Well, Dad," he said, "it's cured Ma of bragging about me."   —*Grit*

~

Paul Lacy, Dean of Faculty at Earlham College, Richmond, Indiana, in 1982: "Chairing a meeting of the Earlham faculty is like trying to take eighty kangaroos for a walk."

~

Henry Merritt Wriston, president of Brown University from 1937–1955, described his job as follows: "The president [of a university] is expected to be an educator, to have been at some time a scholar, to have judgment about finance, to know something of construction, maintenance and labor policy, to speak virtuously and continuously in words that charm and never offend, to take bold positions with which no one will disagree, to consult everyone and follow all proffered advice, and to do everything through committees, but with great speed and without error."

COMMITTEES

Outside of traffic, there is nothing that has held the country back as much as committees.   —Will Rogers

COMMUNICATING

James Schlesinger discovered that in managing the Department of Defense there were many unexpected communications problems. For instance, when the Marines are ordered to secure a building, they form up and assault it. On the other hand, the same instructions will lead the Army to occupy the building

The
BORDERLINE™   By Gabe Martin
                                borderln@cts.com

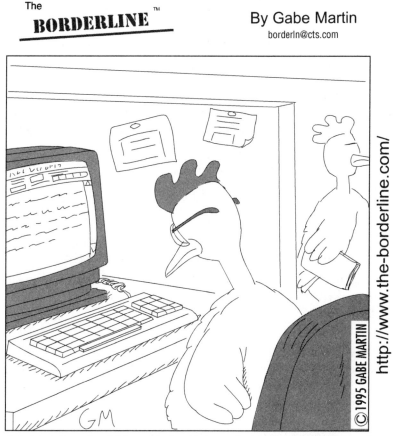

http://www.the-borderline.com/

© 1995 GABE MARTIN

Bob knew he should learn to touch-type, but he'd gotten so used to the "Hunt & Peck" method.

with a troop of infantry, and the Navy will characteristically respond by sending a yeoman to assure that the building lights are turned out. When the Air Force acts on these instructions, what results is a three-year lease with an option to purchase.

—

A young student was trying to earn some money over the summer. He knocked at the door of a rich man's house and asked if there was anything he could do. "Yes, the man replied, you can paint the porch. The paint and brushes are in the garage." Three hours later, the student came back and reported, "Well, it's all painted, but I gotta tell you, that's not a Porsche; it's a Ferrari."

—Eric W. Johnson, *A Treasury of Humor* II

—

Uncle Herbert from Vermont mailed an order to his butcher in Boston. First he began the note, "Kindly send two gooses." That didn't seem right, so he started over again with "Kindly send two geeses." Still he wasn't satisfied. He settled his dilemma by writing finally, "Kindly send me a goose." Then he signed his name and added a P.S.: "Send another one with it."

—

My Aunt Laura was in charge of last month's luncheon for her bridge club. She chose an expensive restaurant. However, after her group of elegantly dressed socialites was seated, Aunt Laura had no luck getting the waiter's attention. So, borrowing a cellular phone from a realtor who happened to be seated at the next table, she called the restaurant and asked to have menus sent to her table. It worked!

—

For many years I was a university theater director. My wife was once asked by one of her clients about her plans for the upcoming weekend. "I think I'm going to watch my husband's play," she replied. "Oh," the client said, "How many do you have?"

—Robert M. Putnam

—

Letter to a school principal: "I am annoyed to find out that you branded my child illiterate. It is a dirty lie as I married his father a week before he was born."

—Bob Terrell, *Fun Is Where You Find It*

—

Two tourists were driving through Louisiana. As they were approaching Natchitoches, they started arguing about the pronunciation of the town. They argued

C

back and forth until they stopped for lunch. As they stood at the counter, one tourist asked the gal at the cash register, "Before we order, could you please settle an argument for us? Would you please pronounce where we are . . . very slowly?" The young woman leaned over the counter and said, "Burrrrrrr, gerrrrrrr, Kiiiiing."

About a year ago my sister, who lives in Virginia, was talking with her four-year-old son, Brent. He was asking her why all their relatives from Wisconsin talk funny and sound like their noses are plugged up. "They think we have an accent," she replied. "But they have an accent, right?" Brent asked. "They talk funny?" "Everybody talks in different ways," she tried to explain. "To them, we sound like we talk very slow and all our words are d-r-a-w-n out." His eyes got big, and he whispered seriously, "Oh, no. You mean they hear funny too?"

The
BORDERLINE ™

By Gabe Martin
borderln@cts.com

For the first time, the head of the Jamaican Tourist Board really took the time to read their new slogan out-loud.

SOME ENGLISH SIGNS SEEN IN NON-ENGLISH SPEAKING COUNTRIES:

- In a Paris hotel elevator: Please leave your values at the front.
- In a hotel in Athens: Visitors are expected to complain at the office between the hours of 9 and 11 A.M. daily.
- In a Yugoslavian hotel: The flattening of underwear with pleasure is the job of the chambermaid.
- In a Hong Kong supermarket: For your convenience, we recommend courteous, efficient self-service.
- In an East African newspaper: A new swimming pool is rapidly taking shape since the contractors have thrown in the bulk of their workers.
- A sign posted in Germany's Black Forest: It is strictly forbidden on our Black Forest camping site that people of different sex, for instance, men and women, live together in one tent unless they are married with each other for the purpose.
- In an advertisement by a Hong Kong dentist: Teeth extracted by the latest Methodists.
- In a Rome laundry: Ladies, leave your clothes here and spend the afternoon having a good time.
- Detour sign in Kyushi, Japan: Stop: Drive Sideways.
- In a Swiss mountain inn: Special today—no ice cream.
- In a Norwegian cocktail lounge: Ladies are requested not to have children in the bar.
- At a Budapest zoo: Please do not feed the animals. If you have any suitable food, give it to the guard on duty.
- In the office of a Roman doctor: Specialist in women and other diseases.
- In a Tokyo hotel: Is forbitten to steal hotel towels please. If you are not person to do such thing is please not to read notis.
- In a Japanese hotel room: Please to bathe inside the tub.
- In a Bucharest hotel lobby: The lift is being fixed for the next day. During that time we regret that you will be unbearable.
- In a Leipzig elevator: Do not enter the lift backwards, and only when lit up.
- In a Belgrade Hotel Elevator: To move the cabin, push button for wishing floor. If the cabin should enter more persons, each one should press a number of wishing floor. Driving is then going alphabetically by national order.
- In the lobby of a Moscow hotel across from a Russian Orthodox Monastery: You are welcome to visit the cemetery where famous Russian and Soviet composers, artists, and writers are buried daily except Thursday.
- In an Austrian hotel catering to skiers: Not to perambulate the corridors in the hours of repose in the boots of ascension.
- On the menu of a Swiss restaurant: Our wines leave you nothing to hope for.
- On the menu of a Polish hotel: Salad a firm's own make; limpid red beet soup with cheesy dumplings in the form of a finger; roasted duck let loose; beef rashers beaten up in the country people's fashion.
- Outside a Hong Kong tailor shop: Ladies may have a fit upstairs.
- In a Bangkok dry cleaner's: Drop your trousers here for best results.

- In a Rhodes tailor shop: Order your summers suit. Because is big rush we will execute customers in strict rotation.
- In a Zurich hotel: Because of the impropriety of entertaining guests of the opposite sex in the bedroom, it is suggested that the lobby be used for this purpose.
- In a Vienna hotel: In case of fire, do your utmost to alarm the hotel porter.
- From a brochure of a car rental firm in Tokyo: When passenger of foot heave in sight, tootle the horn. Trumpet him melodiously at first, but if he still obstacles your passage then tootle him with vigor.

An American tourist in Tel Aviv picked up a hotel telephone one night and asked for a 7-Up. The switchboard operator answered in a charming accent, "7-Up? Yes, sir." The beverage never arrived, but the next morning the tourist was awakened punctually at seven o'clock.   —Moshe Brilliant

Secretary of Commerce Malcolm Baldrige likes to tell how one high-ranking official once responded to a subordinate's request for a raise by saying: "Because of the fluctuational predisposition of your position's productive capacity as juxtaposed to government standards, it would be monetarily injudicious to advocate an increment." The staff person said, "I don't get it." The official responded, "That's right."

From a perplexed father: "I've got TV, cable, two phone lines, a phone in my car, a fax—and my kids tell me I'm out of touch.

Theatre Arts magazine reports a frustrating conversation. It seems a subscriber called "Information" for the magazine's number. "Sorry," drawled the operator, "but there is nobody listed by the name of 'Theodore Arts.'" "It's not a person; it's a publication," insisted the subscriber. "I want *Theatre Arts*." "I told you," repeated the operator in a voice a few decibels higher, "we have no listing for Theodore Arts." "Confound it," hollered the subscriber, "the word is Theatre: T-H-E-A-T-R-E." "That," replied the operator with crushing finality, "is not the way to spell Theodore."

—Msgr. Arthur Tonne. *Jokes Priests Can Tell,* Volume 8,
Multi Business Press, Hillsboro, Kansas, October, 1990.

COMPETITION

A Methodist minister and a Baptist minister were fierce competitors. Their churches were across the street from each other and were roughly the same size. They were constantly vying for the attention of the community and, unfortunately, the competition had caused a great deal of tension between them. A rich businessman in the community wanted to see the two pastors

get together in a spirit of Christian love. So he paid for the two of them to go on a hunting trip together to the Rockies. For several days they shared the same tent and cooked their meals over the same fire. A good spirit of camaraderie developed between them. Until one night they heard a giant grizzly bear clawing at their tent. They realized that the bear was angry. The Methodist preacher yelled, "Let's run for it!" The Baptist preacher protested. "You can't outrun a grizzly," he said. "I don't have to outrun the grizzly," said the Methodist. "All I have to do is outrun you!"

COMPLAINTS

During a power failure, he complained of having gotten stuck for hours on the escalator.

~

My daughter lives in Los Angeles. A few years ago she was dining out with a friend after work. Suddenly she interrupted her conversation and summoned the headwaiter. "That's Brad Pitt at the bar, isn't it?" she asked. He assured her that it was. "He's annoying me," she said. "Annoying you?" The headwaiter raised an eyebrow. "Why, he hasn't even looked at you!" "That," said my daughter, "is what's annoying me."

~

A commuter sitting on a subway train reading a paperback was so sprawled out in the seat that the woman next to him had very little room. When she asked if he could move a bit, he refused. Just then, a man opposite them yelled, "Why don't you sit like a human being?" "What are you going to do if I don't?" came the reply. "Well, for one thing, I'll tell you how that book ends."   —Catherine Romano

~

It pays to complain. After all, it's the surly bird that gets the worm.
                                                    —Shelby Friedman

~

A man who lived in Warsaw, Poland, went to the police station to ask for permission to emigrate to Western Europe. "Aren't you happy here?" the police asked. "I have no complaints," said the man. "But are you dissatisfied with your work?" "I have no complaints." "Are you discontented with the living conditions?" "I have no complaints." "Then why do you want to go west?" "Because there I can have complaints."   —*Times,* Hong Kong

COMPLIMENTS

A friend of mine, who is a radio announcer, has such a deep, warm, smooth voice that it could melt ice on the tundra. Even when he was a teenager, people were always telling him that with his voice he should have a career in broadcasting. One day after many years at the radio mike, my friend drove to the drive-up window of a fast food restaurant, placed his order into the electronic intercom, then drove ahead to pick up his food. When he reached for his change the restaurant employee commented, "You sure do have a nice voice. You know what you should be?" Undaunted by yet another fan who probably recognized his voice but not his face, he nodded understandingly. "A bingo caller!" the woman declared.   —*Catholic Digest*

My wife rushed into the supermarket to pick up a few items. She headed for the express line where the clerk was talking on the phone with his back turned to her. "Excuse me," she said, "I'm in a hurry. Could you check me out, please?" The clerk turned, stared at her for a second, looked her up and down, smiled and said, "Not bad."

Helen and George, a young married couple, were sitting on a porch swing. Helen asked, "George, do you think my eyes are beautiful?" He answered, "Uh-huh." In a few moments, she asked: "George, do you think my hair is attractive?" Again he answered, "Uh-huh." A few minutes later, Helen asked, "George, would you say that I have a nice figure?" Once again he answered, "Uh-huh." "Oh, George," she said, "You say the nicest things."

COMPROMISE

Compromise is the art of dividing a cake so that everybody believes he or she got the biggest piece.   —Ludwig Erhard in *The Observer,* London

COMPUTERS

Applying computer technology is simply finding the right wrench to pound in the correct screw. Having heard stories of E-mail messages vitriolic enough to acid-etch the recipient's monitor, I've decided people who fume through their word processors feel invulnerable, like little kids shouting challenges and insults to an empty room. Thus, someone can launch a cluster bomb toward a colleague's computer and still be astonished to find that its arrival on target has left the recipient wounded and hungry for revenge.

—Owen Edwards

Humans do not naturally communicate by moving a device around on a tabletop.   —Ronald D. Rotstein, speaking of mice

I know that every computer has exactly the same available memory: too little.

—Ken Skier, 1981

NEW COMPUTER VIRUSES:

- GOVERNMENT ECONOMIST VIRUS: Nothing works, but all your diagnostic software says everything is fine.
- NEW WORLD ORDER VIRUS: Probably harmless, but it makes a lot of people mad just thinking about it.
- FEDERAL BUREAUCRAT VIRUS: Divides your hard drive into hundreds of little units, each of which do practically nothing, but all of which claim to be the most important part of the computer.
- PAUL REVERE VIRUS: This revolutionary virus does not horse around. It warns you of impending hard disk attack—once if by LAN; twice if by C:\>.
- POLITICALLY CORRECT VIRUS: Never calls itself a virus, but instead refers to itself as an electronic microorganism.
- AT&T VIRUS: Every three minutes it tells you what great service you are getting.
- THE MCI VIRUS: Every three minutes it reminds you that you are paying too much for the AT&T virus.
- TED TURNER VIRUS: Colorizes your monochrome monitor.
- ARNOLD SCHWARZENEGGER VIRUS: Terminates and stays resident. It'll be back to erase your data and say, Hasta la vista, baby!
- GALLUP VIRUS: Sixty percent of the PCs infected will lose 38 percent of their data 14 percent of the time (plus or minus a 3.5 percent margin of error).

You've got to feel sorry for the small group within the computer industry that actually has to face the end user.   —Eri Golembo

The first business to use computers was the computer business. Its projections told it that no one would buy a computer.

There is reason to hope that machines will use us kindly, for their existence will be in a great measure dependent on ours; they will rule us with a rod of iron, but they will not eat us.   —Samuel Butler

~

We may be saving trees—but we're starting to drown people.
                                                    —Esther Dyson on e-mail

~

When a clerk at the local power company or at your favorite department store or in your company's payroll department, says, "The computer made a mistake," you have reason to assume that either that person is stupid or thinks you are.   —Marvin Grosswirth

~

It's supposed to do that.   —Anonymous help-line response, 1982

The
BORDERLINE™   By Gabe Martin
                                    borderln@cts.com

And so, another 21-inch monitor is ordered.

A bachelor called a computer dating service and listed his specifications: He wanted someone who likes water sports, is gregarious, likes formal dress, and is small. They sent him a penguin.

~

There was this fully computer-automated bank in Miami. Seems somebody sent it a card saying, "THIS IS A HOLDUP," and the computer mailed the fellow $200,000 in unmarked bills.

~

One business executive to another, talking about the office computer: We can't sell it—it knows too much!

~

Wife, sitting at home computer, excitedly tells husband, "I did it! I broke into the Fitzsimmon's computer and got Edith's recipe for lasagna!"
—How the Platform Professionals Keep 'em Laughin'

The
BORDERLINE ™

By Gabe Martin
borderln@cts.com

http://www.the-borderline.com/

"Management finally figured out we weren't doing anything with our legs."

One of the most important things to consider with any information system is your backup plan. A consultant asked a group of people how many of them had one. One brave soul raised his hand and said, "I've got a disaster plan—complete and ready to go into action. It's real simple—just one page." And the consultant said, "A one-page disaster plan? What would you do if your computer center blew up, or flooded, or caught on fire? How could you recover with just a one-page disaster plan?" He said, "Well, it's really very simple. It's a two-step plan. First, I maintain my resume up-to-date at all times. And second, I store a backup copy off-site."

Thank you for calling the tech-support hotline. If your computer becomes obsolete while you're holding, press 1 to reach our sales department.

Three IBM staffers were on a long car trip when they got a flat tire. After they stopped and studied the situation, the sales rep said, "That does it. We need a new car." The service rep said, "Wait! Let's switch some parts around until it works again." The software rep said, "No. Just turn the car on and off to see it that fixes the problem."   —*The Jokesmith*

HOW TO TELL IF YOU'RE "ADDICTED TO THE INTERNET"

- You find yourself typing "com" after every period when using a word processor.
- You turn off your modem and get this awful empty feeling, like you just pulled the plug on a loved one.
- You start introducing yourself as "Jon at I-I-Net.com"
- Your wife drapes a blond wig over your monitor to remind you of what she looks like.
- All of your friends have an @ in their names.
- You can't call your mother . . . she doesn't have a modem.
- Your phone bill comes to your doorstep in a box.
- You laugh at people with 2400 baud modems.
- You move into a new house and decide to Netscape before you landscape.
- You tell the cab driver you live at "http://123.elm.street/house/bluetrim.html".
- Your spouse makes a new rule: "The computer cannot come to bed."
- You ask a plumber how much it would cost to replace the chair in front of your computer with a commode.
- You start tilting your head sideways to smile. :)
- You turn on your computer and turn off your spouse.
- Your spouse says communication is important in a marriage . . . so you buy another computer and install a second phone line so the two of you can chat.

- You begin to wonder how on earth your service provider is allowed to call 200 hours per month "unlimited."
- And the #1 clue that you are addicted to the Internet is . . . Your dog has its own home page.

A man goes into a pet shop to buy a parrot. The shop owner points to three identical looking parrots on a perch and says, "The parrot on the left costs $500." "Why does the parrot cost so much?" asks the first man. The owner says, "Well, the parrot knows how to use a computer." The man then asks about the next parrot to be told that this one costs $1,000 because it can do everything the other parrot can do plus it knows how to use the UNIX operating system. Naturally, the increasingly startled man asks about the third parrot, to be told that it costs $2,000. Needless to say this brings the question "What can it do?" To which the owner replies, "To be honest I have never seen it do a thing, but the other two call him boss!"

~

Customer to computer salesman. "I would like to return my laptop. My cat is jealous of it."

~

Compaq is considering changing the command "Press Any Key" to "Press Return Key" because of the flood of calls asking where the "Any" key is.

~

Part of the inhumanity of the computer is that, once it is competently programmed and working smoothly, it is completely honest.

—Isaac Asimov, *Change!*

~

Many pharmaceutical firms supply pharmacies with order forms listing products and their costs. When one company neglected to do this, despite repeated requests, a pharmacy employee attached a note to an order, stating: "Your computer and I are having communication difficulties. If you no longer supply order forms, please let us know—that is, if you still employ real, live people." With the next delivery of merchandise there was this note: "Enclosed please find six order forms. Please forgive the delay. Yes, we do still employ people. Therein lies our problem. Signed, IBM 402."   —Matt Weinstock

CONCEIT

He was so conceited it was beneath his dignity even to talk to himself.

—Sholom Aleichem

CONFIDENCE

Some years ago *Time* magazine reported on a nervous motorist in Lambertville, New Jersey. This man, on being stopped by the police, explained that he had been driving on two hundred and twenty-four consecutive learner's permits over the last twenty-five years. He had flunked his first driver's test and had been unsure of himself ever since.   —George F. Regas

Two developers met on a golf course one Sunday afternoon, and the first one asked the second one what he'd been doing lately. "Not much," he replied. "What with this overbuilt market and the lack of tenants, I've been spending a lot of time working on my golf game. How about you?" The second developer preened with pride. "I'm building a $40 million church," he said. "It's going to have marble floors from the same quarry as the marble in St. Peter's, stained glass from Stuttgart, Germany, and the pews are made of inlaid wood from the Far East." The first developer gaped in awe and admiration. "That's incredible," he said. "What's the denomination?" And the second developer said, "I'm not sure yet. It's on spec."

CONGRESS

A member of the House of Representatives asserted pompously his conviction that he could not be wrong. "I know I am right," he thundered. "And I'd rather be right than be President!" "Don't worry," retorted the honorable opponent. "You'll never be either."

If you're hanging around with nothing to do and the zoo is closed, come on over to the Senate. You'll get the same kind of feeling and you won't have to pay.   —Bob Dole

Jay Leno says, "I saw a Senator on a Sunday-morning talk show who said that the actions of the Senate have created jobs for a lot of citizens." He paused for a moment. "But let's face it," he continued, "you can't make a career out of jury duty."

My dog can bark like a congressman, fetch like an aide, beg like a press secretary and play dead like a receptionist when the phone rings.
      —Gerald B. H. Solomon

Senate office hours are from twelve to one, with an hour off for lunch.

—George S. Kaufman

Senators are a prolific source of advice, and most of it is bad.

—Dean Acheson

You know, Congress is a strange place. A man gets up to speak and says nothing. Nobody listens. And then everybody disagrees.   —Will Rogers

Software reviewer describing a very slow computer program: . . . it ran with the speed of a congressman getting to the point.   —Paul Cilwa

There was a fellow who applied for a job as a press aide for a congressman. Not long after he submitted his application, he received word from the official's office: "Your resume is full of exaggerations, distortions, half-truths and lies. Can you start work Monday?"

Senator to newspaper reporter: "I spent $3 million to get elected to a $125,000-a-year job, and you expect me to help balance the budget?"

—Bucella, King Features Syndicate

Richard Armey, majority leader of the House of Representatives, tells how he decided to run for Congress. One evening several years ago, he and his wife were at home watching the government at work on C-Span. "Honey," Armey remarked, "these people sound like a bunch of damn fools." "Yeah," she responded, "you could do that."

The mistakes made by Congress wouldn't be so bad if the next Congress didn't keep trying to correct them.   —Cullen Hightower

CONSCIENCE

Your conscience may not keep you from doing wrong, but it sure keeps you from enjoying it. A man with a nagging secret couldn't keep it any longer. In the confessional he admitted that for years he had been stealing building supplies from the lumberyard where he worked. "What did you take?" his parish priest asked. "Enough to build my own home and enough for my son's house. And houses for our two daughters. And our cottage at the lake." "This is very serious," the priest said. "I shall have to think of a far-reaching penance. Have you ever done a retreat?" "No, Father, I haven't," the man replied. "But if you can get the plans, I can get the lumber."

CONSERVATION

There are three reasons for being a conservationist. (1) You will help prevent the destruction of the world as you know it. (2) You will save hundreds of endangered species from extermination. And (3) You'll finally have reason not to buy your wife a fur coat.

—Robert Orben, *2500 Jokes To Start 'Em Laughing*

CONSUMERS

CONSUMER ALERT: At the top of the list of newly released products you should not buy are the new inflatable dart boards.   —Ron Dentinger

CONTRACTORS

A woman wants the inside of her house painted and she calls a contractor in to help her. They wander around the house, and she points out the colors she wants. She says, "Now, in the living room, I'd like to have a neutral beige, very soft and warm." The contractor nods, pulls out his pad of paper and writes on it. Then he goes to the window, leans out and yells, "Green side up!" The woman is most perplexed but she lets it slide. They wander into the next room. She says, "In the dining room I'd like a light white, not stark, but very bright and airy." The contractor nods, pulls out his pad of paper and writes on it. Then he goes to the window, leans out, and yells "Green side up!" The woman is even more perplexed but still lets it slide. They wander further into the next room. She says, "In the bedroom, I'd like blue. Restful, peaceful, cool blue." The contractor nods, pulls out his pad of paper and writes on it. Then once more he goes to the window, leans out and yells "Green side up!" This is too much. The woman has to ask. So she says, "Every time I tell you a color, you write it down, but then you yell out the window 'Green side up.' What on earth does that mean?" The contractor shakes his head and says, "I have four guys laying sod across the street."

COOKING

Couples who cook together stay together. Maybe because they can't decide who'll get the Cuisinart.   —Erica Jong

Cousin Wendy was very economy minded. During her first month of marriage, she had been preparing ground beef in as many different ways as she knew how—hamburgers, Salisbury steak, tacos, meat loaf, spaghetti and meatballs, etc. On the twelfth straight night, as she served chopped meat, her husband surveyed it and sighed: "How now, ground cow?"

Shortly after they were married, Heather said to Mark, "The two best things I cook are meat loaf and apple dumplings." Mark sheepishly replied, "Um, which one is this?"

The family, knowing how dangerous my cooking is, lets grace last 45 minutes.

There is one thing more exasperating than a wife who can cook and won't and that's a wife who can't cook and will.   —Robert Frost

My neighbor said he figured his wife was not much of a cook when she kept referring to the oven as: "That square thing in the kitchen." —Ron Dentinger

My wife does wonders with leftovers—she throws them away.
                                                —Herb Shriner

Today's housewife enjoys cooking—especially when it's done by the chef at one of the better restaurants in town.

The owner of a restaurant was carefully checking out the work of his new cook, my brother Scott. "You say you were an army cook during the Vietnam war?" "Yes, sir," the cook said. "I cooked for the officers' mess for over two years and was wounded three times." "Huh," said the boss. "You're lucky they didn't kill you."

Ever notice . . . that you can never make the right number of pancakes?
                                —Executive Speechwriter Newsletter

Uncle Sid claims, "My wife's cooking was so bad the flies got together to mend the screens."

REVEREND FUN

Having lost the recipe, Don tried to make an angel food cake from memory.

'Tis an ill cook that cannot lick his own fingers.　　—William Shakespeare

The weary husband was met at the door with sad news. "We'll have to go out for dinner," his wife said cheerily. "I couldn't fix anything because the electricity went off." "Electricity!" growled the husband. "We have a gas range." "I know," the wife went on, "but our can opener is electric."

—Arkansas Baptist

COURTROOM

Carl, an accused debtor, chose to act as his own attorney. He concluded his case with an impassioned plea, "As God is my judge, I do not owe the money!" The judge responded, "He isn't, I am, and you do."

A litigant is a person about to give up his skin for the hope of retaining his bones.　　—Ambrose Bierce

A man, when tried for stealing a pair of boots, said he merely took the boots as a joke. It was found that he was captured with them forty yards from the place he had taken them. The judge said he had carried the joke too far.

Question: "Have you ever been cross-examined before?"
Answer: "Yes, Your Honor, I'm a married man."

~

The prosecuting attorney faced the witness. "Isn't it true the defendant talks to himself when alone?" "Couldn't say. Never been with him when he was alone."

~

It was a lengthy trial. Testimony was heard for six months. The attorneys took an entire week to present their respective summations. After a three-hour charge to the jury, the presiding judge finally said: "Are there any other questions before the jury retires?" "Your Honor," said a juror, "please tell us, what is a plaintiff and what is a defendant?"

~

It was a sensational murder trial, one that the media covered with morbid fascination. When the jury was being selected, Judge Reynolds asked one prospective juror, "Have you formed any opinion concerning the guilt or innocence of the prisoner?" "No, Your Honor, I have not." "Have you any conscientious objections against imposing the death penalty if the prisoner is found guilty?" "Not considering what the defendant did, Your Honor," replied the prospective juror.

~

It's getting to the point where actual court cases are turning into television productions. The following dialogue is not far from the truth:

Judge: "Are all the TV cameramen here?"
Bailiff: "Yes, Your Honor."
Judge: "Is the lighting set?"
Bailiff: "Yes, Your Honor."
Judge: "Does my makeup look OK?"
Bailiff: "Yes, Your Honor."
Judge: "Is the sound good?"
Bailiff: "Yes, Your Honor."
Judge: "Are Connie Chung, Barbara Walters, and Tom Brokaw in their
        seats?"
Bailiff: "Yes, Your Honor."
Judge: "Is my press agent here?"
Bailiff: "Yes, Your Honor."
Judge: "Good! Then let justice be done!"

Lawyer Ernest Phelps was questioning Theodora Sampson in a court trial involving slander. "Please repeat the slanderous statements you heard, exactly as you heard them," instructed the lawyer. The witness hesitated. "But they were unfit for any respectable person to hear!" "Then," said the attorney, "just whisper them to the judge."

Milton Brown, the defense attorney, was cross-examining the prosecution's main witness, a bus driver named Jim Samson. "You say your only meeting with the defendant was on the municipal bus you were driving and that he had been drinking and gambling?" "Yes," replied Samson. "Did you see him take a drink?" asked Brown. "No," replied Samson. "Did you see him engage in any form of gambling?" asked the lawyer. "No," admitted the bus driver. "Then how do you know," demanded the attorney, "that the defendant had been drinking and gambling?" "Well," explained Samson, "he gave me a blue chip for his bus fare and told me to keep the change."

Mr. Dewey was briefing his client, who was about to testify in his own defense. "You must swear to tell the complete truth. Do you understand?" The client replied that he did. The lawyer then asked, "Do you know what will happen if you don't tell the truth?" The client looked back and said, "I imagine that our side will win."

From an actual courtroom transcript:

Question: "Mrs. Jones, is your appearance this morning pursuant to a deposition notice which I sent to your attorney?"

Answer: "No, this is how I dress when I go to work."

From an actual courtroom transcript:

Question: "Officer, what led you to believe the defendant was under the influence?"

Answer: "Because he was argumentary and he couldn't pronunciate his words."

Robarts, the defense attorney, was trying to get the prosecution witness to lose her temper. In his line of questioning, he mocked, insulted, and derided her constantly. Despite his tactics, the witness remained calm. Finally, Robarts asked sarcastically: "You say you had no education, but you answered my questions smartly enough." "You don't have to be a Rhodes scholar to answer stupid questions," replied the woman.

The convicted bank robber later admitted, "I think my mistake was yelling 'Hi' to the eyewitnesses as they filed into court."

The lawyer was beginning to grasp at straws during his cross-examination. "You say, Mr. Dyson, that this took exactly five minutes?" The witness replied that he was sure. "I am going to give you a test. I want you to tell me when exactly five minutes has passed, starting . . . now." The lawyer was intently watching a stopwatch taken from his briefcase. At five minutes, to the second, the witness gave the signal. The lawyer told him, "That's quite remarkable. How did you gauge the time so accurately?" Mr. Dyson replied, "I watched the clock on the wall behind you."

The plaintiff and defendant in an action at law, are like two men ducking their heads in a bucket, and daring each other to remain longest under water.

—Samuel Johnson

The reason that there is a penalty for laughing in court is that otherwise the jury would never be able to hear the evidence.　　　—H. L. Mencken

Defense Attorney to Court: "To save the state the expense of a trial, Your Honor, my client has escaped."　　　—Chon Day

Treat the bailiff with respect. He has a gun.　　　—Malcolm Lewis

The plaintiff's medical malpractice attorney was famous for his use of trick questions to gain an advantage over his opponents. He was overheard telling Brubaker, another plaintiff's attorney, of the time a trial judge limited him to a single hypothetical question of the defendant's expert medical witness. My office worked on the question for days. We checked all possible answers against the most authoritative medical opinions, texts and experts. Finally, in court, I took two full hours to ask the question. So?" asked Brubaker. "And then I finished." "Yes?" "The witness asked me. . . ." "Yes, yes?" ". . . if I would mind repeating the question."

❧

From an actual courtroom transcript:

Question: "Were you acquainted with the deceased?"
Answer: "Yes, sir."
Question: "Before or after he died?"

❧

"Weren't you up before me on another drunk driving charge only a few weeks ago?" asked the judge sternly. "I thought you told me you were a recovering alcoholic." "Oh I am," the drunk reassured him sincerely. "I only drink on weekends, and I recover the other five days."

The
BORDERLINE™   By Gabe Martin
                                 borderln@cts.com

"Your Honor, I motion for dismissal of the charges. The witness is obviously lying."

From an actual courtroom transcript:

Question: "What happened then?"

Answer: "He told me, 'I have to kill you because you can identify me.'"

Question: "Did he kill you?"

Answer: "No."

~

From an actual courtroom transcript:

Question: "What is your name?"

Answer: "Ernestine McDowell."

Question: "And what is your marital status?"

Answer: "Fair."

~

From an actual courtroom transcript:

Question: "When he went, had you gone and had she, if she wanted to and were able, for the time being excluding all the restraints on her not to go, gone also, would he have brought you, meaning you and she, with him to the station?"

Mr. Brooks: "Objection. That question should be taken out and shot."

~

The judge says to the plaintiff, "Explain what happened." The plaintiff says, "I was in a phone booth talking to my girlfriend when the defendant opened the door and dragged me out." The defendant says, "The only reason I dragged him out is because he refused to get out, and I needed to make a phone call." The judge asks, "How long were you talking to your girlfriend?" The plaintiff says, "I don't know, Your Honor, but I want to add that he dragged my girlfriend out too."

~

From an actual courtroom transcript:

Question: (Showing man picture.) "That's you?"

Answer: "Yes, sir."

Question: "And you were present when the picture was taken, right?"

~

"Has the jury reached a verdict?" "Yes, Your Honor. We find the defendant . . . dumber than the law allows."

~

A man was sued by a woman for defamation of character. She charged that he had called her a pig. The man was found guilty and fined. After the trial he asked the judge, "This means that I cannot call Mrs. Johnson a pig?" The judge said that was true. "Does this mean I cannot call a pig Mrs. Johnson?" the man asked. The judge replied that he could indeed call a pig Mrs. Johnson with no fear of legal action. The man looked directly at Mrs. Johnson and said, "Good afternoon, Mrs. Johnson."

~

The following are things people actually said in court, word for word:

Q: "What is your date of birth?"
A: "July fifteenth."
Q: "What year?"
A: "Every year."

Q: "What gear were you in at the moment of the crash impact?"
A: "Gucci sweats and Reeboks."

Q: "This myasthenia gravis—does it affect your memory at all?"
A: "Yes."
Q: "And in what ways does it affect your memory?"
A: "I forget."
Q: "You forget. Can you give us an example of something that you've forgotten?"

Q: "All your responses must be oral, OK? What school did you go to?"
A: "Oral."

Q: "How old is your son—the one living with you."
A: "Thirty-eight or thirty-five, I can't remember which."
Q: "How long has he lived with you?"
A: "Forty-five years."

Q: "And where was the location of the accident?"
A: "Approximately milepost 499."
Q: "And where is milepost 499?"
A: "Probably between milepost 498 and 500."

Q: "Sir, what is your IQ?"
A: "Well, I can see pretty well, I think."

Q: "Trooper, when you stopped the defendant, were your red and blue lights flashing?"
A: "Yes."
Q: "Did the defendant say anything when she got out of her car?"
A: "Yes, sir."
Q: "What did she say?"
A: "What disco am I at?"

Recently reported in the Massachusetts Bar Association Lawyers journal, the following are questions actually asked of witnesses by attorneys during trials and, in certain cases, the responses given by insightful witnesses:

Q: "Now doctor, isn't it true that when a person dies in his sleep, he doesn't know about it until the next morning?"

Q: "The youngest son, the twenty-year old, how old is he?"

Q: "Were you present when your picture was taken?"

Q: "Was it you or your younger brother who was killed in the war?"

Q: "Did he kill you?"

Q: "How far apart were the vehicles at the time of the collision?"

Q: "You were there until the time you left, is that true?"

Q: "How many times have you committed suicide?"

Q: "Are you qualified to give a urine sample?"

Q: "So the date of conception (of the baby) was August 8th?"
A: "Yes."
Q: "And what were you doing at that time?"

Q: "She had three children, right?"
A: "Yes."
Q: "How many were boys?"
A: "None."
Q: "Were there any girls?"

Q: "You say the stairs went down to the basement?"
A: "Yes."
Q: "And these stairs, did they go up also?"

Q: "Mr. Slatery, you went on a rather elaborate honeymoon, didn't you?"
A: "I went to Europe, sir."
Q: "And you took your new wife?"

Q: "How was your first marriage terminated?"
A: "By death."
Q: "And by whose death was it terminated?"

And Best of All . . .

Q: "Doctor, how many autopsies have you performed on dead people?"
A: "All my autopsies are performed on dead people."
Q: "Do you recall the time that you examined the body?"
A: "The autopsy started around 8:30 P.M."
Q: "And Mr. Dennington was dead at the time?"
A: "No, he was sitting on the table wondering why I was doing an autopsy."

Q: "Doctor, before you performed the autopsy, did you check for a pulse?"
A: "No."
Q: "Did you check for blood pressure?"
A: "No."
Q: "Did you check for breathing?"
A: "No."
Q: "So, then it is possible that the patient was alive when you began the autopsy?"
A: "No."
Q: "How can you be so sure, Doctor?"
A: "Because his brain was setting on my desk in a jar."
Q: "But could the patient have still been alive nevertheless?"
A: "It is possible that he could have been alive and practicing law in this particular case."

∼

From an actual courtroom transcript:

Question: "What is your relationship with the plaintiff?"
Answer: "She is my daughter."
Question: "Was she your daughter on February 13, 1979?"

∼

One day Mel Martin stopped by the chambers of a judge with whom he had a lunch appointment. As his friend changed from robe to jacket, Martin noticed a shiny black pistol holstered to the judge's shoulder. The judge was not a firearms enthusiast, so Martin asked him why he was carrying it. His friend said that because of recent threats he had borrowed the pistol from the repository of confiscated weapons. Holding it up, the judge said, "I chose this one because it's so mean-looking, yet it hardly weighs a thing. I hope I don't need it, because I don't even know how to load it." "It's not hard," Martin said examining it closely. "We can fill it at the water fountain on the way out."

—ABA Journal

∼

Judge to defendant: "I note that in addition to stealing money, you took watches, rings and pearls." "Yes, your honor," he replied. "I was taught money alone doesn't bring happiness."   *—Joey Adams*

∼

Judge Gerald Kalina of Burnsville, Minnesota, was asking prospective jurors if any of them had illnesses that might prevent their serving. One candidate raised his hand. "I suffer from narcolepsy," he said, "and I'm worried that if I'm chosen, I might nod off during part of the trial." "We can't have that," Kalina replied. "That's the job of the judge." *—ABA Journal*

❧

The following dialog took place at family court in Australia:

Question: "What was the first thing your husband said to you when he woke up that morning?"

Answer: "He said, 'Where am I, Cathy?'"

Question: "And why did that upset you?"

Answer: "My name is Susan." *—Beverley Tait, Court in the Act*

❧

Attorney Peter V. MacDonald tells about a murder trial in Texas, during which the first words of the assistant district attorney's address to the jury were as follows: "Ladies and gentlemen, have any of you ever been the victim of a homicide?" *—Sunday Star, Toronto*

❧

The following testimony is from a trial of a contest over two wills left by the late Mr. Walter:

Question: "When did you last see Walter?"

Answer: "At the funeral."

Question: "Did he make any comment to you at that time?"

—Jerry Buchmeyer in Texas Bar Journal

❧

In a sensational court case, the plaintiff, who was all twisted and bent over, won $3 million from the driver of another car. The defendant knew the "injured party" was faking, so after the trial he followed the guy around everywhere, even trailing him to France. "Where do we go now?" the defendant taunted the plaintiff. "Off to Lourdes! If you watch closely, you'll see one of the greatest miracles of all time!" *—Alex Thien in Milwaukee Sentinel*

COWBOYS

On a visit to Cody, Wyoming, I met Bobby Lee Earl, age 91, the retired sheriff of a nearby small town. I asked Earl to tell me some of his most memorable experiences in law enforcement. He said: "Well, sir, once I was sitting at the bar in the local saloon, keeping an eye on a high-stakes poker game, when all of a sudden this feller moseys in all dressed in, in . . ." "White linen?" I suggested, trying to be helpful. "No, son," Earl continued, "this galoot was wearing brown wrapping paper. His hat was brown wrapping paper. His pants was brown wrapping paper. His shirt was brown wrapping paper. He wore a newspaper vest and newspaper boots. So I arrested him." "What for?" I asked. "Rustling," Earl replied with a wink in his eye.

⌒

One Sunday a cowboy went to church. When he entered, he saw that he and the preacher were the only ones present. The preacher asked the cowboy if he wanted him to go ahead and preach. The cowboy said, "I'm not too smart, but if I went to feed my cattle and only one showed up, I'd feed him." So the minister began his sermon. One hour passed, then two hours, then two-and-a-half hours. The preacher finally finished and came down to ask the cowboy how he liked the sermon. The cowboy answered slowly, "Well, I'm not very smart, but if I went to feed my cattle and only one showed up, I sure wouldn't feed him all the hay."

⌒

A pastor at a frontier church ended a stirring sermon with, "All those who want to go to heaven, put up your hands!" Everybody enthusiastically raised their hands . . . everybody except a grizzled old cowboy who had been slouching against the doorpost at the back of the room. All heads turned as he sauntered up to the front, spurs jangling and said, "Preacher, that was too easy. How d'ya know if these folks are serious? I c'n gar-an-tee to prove who really means it an' who don't!" Bemused and not a little frightened the preacher said, "OK, stranger, go ahead and put the faith of these good people to the test. Ask them anything you want." At that the cowpoke pulled his twin six-shooters, turned to the audience and said, "All right . . . who wants to go heaven . . . raise your hands!"

⌒

A cowboy fell off his horse and broke his leg while he was out on the prairie. The steed grabbed his master's belt in his teeth, carried him to shelter and then went to fetch the doctor. Talking it over a few weeks later, a friend praised the horse's intelligence. "Heck, he's not so smart," replied the cowboy. "He came back with the veterinarian." —Art Pierce

⌒

A cowboy applied for an insurance policy. "Have you ever had any accidents?" asked the agent. "Nope," replied the applicant, "though a bronc did kick in two of my ribs last summer, and a couple of years ago a rattlesnake bit me on the ankle." "Wouldn't you call those accidents?" replied the puzzled agent. "Naw," the cowboy said, "they did it on purpose!"   —*Our Daily Bread*

COWS

When cows laugh, does milk come out of their noses?   —Jeff Marder

A big city lawyer was called in on a case between a farmer and a large railroad company. A farmer noticed that his prize cow was missing from the field through which the railroad passed. He filed suit against the railroad company for the value of the cow. The case was to be tried before the justice of the peace in the back room of the general store. The attorney immediately cornered the farmer and tried to get him to settle out of court. The lawyer did his best selling job, and the farmer finally agreed to take half of what he was claiming to settle the case. After the farmer signed the release and took the check, the young lawyer couldn't help but gloat a little over his success. He said to the farmer, "You know, I hate to tell you this but I put one over on you in there. I couldn't have won the case. The engineer was asleep and the fireman was in the caboose when the train went through your farm that morning. I didn't have one witness to put on the stand." The old farmer replied, "Well, I'll tell you, young feller, I was a little worried about winning that case myself because that durned cow came home this morning!"

CREDIT CARDS

Two guys were chatting at a cocktail party. "Your wife certainly brightens the room," one said to the other. "Her mere presence is electrifying." "It ought to be," the other man replied. "Everything she's wearing is charged."

—Ron Dentinger

I was signing the receipt for my credit card purchase when the clerk noticed that I had never signed my name on the back of the credit card. She informed me that she could not complete the transaction unless the card was signed. When asked why, she explained that it was necessary to compare the signature on the credit card with the signature I just signed on the receipt. So, I signed the credit card in front of her. She carefully compared that signature to the one I signed on the receipt. As luck would have it, they matched.

Santa Claus comes to us under many names: Kris Kringle, Saint Nicholas, MasterCard.   —Phyllis Diller

C

CRIME

Before we moved, we lived in a town where no one worried about crime in the streets. The criminals make house calls.

~

Several years ago, Andy was sentenced to prison. During his stay, he got along well with the guards and all his fellow inmates. The warden saw that deep down, Andy was a good person and made arrangements for Andy to learn a trade while doing his time. After three years, Andy was recognized as one of the best carpenters in the local area. Often he would be given a weekend pass to do odd jobs for the citizens of the community, and he always reported back to prison before Sunday night was over. The warden was thinking of remodeling his kitchen and in fact had done much of the work himself. But he lacked the skills to build a set of kitchen cupboards and a large countertop which he had promised his wife. So he called Andy into his office and asked him to complete the job for him. But, alas, Andy refused. He told the warden, "Gosh, I'd really like to help you but counter fitting is what got me into prison in the first place."

~

An Illinois man pretending to have a gun kidnapped a motorist and forced him to drive to two different automated teller machines. The kidnapper then proceeded to withdraw money from his own bank accounts.

~

A man walked into a Topeka, Kansas, Kwik Shop, and asked for all the money in the cash drawer. Apparently, the take was too small, so he tied up the store clerk and worked the counter himself for three hours until police showed up and grabbed him.

CRITICS

After church one Sunday at St. Philip's, two members were critiquing Father Thompson's sermon. The first member said, "I thought the sermon was divine. It reminded me of the peace of God. It passed all understanding." The second member observed, "It reminded me of the mercy of God. I thought it would endure forever."

~

Comment by a drama critic: "The play is one big piece of Swiss cheese, minus the cheese."

This is not a novel to be tossed aside lightly. It should be thrown with great force.
—Dorothy Parker

Critic: One who finds a little bad in the best of things.

He writes his plays for the ages—the ages between four and twelve.
—George Jean Nathan

Drama critic Clive Barnes, reviewing a Broadway play: "I realized it was not a particularly distinguished play when, at the intermission, I found myself rushing up the aisle for a cigarette outside. It was not until I got out there that I remembered that I don't smoke. The cast was well balanced—they were all rotten."

One of the shortest music criticisms on record appeared in a Detroit paper: "An amateur string quartet played Brahms here last evening. Brahms lost."

Another pithy review lasted much longer than the play called *Dreadful Night*. The account: "Dreadful night: PRECISELY!"

This actor did a one-man show and the critic wrote: "There were too many in the cast."

Heywood Broun on a play: "It opened at 8:30 sharp—and closed at 10:50 dull."

Alexander Woollcott: "The scenery was beautiful, but the actors got in the way of it."

The show had one strike against it: The seats faced the stage.

Monty Woolley: "For the first time I envied my feet—they were asleep."

One critic admits: "I never read a book before reviewing it—it prejudices me so."

A playwright was having lunch with his friends the night after his new play opened on Broadway. They asked him how it was going. His reply: "The show got divided notices. We liked it, but the critics didn't."

❧

The producer came to his wife and gleefully announced, "I think I've got a hit." "How do you know? I met three of the critics and they each told me if I change one of the acts, I'll have a hit." "That's wonderful." "Yeah, but each picked a different act."

❧

Two shipwrecked critics were drifting for weeks on a raft. The more frightened of the two started seeking forgiveness for his sins. "I've been a louse all my life," he said. "I've been cruel to actors. Too often I went out of my way to hurt them. If I'm spared, I promise—" "Just a moment," interrupted the other critic, "don't go too far. I think I see smoke from a ship!"

❧

I saw the show at a disadvantage—the curtain was up.

❧

If there is a hero in this book, he should kill the author.

❧

The show had a cast of ten—buried in one plot.

❧

For years I was my own worst critic, then I got married.   —Ron Dentinger

❧

According to David Frost, what a writer means by constructive criticism is six thousand words of closely reasoned adulation.

❧

James Agee's comment on a film: "Several tons of dynamite are set off in this picture—none of it under the right people."

❧

One mustn't criticize other people on grounds where he can't stand perpendicular himself.   —Mark Twain

❧

From a film review: "It's the kind of movie that grips you by the eyelids and won't let go until you've fallen asleep."
    —Thomas Mallon, *Rocketts and Rodeos and Other American Spectacles*

Movie critic Richard Harrington: "The plot must have been scripted on a napkin over lunch at a fast-food restaurant."   —*Washington Post*

~

Comment on a film: "Most of the actors came into this project anonymously and that's how they'll leave it, if they're lucky."
                                          —Julie Salamon in *The Wall Street Journal*

~

Comment by a filmgoer: "The movie should have been rated DG for 'Don't Go.'"   —Quoted by James Dent in Charleston, W.Va., *Gazette*

~

From a movie critique: "It probably would have been all right if only they had eliminated the plot."   —Henry Tenenbaum, *WJLA*, Kensington, Md.

~

Headline above article about a Tennessee Williams Revival: "This 'Streetcar' Doesn't Travel Far Enough."

~

Nature, not content with denying him the ability to think, has endowed him with the ability to write.   —A. E. Housman

~

Being attacked by him is like being savaged by a dead sheep. —Dennis Healy

~

From a review: "Television is so dull this season that children are doing their homework."   —Pembroke, Mass., *Silver Lake News*

~

Author Christopher Andersen referred to Madonna as "Our Lady of Perpetual Promotion."

~

About an adventure-film actor's performance: "He is wooden enough on screen to make an annual termite inspection mandatory."
                                          —Desmond Ryan in *Philadelphia Inquirer*

~

Of a movie script: "The screenwriters apply personality traits to the characters like Post-It notes."   —David Ansen in *Newsweek*

Comment on record album by Barbara Streisand: "Each song is delivered with the delicacy of a sonic boom."   —Jay Cocks in *Time*

A TV sequel to a mini-series elicited the following: "This offers further proof— as if it were needed—of a venerable television axiom: The only thing that pays better than having no taste is having no shame."

—Tom Shales in *Washington Post*

CYNICS

A cynic is a man who, when he smells flowers, looks around for a coffin.

—H. L. Mencken

The cynics are right nine times out of ten.   —H. L. Mencken

----------------------------------- **D** -----------------------------------

DANCING

You go to the ballet and you see girls dancing on their tiptoes. Why don't they just get taller girls?   —Greg Ray

Rumba is a dance where the front of you goes along nice and smooth like a Cadillac and the back of you moves like a Jeep.   —Bob Hope

It happened in one of those dance places popular with the younger set: A waitress dropped a tray of dishes and everybody jumped up and started dancing.

—Journeyman Barber

DARKNESS

It's always darkest right before you stub your toe.   —Al Batt

DATING

I met a new girl at a barbecue, very pretty, a blond I think. I don't know, her hair was on fire, and all she talked about was herself. You know these kind of girls: "I'm hot, I'm on fire." Me, me, me. You know. "Help me, put me out." Come on, could we talk about me just a little bit?   —Garry Shandling

She was a lovely girl. Our courtship was fast and furious—I was fast and she
was furious. —Max Kauffmann

My grandmother's ninety. She's dating. He's ninety-three. They're very happy.
They never argue. They can't hear each other. —Cathy Ladman

Ricky was telling his father about his new girlfriend. He said, "Since I met her
I can't eat, drink, or sleep." "Why's that?" asked his father. "Because," he said,
"I'm broke."

If men acted after marriage as they do during courtship, there would be fewer
divorces—and more bankruptcies. —Frances Rodman

When Barbara and Jim were dating, Barbara became concerned over the lavish
amount of money Jim was spending on her. After an expensive dinner date,

she asked her mother, "What can I do to stop Jim from
spending so much money on me?" Her mother replied
simply, "Marry him."

At the girl's college, dates were permitted only on Saturday
night. One young man showed up on a Tuesday evening,
explaining to an older woman in the lobby of the dorm
that it was imperative he see a certain young lady immediately. "I want to surprise her. You see, I'm her brother."
"Oh, she'll be surprised, all right," said the woman. "But think of how I feel.
I'm her mother." —*Liguorian*

Young woman to friend: "I'm all in from going out." —Judith A. Mollner

Bachelor to mirror: "Mirror, mirror, on the wall, who's the fairest one to call?"
—Gregory Scott Billstone

Customer to computer-dating service: "Your machine just matched me up
with my ex-wife!" —Al Kaufman

Woman about date: "He's a regular Don Yawn."
—Lou Erickson in *Atlanta Journal*

Man to girlfriend's lawyer: "Fifty thousand for a broken heart? What's she getting—a transplant?"
                                                              —Reamer Keller

Never date a man whose belt buckle is bigger than his head.
                                              —"Grace Under Fire," ABC-TV

I was on a date recently; we went horseback riding. It was kind of fun, until we ran out of quarters.
                                                              —Susie Loucks

A middle-aged widower was dating an attractive young woman of 18. When he got inquiries about his new romance, he commented, "I've found myself asking new questions about life, like, 'What kind of wine goes well with peanut butter?'"
                                                              —Leo Aikman

DAUGHTERS

At the national prayer breakfast held in Washington, D.C., Representative Tribble told a story about his own family. He said that wherever his little daughter went, she was constantly being associated with him. People would say, "Oh, you must be Representative Tribble's little girl." She quietly explained to her parents that she wanted to be herself, not just known as someone else's daughter. Her father told her not to worry about it. Her mother, on the other hand, who was more understanding, said to her, "The next time that happens, just stand right up and say, I am Constance Tribble!" Sure enough a few days later, a group of people met her and when they heard her name, they said, "Why, Congressman Tribble must be your father!" The little girl looked right back at them and said, "Oh, no! That's not what my mother says!"

When my daughter talks on the telephone she talks for over an hour. Yesterday she hung up after only thirty minutes. I asked her why. She said, "Wrong number."
                                                              —Ron Dentinger

Father welcomed his daughter's boyfriend at the door. "She will be right down. Care for a game of chess?"

You don't realize how many junk cars there are until your daughter starts dating.

Daughter: "Is it true that Santa Claus brings us presents?"
Mother: "Yes, that's true."
Daughter: "And the stork brings us babies?"
Mother: "Yes, that's true."
Daughter: "And the Police Department protects us?"
Mother: "That's right."
Daughter: "Then what do we need Daddy for?"

My daughter-in-law Dalacie asked her daughter Jessica: "Did you say your prayers last night?" Jessica: "Well, I got down on my knees and started to say them and all of a sudden I thought: *I bet God gets awfully tired hearing the same old prayer over and over.* So I crawled into bed and told Him the story of the three bears."

Years ago when my daughter Susan was sixteen, I was apprehensive about the date she was getting ready for, "Are you sure he's a good driver?" Susan's reply: "Oh, yes, Dad. He has to be. If he gets arrested one more time, he loses his license."

A minister was explaining the facts of life to his daughter. The youngster listened attentively as her father told her about the birds and bees, then asked, "Does God know about this?"

DEATH

Death is God's way of telling you not to be such a wise guy.

You can't take it with you. You never see a U-Haul following a hearse.
—Ellen Glasgow

I know a guy who saved all his life to buy a cemetery plot. Then he took a cruise and was lost at sea.
—Norm Crosby

What do you call falling out of an airplane at ten thousand feet without a parachute? Jumping to a conclusion!

Mrs. Pulaski was telling me: "I heard about one small child saying, 'Night-night' to a body at the funeral home. It reminded me of our small daughter. We took her to view her great-grandmother, and she asked, 'Why did they put Great-grandma in a jewelry box?'"

~

I don't usually pass on news like this because I know how busy you are. Sometimes we have to pause and truly remember what life is about. So I will pass on this sad, sad news. There was a great loss today in the entertainment world. The man who wrote the song Hokey Pokey died. What was really horrible is that they had trouble keeping the body in the casket. They'd put his left leg in and . . . well, you know the rest.

~

Teacher: "There's an old saying that cats have nine lives. Does any animal have more than that?"
Pupil: "Sure, frogs. They croak every night."   —*Capper's Weekly*

~

Old realtors never die; they just get listless.

~

Why do they sterilize the needles for lethal injections?

~

Old bankers never die; they just yield to maturity.   —Susan M. Weschler

~

Old lecturers never die; they know they'll see better dais.
                                                    —Shelby Friedman

~

Old dictators never die; they just fly the coup.   —C. P. Miscavish

~

Old politicians never die; they just harangue in there.   —Shelby Friedman

DECISIONS

A young man of 32 had been appointed president of the bank. He'd never dreamed he'd be president, much less at such a young age. So he approached the venerable chairman of the board and said, "You know, I've just been appointed president. I was wondering if you could give me some advice." The old man came back with just two words: "Right decisions!" The young man had hoped for a bit more than this, so he said, "That's really helpful, and I appreciate it, but can you be more specific? How do I make right decisions?"

The wise old man simply responded, "Experience." The young man said, "Well, that's just the point of my being here. I don't have the kind of experience I need. How do I get it?" Came the terse reply, "Wrong decisions!"

DEFINITIONS

Bulldozer: Someone who sleeps through a political address.

Gadget: Any mechanical device that performs a kitchen task in one-twentieth the time it takes to find it.

Taxpayers: A special class of people who don't have to pass civil service examinations in order to work for the government.

Economics: The science of telling you things you've known all your life, but in a language you can't understand.   —Rep. Dick Armey

Ecstasy: Discovering a second layer of chocolates under the first.

Perfectionist: A person who takes great pains—and gives them to others.

Summer vacation: When parents suddenly realize that teachers are grossly underpaid.

Buffet: A French word that means "Get up and get it yourself."
                                          —Ron Dentinger

DAFFY DEFINITIONS

- Classy canine: Gucci poochie.—Joyce Chudy
- Noncommittal: bland stand.—Daisy Brown
- Marathon: fleet feet feat.—WLWT, Cincinnati
- Brothers and sisters: quibblings.—Barbara A. Selenke
- Counter-attack: January sales.—G. Pearson
- Fur coat: wrapture.—Rae Gardner
- Hospital gown: ward robe.—Susie Hillyer

- Raincoat: thunderwear.—Hank Ketcham
- High heels: arch enemies.—Edith Ogutsch
- Perseverance: the eternal try-angle.
- Apathy: smother of good intentions.—Morris Bender
- Hysteria: fancy stress bawl.—Jane Hunt Clark
- Conscience: God's little acher.—Shelby Friedman
- Hemlock: refusal to accept changing fashions.
  Forelock: overcrowded golf course.
  Wedlock: inability to give an inch in marriage.
  Padlock: apartment shortage.—Kathryn Lance, Nan Schubel and Dan Weicher
- World: a big ball that revolves on its taxes.—Wayne Mackey in *Oklahoma City Times*
- Debt: the first thing a person runs into when he buys a new car.—Evan Esar
- Disinheritance: a leading cause of ill will.—Frank Tyger in *New Jersey Lawyer*
- Revolving charge: the kind of credit that keeps your interest up.—Ray A. Cates
- Bartlett: a small, familiar quotation by the Simpsons' son.—Jacqueline Schiff
- Tentacles: a linebacker's dream for every game.—Aaron Bigelow
- Stagnation: country without women.—John Dratwa
- Pessimist: someone who complains about the noise when opportunity knocks.—*Farmer's Digest*
- Accountant: Someone who tells you approximately how much you are worth and exactly what you owe him.
- Bachelor: Someone who is footloose and fiancee free!
- Credit Card: What you use when you discover money can't buy everything!
- Hypochondriac: Someone with an infinite capacity for faking pains
- Acquaintance: Someone you know well enough to borrow from but not to lend to!
- Consultant: Someone you call in at the last minute to share the blame!
- Consultant: Someone who takes the watch off your wrist and tells you the time.
- Conservative: Someone who believes that nothing should be done for the first time.
- Egotist: a person more interested in himself than in me.—Ambrose Bierce
- A narcissist is someone better looking than you are.—Gore Vidal
- Fanatic: A person who's enthusiastic about something in which you have no interest.—Albert J. Nimeth, *Grow Old Gracefully*
- Flattery: The art of telling a person exactly what he thinks of himself.—Paul H. Gilbert
- Bore: A person whose life is an open book . . . that you don't want to read.—Joey Adams
- Wallet: a device that permits you to lose all your valuables at the same time.—Los Angeles Times Syndicate
- M.B.A: a businessman who is often wrong but seldom in doubt.—Robert Buzzell
- Atheist: a man who watches Notre Dame play Southern Methodist and doesn't care who wins.—*Sports Illustrated*
- Bargain: Something you can't use at a price you can't resist.—Franklin P. Jones

Show me an after-dinner walk and I'll show you a digestive trek.

—Bert Murray

Show me a Confederate bugler and I'll show you a rebel rouser.

—Murray Young

Show me buried treasure and I'll show you sleeping booty.

—Findley E. Brown

Flattery: the power to describe others as they see themselves.

—*The Farmer—Stockman of the Midwest*

Bargain: a transaction in which each party thinks he has cheated the other.

—Los Angeles Times Syndicate

Compromise: an arrangement whereby people who can't get what they want make sure nobody else does either.

—Dick Cavett with Christopher Porterfield, *Eye on Cavett*

Grapevine: The only communications system in no danger of being replaced by electronics.

Diet: A plan for putting off tomorrow what you put on today.   —Ivern Ball

Hospital: A place where a patient's friends meet to tell him their symptoms.

—Vernon Hagelin, *The Furrow*

Banker: A person who lends you his umbrella when the sun is shining and wants it back the minute it rains.   —Mark Twain

Communism: The longest and most painful route from capitalism to capitalism.

Pessimist: Someone who can look at the land of milk and honey and see only calories and cholesterol.

DENTISTS

My Uncle Irv and my Aunt Harriet interrupted their vacation to go to a dentist. "I want a tooth pulled, and I don't want Novocaine because I'm in a big hurry," my aunt insisted. "Just extract the tooth as quickly as possible, and we'll be on our way." The dentist was quite awestruck. "You're certainly a brave woman," he said. "Which tooth is it?" Aunt Harriet turned to Uncle Irv and said, "Show him your tooth, dear."

~

A story along similar lines: One day a man walks into a dentist's office and asks how much it will cost to extract wisdom teeth. "Eighty dollars," the dentist says. "That's a ridiculous amount," the man says. "Isn't there a cheaper way?" "Well," the dentist says, "if you don't use an anaesthetic, I can knock it down to $60." "That's still too expensive," the man says. "Okay," says the dentist. "If I save on anesthesia and simply rip the teeth out with a pair of pliers, I could get away with charging $20." "Nope," moans the man, "it's still too much." "Hmm," says the dentist, scratching his head. "If I let one of my students do it for the experience, I suppose I could charge you just $10." "Marvelous," says the man, "book my wife for next Tuesday!"

~

Patient: "How much to have this tooth pulled?"
Dentist: "Ninety dollars."
Patient: "Ninety dollars for just a few minutes work?"
Dentist: "I can extract it very slowly if you like."

~

My dentist keeps his prices down by keeping his overhead down. No unnecessary extras. Instead of laughing gas, he tickles you.   —Ron Dentinger

~

A woman phoned her dentist when she received an exorbitant bill. "I'm shocked," she complained. "This is three times what you normally charge." "Yes, I know," said the dentist. "But you yelled so loudly, you scared away two other patients."

DIETS

I've been on a diet for two weeks and all I've lost is two weeks.
                                                        —Totie Fields

If I am ever stuck on a respirator or a life-support system, I definitely want to be unplugged—but not till I get down to a size 8.   —Henrietta Mantel

The two women were on their coffee break and the conversation drifted to efforts to try to lose a few pounds. But then one of them produced a humongous sweet roll and began to devour it. "Is that allowed on your diet?" the other asked. "It's only okay on my second diet," the first woman explained. "You mean you're on two diets?" "Uh hum. I don't get it." "The first diet didn't give me enough to eat."

DIET TIPS:

- If no one sees you eat it, it has no calories.
- If you drink a diet soda with a candy bar, they cancel each other out.
- When eating with someone else, calories don't count if you both eat the same thing.
- Food used for medicinal purposes NEVER counts, such as hot chocolate, brandy, toast, and Sara Lee cheesecake.
- If you fatten up everyone else around you, you look thinner.
- Movie-related foods don't count because they are simply part of the entertainment experience and not a part of one's personal fuel, such as Milk Duds, popcorn with butter, and Junior Mints.
- Enjoy your Diet!!!!

Malcolm Kushner, How to Use Humor for Business Success

You can lead a person to cottage cheese, but you can't make him shrink.
                              —*New York Magazine*

If you're thin, don't eat fast; if you're fat, don't eat—fast!
                              —*Classic Crossword Puzzles*

One friend to another: "I'm twice the man I used to be— and I've got the bathroom scale to prove it."

A secretary ran into a friend at a lunch counter and noted the friend was nibbling at a cottage cheese salad. "Trying to lose weight?" asked the secretary. "No," replied the friend. "I'm on a low-salary diet."

DIPLOMACY

Diplomacy is the art of saying "Nice doggie" until you can find a rock.

—Will Rogers

Do not insult the mother alligator until after you have crossed the river.

—Haitian proverb

Diplomacy gets you out of what tact would have kept you out of.

Diplomacy: Letting someone else have your way.   —Lester B. Pearson

DISASTERS

A young man came home from work and found his bride upset. "I feel terrible," she said. "I was pressing your suit and I burned a big hole in the seat of your trousers." "Forget it," consoled her husband. "Remember that I've got an extra pair of pants for that suit." "Yes," said the woman, cheering up. "And it's lucky you have. I used them to patch the hole."   —Bob Phillips

DIVORCE

My cousin Bill once sent out a thousand perfumed Valentines signed, "You Know Who . . ." He's a divorce lawyer.

My cousin Wendy is extremely sentimental. She wants to get divorced in the same dress her mother was divorced in.

My aunt Sonia's been married six times now. For her last wedding, I bought her a wash-and-wear bridal gown.

Many a man owes his success to his first wife and his second wife to his success.   —Jim Backus

"The rapidly increasing divorce rate," remarked my Uncle Irv, the wit, "indicates we are indeed becoming the land of the free." "Yes," replied his practical wife, "but the continuing marriage rate suggest this is still the land of the brave."

～

It's always the other person who is incompatible.   —Bruce Lansky

～

Most marriage failures are caused by failures marrying.   —Henry Youngman

～

My ex-husband is the kind of guy who would watch a fishing show on television and pay attention to it.   —Brett Butler

～

One woman to another at a singles bar: "I'm not as optimistic about relationships as I once was. These days, when I meet a man, I ask myself, *Is this the guy I want my children to spend every other weekend with?*
                                        —*Executive Speechwriter Newsletter*

～

A father was driving home late one evening when he suddenly realizes that it is his daughter's birthday and that he hasn't bought her anything. Out the corner of his eye he sees a shopping mall, and pulling his car through three lanes of traffic, finds a parking spot and runs into the mall. After a frantic search he finds a toy store, goes inside and attracts the attention of a salesman. When asked what he would like, he simply says "a Barbie doll." The salesman looks at him in the particularly condescending manner that only salesmen can muster and asks "Which Barbie would that be, sir?" As the would be shopper looked disconcerted the assistant continues, "We have: Barbie Goes to the Gym for $19.95. Barbie Goes to the Ball for $19.95. Barbie Goes Shopping for $19.95. Barbie Goes to the Beach for $19.95. Barbie Goes Night Clubbing for $19.95, and Divorced Barbie for $265.00." The man can't help himself and asks, "Why is Divorced Barbie $265.00 when all the other Barbies are selling for $19.95?" "That's obvious!" says the salesman. "Divorced Barbie comes with Ken's house, Ken's car, Ken's furniture . . ."

DOCTORS (*See also* MEDICINE)

I try to remember the case of the gentleman who went in for a physical examination and then said to the doctor, "O.K. Give it to me straight. I can take it." And the doctor said, "Let me put it to you this way. Eat the best part of the chicken first."   —Ronald Reagan

OVERHEARD AT THE DOCTOR'S OFFICE:

- "Excuse me, but what medical journal is this going to be in?"
- "Do you by any chance still have some of those pills I gave you last week? They were a string of beads my wife wanted restrung."
- "Yours is a common enough personality problem, Mr. Rankley—you're obnoxious."
- "Imagine! Telling me I'm in perfect health. How does a 'quack' like you stay in business?"
- "Pulse, 80; temperature, 103; income, $100,000 net."
- "There's really nothing unusual about your condition, Mr. Lerch, except for the fact that it is so seldom encountered in a person who is still living."
- "Nurse Locke, I wish you wouldn't refer to hypodermic injections as your needle work."
- "Dear me, I've been waiting so long I think I've recovered."
- "Take one upon going to bed, and the other if you wake up in the morning."
- "Don't worry about the hospital bills, dear—they're less than you would spend if you were well!"
- "I hope I'll get to the root of your trouble, Mr. Brown, because I've had the same thing myself for years."

Susan Elroy, our congregation's notorious hypochondriac, was so certain that she had an incurable liver condition that she went to the doctor to find out about it. The doctor assured her she was all right. "You wouldn't know if you had this condition, because it causes no discomfort of any kind." "Oh, my goodness," gasped Susan. "Those are my symptoms exactly."

Medical science has made a lot of progress with new miracle drugs. No matter what illness you have, the doctor can keep you alive long enough for you to pay your bill.

—Joey Adams

As the doctor completed an examination of the patient, he said, "I can't find a cause for your complaint. Frankly, I think it's due to drinking." "In that case," said the patient, "I'll come back when you're sober."

I called for an appointment with the doctor. I was told that they couldn't fit me in for at least two weeks. I said, "I could be dead by then." They said, "That's no problem. Just have your wife let us know, and we will cancel the appointment."

—Ron Dentinger

Sid was a nonstop talker. When his wife became ill, the doctor said, "I prescribe absolute quiet for your wife. Here's a bottle of sleeping pills." "When do I give them to her?" asked Sid. "You don't give them to her," said the doctor. "You take them yourself." —Bennett Cerf

My neighbor was telling me about her toddler Allison: "I took Allison to the doctor for her two-year-old checkup. They had her do coordination tests, like stacking blocks, and they watch and see if they walk properly. And then the doctor said, 'Allison, can you stand on one foot for me?' And she walked over and stood on his foot."

After surgery, the doctor told the patient, you can pay $500 down and $300 a month. "But that's like buying a car," the patient remarked. "That's right, I am," said the doctor. —Msgr. Arthur Tonne, *Jokes Priests Can Tell,* vol. 6

WHAT THE DOCTOR SAYS (AND WHAT HE REALLY MEANS):

- This should be taken care of right away. (I'd planned a trip to Hawaii next month but this is so easy and profitable that I want to fix it before it cures itself.)
- Wellllll, what have we here . . . (Since I haven't the the foggiest notion of what it is, I am hoping you will give me a clue.)
- We'll see. (First I have to check my malpractice insurance.)
- Let me check your medical history. (I want to see if you've paid your last bill before spending any more time with you.)
- Why don't we make another appointment later in the week. (I'm playing golf this afternoon, and this is a waste of time.—or—I need the money, so I'm charging you for another office visit.)
- I really can't recommend seeing a chiropractor. (I hate those guys mooching in on our fees.)
- Hmmmmmmmmm. (Since I haven't the faintest idea of what to do, I am trying to appear thoughtful while hoping the nurse will interrupt. [Proctologist also say this a lot.])
- We have some good news and some bad news. (The good news is I'm going to buy that new BMW, and the bad news is you're going to pay for it.)
- Let's see how it develops. (Maybe in a few days it will grow into something that can be cured.)
- Let me schedule you for some tests. (I have a 40% interest in the lab.)
- I'd like to have my associate look at you. (He's going through a messy divorce and owes me a small fortune.)
- I'd like to prescribe a new drug. (I'm writing a paper and would like to use you for a guinea pig.)

- If it doesn't clear up in a week, give me a call. (I don't know what it is. Maybe it will go away by itself.)
- That's quite a nasty looking wound. (I think I'm going to throw up.)
- This may smart a little. (Last week two patients bit through their tongues.)
- Well, we're not feeling so well today, are we? (I can't remember your name, nor why you are here.)
- This should fix you up. (The drug salesman guaranteed that it kills all symptoms.)
- Everything seems to be normal. (I guess I can't buy that new beach condo after all.)
- Do you suppose all of this stress could be affecting your nerves? (I think you are crazy and am hoping to find a psychiatrist who will split fees.)
- If those symptoms persist, call for an appointment. (I've never heard of anything so disgusting. Thank God I'm off next week.)
- There is a lot of that going around. (That's the third one this week. I'd better learn something about this.)
- It could be one of several things. (I haven't the foggiest idea what's wrong with you.)
- Are you sure you haven't had this before? (Because you've got it again.)
- I'd like to run that test again. (The lab lost your blood sample.)
- Insurance should cover most of this. (You'll have to sell your house to cover the rest.)
- These pills have very few side effects. (You may experience sudden hair growth on your palms.)
- Why don't you go over your symptoms with me one more time. (I can't remember who you are.)

—*David Grimes in* Sarasota Herald-Tribune

My car skidded on wet pavement and struck a light pole. I was stunned and momentarily unable to speak. Several bystanders ran over to help me. A tall, middle-aged woman was the first to reach my car. She started to speak when a burly truck driver rushed in and pushed her back. "Step aside, lady," he shouted. "I've taken a course in first aid." The woman watched him for a few minutes, then tapped his shoulder. "Pardon me," she said. "But when you get to the part about calling a doctor, I'm right here."

Physician to patient: "If I've told you once, I've told you a hundred times—I do not treat amnesia cases!"

—Baloo in *Corlandt Forum*

Receptionist to physician: "The patient is in the middle of a magazine article and will see you soon, doctor."

—Earl W. Engleman in *Medical Economics*

My doctor takes no chances. Before operating on me, he gave me a pre-surgery credit-scan.

～

My opthalmologist Peter Nelson tells me: I was performing a complete physical, including the visual acuity test. I placed the patient twenty feet from the chart and began. "Cover your right eye with your hand." He read the 20/20 line perfectly. "Now your left." Again, a flawless read. "Now both," I requested. There was silence. He couldn't even read the large E on the top line. I turned and discovered that he had done exactly what I had asked. He was standing there with both his eyes covered. I was laughing too hard to finish the exam.

～

A distraught patient phoned her doctor's office. "Was it true, the woman wanted to know, that the medication the doctor had prescribed was for the rest of her life?" She was told that it was. There was a moment of silence before the woman continued, "I'm wondering, then, just how serious my condition is. This prescription is marked 'NO REFILLS.'"

～

Isn't it a bit unnerving that doctors call what they do "practice"?

～

A true story. After I survived a very serious illness I went to see my doctor. As his nurse was taking my vital signs and checking my weight and height, I discovered that I was only 5 foot 8 instead of my former 5 foot 10. When the doctor entered the examination room, I reported with alarm, "Doctor! I think I'm shrinking!" The doctor calmly responded, "Now, settle down. You'll just have to be a little patient."

～

I was in the waiting room of my doctor's office the other day when the doctor started yelling, "Typhoid! Tetanus! Measles!" I went up to the nurse and asked her what was going on. She told me that the doctor liked to call the shots.

～

"That was close!" exclaimed the surgeon as he left the operating room. "What do you mean?" asked a nurse. "An inch either way and I would have been out of my specialty!"　　　　　　　　　—*The Toastmaster's Treasure Chest,* edited by
　　　　　　　　　Herbert V. Prochnow and Herbert V. Prochnow, Jr.

～

The hospital patient was worried. "Are you sure it's pneumonia, doctor?" he asked. "I've heard of cases where a doctor treated a patient for pneumonia, and he ended up dying of something else." "Don't worry," said the doctor. "When I treat a patient for pneumonia, he dies of pneumonia."

—Winston K. Pendleton, *Funny Stories, Jokes and Anecdotes*

"Your cholesterol level is unbelievably high," a doctor told his patient during a physical examination. "How bad is it?" The doctor pointed out the window. "See that field of oats out there?" "Yes?" "Bon appetit!"

—Parker and Hart, North America Syndicate

The grouchy, short-tempered doctor glared at the new patient. "Have you been to a doctor," he asked, "before you came to me?" "No, sir," replied the meek patient. "I went to a pharmacist." "That shows how much sense some

The
BORDERLINE™

By Gabe Martin
borderln@cts.com

©1995 GABE MARTIN

http://www.the-borderline.com/

"OK men, pass this along—this is our last chance, so at high noon we all make a break for it—but THIS time, don't everybody all go running in the same direction!"

people have," the doctor growled. "And what sort of idiotic advice did he give you?" "He told me to come to see you." —*Rotarian*

~

A young surgeon got a call from a colleague who invited him over for a poker foursome. "Going out, dear?" asked the wife sympathetically. "I'm afraid so," was the brave reply. "It's a serious case. There are three doctors there already!"

~

Patient: "Doc, what I need is something to stir me up, give me energy, put me in fighting spirit. Did you put something like that in the prescription?"
Doctor: "No—you'll find that in the bill." —Hugh Harrison

DOGS

Minnie said to her friend Marge, "Our dog is just like a member of the family." "Which one?" Marge asked.

~

My husband and I are either going to buy a dog or have a child. We can't decide whether to ruin our carpet or ruin our lives. —Rita Rudner

HOW TO PHOTOGRAPH A PUPPY

- Remove film from box and load camera. Remove film box from puppy's mouth and throw in trash.
- Remove puppy from trash and brush coffee grounds from muzzle.
- Choose a suitable background for photo.
- Mount camera on tripod and focus.
- Find puppy and take dirty sock from mouth.
- Place puppy in prefocused spot and return to camera.
- Forget about spot and crawl after puppy on knees.
- Focus with one hand and fend off puppy with other hand.
- Get tissue and clean nose print from lens.
- Take flash cube from puppy's mouth and throw in trash.
- Put cat outside and put peroxide on the scratch on puppy's nose.
- Put magazines back on coffee table.
- Try to get puppy's attention by squeaking toy over your head.
- Replace your glasses and check camera for damage.
- Jump up in time to grab puppy by scruff of neck and say "No, outside! No, outside!"
- Call someone to help clean up mess.
- Fix a cold glass of soda.
- Sit back in Lazy Boy with large, cold drink and resolve to teach puppy "sit" and "stay" the first thing in the morning.

There's a guy with a Doberman pinscher and a guy with a Chihuahua. The guy with the Doberman pinscher says to the guy with the Chihuahua, "Let's go over to that restaurant and get something to eat." The guy with the Chihuahua says, "We can't go in there. We've got dogs with us." The guy with the Doberman pinscher says, "Just follow my lead." They walk over to the restaurant, the guy with the Doberman pinscher puts on a pair of dark glasses, and he starts to walk in. A guy at the door says, "Sorry, Mac, no pets allowed." The guy with the Doberman says, "You don't understand. This is my seeing-eye dog." The guy at the door says, "A Doberman pinscher?" He says, "Yes, they're using them now,

they're very good." The guy at the door says, "Come on in." The guy with the Chihuahua figures, "What the heck," so he puts on a pair of dark glasses and starts to walk in. The guy at the door says, "Sorry, pal, no pets allowed." The guy with the Chihuahua says, "You don't understand. This is my seeing-eye dog." The guy at the door says, "A Chihuahua?" He says, "You mean they gave me a Chihuahua?"

❧

The constant barking of my neighbor's dog was driving me out of my mind. Appeals to my neighbor proved fruitless. Finally I called the police. A police officer arrived at my home and asked me to accompany him to our neighbor's house. My neighbor was highly insulted. "My dog," she protested coldly, "never disturbs anybody. Mr. Streiker has no proof at all, Officer." I thought for a moment and then asked my neighbor, "Do you have any objection to the officer seeing the dog?" "Of course not," said my neighbor. "Here, Barky, Barky!"

❧

I took my dog Nehi to obedience school, and the dog got a higher grade than I did.

❧

A little four-year-old brought his puppy to visit his grandmother. She was busy fixing dinner and paid no attention to the pup. After a while the boy, his eyes filling with tears, asked her reproachfully: "Aren't you even going to speak to your granddog?"

One day a letter carrier was greeted by a boy and a huge dog. The mailman said to the boy, "Does your dog bite?" "No," replied the boy. Just then the huge dog bit the mailman on the ankle. The letter carrier yelped, "I thought your dog doesn't bite!" "He doesn't," replied the boy. "This is not my dog!"

What is a dog? They follow you around with their tongues out. They only respond to simple commands. Their needs are basic and predictable. They whine when their needs are not met. They always need to have something in their mouth. They scratch a lot and sometimes drool. They make loud noises and sometimes smell bad. They need to be trained. You can always tell when one has lived in a house for a long time. They're rude and rowdy, especially when they're with others like them. Conclusion: They're little men in fuzzy boxes.

A farmer was bitten on the leg by one of his dogs. At the clinic, the nurse asked him if he had put anything on it. "No," replied the puzzled farmer, "the dog liked it just as it was."

—Don Bosco in *Salesian Bulletin*

One good thing about a dark skirt is that it's the best thing for removing dog hairs from the sofa. —Jane Goodsell, Press Associates

The dog has got more fun out of man than man has got out of the dog, for the clearly demonstrable reason that man is the more laughable of the two animals. —James Thurber, *Thurber's Dogs*

If you think dogs can't count, try putting three dog biscuits in your pocket and then giving Fido only two of them.

—Phil Pastoret, Newspaper Enterprise Assn.

A fellow walked into a saloon with his dog under his arm. "No dogs allowed," said the bartender. "But this dog can talk," said the man. "Listen, I'll ask him three questions and if he answers, I drink free here tonight." The bartender agreed. "Spot," called the man, "what's the opposite of smooth?" "R-r-ruff," barked the dog. "What's on top of a house?" "R-r-ruff," the dog responded. "Right again!" cried the fellow. "Now, who's the best baseball player?"

R-r-ruth," said the dog. The bartender picked up the fellow and the dog by the scruff of their necks and threw them both out in to the alley. As they lay there, the dog looked quizzically at the fellow and said, "Aaron?"

—James Dent in Charleston, W.VA., *Gazette*

It's not the size of the dog in the fight; it's the size of the fight in the dog.

—Mark Twain

If you can start the day without caffeine, if you can get going without pep pills, if you can always be cheerful, ignoring aches and pains, if you can resist complaining and boring people with your troubles, if you can eat the same food everyday and be grateful for it, if you can understand when your loved ones are too busy to give you anytime, if you can overlook it when those you love take it out on you when, through no fault of yours, something goes wrong, if you can take criticism and blame without resentment, if you can ignore a friend's limited education and never correct him, if you can resist treating a rich friend better than a poor friend, if you can face the world without lies and deceit, if you can conquer tension without medical help, if you can relax without liquor, if you can sleep without the aid of drugs, if you can say honestly that deep in your heart you have no prejudice against creed, color, religion or politics, then, my friend, you are almost as good as your dog.

The first thing that veterinary doctors learn about treating pit bulls is that you should never try to force a pit bull to open his mouth and say, "Ahhh."

TURTLE WAX

One reason a dog can be such a comfort when you're feeling blue is that he doesn't try to find out why.

~

A man came into our grocery store and asked what kind of dog food we carried. I showed him the two brands, and he bought a few cans of the cheaper food. Almost immediately he was back—his dog didn't like that brand. When I told him he could exchange the cans, he said, "I'd better check first to see if he'll like the other one." Puzzled, I watched as the man went out to his car, tapped on the window, held the can up for his dog to see, and then returned to the store. "We're in luck," he said, smiling. "He likes this one. I'll take it."

—Mrs. Jesse Holmes in *The Star*

~

Whoever said you can't buy happiness forgot about puppies.   —Gene Hill

~

They say animal behavior can warn when an earthquake is coming. Like the night before the last earthquake hit, our family dog took the car keys and drove to Arizona.   —Gene Perret

~

A man wrote to a hotel to ask if his dog would be allowed to stay there. He received the following answer: "Dear Sir—I have been in the hotel business for over 30 years. Never yet have I had to call in the police to eject a disorderly dog in the small hours of the morning. No dog has ever attempted to pass off a bad check on me. Never has a dog set the bedclothes on fire through smoking. I have never found a hotel towel in a dog's suitcase. Your dog is welcome. P.S.—If he will vouch for you, you can come, too."   —*Ireland's Own*

DREAMS

After she woke up, a woman told her husband, "I just dreamed that you gave me a pearl necklace for Valentine's day. What do you think it means?" "You'll know tonight," he said. That evening, the man came home with a package and gave it to his wife. Delighted, she opened it—to find a book entitled, *The Meaning of Dreams.*

~

My aunt said to her husband, "Max, last night I dreamed you bought me a fur coat." Her husband said, "In your next dream, wear it in good health."

—Henny Youngman

DRIVING

Police arrested 56-year-old Joe Shaw near White River Junction, Vermont, in April after he tried to break through a rolling roadblock on I-89. Shaw, who was charged with DUI and other offenses, said, "I saw it so many times in the movies, I had to try it."

D

An applicant for driver's license came to the questions: "How many feet are required to stop car traveling 30 mph?" He answered straightforwardly: "Two feet, one for the clutch, one for the brake." He got his license.

—The Railway Clerk

On the walls of the men's room at a Kansas truck stop were scribbled the words from Romans 8: "If God be for us, who can be against us?" Scrawled beneath someone had added: "The Highway Patrol!"

A car headed out of Calgary was stopped by a Canadian Mountie. He told the driver: "Congratulations, you have just won a $100 prize for the hundredth car passing through here today with all occupants buckled up with seat belts. Now, what are you going to do with the money?" "Well," said the motorist, "I think I'll go and get a driver's license, now that I can afford it."

It's some kind of unwritten law that drivers under 30 drive over 70 and drivers over 70 drive under 30.   —Ron Dentinger

A man is driving up a steep, narrow mountain road. A woman is driving down the same road. As they pass each other the woman leans out the window and yells, "PIG!!" The man immediately leans out his window and yells out, "IDIOT!!" They each continue on their way, and as the man rounds the next corner, he crashes into a pig in the middle of the road.

Driving Tip: If you're driving while you're tired, you can take the edge off when you get to a stoplight. Close your eyes and rest while the light is red. When you hear horns, you'll know that it's time to go.

A motorist whose car was weaving was ordered to pull off the road into a parking lot, and the policeman told the obviously drunk motorist to walk down a straight line painted on the pavement. "I'm sorry, sir, but I will not walk it unless you put a net under it," said the motorist.   —*Ohio Motorist*

❧

A motorist in Washington, D.C., stopped to help a woman driver stalled on one of the main thoroughfares. He found her taking sand out of the trunk of her car and sprinkling it around the front wheels. "It ought to go under the back wheels," he said. Sneering at his stupidity, she replied, "The back wheels go around all right. It's the front wheels that won't turn."

—*Minneapolis Tribune*

❧

A speaker was talking to a group of teenagers about the old West. He remarked that Billy the Kid had killed 21 men by the time he was 21 years old. "Good heavens," exclaimed one of his listeners. "What kind of a car did he drive?"

—*Far East*

E

ECONOMISTS

An economist was asked to talk to a group of business people about the recession. She tacked up a big sheet of white paper. Then she made a black spot on the paper with her pencil and asked a man in the front row what he saw. The man replied promptly, "A black spot." The speaker asked every person the same question, and each replied, "A black spot." With calm and deliberate emphasis the speaker said: "Yes, there is a little black spot, but none of you mentioned the big sheet of white paper. And that's my speech."

❧

If all the financial experts in this country were laid end to end, they'd still point in all directions.   —Sam Ewing

❧

A pair of economists went to a restaurant for lunch. "Never mind the food," one said to the waitress. "Just bring us the bill so we can argue about it."

—Carol Simpson in *Funny Times*

EDUCATION

Mr. Gray, the professor asked, what three words are used most among college students? The student answered, "I don't know." The professor responded, "Correct."   —*Irish Grit*

Who's going to do all the work in this world when the trend toward longer education meets the trend toward early retirement?
—Don Reber in Reading, Pennsylvania, *Times*

Education is learning what you didn't even know you didn't know.
—Daniel J. Boorstin, *Democracy and Its Discontents*

E

Learning sleeps and snores in libraries, but wisdom is everywhere, wide awake, on tiptoe.   —Josh Billings

A historian who held a Ph.D. spent a few days in a small town. The elderly postmaster, curious about the visitor's background, asked what kind of doctor she was. "I'm a doctor of philosophy," she answered. "Hmmm," he said, scratching his bald head, "I don't recall that we've ever had a case of that around here."

EFFICIENCY

According to a story of uncertain origin, an efficiency expert was hired to make a report on the New York Philharmonic Orchestra. As a part of this preparation, he attended several concerts. At last, he issued his report, which read in part as follows:

Report on the New York Philharmonic Orchestra—"For considerable periods, the four oboe players have nothing to do. Their number should be reduced and the work spread more evenly over the whole of the concert, thus eliminating peaks of activity . . . All twelve first violins were playing identical notes. This seems unnecessary duplication . . . Much effort was absorbed in the playing of semiquavers. This seems an excessive refinement. It is recommended that all notes be rounded up to the nearest quaver . . . No useful purpose is served by the repeating on the horns a passage which has already been played by the strings . . . It is estimated that if all redundant passages were eliminated, the whole concert time of two hours could be reduced to twenty minutes and there would be no need for an intermission."

EFFORT

If at first you don't succeed, try, try, a couple of times more. Then quit. There's no sense making a fool of yourself.
—W. C. Fields

By trying, we can easily learn to endure adversity. Another man's, I mean.

—Mark Twain

EGO

Field Marshall Lord Montgomery was reported to have started his reading of the Gospel at Matins one Sunday with the words: "'And the Lord said unto Moses,'—and, in my opinion, quite rightly—"

—Norman Broadbridge in *Manchester Guardian Weekly*

Senator Blowright was quite full of himself. He took every opportunity to remind everyone how important he was. At the county fair he extolled, "All that I now am I owe to my fine parents." An anonymous voice from the back of crowd expressed the sentiment all present: "Then why don't you give them twenty cents and pay off your debt?"

My Uncle Irv has such an ego that when he prays he says, "Dear God, do you need anything?"

My Uncle Irv admits he has no humility, but if he did have it he says it would better than everybody else's.

"I made the mistake of telling him to get his hair out of his eyes."

My cousin Ed says, "I know a lot of people with inferiority complexes, but theirs are all better than mine."

E

Self-love seems so often unrequited.   —Anthony Powell

A very boastful explorer was boring his dinner guests with accounts of a South African trip he had made. "And just as I looked inside my tent when I retired," he boomed, "I saw a ferocious ape."

"What do you suppose I did?" A weary voice replied, "Took the mirror down?"   —Quote

You can always recognize an egotist by the gleam in his I.   —Amy Griffin

The nice thing about egotists is that they don't talk about other people.
                                                              —Lucille S. Harper

Sir Arthur Eddington, a British astronomer, was once asked: "Is it true, Professor Eddington, that you are one of the three people in the world who understands Einstein's theory of relativity?" The astronomer appeared reluctant to answer. "Forgive me," said his questioner. "I should have realized a man of your modesty would find such a question embarrassing." "Not at all," said Eddington. "I was just trying to think who the third could be."
                            —Toastmaster's Quips & Stories and How to Use Them,
                                               edited by Herbert V. Prochnow

An egotist is someone who is always me-deep in conversation.
                                                              —George Goldtrap

ELKS

A friend who teaches the first grade asked her class, "What do elks have that no other animals have?" Little Bobbie answered, "Parades."   —Quote

ELVIS

If life was fair, Elvis would be alive and all the impersonators would be dead.
                                                              —Johnny Carson

Sorry guys, but there is now definitive, undeniable proof that Elvis is, indeed, dead. He was registered to vote in Chicago.

E-MAIL

Consider the case of the Illinois man who left the snow-filled streets of Chicago for a vacation in Florida. His wife was on a business trip and was planning to meet him there the next day. When he reached his hotel, he decided to send his wife a quick e-mail. Unable to find the scrap of paper on which he had written her e-mail address, he did his best to type it from memory. Unfortunately, he missed one letter, and his note was directed instead to an elderly preacher's wife, whose husband had passed away only the day before. When the grieving widow checked her e-mail, she took one look at the monitor, let out a piercing scream, and fell to the floor in a dead faint. At the sound, her family rushed into the room and saw this note on the screen: "Dearest Wife, Just got checked in. Everything prepared for your arrival tomorrow. Signed, Your eternally loving husband. PS. Sure is hot down here!"

EMERGENCIES

Nothing seems to bring on an emergency as quickly as putting money aside in case of one.
　　　　　　　　　　　　　　　　　　　　　　　—Lynne Youdin

ENEMIES

A few years back, Comedian Mort Sahl said of former Secretary of State Alexander Haig: "I was with him when he lit up a Havana cigar, and I asked him, 'Isn't that trading with the enemy?' He told me, 'I prefer to think of it as burning their crops to the ground.'"

～

Never interrupt your enemy when he is making a mistake.
　　　　　　　　　　　　　　　　　　　　—Napoleon Bonaparte

～

He made enemies as naturally as soap makes suds.　　　—Percival Wilde

ENGLISH

English is used by one of every seven human beings on earth. Half of the world's books are written in English. The majority of international phone calls are made in English. Over 60% of the world's radio programs are broadcast in English. Over 70% of international mail is written in English. Eighty percent of all computer text is stored in English. English has the world's largest vocabu-

lary—about two million words. And yet English is a strange language. For example: sharp and blunt speech are the same; overlook and oversee are opposites; your nose runs and your feet smell; a vegetarian eats vegetables, but what does a humanitarian eat? Yesterday the teacher taught, but last Sunday the preacher didn't praught; there are no peas in peanuts, no pine or apple in pineapple, no mush or room in mushroom, no grape in grapefruit, no butter in buttermilk, no egg in eggplant, no bread in shortbread; a woman can man a station, but a man can't woman one; a man can father a movement, but a woman can't mother one; a king rules a kingdom, but queens don't rule a queendom.
                                        —Eric W. Johnson, *A Treasury of Humor II*

Isn't it strange that the words ruly, ert, ept, ane, sipid, and mune do not exist in English, whereas their negatives unruly, inert, inept, inane, insipid and immune do?

ENVY

Mrs. Felton asked the artist to paint a portrait of her covered with jewels. "Then put them on," said the artist. Replies Mrs. Felton, "You don't understand, I don't have any jewels, but if I die and my husband remarries, I want his next wife to go crazy looking for the jewels."

REVEREND FUN

"Hey, this burnt-offering sauce was made in NEW YORK CITY!!!"

EPITAPHS

Seven wives I've buried with as many a fervent prayer;
If we all should meet in heaven, won't there be trouble there?

~

Here lies the preacher, judge, and poet Peter,
Who broke the laws of God and man and meter.

~

Matilda Graham has gone to rest.
She now reclines on Abraham's breast.
Peace at last for Matilda Graham,
But not for Father Abraham.

~

Norman Zierold of Long Island, N.Y., *Newsday,* asked many celebrities to write their own epitaphs. What follows is a sampling:

Comedienne Pat Carroll: "Could I leave a wake-up call?"

Baritone Robert Merrill: "One more encore, please."

Mark Russell: "A comedian. It's not the first time he died."

Author James Michener: "Here lies a man who never showed home movies or served vin rosé."

Comic Joan Rivers: "Wait—can we talk?"

ERRORS

Admit your errors before someone else exaggerates them.

—Andrew V. Mason, M.D.

~

From Father Ferreira's bulletin from Our Lady of Good Council in San Leandro, California, there's this poignant note: "If you find errors, please consider that they appear for the benefit of those readers who always look for them . . . We try to print something for everybody!"   —*The Priest Magazine*

ESP

Notice: The ESP Society will not be meeting this month due to unforeseen circumstances.   —Ron Dentinger

ETERNITY

Eternal rest sounds comforting in the pulpit . . . Well, you try it once, and see how heavy time will hang on your hands.   —Mark Twain

ETHICS

My doctor has ethics. He won't operate unless he really needs money.
—Ron Dentinger

EVIL

If there isn't a devil, there's sure somebody getting his work done for him.

E

EXAMPLE

Few things are harder to put up with than the annoyance of a good example.
—Mark Twain

EXCELLENCE

If you pursue excellence, happiness sneaks up behind you and touches you
on the shoulder. If you pursue mediocrity, you're sure to catch it.
—Kenneth Boulding

EXCUSES

An Prohibition-era story from the South tells about the time a police officer
caught a bootlegger with a lot of jugs in his truck. The officer asked what was
in them. The bootlegger said, "Water." The police officer did not believe him.
So he opened one of the jugs and took a gulp. He said to the bootlegger, "This
looks like wine. And it tastes exactly like wine." The bootlegger exclaimed,
"Praise the Lord! He's done it again!"

～

Little Ted was told not to go swimming in a nearby pond. He came home with
his hair wet and told his mother he had fallen into the water. "Then why aren't
your clothes wet too?" she asked. "Well," he replied, "I had a hunch I might
fall in so I took off my clothes and hung them on a limb."

～

While we still lived in Foster City, California, I had the following adventure:
Seven houses down from ours is a park with a nice sandy beach. It is an
attractive little park which is heavily infested with
snails. A few years ago, my wife and I were having
a dinner party for all the major shakers and movers
in our church. My wife was very excited about
this and wanted everything to be perfect. At the very
last minute, she realized that she didn't have any snails for hors d'oeuvres
for the dinner party, so she instructed me to run down to the beach with the

bucket she was handing me to gather some snails. Very grudgingly I agreed, took the bucket, walked out the door, down the steps, went past the seven intervening houses, through the park, and down to the beach. As I was collecting the snails, I noticed a neighbor, whom I hadn't seen in some time, strolling alongside the water just a little further down the beach. I greeted her and we got into a long and pleasant conversation as the result of which I lost track of time. As the sun began to set, I realized that it was nearly time for my wife's dinner party! So I scooped up as many snails as I could find and ran through the park and toward my house. I ran up the front stairs of my house, but I was in such a hurry that when I got to the top stair, I dropped the bucket of snails. There were snails all down the stairs. The door opened just then, and there was a very angry wife standing in the doorway wondering where I'd been all this time. I looked at the snails all down the steps, then I looked at her, then back at the snails and said: "Come on guys, we're almost there!"

EXERCISE

I'm not working out. My philosophy: No pain, no pain.   —Carol Leifer

Professor in lab: "Researchers have announced that exercise kills germs."
New student: "Sure, sure. But how do you get germs to exercise?"

—*Capper's Weekly*

I developed a great incentive for doing sit-ups. I put M & Ms between my toes.

EXPERIENCE

We should be careful to get out of an experience only the wisdom that was in it—and stop there, lest we be like the cat that sits on a hot stove-lid. She will never sit down on a hot stove-lid again—and that is well, but also she will never sit down on a cold one anymore.   —Mark Twain

EXPERTS

A friend of mine used to spend summer vacations as a ranger at Lassen Volcanic National Park in California. He was on duty one morning when a tourist approached, gave a brief description of an unusual bird he had just seen and asked whether my friend could identify it. "No," my friend replied, "I don't recognize it either, but I can help you. I have here a copy of Roger Tory

Peterson's *Definitive Field Guide to Western Birds*." "That won't help," replied the disappointed tourist. "That bird's not in there. I'm Roger Tory Peterson."
—Stephen L. Brown, Sr.

~

Even more exasperating than the guy who thinks he knows it all is the one who really does.
—Al Bernstein

~

An expert is someone called in at the last minute to share the blame.
—Sam Ewing in *Mature Living*

------------------------- **F** -------------------------

FACTS

Fact: 50% of doctors practicing in this country today graduated in the lower half of their class.
—Ron Dentinger

FAMILIES

George Burns: "This family of yours—they all lived together?"
Gracie Allen: "Yes, my father, my uncle, my cousin, my brother, and my nephew used to sleep in one bed, and my—"
George: "I'm surprised your grandfather didn't sleep with them."
Gracie: "Oh, he did, but he died and they made him get up."

~

Home, nowadays, is a place where part of the family waits till the rest of the family brings the car back.
—Earl Meltzer

~

Johann Andersen tells me, "We've got so many kids that we wore out four storks."

~

Lord have mercy, Mrs. Tugwell just had her sixteenth young 'un. She said she had so many young 'uns she'd run out of names—to call her husband.
—Minnie Pearl

~

Nothing in life is fun for the whole family.

~

The trouble with the average family is it has too much month left over at the end of the money.
—Bill Vaughan

Watching a particular romantic ending to a Disney animated video, five-year-old Tiffany sighed, "I hope I meet my prince someday." "Of course you will," her mother reassured her. "You know, I met my prince the day I met your daddy." Puzzled, she turned to Mom. "Who was he?" she asked.

~

My father's Aunt Rose was a real character. The first time I met her was at a family reunion. I was 30 and she was 80. "Hey, good looking," she exclaimed as she pinched my bottom, "if I had known you were coming along, I would have waited." Her three middle aged children, all Japanese Americans and all strikingly attractive, were there. She proudly pointed to them and said, "People often ask me about my children. You see, good looking, when I got married I was so poor that I had to have my babies made in Japan!"

~

During a long car ride, my Uncle Jack was driving the family crazy with a continuous lament: "Oh, am I thirsty! Oh, am I thirsty! . . ." At the next rest stop, his son rushed out and brought him a large seltzer water. As my dad started the car to continue the ride, the silence was broken by Uncle Jack: "Oh, was I thirsty! Oh, was I thirsty! Oh, was I thirsty! . . ."

~

The phone rings and, in a whisper, a six-year-old boy says, "Hello." The caller says, "Can I talk to your mother?" The kid whispers, "She's outside." The caller says, "Can I talk to your father?" The kid whispers, "He's outside too." The caller says, "Is there anyone else there?" The kid whispers, "The police are here." The caller says, "The police are at your house?" The kid whispers, "Yea. They're outside." The caller says, "What's everybody doing outside?" The kid whispers, "Looking for me."

—Ron Dentinger

~

A young couple had their first baby. When it was one year old, it hadn't said a word; one and a half years, still not a word. The parents took the baby to a pediatrician, who said, "Everything's perfectly normal. Just be patient." And so it went until the child's 25th month. They were all having breakfast and the kid turned to his mother and said, "This oatmeal is too darn lumpy." The parents were amazed, and so they said, "Why haven't you talked before?" The kid replied, "Up till now, things have gone very well."

—Eric W. Johnson, *A Treasury of Humor II*

The other day my daughter came home from school and asked a question of my wife. My wife said, "Why not wait until your dad comes home and ask him." To which my daughter replied: "But, Mom, I don't want to know that much about it!"
                                                        —King Duncan

My friend Ralph complained to me: "Things were a lot different when you and I were boys. In his room my son has a color TV, a computer, VCR, a refrigerator, a stereo, several radios, and his telephone. When I want to punish him, I have to send him to my room!"

Grandma Betty was saying good-night to her granddaughters when six-year-old Beth remarked, "Mommy and Daddy are entertaining some very important people downstairs." Grandma said, "Yes, I know they have guests. But what makes you thing they are important?" The little girl responded, "Just listen. Mommy is laughing at all of Daddy's jokes."

Agnes and Beverly were discussing their respective families. "Do you mean to tell me that your son and daughter-in-law were married six months ago and you haven't visited them yet?" exclaimed Agnes. "I'm shocked!" "What's there to be shocked about?" demanded Beverly. "I'm waiting until they have their first baby. Everybody knows that a grandma is always more welcome than a mother-in-law."

I never liked hide-and-seek since the time I hid in the closet and my family moved.

Having a family is like having a bowling alley installed in your brain.
                                                        —Martin Mull

A mother asked her son why he didn't take his little sister along as he left to go fishing, and he said, "Because the last time I took her I didn't catch a thing." Mother said, "I'm sure she'll be quiet if you explain to her." "Oh, it wasn't the noise," the boy replied. "She ate the bait."

Two boys were registering for the first grade. They were almost the same height and weight and had the same last name. The teacher asked: "Are you twins?" "No," one of them answered. When she noticed on their birth certificates that there was only six months difference in their ages, she asked: "Are you cousins?" "No, we're brothers," one boy replied. "Well," said the teacher, "please have your mother write down the dates of your birth, and bring it to me. If you aren't twins and you are brothers, one of you would have to be more than six months older than the other." Both boys looked at each other and then one of them said with a smile: "One of us don't have to be older than the other, cuz one of us is adopted. But I don't know which one."

—Msgr. Arthur Tonne, *Jokes Priests Can Tell,* vol. 6

The rich aunt was hurt and said to her nephew, "I'm sorry you don't like your gift. I had asked you if you preferred a large check or a small check." "I know, Auntie," the nephew said contritely, "but I didn't know you were talking about neckties."

—*Irish Grit*

I was preaching in a small Methodist church in Georgia and I asked the congregation, "How many of you folks here this morning are Methodists?" And everybody raised their hand except one little old lady. After the service, she and I were shaking hands and I said, "Ma'am, I noticed you didn't raise your hand; that means you're not a Methodist. Would you mind telling me what

"I showed him one of his old report cards instead of mine. . . . . He was NOT amused."

you are?" She said, "Well, I'm a Baptist." Well, some of the people standing around didn't seem to appreciate her answer.

So, I asked her, "Ma'am, would you mind telling me why you're a Baptist?" She said, "Well, I really don't know, except my mother was a Baptist, my father was a Baptist, my grandmother and my grandfather were Baptists." "Well," I said, "Ma'am, that's really not a good reason to be a Baptist. Suppose your mother and your father, and your grandmother and your grandfather had been morons, what would you have been?" She didn't bat an eye, but said, "I guess I'd have been a Methodist."

The bride brought her new husband up to meet Granny at the family picnic. The old woman looked the young man over carefully and then said to him, "Young man, do you desire to have children?" He was a bit startled by her candid approach, but finally came out with, "Well, yes, as a matter of fact, I do." She looked at him scornfully and then surveyed the very large clan gathered around a half-dozen picnic tables and said, "Well, try to control it."

Ever notice that the laws of household physics are every bit as real as all other laws of the universe? Here are a few examples:

1. A child's eagerness to assist in any project varies in inverse proportion to his ability to actually do the work involved.
2. Leftovers always expand to fill all available containers plus one.
3. A newly washed window gathers dirt at double the speed of an unwashed window.
4. The availability of a ballpoint pen is inversely proportional to how badly it is needed.
5. The same clutter that will fill a one-car garage will fill a two-car garage.
6. Three children plus two cookies equals a fight.
7. The potential for disaster is in direct proportion to the number of TV remote-controls divided by the number of viewers.
8. The number of doors left open varies inversely with the outdoor temperature.
9. The capacity of any hot-water heater is equal to one and one-half sibling showers.
10. What goes up must come down, except bubble gum and slightly used Rice Krispies.

Jo Houser Haring, Notes on the Refrigerator Door

It's hard to say when one generation ends and the next begins—but it's somewhere around nine or ten at night.   —Charles Ruffing in *Family Weekly*

I was admittedly miffed when my children failed to stop by the house for weeks. Finally a visit was arranged, and my sons and their families were due to arrive. "Now don't say anything to them about not visiting when they get here," my husband admonished. I didn't say a word. I just had them fill out name tags as they came in the door. —Angie Papadakis

Leigh, my five-year-old brother, was listening as my mother and I argued. When Mom told me that I was just going to have to live with the consequences, Leigh piped up, "If Dory is going to live with consequences, can I have her room?" —Dory Smith in *Woman's Day*

A very successful businessman had a meeting with his new son-in-law. "I love my daughter, and now I welcome you into the family," said the man. "To show you how much we care for you, I'm making you a 50/50 partner in my business. All you have to do is go to the factory every day and learn the operations." The son-in-law interrupted, "I hate factories. I can't stand the noise." "I see," replied the father-in-law. "Well then you'll work in the office and take charge of some of the operations." "I hate office work," said the son-in-law. "I can't stand being stuck behind a desk all day." "Wait a minute," said the father-in-law. "I just made you half-owner of a money-making organization, but you don't like factories and won't work in a office. What am I going to do with you?" "Easy," said the young man. "Buy me out."

The loaded minivan pulled in to the only remaining campsite. Four children leaped from the vehicle and began feverishly unloading gear and setting up the tent. The boys rushed to gather firewood, while the girls and their mother set up the camp stove and cooking utensils. A nearby camper marveled to the youngsters' father, "That, sir, is some display of teamwork." The father replied, "I have a system; no one goes to the bathroom until the camp is set up."

A journey of a hundred miles starts with an argument over how to load the car.

FANATICS

A fanatic is one who is sure the Almighty would agree with him, if only the Almighty had all the facts.

—Rev. Robert E. Harris, *Laugh with the Circuit Rider*

FARMERS

The other night we went to a local art exhibit put on mainly for the rural folk. I saw a farmer walk up to one abstract picture and look at it from all angles. Finally he told his wife he wanted to buy it. When she asked why, he said: "Best darned picture of the farm situation I have ever seen. No matter which way you look at it, it doesn't make sense."   —*American Opinion*

Two of my uncles, Edwin and Lamar, are sour-faced farmers who love to grumble to each other. "Never did see hay grow so short as mine this summer," sighed Edwin. "You think yours is short," answered Lamar. "I had to lather mine to mow it."

Farmer A: "How close did the electrical storm come to you?"
Farmer B, stammering: "I don't know, but my pipe wasn't lit before!"
—*Capper's Weekly*

The city man bought a farm and was visited by his new neighbor. He asked him, "Can you tell me where the property line runs between our farms?" The farmer looked him over and asked, "Are you talking owning or mowing?"

An efficiency expert was driving through the country side when he noticed an old farmer in an apple orchard feeding his pig. What he saw drove him absolutely crazy, for the farmer was holding the pig over his head and moving him from apple to apple while the pig ate happily. He turned around, parked and walked up to the farmer saying "Hey, there, old timer, have I got a good idea for you." The farmer asked him what it was and the Expert continued, "Just put the pig on the ground, get a stick, knock the apples to the ground and let the pig eat them there. It sure will save a lot of time." The old farmer thought about this while he moved his pig to another apple and finally said "Aw shucks, mister, what's time to a pig?"

An Amish Farmer and his son, traveling by horse and buggy up a narrow lane, met a motorist going the other way. There was no room to pass for two miles in either direction. The motorist, in a hurry, honked his horn. "If you don't back up," said the Amish man, rolling up his sleeves, "I won't like what I'm going to have to do." The surprised driver put his car in reverse and backed up two miles, allowing the horse and buggy to go by. "What was it you wouldn't have liked to have done back there?" asked the Amish man's son. "Back up two miles," replied the farmer.   —AP

A farmer wakes his new hired man at four in the morning for his first day. Five minutes later the new hired man is dressed and walking out the door. The farmer says, "Wait. Let's eat breakfast before we go to work." The hired man says, "I'm not going to work. I'm gonna find someplace where I can spend the rest of the night."

A farmer came to a restaurant and bought four hamburgers and had them put into a bag and left the store. He was soon back and bought eight more. As he started out the door the restaurant owner asked him what he was doing with the sandwiches. "Oh," said the farmer, "I sell them down on the corner for twenty-five cents a piece." "My gosh," said the restaurant man. "I charge you fifty cents each. You are taking a 25 cent loss." "I know," said the man, "but it sure beats farming."   —Paul Meysing

Signs! Folks used to farm by them a lot. I'm reminded that one sign it was time to plant corn was when you saw folks sitting on the banks fishing. If the ground was warm enough to sit on, they figured it was warm enough to make corn come up. If the fishing was fine, the corn planting was liable to be a little late, though.   —*Anderson Independent*

FATHERS

A college professor congratulated a man on his daughter's brilliant paper on the influence of science on the principles of government. The father exclaimed, "Good! Next I want her to begin to work on the influence of the vacuum cleaner on the modern carpet!"

"I can't figure it out," said ten-year old Mitchell, trying to get his father to help him with his arithmetic. "If a carpenter is paid $13 a day, how much does he earn in four days?" "No wonder you can't figure it out," replied the father. "That's not arithmetic, that's ancient history!"

I knew I was taking too many business trips away from home when my kids started calling me Uncle.

~

Jack and Wendell commuted to work together on the Illinois Central. One day they began conversing for the first time. They talked about world problems, high taxes, the cost of living, and finally, their families. Jack proudly announced, "I have three boys." "That's a nice family," sighed Wendell. "I wish to heaven I had three children." "Don't you have any children?" the proud father asked with a touch of sympathy in his voice. "Oh, yes," sighed Wendell, "I have six."

~

My father used to tell me, "When Abraham Lincoln was your age, Abraham Lincoln had a job. When Abraham Lincoln was your age, he walked twelve

The
BORDERLINE™   By Gabe Martin
                                     borderln@cts.com

http://www.the-borderline.com/

"All returns must be accompanied by receipt and returned in their original packaging. . . ."

miles to get to school." I said, "Dad, when Abraham Lincoln was your age, he was President, okay?"

—Andy Andrews

~

The Wall Street attorney sent his only son to his alma mater law school, promising him a gift of $10,000 if he would make the Law Review in one year. At the end of the son's first year, the law student called his father and told him that he had wonderful news for him. "Dad! I've saved you $10,000!"

~

Two schoolgirls were having an argument. "My dad's better than your dad. He's a carpenter and makes buildings." The other girl replied, "My dad does better than that. He's a lawyer, and makes loopholes."

~

A father has just learned of his only daughter's plans to get married to some guy that she barely even knows. He asks, "Does he have any money?" She says, "Men are all alike . . . that's exactly what he asked about you."

—Ron Dentinger

~

Two explorers met in the heart of the jungle. "I'm here," declared one, "to commune with nature in the raw, to contemplate the eternal verities and to widen my horizons. And you, sir?" "I," sighed the second explorer, "came because my son has begun playing the saxophone." —King Duncan

~

The little boy asked his father, "Daddy, where did I come from?" The embarrassed father gulped and proceeded to go into a long-winded explanation of the birds, the bees, the stork and anything else he could think of. Finally, the father turned to his son and asked, "Why do you want to know?" "Oh," he replied, "there's a new kid in the neighborhood and he's from Nashville, and I just wondered where I came from." —King Duncan

~

What's wrong with kids today? My friend Mort explains: "When we were kids we were very disciplined. My father was very strict, but along came the electric razor and took away the razor strap. Then furnaces took away the woodshed. And along came taxes and the worries of it took away my Dad's hair and with that the old hair brush disappeared. And that's why kids today are running wild, the old man has run out of weapons!"

Twenty-five-years ago, I was concerned that my Donny Osmond-doting daughter was growing up too quickly until I saw her wetting her hair rollers with a water pistol.

～

It is not easy being a father. One cynic, speaking from his own experience, noted that children go through four fascinating stages. First they call you Da-Da. Then they call you Daddy. As they mature they call you Dad. Finally they call you collect. —King Duncan

F

～

Then there's the father who laments the fact that three of his children are in graduate school. He's getting poorer by degrees.

～

Hal Adams, a Kentucky farmer, had an ambitious son who graduated from Princeton University and upon his graduation (magna cum laude), he went to New York to make his fortune. The breaks were against him, however, and he ended up as a bootblack in Grand Central Station. Hal continued to work his farm. Now the father makes hay while the son shines.

～

When I moved from Pacifica to Cottonwood, my son suggested a new sign for the road leading into town: "Cottonwood—Home of 3,041 happy people and 1 old sorehead."

～

You show me a child who doesn't play with toys and I'll show you a father who's not done with them yet. —Gene Perret

～

My father became a podiatrist. When he was going to medical school he couldn't afford to buy the whole skeleton.

～

My dad really wanted to become a tree surgeon but discovered that he couldn't stand the sight of sap.

～

My Cousin Victor had just been graduated from Yale but was unable to find a job. So he went to work for his father, my Uncle Hank, at the steel shelving factory my uncle owned. Catching Victor napping in a supply closet, Uncle

Hank commanded, "Go out and sweep the sidewalk." "But dad," Victor protested, "I'm a college graduate!" "Oh, I forgot about that," Uncle Hank replied. "I'll come out and show you how."

During his freshman year, my son Steve couldn't get home for Christmas. So he sent me a set of inexpensive cuff links and a note reading: "Dear Dad, This is not much, but it's all you could afford."

One little boy defined Father's Day like this: "Father's Day is just like Mother's Day, only you don't spend as much on a present."

FATHERHOOD IS NOT PRETTY

- Non-fathers wear expensive Italian shoes. Fathers wear vinyl loafers that are made nowhere near Italy.
- Non-fathers drive cars that hold the turns. Fathers drive cars that hold the kids.
- Non-fathers fly to Switzerland. Fathers drive to Disneyland.
- Non-fathers spend weekends taking in the theater. Fathers spend weekends taking out the trash.
- Non-fathers eat seafood quiche. Fathers eat macaroni and cheese—from the box.
- Non-fathers play tennis. Fathers play pat-a-cake.
- Non-fathers live in the fast lane. Fathers live in a subdivision near a good school, an all-night grocery, a clinic and a gas station.
- Non-fathers wear silk ties with subtle designer logos. Fathers wear whatever they got last Father's Day, something in a palm tree, perhaps.
- Non-fathers invest in certificates that mature in a year. Fathers invest in shoes for feet that mature in six weeks.

Gary D. Christenson

One teenage boy to another: "My Dad had a long talk with me about girls last night. He doesn't know anything about them either."

Three boys are in the schoolyard bragging about their fathers. The first boy says, "My Dad scribbles a few words on a piece of paper, he calls it a poem, they give him $50." The second boy says, "That's nothing. My Dad scribbles a few words on a piece of paper, he calls it a song, they give him $100." The third boy says, "I got you both beat. My Dad scribbles a few words on a piece of paper, he calls it a sermon. And it takes eight people to collect all the money!"

A doting father used to sing his little children to sleep until he overheard the four-year-old tell the three-year-old, "If you pretend you're asleep, he stops."

~

Kevin's father kept bringing home office work just about every night. Finally his first grader son asked why. Daddy explained that he had so much work he couldn't finish it all during the day. Asked Kevin, "In that case, why don't they put you in a slower group?"

~

Mark Twain's best known remark is always worth repeating: "When I was a boy of fourteen, my father was so ignorant I could hardly stand to have the old man around. But when I got to be twenty-one, I was astonished at how much the old man had learned in seven years."

~

A local Romeo's face appeared in the window of his beloved's bedroom. "Get a move on," he hollered, "and let's get this eloping business over with." Be quiet," cautioned his Juliet. "Daddy will hear us and spoil our plans." "I wouldn't worry about that," said Romeo. "He's down on the ground holding the ladder."

~

Father to son: "Of course we have faith in your generation. Just look at the size of the national debts we expect you to pay." *—The Milwaukee Journal*

~

Comedian Myron Cohen tells about the 80-year-old man, retired in Florida and visited frequently by his son. One night, son shows up to find father watching television. "What are you watching, Pop?" asks son. "Basketball," says old man. "What's the score?" asks son. "Eighty-six to eighty-two," father replies. "Who's winning?" asks son. "Eighty-six," says father.

—Phil Pepe in *New York Daily News*

~

Overheard: "I don't mind that my son is earning more than I did on my first job. What disturbs me is that he's six and it's his allowance."

—*Business to Business*

~

My Dad never throws anything out," says comedian Jonathan Katz. "He has coffee in his apartment that's pre-Colombian." —"Comic Strip Live," Fox TV

My neighbor Sam was telling me, "My father is a very highly respected accountant—a ledger in his own time."

~

A man was complaining to his co-worker about the expense of keeping two kids in college. "About all I can afford to put aside for a rainy day," he sighed, "is a pair of dry socks."

~

Two fathers were discussing how their sons were doing in college. One father said, "My son is so smart that when he writes home I have to go to the dictionary." "You're lucky," the other father responded. "When my son writes home I have to go to the bank!"   —Henry Boys

~

An explorer on a trip to Africa visited a village of pygmies, and the most unforgettable experience was listening to a pygmy father three feet high lecturing his two-foot pygmy sons. He said, "When are you going to grow up?"
                                                                    —*Laugh Parade*

~

Downcast father: "I finally talked my son into getting his hair cut, and I'm so sorry. Now I can see his earrings."   —*Southeastern Oil Review*

~

Jan Murray informed his children that he was boss, and they were to obey him. After a long silence his small son spoke up and said, "Gosh, Daddy thinks he is Mommy!"   —*Grit*

~

On my birthday I was cutting the lawn when my teenage son came home from a baseball game. Seeing me behind the mower, he exclaimed, "Oh, Dad, you shouldn't have to mow the lawn on your birthday." Touched, I was about to turn the mower over to him, when he added, "You should wait until tomorrow!"   —Ernest Blevins

FEAR

Common sense gets a lot of credit that belongs to cold feet.
                                                                    —Arthur Godfrey

FEELINGS

One thing I like is long walks—especially when they're made by people who annoy me.   —Fred Allen

One of the symptoms of an approaching nervous breakdown is the belief that one's work is terribly important.   —Bertrand Russell

FEET

My father retired a few years ago after a long career as a podiatrist (foot doctor). Once he was visited by a rather stout woman. After he pried her foot loose from a dainty shoe, he asked her what her trouble was. "It seems my feet are always swollen," she complained. "I wonder what causes this." Dad glanced at her feet, then at the shoes. "Well," he mused, "it could be pride in accomplishing the impossible."

FISHING

While sports fishing off the Florida coast in Key West, a tourist capsized his boat. He could swim, but his fear of alligators kept him clinging to the overturned craft. Spotting an old beachcomber walking on the shore, the tourist shouted, "There wouldn't by chance be any alligators in these waters?!" "No," the old man hollered back, "haven't been any for years!" Feeling relieved, the tourist started swimming leisurely toward the shore. About halfway toward shore he asked the old man, "Say, how'd you get rid of the gators, anyway?" "We didn't do anything," the old man said. "The sharks got 'em."   —H. Aaron Cohl, *The Friars Club Encyclopedia of Jokes*

CORRECTION: In last week's paper we ran a story about a local man who injured himself while fishing. This was an error. We have since learned that it didn't happen while he was fishing. He dislocated his shoulders the next day, while describing a fish that got away.   —Ron Dentinger

Granddad and I went fishing one time up at the North Avenue Pier in Chicago. We fished all day, tried every kind of bait—worms, flies, minnows, doughballs, shad guts—but couldn't catch anything. Didn't get a nibble all day. Just about sundown—sunburned, hot, thirsty, tired, and we hadn't got a bite yet—Granddad finally just reached in his pocket and got a handful of change and just threw it all out into the lake and said, "Here, go buy something you like."

My Aunt Edna tells me: "As we were preparing for a fishing trip, I noticed my husband looking at me lovingly. 'What's on your mind?' I asked. 'Oh,' he replied, 'I was just thinking what great lures your earrings would make.'"

The young wife on her first fishing trip was working busily over her line. Finally her husband asked her what she was doing. "I'm changing corks, dear," she replied sweetly. "This one keeps sinking." —*Quote*

The main reason that comparatively few females go fishing is that women have more important things to lie about.

Give a man a fish and he eats for a day. Teach him how to fish and you get rid of him for the whole weekend. —Zenna Schaffer

A fishing enthusiast thinks that fish should bite on a fancy lure just because he did. —Quin Ryan in "Line O'type," *Chicago Tribune*

A fisherman accidentally left his day's catch under the seat of a bus. The next evening's newspaper carried an ad: "If the person who left a bucket of fish on the No. 47 bus would care to come to the garage, he can have the bus."

—*Sri Lanka Sunday Island*

A stranger stopped his car to watch the odd behavior of a fisherman on a river bank. First, he hooked a big pike, but threw it back. Then he landed a beautiful large trout, but threw it back, too. Finally, he reeled in a tiny perch, and with a grunt of satisfaction, deposited it in his bag. The stranger couldn't resist calling out, "Why on earth did you throw those two big ones back and keep this tiny one?" The fisherman explained tersely, "Small frying pan." —Hugh Harrison

After fishing for walleye all day and not getting so much as a bite, the fisherman went back to shore, loaded up his boat and began driving home. He stopped at a fish market. "Throw me six of the biggest fish you have," he said to the proprietor. "Throw them? Why?" "Because I'm going to catch them. I may be a lousy fisherman, but I'm not a liar." —*Ohio Motorist*

FLORIDA

"The weather here in Florida is so wonderful," said the old lady, "how do you tell summer from winter?" Replied the hotel clerk, "In winter, we get Cadillacs, Lincolns and stuffed shirts. In summer we get Chevrolets, Fords and stuffed shorts."
—Automotive Service Digest

FOOD

I'm not against using some preservatives in food. What I'm against is any loaf of bread that has a life expectancy greater than my own.
—Orben's Current Comedy

After a delicious lunch in an Italian restaurant, the well-traveled businesswoman called the chef over to compliment him on the meal. "Frankly, your eggplant parmesan was better than the one I ate in Milan last Tuesday," she told him. "It's not surprising," said the chef proudly. "They use domestic cheese. Here we use imported!"

French onion soup is like some romances. You know you're going to make a fool of yourself, but it's so good that you don't care.
—Judith Martin, United Feature Syndicate

Trouble in the land of milk and honey

Sign in restaurant window: "Try our Lautrec cocktail. What have you got Toulouse?"
—Ben Slutsky

~

Don't fight a good breakfast. Go with the grain.
—"Graffiti"

~

Garlic: It may build you up physically, but it shoots you down socially.

~

Never eat any product on which the listed ingredients cover more than one-third of the package.

~

A lady was entertaining her friend's small son. "Are you sure you can cut your meat?" she asked, after watching his struggles. "Oh, yes," he replied, without looking up from his plate. "We often have it as tough as this at home."
—*Grit*

FOOLS

He's nobody's fool. On the other hand, maybe someone will adopt him.
—Ron Dentinger

~

Let us be thankful for the fools. But for them the rest of us could not succeed.
—Mark Twain

~

Only a fool tests the depth of the water with both feet.
—African proverb

~

Foolproof systems don't take into account the ingenuity of fools.
—Gene Brown in Danbury, Conn., *News-Times*

~

Wise men make proverbs, but fools repeat them.
—Samuel Palmer

~

Everyone is a damn fool for at least five minutes every day. Wisdom consists in not exceeding the limit.
—Elbert Hubbard

~

King Arthur: "What is an unemployed jester?"
Merlin: "Nobody's fool."
—Edward Tecklin in *Boys' Life*

FOOTBALL

A Harvard University boy got his old father in Maine to come to Cambridge and see the football game between Yale and Harvard. As they sat down, the boy slapped his father on the back and said, "Dad, for three dollars you are going to see more fight, more life, and more enthusiasm then you ever saw before." The old man smiled and replied, "I am not so sure about that, Son. That's what I paid for my marriage license."

—Rev. James Whitcomb Brougher, Sr.

The wife is complaining to her husband, "You seem to know every single football statistic, but you can't remember our wedding anniversary or the year that we got married." He says, "I can too. It was the same year that the Packers traded Williams for a first round draft choice." —Ron Dentinger

Army doctor to recruit: "Did this injury occur when you were on the football team?"

Recruit: "No, Sir. It happened when the football team was on me."

—Liguorian

～

Football coach, on job security: "I have a lifetime contract. That means I can't be fired during the third quarter if we're ahead and moving the ball."

～

Following a 34-27 loss to Cleveland, the Tampa Bay coach was asked about what he thought of his team's execution: "I think it's a good idea."

～

Coach Bum Phillips explains: "Football isn't complicated. You push. The other team pushes back. The one that pushes hardest wins."

～

The football coach at our community college is an incorrigible optimist. Last week, he came into the locker room to give his team a pre-game pep talk. "All right, boys," he cried cheerfully, "here we are, unbeaten, untied, and unscored upon—and ready for the first game of the season!"

～

A triple threat in pro football today is the star who is equally at home running, passing, or endorsing products.

～

A minister stopped John McKay, coach of the Tampa Bay Buccaneers, and said sternly, "Sir, don't you know that it is a sin to play football on Sunday?" "Well," said McKay glumly, "the way the Bucs are playing, it sure is."

～

Two armchair quarterbacks were discussing how much their football watching on TV irritated their wives. "My wife won't say much if I watch just one game on Sunday, but if I watch two, she hits the ceiling!" said one guy. "Mine, too! Say, what's her hang time?"

—How the Platform Professionals Keep 'em Laughin'

～

A ticket scalper was trying to buy a ticket off a guy who had two 50-yard-line seats. The scalper asked, "Is your wife with you?" "Oh, no," was the reply. "Well, listen. I'll give you $150 for that extra ticket of yours." "No way," the guy said, "I'm gonna go to that game and I'm gonna have a few drinks and I'm gonna yell a lot. And then I'm gonna have a few more drinks. And then I'm probably gonna get into a fight. And then they're gonna come and get me and throw me out of the stadium. And then I'm gonna need this extra ticket to get back in."   —James Dent

～

The shivering wife was sitting in the stands with the screaming football maniacs all around her. "Tell me again how much fun we're having," she said to her husband. "I keep forgetting."

～

I heard two high school superintendents from different school systems talking recently. One asked the other how their football season turned out. The superintendent replied: "We had a 5 and 5 season. We lost 5 at home and 5 on the road."   —Doc Blakely

～

When college football's undefeated Notre Dame was about to play Miami in 1989, an impromptu theological debate occurred between Fighting Irish coach Lou Holtz and Miami's chaplain, Father Leo Armbrust. In his invocation at a booster luncheon, Armbrust assured his audience that the Almighty was impartial. When Holtz got up to speak, he agreed with Father Leo. "I don't think God cares who wins tomorrow either," said Holtz. "But His mother does."

～

Joe Montana, on the disabled list with a hand injury, was having lunch with his wife and children at a hotel on Maui. "You poor thing!" the waitress gushed. "How did it happen?" "I broke it playing football," Montana explained. "Really?" replied the waitress. "Aren't you a little old to be playing football?"

～

George Motz, in the Polk County, Wisconsin, Ledger: "I once coached the worst team in all of football. I won't tell you how inept they were, but once, while they were playing a game, a train ran through town tooting its whistle. The opposing team thought it was half time and ran off field. Four plays later my team scored."   —Bob Talbert in St. Louis *Globe-Democrat*

～

Pfugerville High School in Texas once won 55 football games in a row for a state record. When a game was lost, the Waco *News Tribune* had the following headline: "Pflugerville Pfinally Pfalters."   —*Texas Coach Magazine*

After some striking failures in his attempt to pick winning football teams, a columnist for the Dallas *Morning News* suggested last fall that a monkey at the zoo could probably do better and pick at least half the games right. So a year-old gorilla named Kanda was given a chance. A zookeeper wrote the names of the opposing teams on slips of paper and held one in each hand. The hand Kanda slapped was Kanda's choice. For the first week the gorilla's record was 10-3-1. The newspaper was so impressed that it added Kanda to its six-man selection panel. By the end of the third week, the gorilla's record was 27-14-1, giving him a .642 winning percentage as compared with the panel's lackluster .464.   —UPI

We didn't lose the game; we just ran out of time.   —Vince Lombardi

Before he was terminated by the Dallas Cowboys football team, Coach Barry Switzer was seeking advice all around the NFL on what ingredient makes for a winning football team. He eventually sought out Steve Mariucci of the San Francisco Forty-Niners, who told him that the MOST important thing to having a winning football team was to have a quarterback who was extremely smart and as proof he took him over to quarterback, Steve Young, and asked Steve this question: "Who is your father's brother's nephew?" Steve Young without hesitating a moment answered, "I am." When Switzer returned to the Cowboys practice facilities, he went over to Troy Aikman and asked him the same question: "Who is your father's brother's nephew?" Troy thought about it for a moment and told the coach he needed some more time to come up with the right answer. Then Troy went over to Deion Sanders and asked Deion the same question. Deion, replied, "Why it's me!" So Troy Aikman went back to coach Switzer and said, "I have the answer, it's Deion Sanders." "No, No!" replied Switzer, "you're wrong, it's Steve Young."

John Brodie, former San Francisco 49er, was asked by a fan, "How come a great quarterback like you has to hold the ball for kickers?" Replied Brodie, "Because if I don't, it would fall over."

Several years ago, a dejected football coach entered a telephone booth just after his team had lost the big game of the season. When he discovered that he didn't have the necessary dime, he called to a passing student, "Oh, Roger! Will you lend me a dime so I can call a friend?" The student grinned sourly and reached in his pocket. "Here's two dimes, coach," he replied. "Call all your friends."

Before the 100th meeting in the intense rivalry of the Green Bay Packers and the Chicago Bears, my crew and I were in our pew at Green Bay's St. Willibrod's. In front of us say George Halas and his Monsters of the Midway. Across the aisle were Vince Lombardi and his heroes, Paul Hornung in the front row. The priest launched into a stirring homily on the Good Samaritan and brotherly love. It was a fine sermon, and it ended with a powerful punch-line: "Now go out and beat those Bears!"

—Jim Turner

FORGIVENESS

Quite often it's easier to get forgiveness than to get permission.

—Ron Dentinger

Forget and forgive. This is not difficult, when properly understood. It means that you are to forget inconvenient duties, and forgive yourself for forgetting. In time, by rigid practice and stern determination, it comes easy.

—Mark Twain

Heinrich Heine (1797–1856), a great German poet, was famous for his barbed wit. About religion, he wrote: "I love to sin. God loves to forgive sin. Really, this world is admirably arranged."

FREEDOM

It is by the goodness of God that in our country we have those three unspeakably precious things: freedom of speech, freedom of conscience, and the prudence never to practice either of them.   —Mark Twain

People demand freedom of speech to make up for the freedom of thought which they avoid.   —Soren Kierkegaard

FRIENDS

There is nothing so disturbing to one's well-being and judgment as to see a friend get rich.

—Charles P. Kindleberger

He's really a wonderful guy. Why, if I asked him to, he'd give me the shirt off his back. After all, it's mine.

Former U.C.L.A. football coach Pepper Rodgers, after a disastrous season: "I had only one friend—my dog. Even my wife was mad at me, and I told her a man ought to have at least two friends. She agreed, and bought me another dog." —*Quote*

~

It takes your enemy and your friend, working together, to hurt you to the heart: one to slander you and the other to get the news to you.

—Mark Twain

~

Friends are the chocolate chips in the cookie of life. —Taste of Home

~

Lots of people want to ride with you in the limo, but what you want is someone who will take the bus with you when the limo breaks down.

—Oprah Winfrey

~

In the end, we will remember not the words of our enemies, but the silence of our friends. —Martin Luther King Jr.

~

She is such a good friend that she would throw all her acquaintances into the water for the pleasure of fishing them out again. —Charles Talleyrand

~

Before you borrow money from a friend, decide which you need more.

—Gene Brown in Danbury, Conn., *News-Times*

~

The surest way to lose a friend is to tell him something for his own good.

—Sid Ascher

~

The holy passion of Friendship is of so sweet and steady and loyal and enduring a nature that it will last through a whole lifetime, if not asked to lend money. —Mark Twain

FRUGALITY

You can always identify the pastor of any parish. He's the one who goes around turning out the lights.

~

Two young priests were discussing how frugal their senior pastor was. Said one: "When he dies, if he sees light at the end of the tunnel, he'll put it out."

—Msgr. Charles Dollen

FRUSTRATION

In the late 1800s in the eastern part of Tennessee, there was a famous moonshiner known as Big Haley. The woman's real name was Mahalia Mullins, but since she weighed somewhere around 500 pounds, Big Haley was not an inappropriate name. Big Haley and her sons ran a reliable operation. They were renowned for the quality of their product. They didn't dilute their moonshine and were known to deal honestly. That fact, coupled with the problems of arresting a mountain clan, caused local government officials to pretty much leave them alone. However, a newly elected sheriff did once attempt to arrest Mahalia and make a name for himself. The judge who signed the arrest warrant just smiled and told the sheriff to be sure to bring her in. The sheriff and his deputies had no trouble finding Mahalia's cabin. He knocked on the cabin door, entered, and informed Mahalia she was under arrest. What he discovered, though, was that Mahalia was bigger than the cabin's doorway. After some futile efforts, he decided not to arrest her after all. When the judge later asked the sheriff about Mahalia, the officer complained that, "She's catchable but not fetchable." There are some things in life that are like that. They may be catchable, but in the vernacular of the mountains, they are not fetchable.

—Fred Brown, Knoxville *News-Sentinel*

Frustration is when the same snow that covers the ski slopes makes the roads to them impassable.　　　　—James Holt McGavran in *The Homesteader*

G

GAMES

"I think it's wrong," says comedian Steven Wright, "that only one company makes the game Monopoly."

GARBAGE

During the garbage workers strike in New York a modern Houdini figured out a way to get rid of his garbage and trash. He gift-wrapped it in several packages and left it in his unlocked car. Every day somebody would steal it.

—Brian O'Hara

GARDENING

I'm glad I didn't throw away my empty seed packages. It turns out they're just the right size for storing my first year's crop!

One way to get your tomatoes to ripen is to go on vacation. The moment you leave, the tomatoes sense your absence, ripen, rot, and fall to the ground before you get back. Even if you're only gone two days.

—*The Milwaukee Journal*

❧

Excellent gardening advice: "To plant asparagus, dig a ditch three years ago."

—E. B. White

❧

One of the worst mistakes you can make as a gardener is to think you're in charge. —Janet Gillespie, Quoted by Lindsay Bond Totten, Scripps-Howard News Service

❧

A weed is a plant with nine lives. —Arnold H. Glasow

❧

If God had wanted us to plant gardens, he wouldn't have created supermarkets. —James Dent in Charleston, W.VA, *Gazette*

"MOM, have you been messing with my Nintendo?"

A lot of homeowners have discovered that trees grow on money.   —Fred Houston in *Look*

~

The one thing every good gardener has is a green thumb. It comes from pulling twenties out of your wallet at the garden supply shop.
       —Robert Orben, *2500 Jokes To Start 'Em Laughing*

GENIES

A despondent woman was walking along the beach when she saw a bottle on the sand. She picked it up and pulled out the cork. Whoosh! A big puff of smoke appeared. "You have released me from my prison," the genie told her. "To show my thanks, I grant you three wishes. But take care, for with each wish, your mate will receive double of whatever you request." "Why?" the woman asked. "That bum left me for another woman." "That is how it is written," replied the genie. The woman shrugged and then asked for a million dollars. There was a flash of light, and a million dollars appeared at her feet. At the same instant, in a far-off place, her wayward husband looked down to see twice that amount at his feet. "And your second wish?" "Genie, I want the world's most expensive diamond necklace." Another flash of light, and the woman was holding the precious treasure. And, in that distant place, her husband was looking for a gem broker to buy his latest bonanza. "Genie, is it really true that my husband has two million dollars and more jewels that I do, and that he gets double of whatever I wish for?" The genie said it was indeed true. "Okay, genie, I'm ready for my last wish," the woman said. "Scare me half to death."

~

A secretary, a paralegal and a partner in a city law firm are walking through a park on their way to lunch when they find an antique oil lamp. They rub it and a genie comes out in a puff of smoke. The genie says, "I usually only grant three wishes, so I'll give each of you just one." "Me first! Me first!" says the secretary. "I want to be in the Bahamas, driving a speedboat, without a care in the world." Poof! She's gone. In astonishment, "Me next! Me next!" says the paralegal, "I want to be in Hawaii, relaxing on the beach with my personal masseuse, an endless supply of pina coladas and the love of my life." Poof! She's gone. "You're next," the genie says to the partner. The partner says, "I want those two back in the office after lunch."

GENIUS

Everyone is a genius at least once a year; a real genius has his original ideas closer together.   —Georg Lichtenberg

GIFTS

At a drugstore, a wife wanted to buy shaving lotion for her mate. "What kind?" asked the clerk. "Well," explained the wife, "he's seventy years old. Have you got any of that Old Spouse?" —James Dent

A famous author was autographing copies of his new novel in a department store. One gentleman pleased him by bringing up not only his new book for signature, but two of his previous ones as well. "My wife likes your stuff," he remarked apologetically, "so I thought I'd give her these signed copies for a birthday present." "A surprise, eh?" hazarded the author. "I'll say," agreed the customer. "She's expecting a Mercedes."

GLORY

Glory is fleeting, but obscurity is forever. —Napoleon Bonaparte

GOD

If there is no God, who pops up the next Kleenex? —Art Hoppe

"Gramma, know what you and God have in common?" asked the three-year-old Devon. Mentally polishing her halo and looking as saintly as possible,

REVEREND FUN

NOW SERVING NUMBER:
714,891,541
426,730,102
578,625,448

PLEASE TAKE A NUMBER

Gramma waited for the expected compliment. "You're both old," Devon replied.   *—Family Digest*

~

At a theological seminar in Kentucky, students entering the room for lunch were greeted by a sign which read: "Take only one apple. God is watching you." At the other end of the table was a large tray of chocolate cookies with a hastily scribbled sign which read: "Take as many as you want—God is back there watching the apples."   —Colin Jeffrey

GOLF

A guy is standing in front of his locker at the country club admiring a golf ball he has in his hand. One of his golfing buddies says to him, "What'd you do, get some new golf balls?" And the guy says, "Would you believe that this is the greatest golf ball ever made. You can't lose it. You hit it into the rough and it whistles. You hit it into the woods and a bell inside goes off. If you drive it into a lake, a big burst of steam shoots up six feet in the air for two minutes." And his friend says, "That's great. Where did you get it?" And the guy says, "I found it."   —Soupy Sales

~

After a long day on the course, the exasperated golfer turned to his caddie and said, "You must be the absolute worst caddie in the world." "No, I don't think so," said the caddie. "That would be too much of a coincidence."

~

An avid golfer came home to dinner. During the meal his wife said: "Michael tells me he caddied for you this afternoon." "Well, what do you know?" said Michael's father, "I thought I'd seen that boy before."

~

A: "Why aren't you playing golf with the colonel any more?"
B: "What! Would you play with a man who swears and curses with every shot, who cheats in the bunkers, and who enters false scores on his cards?"
A: "Certainly not!"
B: "Well, neither will the colonel."   —Freddie Oliver

~

Two Scotsmen were avid golfers and had played together every Thursday for many years. The sixth tee was near the road that led to the local cemetery. One day as they reached that particular tee a funeral passed by, and old Hamish turned and raised his club in salute. "Mon," exclaimed Hector, "in all these years we've been a playing this course, and that's the first time I've seen ye paying any respect for the dead." "Aye, weel," explained Hamish, "when you have been married to a woman for forty years, she's entitled to a wee bit of respect." —H. Aaron Cohl, *The Friars Club Encyclopedia of Jokes*

My neighbor was crying because her husband had left her for the sixth time. I consoled her, "Don't be unhappy, he'll be back." "Not this time," she sobbed. "He's taken his golf clubs." —Joey Adams

A golfer swings his club, but misses the ball entirely. He looks at his partner and says, "Boy, this is a tough course." —Ron Dentinger

If golf had never been invented, how would they measure hail? —Ron Dentinger

Two golfers were about to tee off and one said to the other, "Let's play for a little money, but since you're so much better than I am, why don't you give me two gotcha's." Well, the better golfer agreed to give two gotcha's. As he was about to tee off, the other guy hauled off and kicked him in the rear, knocking him three feet off the tee box. The better golfer got up and said, "Why did you do that?" And the other golfer said, "That's one gotcha." The poorer golfer won the tournament because the other golfer kept waiting for the next gotcha.   —*How the Platform Professionals Keep 'em Laughin'*

Golfer Tommy Bolt had a terrible temper. Once, after missing six straight putts, generally leaving them teetering on the very edge of the cup, Bolt shook his fist at the heavens and shouted, "Why don't you come down and fight like a man!"

G

Many men play golf religiously—every Sunday.
                                        —Jim Reed, *The Funny Side of Golf*

It's good sportsmanship to pick up lost golf balls while they are still rolling.
                                        —Mark Twain

A husband and wife were playing on the ninth green when she collapsed from a heart attack. "Please dear, I need help," she said. The husband ran off saying, "I'll get some help." A little while later he re-turned, picked up his club and began to line up his shot on the green. His wife, on the ground, raised up her head and said, "I may be dying and you're putting?" "Don't worry dear. I found a doctor on the second hole who said he would come and help you." "The second hole? When the heck is he coming?" While practice stroking his putt, he said, "I told you not to worry, everyone's already agreed to let him play through."

You can always spot an employee who's playing golf with his boss. He's the fellow who gets a hole in one and says, "Oops!"   —Bob Monkhouse

Ferris Mack doesn't play golf, but for years he kept a golf ball in the pocket of his overcoat. It ensured him proper identification of the garment in the checkrooms of the restaurants where he regularly lunched.

GOSSIP

Why must the phrase, "It's none of my business," always be followed by the word but?

~

Neighbor to woman: "I hear your husband is in the hospital. What happened?" The other woman replied, "Knee trouble. I found his secretary sitting on it."

~

Gossip: The only thing that travels faster than e-mail.   —Angie Papadakis

~

If you haven't got anything nice to say about anybody, come sit next to me.
—Alice Roosevelt Longworth

~

Trying to squash a rumor is like trying to un-ring a bell.
—Shana Alexander, *Anyone's Daughter*

~

At a cocktail party: "I never repeat gossip, so I'll say this only once."
—*Selected Cryptograms 5*

GOVERNMENT

A government is the only known vessel that leaks from the top.
—James Reston

~

A government that robs Peter to pay Paul can always depend upon the support of Paul.   —George Bernard Shaw

~

An elderly gentleman took his Social Security check to the bank. Although it was clearly marked, "Do not fold, staple or mutilate," the old gentleman had folded it and creased it pretty severely. The teller at the bank cautioned him, "You should be more careful with your check. The government doesn't like it when you mutilate your check like that." The old fellow shook his head and said, "Well, there are some things that the government does that I don't like either."

~

Crime wouldn't pay if the government ran it!

Frederick Wamsley reports: "I had gotten lost in cryptic and ambiguous regulations, and in total desperation called the Internal Revenue Service for some explanations. I got hold of someone thor-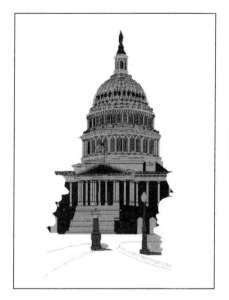oughly familiar with the subject of my questions. He gave me complete and helpful answers. I like to give positive reinforcement when I run across people like that, so I made it a point to say, 'Thank you! You've been really informative and helpful.' To which the IRS agent said, 'I'm sorry.'"

Harry Truman said that after winning his first election to Washington, he spent six months wondering how he made it to the Senate and the rest of his term wondering how the others made it.

If you laid all our laws end to end, there would be no end.

—Arthur "Bugs" Baer

It's getting harder and harder to support the government in the style to which it has become accustomed.

One day at the pearly gates, St. Peter met Chief Justice Earl Warren, who was applying for admission. St. Peter looked at his ledger, and then looked back at the Chief Justice and said, "Uh, there's a little problem. It says here that you were Chief Justice of the United States, yet you had very little regard for the Constitution." The Chief Justice looked positively shocked and hurt, and protested, "Oh, no, St. Peter, I have never had any problem with the Constitution—just the amendments!"

You can criticize the President, you can criticize the Vice President, you can criticize the Congress. But you have to hand it to the IRS.

The government has invented a machine that will do the work of five people. Unfortunately it takes ten people to operate it.

Under current law, it is a crime for a private citizen to lie to a government official, but not for the government official to lie to the people.

Speaking of (and maybe to) dead people, consider the following published by that super-excellent paper *The Philadelphia Inquirer* on March 8, 1992:

> Nothing can screw up your life-style like dying. Just ask a guy who died last month in Greenville, S.C. Some of you might be asking how you can ask a dead guy anything. Well, his being dead didn't stop the Greenville County Department of Social Services from sending him a letter: "Your food stamps will be stopped effective March 1992 because we received notice that you passed away," the letter to the dead guy said. "May God bless you." Despite the nice touch at the end, the letter made it sound as if the decision to stop food stamps was final. But not all public agencies are cold. The department offered the dead guy hope for the future. "You may reapply if there is a change in your circumstances," the letter said.
>
> At first, Al Palanza Jr., brother of the dead guy, read the letter and said he was disgusted. Later he found it funny. He called it "living proof of how screwed up the system is." Robin Kubler, the county's social services director, said it's not her system that's screwed up. She said the form letter was generated by a computer system. And the "May God Bless you"? That was added by a caseworker, she said to soften the statement.

A bureaucrat is a man who shoots the bull, passes the buck, and makes seven copies of everything.

The zip code in Washington will be changed to 00000. Nothing there adds up anyhow.

I know a guy who just retired from civil service after 40 years. As a kind of surprise, the government gave him a retirement banquet and told him what his job had been.

When I get a letter in the mail, it makes me grateful to think that 500,000 people have worked for 14 days just to get it to me!

Most problems don't exist until a government agency is created to solve them.
—Kirk Kirkpatrick

A member of the Los Angeles County Board of Supervisors welcomed a presidential commission on drug trafficking. "I am sure," he declared, "that this commission will do an infinitesimal amount of good." —*The Baltimore Sun*

~

Everyone wants to live at the expense of the state. They forget that the state wants to live at the expense of everyone. —Frederic Bastiat

~

Justice may be blind, but she has very sophisticated listening devices.
—Edgar Argo in *Funny Times*

~

Government investigations have always contributed more to our amusement than they have to our knowledge. —Will Rogers

~

In 1990, Congress sent the Pentagon some 20,000 letters, which required more than 250,000 man-hours to answer. The inevitable happened when Rep. John Conyers, chairman of the Government Operations Committee, demanded to know how a Presidential memorandum entitled "Reducing the Burden of Government Regulation" was being implemented. The Conyers letter was addressed to "John G. Tower, Secretary of Defense" despite the fact that the Senate had refused to confirm Tower the previous year. Conyers' staff said several incorrect letters went out because an old mailing list was used. It is hard to avoid such mistakes, according to one staffer, because "we send out so much stuff." —*The Wall Street Journal*

~

If the government were to ask to have the paper clip invented today, it would probably have seven moving parts, two batteries, three transistors and require servicing at least twice a year.
—Sandy Cooley in New Holstein, Wisconsin, *Reporter*

GRANDCHILDREN

Here are a few I heard from my grandchildren:

- If you can't stand the heat, get a pool.
- If you can't stand the heat, get out of the oven.
- A bird in the hand is messy.
- Don't count your chickens, eat them.
- You can't teach an old dog new math.
- When in Rome, do Roman numerals in math.

- When in Rome, do bulls run around town?
- Too many cooks, so little meals.
- A fool and his money are my best friends.
- A penny saved is one cent.
- Look before you run into a pole.
- A watched pot never disappears.
- A rolling stone makes you flat.
- A rolling stone is a rock group.
- Every cloud has a wet spot.

When my grandsons came home from Sunday school during one of our weekend visits to their home, I asked if either of them could tell me where to find the Ten Commandments. Blank stares and silence were finally broken when one of them said, "Have you looked it up in the Yellow Pages?"

Never have any children, only grandchildren.   —Gore Vidal

I once asked my four-year-old grandson how he liked his Thanksgiving dinner. "I didn't like the turkey much," he replied, "but I sure loved the bread it ate."

Elephants and grandchildren never forget.   —Andy Rooney

A few days ago, I asked my granddaughter which month has 28 days. "Every month has 28 days," she answered, grinning. Guess I ought to rephrase the question.   —*The Milwaukee Journal*

GRANDFATHERS

I was trying to help my grandson with his arithmetic homework. I said to him, "Suppose you reached in your right pocket and found a ten dollar bill, and you reached in your left pocket and found another one, what would you have?" My grandson's answer: "Somebody else's pants."

A five-year-old was amazed by his grandfather's false teeth. He watched as Gramps removed his dentures, washed them and put them back in. He asked to see it done again and again. "Okay," said the grandfather, humoring the child. "Anything else?" "Yeah," said the kid, "Now take off your nose."

A small boy approached a white-haired gentleman in a store and asked, "Are you a grandfather?" "Yes," replied the man with a smile. "Oh, I'm glad," said the boy, "because my own grandfather isn't here and I need a dime."

—*Catholic Digest*

❧

I was helping my grandson Jonathan with his science homework. He and I had just seen the movie, *The Ten Commandments,* on TV. His assignment was to define the Great Divide. "That's easy," said Jonathan. "That's when Moses parted the Red Sea. Right, Grandpa?"

G

❧

My seven-year-old niece had gone fishing with her grandpa. After an hour or so, Grandpa asked, "Are you having any luck?" "No!" she replied indignantly. "I don't think my worm is really trying."   —Thea Lowell

❧

"Grandpa," the child asked, "what year were you born?" "In 1937," the grandfather replied. "Wow!" exclaimed the grandson. "If you were a baseball card, you would be worth lots of money!"   —*The Rotarian*

❧

On boarding the train, the man immediately approached a passenger with a vacant seat beside him, asking "Have you any grandchildren?" When he received an affirmative answer, he went to another and repeated the question. Again, the reply was yes. He continued to question potential seatmates until one passenger said he had no grandchildren. "Move over," grinned the man happily. "I want to tell you about my grandchildren!"   —*Modern Maturity*

GRANDMOTHERS

A guy goes to see his grandmother and takes one of his friends with him. While he's talking to his grandmother, his friend starts eating the peanuts that are on the coffee table, and finishes them off. As they're leaving, the friend says, "Thanks for the peanuts." The grandmother says, "Yeah, since I lost my dentures I can only lick the chocolate off of them."

❧

A grandmother got a note from her son and daughter-in-law that her grandchildren would be coming to spend a week with her. She loved her precious little granddaughter and lively little grandson, and when she thought about the pleasures that awaited her with them in her home, she went to church and put five dollars in the offering plate as a token of thanksgiving. She kept her granddaughter and grandson for that week and what a week it was. When they went home, she went back to church and put in a twenty dollar bill in the offering plate in thanksgiving.

—King Duncan

Paul and Marlene Fredericks attended church with their daughter Samantha every Sunday morning. Then the family headed to Paul's parents' home for Sunday dinner. One Sunday after church, Grandmother Fredericks asked six-year-old Samantha, "How was Sunday school?" Samantha replied, "Oh, it was O.K., I guess." The grandmother persisted, "Just O.K.? Who was your teacher?" Samantha answered, "Well, I don't know. She wasn't our regular teacher but she must have been Jesus' grandmother. He was all she talked about."

GRANDPARENTS

Wanting to take his wife out for the evening, Marty Schell dropped off his ten-year-old son Woody at Grandma's house. As Marty went out the door, Grandma Schell asked, "When do you want him back?" "When he's nineteen!" replied the father.

~

My parents used to send me to spend summers with my grandparents. I hate cemeteries!
—Chris Fonseca

~

When their first grandchild was born, Nancy asked her husband Earl, "Well, Earl, how does it feel to be a grandfather?" Earl replied, "Oh, it feels wonderful, of course, but what feels strange is that I'll have to get used to the idea of sleeping with a grandmother."

~

It's a good idea to have children while your parents are still young enough to take care of them.
—Rita Rudner

~

Helen Aberg used to give generous Christmas presents to her several grand-children, but the kids never sent thank-you notes, despite the urgings of their respective parents. But then one year things changed. Grandma sent a hundred dollar Christmas check to each grandchild. The very next day, each child came over in person to thank her. She was telling this to a friend of hers, who said, "How wonderful! What do you think caused them to become so polite?" Well, said Helen, "It was easy. This year I didn't sign the checks."

~

The reason grandparents and grandchildren get along so well is that they have a common enemy.
—Sam Levenson

~

The simplest toy, one which even the youngest child can operate, is called a grandparent.
—Sam Levenson

GREED

Last August, while we were shopping at the mall, I gave my grandson Jake five dollars to buy ice cream cones for himself and his little sister, Jessica. Jessica waited with me while Jake walked across the food court to the ice cream shop. On the way back, one of the cones slipped out of his hand and landed on the ground. "Hey, Grandpa," he reported upon his return, "I sure was lucky. Even though I dropped Jessica's ice cream cone, I was able to hold on to mine!"

~

My cousin Ed is so greedy he has eight deadly sins. He had one custom-made.

GROUCHES

May Tuohy, a seventy-year-old known for her general grouchiness, called the police about her neighbor who was sunbathing in the nude. "I don't see anything," said the police officer, looking out her window. "Of course not," said the woman. "You have to stand on this chair."

~

My neighbor Eli is a notorious grouch. He spreads good cheer wherever he doesn't go.

GUESTS

Guests will happen even in the best regulated families.

~

Dinner guest: "We hate to eat and run but we're still hungry."

—Ron Dentinger

~

A poor man had an overnight guest, and as he showed him to his humble bedroom in the hayloft he said, "If there is anything you want, let us know, and we'll come and show you how to get along without it."

~

I've had a perfectly wonderful evening. But this wasn't it.   —Groucho Marx

GULLIBLE

I can't believe it. My neighbor just told me they're taking the word gullible out of the dictionary.

—Ron Dentinger

H

HAIR

The man says to his hair stylist, "My hair is falling out. What can I use to keep it in?" The stylist replies, "Might I suggest a shoebox?"

~

Aunt Flo tells this one: "What's happened to you!" exclaimed my husband one evening when I came into the living room with my head bristling with curlers. "I just set my hair," I replied. "Well," he asked, "what time does it go off?"

❧

My uncle knows that the Bible says even the hairs on his head are numbered but each year it gets a little easier for the Lord to take inventory.

❧

Men spend thousands on hair transplants and toupees when what is really needed is more women who like bald men.

❧

Two nice middle-aged ladies were discussing a dance to be held at the yacht club. The theme is to wear something that will match your husband's hair, explained one. "I'm wearing that gray silk dress of mine." "Gracious! I don't think I'll go," said the second.
—*How the Platform Professionals Keep 'em Laughin'*

❧

A bald man took a seat in a beauty shop. "How can I help you?" asked the stylist. "I went for a hair transplant," the guy explained, "but I couldn't stand the pain. If you can make my hair look like yours without causing me any discomfort, I'll pay you $5000." "No problem," said the stylist, and she quickly shaved her head.
—Debbie Costet

HALLOWEEN

Last Halloween was bad for me. I got really beat up. I went to a party dressed as a piñata.
—Jim Samuels

❧

For a good many years court reporter Margaret Tanking and her husband, Bob, were always invited to the same Halloween costume party. Bob never liked dressing up in costume and always did his best to avoid it. Margaret always insisted he would have a swell time once he got there. Well, the invitation came again this year. Bob balked at the idea of dressing up. Margaret said he was being silly. "Just think of something unique and you'll be the hit of the party," she told him. Bob did some thinking. He made a cassette tape of his voice with little tidbits like: "We had a swell time on our vacation, The weather was lousy this summer—too much rain, My golf game is getting better," and so on. He gave the tape to Margaret. "What's this for?" she asked. "It's my Halloween costume," he said. "Your costume!" "Sure. All you do is put this little tape recorder in your purse and turn it on when you're at the party," Bob said, pleased with his solution, "and I'll be the invisible man."

—*Milwaukee Sentinel*

One Halloween night, a neighborhood practical joker decided to frighten the young trick-or-treaters who rang his doorbell. He put on a floor-length black

 cape, a black hat fitted with devil's horns, and a hideous mask that seemed to combine the most gruesome features of Dracula, Frankenstein, and the Wolf Man. Then he waited. Finally, his doorbell rang. He turned off all the lights and, shining a flashlight on his mask, he opened the door and pierced the night air with an eerie scream. Then he looked down and saw standing before him a tiny, golden-haired five year old, dressed as a dainty fairy. The little tyke stared wide-eyed for a moment. Then she raised her eyes up along the massive black cape, looked straight into the hideous mask, smiled and said, "Is your mommy home?"

HANDKERCHIEFS

A little boy riding the bus had been sniffling for several blocks. The lady sitting next to him said, "Little boy, do you have a handkerchief?" "Yes, ma'am," he replied, "but I never lend it to strangers."

—*Irish Grit*

HAPPINESS

It's never too late to have a happy childhood.

There are people who can do all fine and heroic things but one; keep from telling their happiness to the unhappy.

—Mark Twain

Action may not always bring happiness, but there is no happiness without action.

—Benjamin Disraeli

When asked what is the secret of a long and happy life, the Duchess of Windsor responded, "Fill what's empty, empty what's full, and scratch where it itches."

Happiness is good health and a bad memory.   —Ingrid Bergman

The secret of happiness is to count your blessings—not your birthdays.
                                                         —Shannon Rose

HATE

I know that there are people in this world who do not love their fellow man,
and I hate people like that!   —Tom Lehrer

You had to stand in line to hate him.   —Hedda Hopper

HATS

Her hat is a creation that will never go out of style. It will look ridiculous year
after year.   —Fred Allen

Joan: Whenever I get down in the dumps, I buy myself a new hat. Jack: So
that's where you get them!   *—Pen*

"Isn't it darling?" bubbled the young matron, showing her husband a new
lampshade. "Darling or not," said the husband, "wear it to church and you go
alone."   *—Grit*

HEADACHES

The strong man appeared at an agent's office carrying a stone, a big hammer,
and a huge suitcase. "This big stone," he explained, "is placed on my head,
then my assistant takes the hammer and swings it as hard as he can, and breaks
the stone." The agent's head nearly ached just from the description and he
was quite enthusiastic. "Sounds wonderful!" he shouted. "But if you need
only the hammer and the big stone, why did you bring this suitcase?" The
strong man replied, "It's full of aspirin."   *—Quote*

HEADLINES

ACTUAL NEWSPAPER HEADLINES:

Safety Experts Say School Bus Passengers Should Be Belted
Survivor Of Siamese Twins Joins Parents

June Babies Flood Ottawa Hospital
Officers' Wives To Select New Officers
Panda Mating Fails—Veterinarian Takes Over
Teacher Strikes Idle Kids
Juvenile Court To Try Shooting Defendant
2 Sisters Reunited After 18 Years In Checkout Counter
Protestor Tried To Spoil Play But Actors Succeeded
20-Year Friendship Ends At The Altar
Prisoners Escape After Execution
Sisters Wed Brothers Have Babies, Same Day
Fidelio Only Opera
Beethoven Wrote On Monday Evening
Passengers Hit By Canceled Trains
Buffalo Swept Off Feet By Mendelssohn Choir
Fried Chicken Cooked In Microwave Wins Trip
Tester Links Pygmy Defect To Shortness
Navy Finds Dead Pilots Flying With Hangovers
Drug Abuse Draws Nancy Back To Acting Humane
Fish Fry Set Fire Officials Grilled Over Kerosene Heaters
Lower Age For Elderly Opposed
Sewer Input Sought Man Shot To Death In Cavalier Manor
Reader Is Upset Over Dog Eating Filipinos
Socks Fall Amid Interest-Rate Worries
Outside Consultant Sought For Test Of Gas Chamber

HEALTH

I tried Flintstones vitamins. I didn't feel any better but I could stop the car with my feet.

—Joan St. Once

It's no longer a question of staying healthy, it's a question of finding a sickness you like.

—Jackie Mason

Doris Hall, our church treasurer, was telling me: "Not too long ago we received a memorial gift to the church. There was a short note written on a beautiful little card that described whom the memorial was for. It said the usual thing, 'Enclosed you will find a check to be used as a memorial for . . .' Unfortunately, the person who sent it forgot to sign the note AND to enclose the check. And to top it all off, the card had been purchased from the Alzheimer's Foundation."

~

Herb Uttley came home from work after a very long and terrible day. Everything had gone wrong. His secretary had not shown up for work. He couldn't figure out how to use the fax machine. The photocopier jammed and the paper caught on fire. The district manager scolded him for not meeting his monthly quota. He plopped himself down in his favorite easy chair and said to his wife, "I've had nothing but bad news at the office today. If there is one thing I don't want, it is more bad news." His wife gently replied, "In that case, you'll be glad to know that three out of four of your children did not break their arms today."

~

From under a beach umbrella: "Just when I can afford to lie in the sun, they decide it's hazardous to my health."

~

My allergy tests suggest that I may have been intended for life on some other planet.

~

A health nut is talking to his co-worker. The only thing he likes more than jogging is telling people about his jogging. He says, "I now jog to work behind the bus in which I used to ride to work. I feel great and I save $2.00 a day." The friend says, "Why don't you save $20 and jog behind a cab?"

—Ron Dentinger

~

Health care is getting far too expensive. I just got a prescription. The instructions read: "Take one every time you can afford it."   —Ron Dentinger

~

You may not know that the greatest cause for heart attacks in men over 60 is women under 30.

~

It's hard to be fit as a fiddle when you're shaped like a cello.

Joined a health club last year, spent four hundred bucks. Haven't lost a pound.
Apparently, you have to show up. —Rich Ceisler

~

Attention to health is life's greatest hindrance. —Plato (427–347 B.C.)

~

You have to hand it to the modern-day health clubs. They've learned how to
make a fortune at our expanse. —*Liguorian*

~

The U.S. government's High Blood Pressure Information Center uses this carefully calculated address: 120/80 National Institutes of Health, Bethesda, Maryland. —*The Wall Street Journal*

~

"How do you account for your longevity?" asked the reporter on Harvey's
110th birthday. "You might call me a health nut," Harvey replied. "I never
smoked. I never drank. I was always in bed and sound asleep by ten o'clock.
And I've always walked three miles a day, rain or shine." "But," said the reporter,
"I had an uncle who followed that exact routine and died when he was 62.
How come it didn't work for him?" "All I can say," replied Harvey, "is that he
didn't keep it up long enough." —*Lutheran Digest*

~

Life expectancy would grow by leaps and bounds if green vegetables smelled
as good as bacon.

HEARING

Uncle Doug was perplexed by his wife's refusal to admit her hearing problem.
Speaking with his doctor one day, he exclaimed, "How can I get my wife to
admit that she is hard of hearing?" I'll tell you what you need to do," his
doctor replied. "When you arrive home this evening, peek your head through
the door and ask, 'Honey, what's for dinner tonight?' If she doesn't answer,
go into the living room and say, 'Honey, what's for dinner?' If she still does
not answer, walk into the kitchen and ask, 'Honey, what's for dinner?' If she
still does not hear you, then walk right up behind her and speak directly in
her ear. 'Honey, what's for dinner?' Then you will be able to convince her of
her need for a hearing exam." "Great!" Doug responded. "I think it will work!"
That evening Doug arrived home from work. Just as he had been instructed,
he opened the front door and called out: "Honey, what's for dinner tonight?"
He listened carefully, but there was no reply. He walked into the living room
and repeated, "Honey, what's for dinner?" He still received no answer. He
then walked into the kitchen and asked, "Honey, what's for dinner?" Still there

was no answer. The man walked right up behind his wife and spoke directly into her ear: "Honey, what's for dinner?" At this the wife turned around and resolutely replied: "For the fourth time, I said we are having spaghetti!"

HEAVEN (*See also* AFTERLIFE)

A woman died and went to heaven. At the pearly gates, St. Peter was quizzing the new arrivals. "Before you may enter, can you tell me God's first name?" he asked. After thinking a moment, the woman smiled and said, "Andy? Andy?" St. Peter replied. "Where'd you get Andy?" "We sang it in church all the time: 'Andy walks with me, Andy talks with me, Andy tells me I am His own . . .'"

As they walk along the sea shore the young boy points to a dead seagull lying on the beach. He looks up at his father and says, "What happened?" The father offers a gentle explanation, "The sea gull went up to heaven." The boy says, "And God threw him back?"

The
BORDERLINE ™

By Gabe Martin
borderln@cts.com

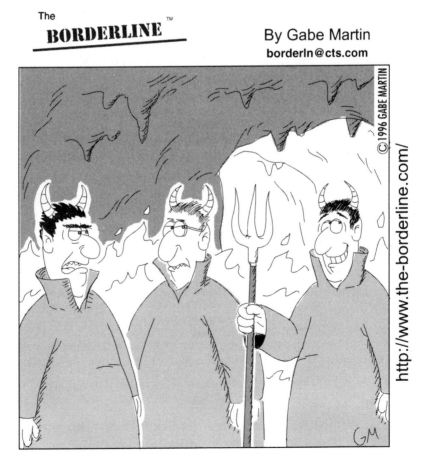

© 1996 GABE MARTIN

http://www.the-borderline.com/

"Phew! Man! Alright, who burned the brimstone?!"

Mrs. Troutman, the Sunday school teacher, asked her preschool class, "Now, how many of you would like to go to heaven?" All the children raised their hands except Justin. The teacher asked Justin why he wouldn't like to go to heaven. Justin's reply: "I'm sorry, but I can't. My mother told me to come right home after Sunday school."

～

"How's your wife?" the man asked an old friend he hadn't seen for years. "She's in heaven," replied the friend. "Oh, I'm sorry." Then he realized that was not the thing to say, so he added, "I mean, I'm glad." And that was even worse. He finally came out with, "Well, I'm surprised."

HECKLERS

Once, when Al Smith had paused in a speech because a heckler kept interrupting him, the man shouted, "Go ahead, Al, don't let me bother you. Tell 'em all you know. It won't take you long." Smith, always quick on the trigger, replied: "If I tell 'em all we both know it won't take me any longer."

HELL

Hell is a half-filled auditorium.

—Robert Frost

HELP

Walking across a parking lot, a woman saw a driverless car slowly rolling toward her. With unusual agility, she sprinted to it, opened the door and pulled the emergency brake, bringing the car to a halt. As she got out, a man in coveralls was among the fast-gathering crowd that approached her. "Well, I stopped the car!" she announced with pride. "Yeah, I know," replied the man. "I was pushing it."

—*The Rotarian*

HIGH TECH

The Electronic Mail Association estimates that the volume of e-mail will grow by more than half this year, to 6 billion messages. And with my luck, they'll all have my name on them.

—Mike Hogan

～

High tech has gotten out of hand. My grandson has an imaginary playmate that requires batteries.

～

A woman called the Canon help desk with a problem with her printer. The tech asked her if she was running it under Windows. The woman then responded, "No, my desk is next to the door. But that's a good point . . . The man sitting in the cubicle next to me is under a window, and his is working just fine."

～

Overheard in a computer shop:

Customer: "I'd like a mouse mat, please."

Salesperson: "Certainly sir, we've got a large variety."

Customer: "But will they be compatible with my computer?"

～

I once received a fax with a note on the bottom to fax the document back to the sender when I was finished with it, because he needed to keep it.

～

Customer: "Can you copy the Internet for me onto this diskette?"

"I've found the problem, Ma'am, and you were right: It just doesn't like you."

Customer: "So, that will get me connected to the Internet, right?"
Tech Support: "Yeah."
Customer: "And that's the latest version of the Internet, right?"
Tech Support: "Uhh . . . uh . . . uh . . . yeah."

~

Tech Support: "All right. Now double-click on the File Manager icon."
Customer: "That's why I hate this Windows—because of the icons. I'm a Protestant, and I don't believe in icons."
Tech Support: "Well, that's just an industry term sir. I don't believe it was meant to . . ."
Customer: "I don't care about any 'Industry Terms.' I don't believe in icons."
Tech Support: "Well . . . why don't you click on the 'little picture' of a file cabinet . . . is 'little picture' OK?"
Customer: [Click]

~

Jay Leno on Campbell's 19 new kinds of soup: "They're trying to attract a hipper, high-tech customer. The alphabet soup now has spell-check."

~

Now wristwatches beep. Alarm clocks beep. Typewriters beep. Beepers beep. We have entered the age of electronic nagging.
—*Changing Times, The Kiplinger Magazine*

~

One of my friends works in the customer service call center of a national pager company. He deals with the usual complaints regarding poor pager

operation, as well as the occasional crank caller demanding to be paged less often, more often, or by more interesting people. The best call came from a man who repeatedly complained that he keeps being paged by "Lucille." He was instructed that he would have to call her and tell her to stop paging him. "She don't never leave no number, so I can't call her back," he said. After three such calls, someone thought to ask how he knew it was Lucille if she didn't leave a number. "She leaves her name" was the reply. After establishing that the customer had a numeric-only pager, the light bulb came on. "How does she spell her name?" the service rep asked. "L-O-W C-E-L-L."

HISTORY

History will be kind to me, for I intend to write it.   —Winston Churchill

In 1991, Rep. Frank Annunzio (D., Ill.) appeared before a House subcommittee to drum up support for legislation authorizing a commemorative coin to honor the 500th anniversary of Columbus's arrival in the New World. Annunzio was questioned by Rep. Al McCandless (D., Calif.), who said his district had a large Scandinavian constituency that believed Leif Ericson discovered America. How would Annunzio respond to them? "Well," Annunzio told McCandless and the audience, "when Columbus discovered America, it stayed discovered."

~

On his way to a reception held in his honor, Ulysses S. Grant got caught in a shower and offered to share his umbrella with a stranger walking in the same direction. The man said he was going to Grant's reception out of curiosity; he had never seen the general. "I have always thought that Grant was a much overrated man," he said. "That's my view also," Grant replied.

—*The Little, Brown Book of Anecdotes*

~

I heard that when Marco Polo first opened the trade routes to China, he was quite impressed with their rockets. Now, these weren't quite the fireworks we now know, but they did shoot into the air, explode and make some pretty patterns. Strangely, no matter where he went, there were people who made fireworks, but he had trouble finding someone to demonstrate them for him. "Not here!" they said . . . very confusing. Until ol' Marc came upon an ancient military fortification at the community of Chu'Lai. Here, fireworks were launched every night, and Marc was very impressed! But still he wondered, "Why here?" At the end of every week, people came from great distances, bringing their own fireworks to launch. So Marco Polo asked his guide why everyone came here to launch their fireworks. Marc's guide replied: "Why honored Sir, . . . We always set off fireworks on the Forts of Chu'Lai."

~

Betsy Ross was a patriotic sew and sew.   —Bob Marshall

~

Question: "What do Catherine the Great, Attila the Hun and Jabba the Hutt have in common?"
Answer: "The same middle name."   —Roger L. Welsch in *Natural History*

HOLIDAYS

Turkeys will be higher this Thanksgiving, except around Washington where there's a surplus.

Americans are putting up Christmas decorations so early, I saw an Easter bunny in a pear tree.

HOME

We have one of those floor lamps with three degrees of brightness: dim, flicker, and out.

～

Some sort of award for tact and diplomacy ought to go to the husband whose wife was giving a crucial dinner party at home and, while carrying the beautifully brown, 15-pound roast into the dining room, dropped it. The meat rolled off the platter and slid along the floor until it reached the opposite wall. The man of the house spoke up calmly: "My dear, just pick it up and carry it back to the kitchen. Then, bring in the other roast."
                    —*How the Platform Professionals Keep 'em Laughin'*

～

Two housekeepers were talking over their problems of work. One said, "This lady I work for says I should warm the plates for our dinner guests, but that's too much work. I just warm hers and she never knows the difference."
                    —*How the Platform Professionals Keep 'em Laughin'*

～

Nothing makes cleaning out the attic such a long job as being able to read.

～

The way some houses are built, the only thing that lasts 30 years is the mortgage.   —Shelby Friedman, *The Wall Street Journal*

HONEYMOONS

On their honeymoon, Eric took Louise by the hand and said, "Now that we're married, dear, I hope you won't mind if I mention a few little defects that I've noticed about you." "Not at all," Louise replied sweetly. "It was those little defects that kept me from getting a better husband."

～

Honeymoon: A short period of doting between dating and debting.
                    —Ray Bandy

～

My cousin Trish and her longtime boyfriend Earl got married and spent their first night at the bride's parents' home. Trish is a very religious girl, so she told

Earl they would have to pray before going to bed. Earl protested, "You're asking the wrong guy. Why, I've never prayed a single prayer in my whole life." "I don't care," she said, "you will tonight." So he did pray. Next morning at breakfast he said, "I did something last night I never did before." That got everybody's attention. Then Trish commented, "Yes, and if you are not good today, I'll tell everybody how awkward you were in doing it."

HORSES

HORSE FOR SALE: What they say in the newspaper ads and what they really mean:

Friendly = Comes up to you in the pasture, but you may not be able to catch him!

Seasoned = Tired.

Bombproof = Ready for retirement.

Gentle = This doesn't mean anything!

Good with kids = Doesn't like adults much; perhaps has a sore back.

Man's horse = You'll have to be a weight lifter to stop this one.

Needs experienced rider = Bucks, spooks, runs away or rears.

Prospect = The horse may be able to perform as required in a few years.

Broke = Green-broke.

Green-broke = Not broke.

Ready to start = Halter broke.

Loves trails = Hates arenas.

Successfully shown = No one was killed at the one schooling show he was taken to.

Horse, USA

HOSPITALITY

Helen Oatley, a wealthy matron, hosted a big luncheon to help launch a new Red Cross drive in Washington, D.C. One of the high dignitaries in attendance patted the hostess' little daughter, Dottie, on the head and said, "Aren't we a big help to our dear mother. What is our task for today?" "Our task for today," snapped the little daughter, "is to see that none of you bozos try to get away with any of the silver."

Hospitality is making your guests feel at home, even if you wish they were.

〜

As the Smiths were about to sit down to dinner, they spotted friends coming up the walk. "Oh, dear," Mrs. Smith moaned, "I'll bet they haven't eaten yet." "Quick!" ordered Mr. Smith, "everybody out on the porch with toothpicks."

—Hugh Harrison

HOSPITALS

One of those high-powered executives was checking into the hospital. Barking orders left and right, he had his own way until he reached the desk of a small, mild-mannered lady. She typed the man's name on a slip of paper, stuck the paper into a plastic bracelet, then snapped it on the man's wrist before he could react. "What's this for?" demanded Mr. Big. "That," replied the woman, "is so we won't give you to the wrong mother when you're ready to leave."

—*Rotary Bulletin*

〜

No matter how much a private room in a hospital costs, they only give you a semiprivate gown.

〜

"What sign were you born under?"
"Neon. My father said he knew the way to the hospital and my mother believed him."

〜

A visitor in Dallas asked, "What's the quickest way to get to the hospital?" "Say something bad about Texas!" came the reply.

〜

Then there was the hospital patient complaining about the cost of some minor surgery. "What this country needs," he griped, "is a good $50 scar."

〜

Statistics disclose that babies are born to every fifth person going into the hospital. If you've already been in four times, be prepared.

〜

Uncle Sid underwent an operation at Mercy hospital and came out of the anesthesia. As he opened his eyes, he asked a nurse, "How come all the shades on the windows are pulled down?" The nurse said, "The house across the street is on fire, and we didn't want you to wake up thinking that the operation was a failure."

~

Nurse: "Did you drink the carrot juice after the hot bath?"
Patient: "I haven't finished drinking the hot bath yet."

~

Hospitalized man to wife: "Do you have any idea what it does to somebody to be 'W. J. Hambley, Senior Vice President' one minute and 'the gall bladder in 403' the next?"

HEARD AT THE HOSPITAL:

- "All that I know is that the ticket broker said they were front row seats to an opening."
- "How are the children and my good dishes?"
- "Bill, go downstairs to the phone booth, call this place, ask them how I'm doing and come back and tell me, will ya?"
- "Let me put it this way—if you were a building you'd be condemned."
- "What you have is a common cold, and there is no known cure for it. But cheer up—it may run into pneumonia—and we know what to do for that!"
- "She's a practical nurse—she only nurses rich old men."
- "I'll have you out of here in a week—one way or the other."

When a hospital runs out of maternity nurses they have a midwife crisis.

~

A small boy swallowed some coins and was taken to a hospital. When his grandmother telephoned to ask how he was, a nurse said, "No change yet."

~

Why do the nurses at hospitals wear masks when it's the cashiers who should? —John Drybred

~

Today's hospitals don't kid around. I won't say what happens if you don't pay a bill—but did you ever have an appendix put back in? —Joey Adams

~

Clarence "Ducky" Nash, who was the voice of Donald Duck for 50 years, once visited a hospital where an undisciplined kid was disturbing everybody in earshot. Nash went to the child and in his Donald Duck voice told the brat: "SHUT UP." The kid shut up and smiled. One of the doctors, hearing about this, made the remark: "That's the first time a quack ever helped a patient."

HOTELS

On a hotel marquee in Commerce, Calif.: "Our towels are so fluffy, it'll be hard to put them in your suitcase."

—

A man walked into a hotel. " I'd like a room for tonight," he told the clerk. "I'm sorry, sir, but we have no vacant rooms," the clerk answered. "Not even one room?" the man asked. "No, sir, we're full tonight," said the clerk. The man thought for a moment. "Please tell me, if the President of the United States came in and asked for a room, would you give him one?" "I guess if the President of the United States asked for a room, I could find one for him," the clerk replied. "Well, the President is not coming here tonight. So give me the room you'd give him!"

—

Overheard at an Atlantic City hotel:

Guest: "When I made this reservation, I specifically requested a room facing the ocean."

Desk Clerk: "Well, you didn't specify which ocean." —Ron Dentinger

—

DESK CLERK TO MAN AT THE COUNTER: "Somebody must have given you the wrong information . . . the Liars Club doesn't meet here."

—Ron Dentinger

—

A Professor from Michigan State University arrived at a hotel in Montreal after a long flight and was told that his confirmed reservation couldn't be honored. There were no rooms. "I'll give you three minutes to find me a room," he told the clerk. "After three minutes, I'm going to undress in the lobby, put on my pajamas and go to sleep on one of the sofas." He got a room.

HOUSEWORK

Newlywed Jennifer told her mother, "Just this morning Ted said I was a terrible housekeeper. I got so angry I ran into the . . . uh . . . what do you call it? . . . oh, yeah, the kitchen."

Way back in the domestic goddess stage of her career, Roseanne observed, "When Sears comes out with a riding vacuum cleaner, then I'll clean the house."

～

Did you see where someone wants to erect a monument to the Unknown Housewife? Isn't that a great idea? A housewife is someone who spends seven days a week scrubbing the floors, shopping for food, cooking the meals, washing the dishes, watering the lawn, weeding the garden, walking the dog, and being a valet, maid, and chauffeur for the kids. But that isn't what hurts. It's when someone asks her husband, "Does your wife work?" And he says, "No!"   —Robert Orben, *2500 Jokes To Start 'Em Laughing*

～

The bride was anything but a tidy housekeeper. It bothered her no end, until one evening her husband called from the hall, somewhat dismayed. "Honey," he shouted, "where's the dust on this table? I had a phone number written on it."   —*Indianapolis Sun Star*

HUMANKIND
Human beings, who are almost unique in having the ability to learn from the experience of others, are also remarkable for their apparent disinclination to do so.   —Douglas Adams

～

There are amusing people who do not interest, and interesting people who do not amuse.   —Benjamin Disraeli

～

There are only two kinds of men: the just who believe themselves sinners; the sinners who believe themselves just.   —Blaise Pascal

～

Man is the only kind of varmit sets his own trap, baits it, then steps in it.
                                                —John Steinbeck, *Sweet Thursday*

～

There are only three kinds of human; those that count, and those that can't.

HUMILIATION
Your worst humiliation is only someone else's momentary entertainment.
                                                                —Karen Crockett

HUMILITY
I asked the avid young friar, "Is your monastic order one I might have heard of?" "Well," replied the friar, "we're not famous as the Jesuits are for scholarship

or the Trappists for silence and prayer. However, when it comes to humility, we're the tops!"

˜

I once heard my Aunt Lou pray: "Lord, help me to believe and accept the truth about myself, no matter how beautiful it is."

˜

Says actor Tom Selleck, "Whenever I get full of myself, I remember that nice couple who approached me with a camera on a street in Honolulu one day. When I struck a pose for them, the man said, 'No, no, we want you to take a picture of us.'"

˜

Don't be humble. You're not that great. —Golda Meir

HUMOR

Mark my words, when a society has to resort to the rest room for its humor, the writing is on the wall. —Alan Bennett

˜

Humor is an affirmation of dignity, a declaration of man's superiority to all that befalls him. —Romain Gary, *Promise at Dawn*

"I think that you have some SERIOUS faith issues."

Satire is traditionally the weapon of the powerless against the powerful.

—Molly Ivins

~

Laughter can be heard farther than weeping.   —Yiddish proverb

~

Humor allows us to step out of the moment, look at it and sum it up with no great reverence. It is a gift nature gives the mature intellect. If a Presidential candidate is lacking in humor, don't vote for him. He lacks the Presidential sensibility, and he'll never succeed with Congress or rally the will of the people.   —Peggy Noonan

HUNTING

Ditsey Baummortal went duck hunting with old Uncle George Tervilliger. A flock of ducks flew overhead and Uncle George took a potshot at them and one fell down on the beach, dead. Ditsey walked over and looked at it. "Hey, Uncle George," he said, "that was a waste of ammunition to shoot that duck. The fall alone would have killed it."   —"Senator" Ed Ford

~

Visiting in Australia, an executive from Texas decided to go on a kangaroo hunt. He climbed into his jeep and instructed his guide to proceed to the plains in quest of a kangaroo. No sooner had they reached the wide open spaces when they spotted one and the driver drove the jeep in hot pursuit. For some time they went at breakneck speed without gaining on the animal. Finally, the executive shouted to his guide, "There's no use chasing that thing." "Why not?" asked the driver. "Cause we're now doing 65, and that critter ain't even put his front feet down yet!"

—*How the Platform Professionals*
Keep 'em Laughin'

~

Ralph and Norris went bear hunting in North Dakota. While Ralph stayed in the cabin, Norris went out looking for a bear. He soon found a huge bear, shot at it but only wounded it. The enraged bear charged toward him. His rifle jammed, so he dropped it and started running for the cabin as fast as he could. Now Norris was pretty fleet of foot but the bear was just a little faster and gained on him with every step. Just as Norris reached the open cabin door, he tripped and fell flat. Too close behind to stop, the bear tripped over him and went rolling into the cabin. Norris jumped up, closed the cabin door and yelled to his friend inside, "You skin this one while I go and get another!"

~

I ask people why they have deer heads on their walls. They always say because it's such a beautiful animal. I think my mother is attractive, but I have photographs of her.   —Ellen DeGeneres

~

Two hunters hire a small plane to take them to a remote area of Canada. Upon dropping off the hunters, the pilot tells them, "Remember only one moose, because the plane wouldn't be able to take off with more weight than that." The hunters go off. A week later when the plane returns to pick them up the

The
BORDERLINE ™

By Gabe Martin
borderln@cts.com

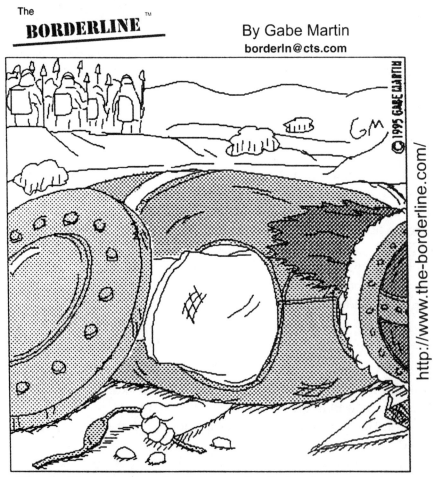

© 1995 GABE MARTIN

http://www.the-borderline.com/

935 B.C.: David becomes the first to realize that, actually, the bigger they are, the harder they fall . . . on you.

two hunters are standing by the lake with two moose. The pilot fumes, "I told you guys only one moose, you'll have to leave one because we won't be able to take off with that much weight." "Oh, c'mon," beg the two hunters, "Last year the pilot let us take two moose on, you're just a chicken." Not wanting to be accused of being a coward, the pilot allows the two to bring both moose on the craft. The plane starts across the lake, straining to take off. The pilot tries and tries to no avail as they run out of room and the plane crashes into the trees at the end of the lake. A while later after coming to one of the hunters gets up and looks at all the scattered debris of the wreck and says, "Where are we?" To which the other hunter replies, "Oh, I'd say about a hundred yards farther than last year."

HURTS

He never bore a grudge against anyone he wronged.   —Simone Signoret

HUSBANDS

Executive overheard talking to a friend: "My wife tells me I don't display enough passion. Imagine! I have a good mind to send her a memo!"

—*Speaker's Idea File*

I met my husband at a travel agency. He was looking for a vacation and I was the last resort.   —Bessie and Beulah

My husband forgot my birthday and my anniversary. I didn't feel bad. On the contrary. Give me a guilty husband any day. Some of my best outfits come from his guilt!   —Betty Walker

Why is the husband who constantly complains he can't get a word in edgewise always so hoarse?   —Peggy Weidman

In a small cemetery on the outskirts of St. Louis, a man is mourning aloud, "Oh, why did you die? Why did you die?" over and over again. My aunt Flo is putting flowers on a nearby grave walks over and asks, "Who died, mister? A close friend of the family?" "No, as a matter of fact, I never met him," the man says and begins to wail again, "Oh, why did you die?" "If you never met him why is his death so painful to you? Who's buried here?" asks Aunt Flo. The man replies, "My wife's first husband."

Husband to wife as he turns on the first football game of the year: "Is there anything you want to say before the season starts?" —Ron Dentinger

～

I began as a passion and ended as a habit, like all husbands.

—George Bernard Shaw

～

At Thanksgiving dinner one wife said, "Who wants to carve the turkey? And her father said, "You carve him, you married him."

～

The man who goes around finding out who is boss in his home might be happier if he didn't know.

～

Every girl should remember in seeking a husband that there are two models: sport and working.

～

Just outside the Pearly Gates is a line of men waiting to get in. A sign overhead read: "For Men Who Have Been Dominated By Their Wives All Their Lives." The line extends as far as the eye could see. There is another sign nearby: "For Men Who Have Never Been Dominated By Their Wives."Only one man was standing under it. St. Peter goes over to him and asks, "Why are you standing here?" The man replies, "I don't know. My wife told me to stand here."

～

Man can climb the highest mountain, swim the widest ocean, fight the strongest tiger, but once he's married, he can barely take out the garbage.

～

A lecturer asked her audience, "Who is wiser than Ann Landers, more controversial than Jerry Springer, wittier than Jerry Seinfeld, and handsomer than Tom Cruise?" From the audience came a forlorn voice: "My wife's first husband!"

～

Woman pedestrian to man: You were too looking at that woman! You had the same look on your face the cat gets when he hears a can opener.

—Art Bouthillier

I went to the hardware store one weekend morning to buy supplies for my latest repair project. A harried-looking man entered and approached the register. "Do you rent carpet-shampooing machines?" he asked. "We do," the clerk said. "But they're all out." "Thank God," the fellow replied in relief.

—Alan Stern

A husband is a man who wishes he had as much fun when he goes on business trips as his wife thinks he does. —Ann Landers

A husband is what is left of the lover after the nerve has been extracted.

—Helen Rowland

Like a lot of married men, I got the "You just don't appreciate me" speech once from Connie. I promised to treat her royally for the remainder of the day. I took her to lunch at Burger King and Dairy Queen for dessert. She's never mentioned it since.

A man spoke frantically into the phone, "My wife is pregnant and her contractions are only two minutes apart!" "Is this her first child?" the doctor asked. "No, you idiot!" the man shouted. "This is her husband!"

Wife, about husband watching TV: "Oh, Fred's interests vary widely—from Channel 2 to Channel 3." —Bob Bugg

HUSBANDS AND WIVES

TWO GUYS ARE TALKING OVER LUNCH: The first guy says, "My wife and I are very happy, but I often overhear her talking about her first husband." The second guy says, "You're lucky. I keep hearing my wife talk about her next husband." —Ron Dentinger

I was telling my friend Al, "My wife should have been a lawyer." "Why do you say that?" he asked. "Well, every time we have a disagreement and I think I'm on the verge of winning, she takes it to a higher court—her mother."

Martha: "Look at the old clothes I have to wear. If anyone came to visit they would think I was the cook."
Herb: "Well, they'd change their minds if they stayed for dinner."

"You," said the doctor to his patient, "are in terrible shape. You've got to do something about it. First, tell your wife to cook more nutritious meals. Stop working like a dog. Also, inform your wife you're going to make a budget, and she has to stick to it. And have her keep the kids off your back so you can relax. Unless there are some changes like that in your life, you'll probably be dead in a month." "Doc," the patient said, "this would sound more official coming from you. Could you please call my wife and give her those instructions?" When the fellow got home, his wife rushed to him. "I talked to your doctor," she wailed. "Poor man, you've got only thirty days to live."

—James Dent in Charleston, W.Va., *Gazette*

When Harold Metzger retired, he and his wife Alice moved to Palm Springs. Shortly thereafter he made an appointment with a local attorney. "I'm here to make a will," Metzger explained. "It's really quite simple and straightforward. Everything goes to Alice—the stocks, the bonds, the cash, the house, the car, the pension, the life insurance—on condition that she remarries within the year." "Whatever you say, Mr. Metzger," said the lawyer. "But do you mind my asking the reason for that condition?" "Simple," said Metzger, "I want at least one person to be sorry I died."

A woman returned home from a holiday shopping spree with her arms loaded with packages. Her husband met her at the door and said, "What did you buy? With prices as high as they are, I'll bet you spent a fortune. I hate to think what has happened to our nest egg." "I'll tell you what happened to our nest egg," his wife said defensively as she began to put her packages on the dining room table. "The old hen got tired of sitting on it."

—*Sunshine Magazine*

There are many things these days, that aren't what they used to be. They bothered me so much that I decided to make a list. My wife said, "Don't forget to include yourself."   —Ron Dentinger

When I first met my wife, she was a schoolteacher. I used to write her passionate love letters—and she'd send them back corrected. I must be the only man in the world who returned from his honeymoon and received a report card. It said, "Dick is neat and friendly and shows a keen interest in fun and games."

—Dick Lord

When my parents were first married more than sixty years ago, my mother dutifully prepared a substantial lunch for my dad to take with him to work. However, no matter what she prepared, he always complained that after eating lunch he was still hungry. I remember one particular week. On Monday, Mother prepared a generous roast-beef sandwich as the main item, and when Dad returned, she asked him what he thought of his lunch. Sourly, Dad replied, "Pretty good—what there was of it." On Tuesday, she made two large sandwiches, but on his return, Dad said once more, in response to her query, "Pretty good—what there was of it." More than a little upset, Mother took a whole loaf of French bread, sliced it lengthwise, and stuffed the entire thing with a variety of cold cuts, cheeses, hard boiled eggs, sardines, anchovies, lettuce, tomato, pickles, and hot peppers. This time, when Dad returned, he did not want to be questioned. He fixed a cold eye on Mother and said, "Back to one sandwich again, eh?"

H

~

My wife is an interior decorator. She wants to get rid of me because I clash with the drapes.   —Morey Amsterdam

~

Every time I leave the house, my wife tells me to call her in case something goes right.   —Rodney Dangerfield

"Brilliant job on the Roberts' proposal, Wilcox! I'm promoting you two cubicles."

I told my wife that a husband is like a fine wine—he gets better with age. The next day she locked me in the cellar.

~

My wife and I have a perfect understanding. I don't try to run her life and I don't try to run mine.

~

One husband knew that every year on the family's way to their vacation spot, just as they would get about eighty miles out of town, his wife would cry out, "Oh, no! I'm sure I left the iron on." Each year they would return home only to find it unplugged. One year, however, was different the man had anticipated what was coming. When his wife gasped, "We must go back, I just know I left the iron on," he stopped the car, reached under his seat, and handed his wife the iron.   —Allen Klein, *The Healing Power of Humor*

~

My Uncle Bill will sit in a boat all day, waiting for fish, then won't hesitate to complain to my Aunt Fern if his dinner is a few minutes late.

~

Uncle Irv loves to complain. He says: "To give you an idea how difficult my wife can be, she bought me two ties for my birthday. To please her I wore one. She hollered, 'What's the matter, don't you like the other one?'"

~

Conversation overheard at a local restaurant:

Was your wife mad when you got home so late last night?

Yes, she was plumb historical.

Don't you mean hysterical?

No, historical. She brought up things that happened forty years ago.

~

One year my Aunt Aurelia told Uncle Floyd, "Honey, I've bought you an unusual birthday present." "What did you buy me?" he asked her. "A cemetery plot." He agreed with her that it was indeed unusual but thanked her anyway. The next year, she didn't buy him a gift, so he asked her why. "Because," she said, "you didn't use the one I bought you last year."

~

My husband said he needed more space, so I locked him outside.

—Roseanne

Give a man enough rope and his wife will steal it for a clothesline.

—Martin A. Ragaway

Abigail Van Buren recently printed the following letter:

Dear Abby: I couldn't believe the letter from the wife who complained about her husband leaving the toilet seat up. She admitted she couldn't count the number of times she had fallen in. And then she said, He still hasn't learned.

Abby's reply: WHO hasn't learned?

Two onetime neighbors met after not having seen one another for some months. "And how are things with you?" asked one of the women. "Oh," said the other, "I'm managing all right, although I lost my husband several months

The
BORDERLINE™   By Gabe Martin
                         borderln@cts.com

Geppeto knew that he should've never bought one of those electric pencil sharpeners.

back." "What happened?" asked the friend. "Well," explained the widow, "I was making dinner and asked him to go out to the garden and pick some corn. After he had been gone a long time, I went to see what the trouble was. There he was dead—a heart attack." "Oh, how awful! What did you do?" "Oh, I had a can of corn in the house, and just used that," said the widow.

～

Aunt Edna was sick, and Uncle Roy, who was fixing her a cup of tea, called out that he couldn't find the tea. "I don't know what could be easier to find," she answered. "It's right in front on the pantry shelf in a cocoa tin marked 'matches.' "

～

By the time the time he whispers, "We were made for each other," she's already planning alterations.

～

Valentine's Day is approaching, a time to recall that your wife still likes candy and flowers. Show her you remember, by speaking of them occasionally.
—Earl Wilson

～

Men do not know their wives well; but wives know their husbands perfectly.
—Raoul-Auger Feuillet

～

My uncle Tim loves art museums. Wherever he travels, he squeezes in a visit to the local art collections. Unfortunately, Aunt Kay is easily bored and tired by them. When Tim and Kay were in Chicago a few years back, Tim dragged Kay to the Art Institute to see the famous Impressionist paintings. After only a few galleries he spotted "Sunday on The Grande Jatte" at the end of the hall. Nearly transported with ecstasy, he danced down the corridor calling: "Kay! Seurat! Seurat!" My aunt shot back, "Whatever will be, will be."

～

Wife to husband looking at garden tools: "Don't buy anything we can borrow."
—Marie Reinke

～

The only time some fellows are ever seen with their wives is after they've been indicted.
—Kin Hubbard

～

Luke's wife bought a new line of expensive cosmetics guaranteed to make her look years younger. After a lengthy sitting before the mirror applying the "miracle" products she asked, "Darling, honestly what age would you say I am?" Looking her over carefully, Luke replied, "Judging from your skin, twenty; your hair, eighteen; and your figure, twenty-five." "Oh, you flatterer!" she gushed. "Hey, wait a minute!" Luke interrupted. "I haven't added them up yet."

~

Woman to friend: "I'm of English descent. My husband's half Scotch and half soda."   —Hoest

~

Jailbird to cellmate: "My wife will get me out—she never lets me finish a sentence."   —Schoenfeld

~

Lawyer to lawyer: "It sure would make things easier if our wives accepted plea bargaining."   —Wilder

~

The stockbroker's secretary answered his phone one morning. "I'm sorry," she said. "Mr. Bradford's on another line." "This is Mr. Ingram's office," the caller said. "We'd like to know if he's bullish or bearish right now." "He's talking to his wife," the secretary replied. "Right now I'd say he's sheepish."

—John Pizzuto, *The Great Wall Street Joke Book*

~

Wife to husband: "Overdrawn, overdrawn, always my fault! Has it ever occurred to you that you might be underdeposited?"   —*Ohio Grange*

HUSTLE
Everything comes to he who hustles while he waits.   —Thomas A. Edison

HYPOCHONDRIACS
All my life I've been a hypochondriac. Even as a little boy, I'd eat my M & Ms one at a time with a glass of water.   —Richard Lewis

---

I

IDEALISTS
An idealist is one who, on noticing that a rose smells better than a cabbage, concludes that it will also make better soup.   —H. L. Mencken

IDEAS

Good ideas are not adopted automatically. They must be driven into practice with courageous impatience.
                                    —Adm. Hyman G. Rickover

IGNORANCE

The older we grow, the greater becomes our wonder at how much ignorance one can contain without bursting one's clothes.   —Mark Twain

It ain't so much the things we don't know that got us in trouble. It's the things we know that ain't so.
                —Artemus Ward, American humorist (1867)

His ignorance covers the world like a blanket, and there's scarcely a hole in it anywhere.   —Mark Twain

His ignorance is encyclopedic.   —Abba Eban

IMAGINATION

You can't depend on your eyes when your imagination is out of focus.
                                    —Mark Twain

Against a diseased imagination demonstration goes for nothing.
                                    —Mark Twain

IMPOSSIBILITY

It is said that many years ago the council of a town in County Cork, Ireland, was having a lot of trouble with criminals, and their jail was overflowing. But the town also had a great shortage of funds. The council dealt with the problem by passing a three-part resolution:
    (1) The city shall build a new jail.
    (2) The jail shall be built out of materials in the old jail.
    (3) The old jail shall be used until the new jail is completed.
                —Eric W. Johnson, *A Treasury of Humor*

INCOME

There are few sorrows, however poignant, in which a good income is of no avail.
                                    —L. P. Smith

e. e. cummings once remarked: "I'm living so far beyond my income that we may almost be said to be living apart." I always suspected that e. e. cummings was undercapitalized!

INDIGNATION

Moral indignation is jealousy with a halo.   —H. G. Wells

INDISPENSABLE

The graveyards are full of indispensable men.   —Charles de Gaulle

INFERIORITY COMPLEX

I had an inferiority complex very early. At birth, when the doctor slapped my bottom I didn't cry. I felt I deserved it.   —Gene Perret

INFLATION

Investment people are telling the story of the fellow who bumped his head and went into a 2-year coma. Awaking refreshed and clearheaded in 2007, the first thing he did was to phone his broker. With the help of a computer setup, it took the broker only a few minutes to report that his 100 shares of General Motors were now worth 5.5 million, and his holdings in Xerox had increased to an amazing $15 million. "Good Lord!" exclaimed the man. "I'm rich!" At which point the telephone operator came on the line and said, "Your 3 minutes are up, sir. Would you please deposit a million dollars?"
                    —*How the Platform Professionals Keep 'em Laughin'*

It's inflation when you pay $10 for the $2 haircut you used to get for $1 when you had hair.

Inflation hasn't ruined everything. A dime can still be used as a screwdriver.

Inflation is the process that enables you to live in a more expensive neighborhood without going to the trouble of moving.

One of the pains of inflation is seeing a youngster start his first job at a salary you once dreamed of as the culmination of your career.
                    —Los Angeles Times Syndicate

IN-LAWS

Her whole family hates me. During the wedding ceremony when they ask, "Is there anyone here who objects to this marriage?" Her side of the family stood up and started forming a double line. —Ron Dentinger

INNOVATION

Two experienced fishermen went ice-fishing. They chopped holes in the ice about twenty-five feet apart, put worms on their hooks, dropped their lines in the water, and got nary a nibble. This went on for several hours, but no luck. Mid-afternoon, a schoolboy arrived, walked confidently onto the ice, and chopped his hole between those of the two men, and caught fish after fish. The men were amazed, and finally one approached the boy and asked, "Tell me, young man, what's your secret?" The boy replied, "Mmmm yymmm mmmms wmmm." "What's that?" asked the man. "Say it again, please." The boy: "Mmmm yymmm mmms wmmm." The man: "I'm sorry. I just can't understand you. Would you speak a little more clearly?" At that, the boy cupped his palms, spat a large amount of substance into them, and said clearly, "Keep your worms warm." —Eric W. Johnson, *A Treasury of Humor*

INSPIRATION

If we expire when we die, shouldn't we inspire while we live?

—George Goldtrap

❧

Inspiration works best when you do.   —Andrew V. Mason, M.D.

INSULTS

A stand-up comic, I was performing at a center for the elderly in the Chelsea section of Manhattan. After my act, a woman, who was probably in her 90s approached me. "Young man," she said, "I want you to know that I saw Milton Berle when he was your age." "That's nice to know," I said. "Yes," she replied. "And he was no good either."

—Bill Gordon

❧

Her face was her chaperone.   —Rupert Hughes

❧

Her family is extremely protective of her—they don't let her out on garbage-collection day.

❧

He does the work of three men: Larry, Curley and Moe.   —Ron Dentinger

❧

I stepped on the drug store scale. The little card read: "You are intelligent, have a magnetic personality, strength of character. You are a leader of men, you are intelligent and handsome and attractive to the opposite sex." My wife said, "Humph! It got your weight wrong, too!"

❧

In an often repeated but apocryphal story, it is reported that Lady Astor once said to Winston Churchill at a party, "Sir, if you were my husband, I would put poison in your tea." To which Churchill retorted, "And, Madame, if you were my wife, I would drink it!"

❧

Oscar Levant, after listening to his friend George Gershwin's monologue about himself, inquired: "George, if you had it to do over, would you fall in love with yourself again?"

❧

His face was as blank as a target after a militia shooting-match.

—Mark Twain

He was good-natured, obliging and immensely ignorant, and was endowed with a stupidity which by the least little stretch would go around the globe four times and tie.   —Mark Twain

He is useless on top of the ground; he ought to be under it, inspiring the cabbages.   —Mark Twain

A mind like Paul Revere's ride—a little light in the belfry.
—Marcus D. Williamson

The only gracious way to accept an insult is to ignore it. If you can't ignore it, top it. If you can't top it, laugh at it. If you can't laugh at it, it's probably deserved.   —Russell Lynes in *Vogue*

I've just learned about his illness. Let's hope it's nothing trivial.
—Irvin S. Cobb

I worship the quicksand he walks in.   —Art Buchwald

 He was either a man of about a hundred and fifty who was rather young for his years, or a man of about a hundred and ten who had been aged by trouble.   —P. G. Wodehouse

I never forget a face, but in your case I'll make an exception.
—Groucho Marx

She not only kept her lovely figure, she's added so much to it.   —Bob Fosse

She was a large woman who seemed not so much dressed as upholstered.
—James Matthew Barrie

Why do you sit there looking like an envelope without any address on it?
—Mark Twain

Why don't you get a haircut? You look like a chrysanthemum.

—P. G. Wodehouse

He has the attention span of a lightning bolt.   —Robert Redford

He has Van Gogh's ear for music.   —Billy Wilder

He is brilliant—to the top of his boots.   —David Lloyd George

He knows so little and knows it so fluently.   —Ellen Glasgow

He loves nature in spite of what it did to him.   —Forrest Tucker

He never said a foolish thing nor never did a wise one.   —Earl of Rochester

He thinks by infection, catching an opinion like a cold.   —John Ruskin

"I'm sorry, Mrs. Jones. He just grabbed his bag and ran out the door."

His golf bag does not contain a full set of irons. —Robin Williams

~

I want to reach your mind—where is it currently located?

—Ashleigh Brilliant

~

I wish I'd known you when you were alive. —Leonard Louis Levinson

~

I would not want to put him in charge of snake control in Ireland.

—Eugene McCarthy

~

If he ever had a bright idea it would be beginner's luck. —William Lashner

~

She is a water bug on the surface of life. —Gloria Steinem

The
BORDERLINE ™

By Gabe Martin
borderln@cts.com

http://www.the-borderline.com/

"Uh-oh—looks like a lynch mob's a'gatherin' . . ."

That young girl is one of the least benightedly unintelligent organic life forms it has been my profound lack of pleasure not to be able to avoid meeting.

—Douglas Adams

What's on your mind? If you'll forgive the overstatement.

—Fred Allen

When you go to the mind reader, do you get half price?

—David Letterman

You've got the brain of a four-year-old boy, and I bet he was glad to get rid of it. —Groucho Marx

Greater love hath no man than this, to lay down his friends for his life.

—Jeremy Thorpe

He could never see a belt without hitting below it. —Margot Asquith

He had delusions of adequacy. —Walter Kerr

He has sat on the fence so long that the iron has entered his soul.

—David Lloyd George

He is as good as his word—and his word is no good. —Seamus MacManus

He was about as useful in a crisis as a sheep. —Dorothy Eden

He's very clever, but sometimes his brains go to his head. —Margot Asquith

I will always love the false image I had of you. —Ashleigh Brilliant

She not only expects the worst, but makes the worst of it when it happens.

—Michael Arlen

She's got such a narrow mind, when she walks fast her earrings bang together.

—John Cantu

~

You have a good and kind soul. It just doesn't match the rest of you.

—Norm Papernick

~

Every time I look at you I get a fierce desire to be lonesome.   —Oscar Levant

~

I feel so miserable without you, it's almost like having you here.   —Stephen Bishop

~

Sometimes I need what only you can provide: your absence.

—Ashleigh Brilliant

~

George Bernard Shaw sent Winston Churchill two tickets for the first night of his play *Pygmalion* with the note: "Here are a couple of tickets for the first night. Bring a friend—if you have one." Mr. Churchill replied, "Sorry, I cannot come to the first night but will come to the second—if there is one."

INSURANCE

After his tour of duty overseas, Corporal Kidman was sent to a stateside induction center where he advised new recruits about their government benefits and options, especially GI insurance. Soon he had an almost one hundred percent sales record. His officers were amazed. Rather than ask him how he did it, an officer stood in the back of the room one day and listened to Kidman's sales pitch. Kidman explained the basics of GI insurance to the new recruits and then said, "If you have GI insurance, and go into battle and are killed, the government has to pay $35,000 to your beneficiaries. If you don't have GI insurance, and go into battle and are killed, the government has to pay only a maximum of $3,000." He concluded, "Now which bunch do you think are going to be sent into battle first?"

~

"Do you know the present value of your husband's policy?" the life-insurance salesman asked his client. "What do you mean?" countered the woman. "If you should lose your husband, what would you get?" The woman thought a minute, then brightened up and said, "A poodle!"   —Frank Eames

INTELLIGENCE

AT&T fired President John Walter after nine months, saying, "He lacked intellectual leadership." He received a $26 million severance package. Perhaps it's not Walter who's lacking intelligence.

INTERRUPTIONS

As two priests traveled along a country road, the first was remonstrating with the second about his habit of constantly interrupting himself. "Tell you what I'll do," said the first priest. "I'll wager you my horse that you won't be able to recite the 'Our Father' through to the end without stopping." The other agreed to the bet and started the prayer. About halfway through, he looked up and asked, "Do I get the saddle too?"

INVENTORS

My dad just invented a new microwave television set. He can watch "60 Minutes" in twelve seconds.

Once, when introducing Thomas A. Edison at a dinner, the toastmaster mentioned his many inventions, dwelling at length on the talking machine. The aged inventor then rose to his feet, smiled, and said gently to his audience: "I thank the gentleman for his kind remarks, but I must insist upon a correction. God invented the talking machine. I only invented the first one that can be shut off."
—Grit

INVESTING

If you use all this financial information diligently, you may even make money. Especially if the market goes up.   —William J. Cook, describing various
stock trading and data software, 1984

October. This is one of the peculiarly dangerous months to speculate in stocks. The others are July, January, September, April, November, May, March, June, December, August, and February.   —Mark Twain

IRELAND

In some parts of Ireland, the sleep which knows no waking is always followed by a wake which knows no sleeping.   —Mary Wilson Little

IRONY

It can be no sufficient compensation to a corpse to know that the dynamite that laid him out was not of as good a quality as it had been supposed to be.
—Mark Twain

IRS

Somehow I sent my utility payment to the IRS and my tax papers to the electric company. Now I just sit here in the dark and wait for a refund.
—Ron Dentinger

Sign in Internal Revenue Service office: "In God we trust, everyone else we audit."

J

JOBS

No job is so simple that is can't be done wrong.

JOCKS

When I was in Indiana a few years back, I walked into a restaurant and was told that there would be a short wait for a table. I was ushered into the bar and told that I would be called in due course. I ordered an ice tea and asked the waitress if she would like to hear a good Notre Dame joke. A look of stern disapproval formed on her face. "Listen," she whispered. "See those 2 big guys on your left? They are both linemen on the Notre Dame football team. And that huge fellow on your right was a world-class wrestler at Notre Dame. That guy in the corner is Notre Dame's all-time champion weight lifter. And that fellow with him lettered in 3 sports at Notre Dame. Now, are you absolutely positive you want to go ahead and tell your joke here?" "Nah, guess not," I replied. "I wouldn't want to have to explain it 5 times."

JOGGING

The human body has several hundred muscles, mostly to tell us we shouldn't have jogged so far.
—*The Idea Treasury*

Jogger: "I can't run today. My headset broke."
—Ralph Dunagin, Tribune Media Services

America is the only country in the world where people jog ten miles a day for exercise and then take elevators up to the mezzanine.
—Robert Orben, *2500 Jokes To Start 'Em Laughing*

JOKES

In Austria in the days following World War II, soldiers from America, France, Britain and Russia shared jeeps for military police duty. One group of them used to kill time by telling jokes. That is, the western soldiers did. The Russians remained silent and sullen. The American asked, "What's the matter with you, Ivan? Doesn't anything funny ever happen in Russia?" "Have you heard of the great canals in Russia?" Ivan asked. "Yes," the American replied. "It must have been a hard job building them." "Exactly," Ivan said. "They were built by people who told jokes."

Sometimes I wish I were Adam. Whatever problems he may have had in days of yore, when he cracked a joke, no one said, "I've heard that one before."

Whenever anything bad happens to me, I write a joke about it. Then it isn't a bad experience, it's a tax deduction.
—Denise Munro

A joke is an epitaph on an emotion.   —Friedrich Nietzsche

~

If you can't remember a joke, don't dismember it.   —Anthony J. Pettito

~

When Secretary of State George Shultz sent a cable to Ronald Reagan, he included a joke so he could check whether the President had read it. If the Secretary got back to Washington and Reagan said, "That was a great joke, George. I've been telling it to everybody," then Shultz knew his message got through to the President.

JOURNALISM

The photographers doing the *Sports Illustrated* swimsuit edition are on strike . . . for longer hours.   —Ron Dentinger

The
BORDERLINE™   By Gabe Martin
                                    borderln@cts.com

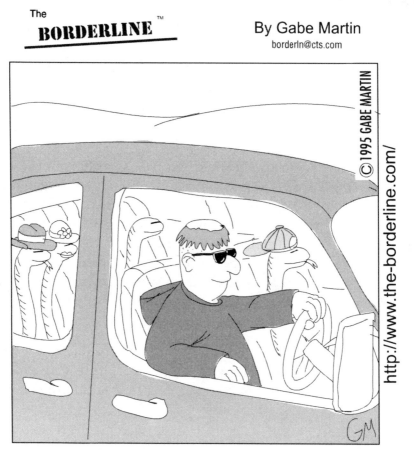

© 1995 GABE MARTIN

http://www.the-borderline.com/

Circa 426: Saint Patrick drives the snakes out or Ireland.

JUDGES

Insulted by the disrespect shown him by lawyer Harvey Smith, the judge thundered, "What do you suppose that I am on the bench for, Mr. Smith?" Smith replied, "It is not for me to attempt to fathom the inscrutable workings of Providence."

JUDGING

A fox should not be the jury at a goose's trial.   —Thomas Fuller

JUNK

The average time between throwing something away and needing it badly is about two weeks.   —Norman Bell

JURIES

A judge in Tulsa was hearing a drunk-driving case and the defendant, who had both a record and a reputation for driving under the influence, demanded a jury trial. It was nearly 4 P.M. and getting a jury would take time, so the judge called a recess and went out in the hall looking to impanel anyone available for jury duty. He found a dozen lawyers in the main lobby and told them that they were a jury. The lawyers thought this would be a novel experience and so followed the judge back to the courtroom. The trial was over in about 10 minutes and it was very clear that the defendant was guilty. The jury went into the jury-room, the judge started getting ready to go home, and everyone waited. After nearly three hours, the judge was totally out of patience and sent the bailiff into the jury-room to see what was holding up the verdict. When the bailiff returned, the judge said, "Well, have they got a verdict yet?" The bailiff shook his head and said, "Verdict? Hey, they're still reciting nominating speeches for the foreman's position!"

~

A jury is a group of twelve men who, having lied to the judge about their hearing, health and business engagements, have failed to fool him.

—H. L. Mencken

~

The judge asked Marty Land, the prospective juror, "Is there any reason why you could not serve as a juror in this case?" "I don't want to be away from my job that long," replied Land. "Can't they get along without you at work?" "I'm sure they can, but I don't want them to realize it."

~

Judge Fielding was interviewing Tom Bailey, a prospective jury member. "Mr. Bailey, have you ever served on a jury?" "No," Bailey replied, "I've been too smart to be on a jury." "I beg your pardon," screamed the judge. "You boast of your smartness in escaping jury duty? Don't you know that service on a jury is the highest calling of a good citizen?" "Your Honor," explained the man, "you misunderstand me. What I mean is that I was always excused because the lawyers thought I wasn't ignorant enough."

❧

Reflecting their firm grasp on the facts of the matter, a jury in West Virginia brought in the following verdict in a suit against the Baltimore and Ohio Railroad: "If the train had run as it should have run; if the bell had rung as it should have rung; if the whistle had blowed as it should have blowed, both of which it did neither—the cow would not have been injured when she was killed."

❧

Rev. Winston Jackson, pastor of the First Assembly of God Church, reported for jury duty. The minister asked to be excused. "On what grounds?" asked the judge. "Because I'm prejudiced," replied the preacher. "I hate to admit it," said the cleric, pointing to the man seated in front of the judge, "but I took one look at those shifty eyes, Your Honor, and I knew right away he was just as guilty as sin." "Sit down," barked the judge. "The man you're pointing at happens to be the defendant's lawyer."

❧

The case against Vera Atkins, the accused shoplifter, was purely circumstantial. Unfortunately, she was convicted. At the time of sentencing her record was placed before the court. It revealed that when the crime in question had been committed, Vera had been in prison. "My God, woman," shrieked her attorney, "why didn't you tell us?" "I thought it might prejudice the jury against me," she explained.

❧

The three-time crook felt a wave of panic come over him as he surveyed the jury in the courthouse. Positive he'd never beat the murder rap, he managed to get hold of one of the kindlier-looking jurors, and bribe her with his life savings to go for a manslaughter verdict. Sure enough, at the close of the trial the jury declared him guilty of manslaughter. Tears of gratitude welling up in his eyes, the young man had a moment with the juror before being led off to prison. "Thank you, thank you—how'd you do it?" "It wasn't easy," she admitted. "They all wanted to acquit you."

—H. Aaron Cohl, *The Friars Club Encyclopedia of Jokes*

We have a criminal jury system which is superior to any in the world and its efficiency is only marred by the difficulty of finding twelve men every day who don't know anything and can't read. —Mark Twain

JUSTICE

Injustice is relatively easy to bear; it is justice that hurts. —H. L. Mencken

K

KIDDING

Reaching the end of a job interview, the Human Resources Person asked a young engineer who was fresh out of MIT, "What starting salary were you thinking about?" The engineer said, "In the neighborhood of $125,000 a year, depending on the benefits package." The interviewer said, "Well, what would you say to a package of 5 weeks vacation, 14 paid holidays, full medical and dental, company matching retirement fund to 50% of salary, and a company car leased every 2 years—say, a red Corvette?" The engineer sat up straight and said, "Wow! Are you kidding?" The interviewer replied, "Yeah, but you started it."

KNEES

When nature designed the male knee, she obviously had neither football nor walking shorts in mind. —Bill Vaughan

KNOWLEDGE

A wise old sea captain stood on the bridge of his ship day in and day out, opening a box and peeking inside, never letting anyone else see the contents. The day he retired, the crew rushed to the bridge, cut the lock and looked inside the box. Hidden inside was a piece of paper that read, "Left—port. Right—starboard."

A priest, a minister, and a rabbi went fishing. The fish weren't biting, so the priest got out of the boat and walked across the water to another spot. Then the minister got out of the boat and walked across the water. The rabbi got out of the boat and he started to sink. He tried again and almost drowned. Finally the priest said to the minister, "Don't you think we should tell him where the rocks are?"

LANGUAGE

A linguistics professor was lecturing to his class one day. In English, he said, a double negative forms a positive. In some languages though, such as Russian, a double negative is still a negative. However, he pointed out, there is no language wherein a double positive can form a negative. A voice from the back of the room piped up "Yeah, right."

❧

Mastery of the art and spirit of the Germanic language—enables a man to travel all day in one sentence without changing cars.   —Mark Twain

❧

Malapropism Lives! Here is a compilation of gaffes overheard in and around New York City: "That job was my bread and water!" "It's going to be nick and tuck from now on." "That's a horse of a different feather." "It's just a kick in the bucket." "You could tell they were alligator tears." "Just what do you want—egg in your beard?" "He was a child progeny." "It takes two to tangle." "These days he's living high as a hog." "It was all over in one full swap." "I guess I'll just have to start from scraps!" "He's got a mind like a trap door." "I slept like a tree!"   —David Diefendorf

❧

A new missionary recruit went to Venezuela for the first time. He was struggling with the language and didn't understand a whole lot of what was going on. Intending to visit one of the local churches, he got lost, but eventually got back on track and found the place. Having arrived late, the church was already packed. The only pew left was the one on the front row. So as not to make a fool of himself, he decided to pick someone out of the crowd to imitate. He chose to follow the man sitting next to him on the front pew. As they sang, the man clapped his hands, so the missionary recruit clapped too. When the man stood up to pray, the missionary recruit stood up too. When the man sat down, he sat down. When the man held the cup and bread for the Lord's Supper, he held the cup and bread. During the preaching, the recruit didn't understand a thing. He just sat there and tried to look just like that man in the front pew. Then he perceived that the preacher was giving announcements. People clapped, so he looked to see if the man was clapping. He was, and so the recruit clapped too. Then the preacher said some words that he didn't understand and he saw the man next to him stand up. So he stood up too. Suddenly a hush fell over the entire congregation. A few people gasped. He looked around and saw that nobody else was standing. So he sat down. After the service ended, the preacher stood at the door shaking the hands of those who were leaving. When the missionary recruit stretched out his hand to greet the preacher, the preacher said, in English: "I take it you don't speak Spanish." The missionary recruit replied: "No I don't. It's that obvious?" "Well, yes," said the preacher, "I announced that the Acosta family had a newborn baby boy and would the proud father please stand up."

~

A woman, wanting to impress two old college chums, took them to dinner at an exclusive French restaurant and ordered for all three in flawless French. Handing the menu back to the waiter with a flourish, she asked, "Would you mind reading our order back to me?" "Oui, madame? No. 4, No. 9, No. 16."

—Leadership

~

Charles Berlitz was asked how a linguist identifies a native tongue. "It probably comes down to what you say when you hit your thumb with a hammer," he replied. "For me, my first reaction is in French."

—Carol Krucoff, Los Angeles Times-Washington Post News Service

LATE

Heard at the bus stop: "Joe's chronically late for everything. His ancestors came over on the Juneflower." —Shelby Friedman

LAUGHTER

Someone at the Food and Drug Administration was heard to say, "If laughter is the best medicine, shouldn't we be regulating it?"

~

I remember we used to be reminded that there are four marks of the Church: One, Holy, Catholic, and Apostolic. I tell the children in my confirmation classes that there is actually a fifth mark—laughter. I think it reflects a maturity in the faith when we are able to laugh at ourselves.

—Archbishop Edward A. McCarthy

~

Life is not a laughing matter—but can you imagine having to live without laughing? —Leonid Sukhorukov

~

Blessed are they who can laugh at themselves for they shall never cease to be amused.

LAUNDRY

If you come out of the laundry with an even number of socks, you have somebody else's laundry. —Laurence J. Peter, *Peter's Almanac*

LAWNS

A midsummer reflection: All you need to grow healthy, vigorous grass is a crack in your sidewalk.
                                        —*The Milwaukee Journal*

~

A man who admits he is allergic to lawn work says, "I long for the day when anybody caught working in the yard will be arrested for disturbing the ecology."
                                        —Red O'Donnell in *The Nashville Banner*

LAWYERS

When the law is on your side, argue the law. When the facts are on your side, argue the facts. When neither the facts nor the law are on your side, holler!
                                        —Albert Gore, Jr.

~

A Russian, a Cuban, an American and his lawyer are on a train. The Russian takes a bottle of the best vodka out of his pack, pours some into a glass, drinks it, and says: "In Russia, we have best vodka in world. Nowhere in world you can find vodka as good as in Russia. And we have so much of it that we can just throw it away." Saying that, he opens the window and throws the rest of the bottle through it. The others are quite impressed. The Cuban takes a box of Havana cigars, lights one of them, and begins to smoke it. He says, "In Cuba, we have the best cigars of the world—Havanas. Nowhere in the world are there such good cigars and we have so many of them, that we can just throw them away." Saying that, he opens the window and throws the box of Havanas on through. Again everyone is quite impressed. Then without saying a word the American stands up, opens the window and throws the lawyer through, too.

~

"How can I ever thank you?" gushed a woman to Clarence Darrow, after he had solved her legal troubles. "My dear woman," Darrow replied, "ever since the Phoenicians invented money there has been only one answer to that question."

~

The phone rang at 3 A.M. Howard Friedkin, the seasoned attorney, was accustomed to occasional midnight calls, especially from clients who were involved in automobile accidents. But he was not prepared for this agitated woman, someone he never met, who was obviously in the middle of a heated argument with her husband. "Can you tell me," she yelled over the noise of her husband's pleading in the background, "if a husband leaves his wife, is she or is she not entitled to the house and its contents?" "I can't give such advice over the phone, especially without knowing the particulars of the case," Friedkin pointed out reasonably. "Call my office in the morning and we'll set up an appointment." He could hear the woman say to her husband, "She's also entitled to the timeshare, both cars, and the joint saving account?" Then she effusively thanked Friedkin and hung up. He never heard from her again.

~

Divorce lawyer: "I have succeeded in making a settlement with your spouse that's completely fair to both of you."
Client: "Fair to both of us! I could have done that myself. Why do you think I hired a lawyer?"   —*The Wall Street Journal*

~

If builders built buildings the way lawyers write laws, the first woodpecker to come along would destroy civilization.

~

If it wasn't for lawyers, we wouldn't need them.

~

Ignorance of the law does not prevent the losing lawyer from collecting his bill.

~

In 1991, terrorists hijacked a Bar Association charter flight. The terrorists issued a press release. They said that, until their demands were met, they would release one lawyer per hour.

~

Irv Karpinski, a noted trial lawyer, was well known for his exhaustive preparation and his exhausting opening statements. In one case, he droned on for two hours until the judge interrupted him. "Mr. Karpinski," said the frustrated judge, "I've been listening to you for over an hour now, and I must confess that I'm none the wiser for it." "That is undoubtedly the case, Your Honor," responded Karpinski with a broad smile on his face, "but you are now far better informed."

~

Phil Williams, the trial lawyer, came dragging in after a hard day at work. He said to his concerned wife Hilda, "It was a terrible day in court—I exhibited moral outrage when I meant to show righteous indignation."

~

Karpinski and Rogers had never liked one another. The divorce trial in which they appeared gave them many opportunities for personal invective. Tired of their constant bickering, the judge called both attorneys to the bench. "Your Honor," began Rogers, the counsel for the husband, "I must object strongly to the comportment of my distinguished colleague, who was clearly badgering the witness. It is clear as day that he has not the slightest acquaintance with the Bill of Rights." "Oh yeah?" retorted Karpinski, his opponent. "I happen to know the Bill of Rights by heart." "Is that so? Well, I've got a hundred dollars that says you can't get out the first sentence." At that Karpinski drew himself up to his full five feet three inches and began, "I pledge allegiance to the flag . . ." "Darn it," muttered Rogers, reaching for his wallet. "I was sure you didn't know it!"

~

Ken Morley, a burly construction worker, watched in horror as the heavy beam fell from the crane and landed on a well-dressed passerby. Morley rushed to the victim, carefully removed the beam, and said, "Hang in there, fellow. Are you badly hurt?" "How should I know?" snapped the victim. "I'm a doctor, not a lawyer."

~

Ludlow Whittaker went into the Chamber of Commerce in Dickinson, North Dakota. He appeared frazzled and desperate. He asked Flora Iverson, the Chamber's receptionist, "Is there a criminal attorney in town?" Flora replied, "Yes, but we can't prove it yet."

~

Mark Twain was at a dinner party where he gave one of his customary after-dinner speeches. When he had finished, a prominent lawyer stood up, shoved his hands in his pockets and said, "Doesn't it strike this company as unusual

"Of course, I can't actually prove anyone's a sinner, as my attorney here will attest . . ."

that a professional humorist should be so funny?" Mark Twain came back with "Doesn't it strike this company as unusual that a lawyer should have both hands in his own pockets?"

~

Marshall Thunderbund made an appointment with Lee Mendelbaum, the famous defense attorney, after his employer had discovered that he had embezzled millions from the company pension fund. Marshall was fearful of going to prison, but the attorney told him, "Don't worry. You'll never go to jail with all that money." The lawyer was right. When Marshall went to prison, he didn't have a dime.

~

The down-on-his-luck attorney was sitting in the bar, nursing his beer. "How's it going?" asked a colleague. "Terrible. I just was evicted from my office. I wrote up the papers myself. I never would have done it if I hadn't needed the money so bad."

~

The minute you read something you can't understand, you can almost be sure it was drawn up by a lawyer.   —Will Rogers

L

UNDERSTANDING LEGALESE

Consider the following:
1. Matters should be held in abeyance pending the meeting in order to determine whether the facts there adduced will warrant a further extension.
2. The administrator has ample power now to frame the remedy to take into consideration any unconscionable delay in bringing a complaint to the attention of the administrator.
3. That dicta, however, is clearly inapposite.
4. Unilateral nullification of the terms and conditions of the expiring agreement absent bona fide impasse is prohibited.

O.K., what they mean in plain English is:
1. We should wait to act until we see what we find out at our next meeting, where we might decide to put it off again.
2. The administrator has the power to decide how to handle late complaints.
3. You are citing the wrong thing.
4. One party cannot leave the contract early without a good reason.

When the armies of lawyers get through settling an estate, the friendless beneficiary doesn't have a legacy to stand on.   —Francis Duffy

Your hourly rate is pretty much determined by how well you dress. No one is going to rent your brain for $300 an hour if you're wearing droopy white socks and a skinny tie, unless skinny ties are in this week. I forget. Keeping up with necktie styles is every bit as important as keeping up with the latest court decisions. Thank God for pin-striped suits, vests and suspenders that have a little more fashion longevity. Looking cool and relaxed in these clothes is even more important than the dress itself. Lawyers who perspire when wearing vests never get their billing much past $100 an hour.

—Herbert I. Kavet

SIZING UP CLIENTS

This is one of the most important skills a lawyer can have. No one wants to represent deadbeats or someone who will always whine about the bill. Likewise a client who calls on weekends and evenings is a terrible inconvenience.

Clients to Avoid:

1. People who ask your going rate before shaking hands.
2. Those who bring a box of tissues to the first meeting.
3. Anyone recommended by your parents.
4. Anyone who brings a pet to your office.
5. Ones that have been fired by four other lawyers.
6. People who claim to have gone to law school.
7. Sales types who want to barter rather than pay.
8. Anyone who brings a video camera with them.
9. Everyone who promises they'll refer more business to you.

Herbert I. Kavet

One lawyer successfully defended a client in a scandalous and highly publicized trial. At a party after the trial ended, he was cornered by an indignant woman. "Is there no client so low, so despicable, so outrageous, that you wouldn't take the case?" she demanded. "It all depends," said the lawyer equably. "What did you do?"

Hell hath no fury like a lawyer of a woman scorned.

The two law partners were having lunch one day, when one of them suddenly jumped up and exclaimed, "Oh, no! I've got to get back to the office! I left the safe unlocked!" The other lawyer looked at his partner calmly and replied, "What are you worried about? We're both here."

~

Lawyer to young client: "You should have signed a contract. A high-five just isn't binding." —Sidney Harris, *So Sue Me!*

~

Definition of a prenuptial agreement: Paper a lawyer prepares to protect the party of the first part from the party of the second part should they discover the party's over. —Rheta Grimsley Johnson, Scripps Howard News Service

~

An investment counselor went out on her own. She was shrewd and diligent, so business kept coming in, and pretty soon she realized she needed an in-house counsel, so she began interviewing young lawyers. "As I'm sure you can understand," she started off with one of the first applicants, "in a business like this, our personal integrity must be beyond question." She leaned forward. "Mr. Peterson, are you an honest lawyer?" "Honest?" replied the job prospect. "Let me tell you something about honest. Why, I'm so honest that my father lent me fifteen thousand dollars for my education, and I paid back every penny the minute I tried my very first case." "Impressive. And what sort of case was that?" The lawyer squirmed in his seat and admitted, "He sued me for the money."

~

Always read the small print—and that goes for lawyers too. A letter sent out by City Attorneys' Association of Los Angeles County announced that the group's next monthly luncheon would be held at a restaurant on South Flower Street. Price: $10 per legal eagle. "No better bargain exists," the letter said. "Find one and your money is cheerfully refunded." A notation at the bottom of the letter read: "Offer limited to bargains within a 10-foot radius of South Flower Street. Offer may be revoked at any time. Offer is hereby revoked."

—Steve Harvey, *Los Angeles Times*

LEADERSHIP

If you want to lead the orchestra, you must turn your back on the crowd.

~

Some church members rise to the occasion, while others merely hit the ceiling.

A railroad agent in India had been reprimanded for making decisions without orders from headquarters. One day his superior received the following startling telegram: "Tiger on platform eating conductor. Wire instructions."

LIBRARIES

Abraham Lincoln once walked 20 miles to borrow a book. Now they close libraries to celebrate his birthday. —Laura Baker, *Quote*

Actual reference queries reported by American and Canadian library reference desk workers:

- "Do you have books here?"
- "Do you have a list of all the books written in the English language?"
- "Do you have a list of all the books I've ever read?"
- "I'm looking for Robert James Waller's book, 'Waltzing through Grand Rapids'." (Actual title wanted: "Slow Waltz in Cedar Bend.")
- "Do you have that book by Rushdie: 'Satanic Nurses'?" (Actual title: "Satanic Verses")
- "Where is the reference desk?" This was asked of a person sitting at a desk who had, hanging above her head, a sign saying "REFERENCE DESK"!
- "I was here about three weeks ago looking at a cookbook that cost $39.95. Do you know which one it is?"
- "Which outlets in the library are appropriate for my hairdryer?"
- "Can you tell me why so many famous Civil War battles were fought on National Park sites?"
- "Do you have any books with photographs of dinosaurs?"
- "I need a color photograph of George Washington [Christopher Columbus, King Arthur, Moses, Socrates, etc.]"
- "I need a photocopy of Booker T. Washington's birth certificate."
- "I need to find out Ibid's first name for my bibliography."
- "Why don't you have any books by Ibid? He's written a lot of important stuff."
- "I'm looking for information on carpal tunnel syndrome. I think I'm having trouble with it in my neck."
- "Is the basement upstairs?" (Asked at First Floor Reference Desk)
- "I am looking for a list of laws that I can break that would send me back to jail for a couple of months."

LIES

The biggest lie in America, according to Norm Chad of *Sports Illustrated* is: "The game's almost over, honey, I'll be there in a minute."

The principal difference between a cat and a lie is that a cat has only nine lives. —Mark Twain

The people who golf have a big advantage over the people who fish. When golfers lie, at least they don't have to show anything to prove it.

—Ron Dentinger

She tells enough white lies to ice a wedding cake. —Margot Asquith

A minister told his congregation, "Next week I plan to preach about the sin of lying. To help you understand my sermon, I want you all to read Mark 17." The following Sunday, as he prepared to deliver his sermon, the minister asked for a show of hands. He wanted to know how many had read Mark 17. Every hand went up. The minister smiled and said, "Mark has only sixteen chapters. I will now proceed with my sermon on the sin of lying."

LIFE

As Arnot L. Sheppard, Jr. once remarked: "Just when you think you see the whole picture of life clearly, the channel changes."

Life may have no meaning. Or even worse, it may have a meaning of which I disapprove. —Ashleigh Brilliant

Life is a public performance on the violin, in which you must learn the instrument as you go along. —E. M. Forester

Among the graffiti on a subway wall: "This life is a test. It is only a test. Had this been an actual life you would have received instructions as to what to do and where to go."

Says one humorist: " Life is unfair. I lost my car keys at a ball game and never found them. I lost my sunglasses at the beach and never found them. I lost my socks in the washing machine and never found them. I lost three pounds on a diet—I found them and five more."

Life is what happens to you while you're busy planning more important things.

Some people just can't enjoy life; the first half of their lives are spent blaming their troubles on their parents and the second half on their children.

—Rev. Denis R. Fakes

I try to take one day at a time, but sometimes several days attack me at once.
—Ashleigh Brilliant

The seven ages of man are spills, drills, thrills, bills, ills, pills, and wills.
—Richard Needham

We're not primarily put on this earth to see through one another, but to see one another through.   —Peter De Vries

The first half of life consists of the capacity to enjoy without the chance; the last half consists of the chance without the capacity.   —Mark Twain

Life resembles a novel more often than novels resemble life.   —George Sand

If all the world's a stage, why do only half of us wear makeup?   —Brad Stein

After taking tea with a parishioner, the bishop said, "I am glad to see in what a comfortable way you are living." "Oh, bishop," replied the man, "if you want to know how we really live, you must come when you're not here."
—Helen Howe, *The Gentle Americans*

Life is like a cobweb, not an organization chart.   —Ross Perot

Life is like a dog-sled team. If you ain't the lead dog, the scenery never changes.
—Lewis Grizzard

Life is a lot like a high-school algebra class. Every time you get one problem solved, the teacher is waiting to give you another.

A first grade teacher collected old, well-known proverbs. She gave each child in her class the first half of a proverb, and asked them to come up with the rest. Here are some choice replies.

- Ambition is a poor excuse for . . . not having enough sense to be lazy.
- As you shall make your bed so . . . shall you mess it up.
- Better be safe than . . . punch a 5th grader.

- Strike while the . . . bug is close.
- Its always darkest before . . . daylight savings time
- You can lead a horse to water but . . . how?
- Don't bite the hand that . . . looks dirty.
- A miss is as good as a . . . Mr.
- You can't teach an old dog new . . . math.
- It you lie down with the dogs . . . you'll stink in the morning.
- The pen is mightier than the . . . pigs
- An idle mind is . . . the best way to relax.
- Where there's smoke, there's . . . pollution.
- Happy the bride who . . . gets all the presents.
- A penny saved is . . . not much.
- Two's company, three's . . . the musketeers.
- Laugh and the whole world laughs with you, cry and . . . you have to blow your nose.
- Children should be seen and not . . . spanked or grounded.
- When the blind leadeth the blind . . . get out of the way.

After I'm dead I'd rather have people ask why I have no monument than why I have one.   —Cato the Elder (234–149 B.C., AKA Marcus Porcius Cato)

L

There are only two ways to live your life. One is as though nothing is a miracle. The other is as though everything is a miracle.   —Albert Einstein

"Your hour will be 3 P.M. next Tuesday."

A sign on a hospital bulletin board read: "Research Shows that the First Five Minutes of Life Can Be Most Risky." Penciled underneath was this anonymous postscript: "The Last Five Minutes Ain't So Hot Either."   —AP

The prime of life is that fleeting time between green and over-ripe.

—Cullen Hightower

LIGHT BULBS

How many pollsters does it take to screw in a light bulb?

Two. One to hold the ladder and one to turn the light bulb. Plus or minus 4 percent.

—Tom Brokaw

How many Stanford researchers does it take to screw in a light bulb?

Three. One to hold the ladder, one to turn the bulb, and one to bill the government for the house.

How many executives does it take to change a light bulb?

Five. One to change the bulb, and four to yank the ladder out from under him.

How many graduate students does it take to change a light bulb?

One—but it takes him nine years.

How many auto mechanics does it take to change a light bulb?

Two. One to screw in the wrong-sized bulb and one to replace the burned-out socket.

How many mystery writers does it take to change a light bulb?

Only one, but it needs a spectacular twist at the end.

How many surrealists does it take to change a light bulb?

Two. One to turn the giraffe and the other to fill the bathtub with multicolored clocks.

LIMITS

Some of our limits exist only in our own minds. A couple of years ago, during a sports clinic at Princeton High School in Cincinnati, Ohio, Dan Woodruff, the softball coach, lent his office to Dave Redding, the strength coach for the Cleveland Browns. Dave wanted to shower before his scheduled appearance at the clinic. Dan showed Dave the facilities, then left while he was in the shower. When Dave finished showering, he went to leave the office, but found he couldn't open the door! He wrote a note and slipped it under the door, then sat back and waited. When Dan went back to his office about an hour later, he heard someone yelling, "Help, help!" Then he found the card outside his door. He opened the door and found Redding. "What's the problem?" Dan asked. Dave told him that he had been locked inside for over an hour. Dan told him the door wasn't locked, that he had only to push a button on the handle to make it open. "We laughed about it a lot when we walked down the hall," said Dan. The 230-pound strength coach of a professional football team being trapped behind an unlocked door.

LISTENING

Good listeners are more than just popular. After a while, they know something.
                                            —*Executive Speechwriter Newsletter*

His thoughts were slow,
His words were few,
And never formed to glisten.
But he was a joy to all his friends—
You should have heard him listen.

LIVING

Let us endeavor so to live that when we come to die even the undertaker will be sorry.   —Mark Twain

Live so that you wouldn't be ashamed to sell the family parrot to the town gossip.   —Will Rogers

LONELINESS

You know what's a real bummer? When you send your picture to the lonely hearts club and they send it back with a note saying: "We're not that lonely."
                                            —Ron Dentinger

LOSER

Believe it or not, the guy who got the bright idea to change the formula for Coca-Cola (probably the most successful product ever to be marketed) still sells Coca-Cola . . . only now he sells it in the bleachers at Cubs games.

LOSERS

The door-to-door salesman reported to his sales manager, I got two orders today—"Get out!" and "Stay out!"

~

What a loser . . . he's the kind of guy who asks for a wine list at McDonalds.

~

There are two sorts of losers—the good loser, and the one who can't act.
—Laurence J. Peter, *Peter's People*

LOSING

It doesn't matter if you win or lose, until you lose.

LOSS

One man's loss is another man's umbrella.   —Sam Ewing in *Mature Living*

LOST

A business man had a tiring day on the road. He checked into his hotel and, because he was concerned the dining room might soon close, left his luggage in the checkroom and went immediately to eat. After a leisurely dinner, he reclaimed his luggage and then realized he had forgotten his room number. He went back to the desk and told the clerk on duty, "My name is W. A. Rolke. Will you please tell my what room I am in?" "Certainly," said the clerk, "you're in the lobby."
—W. A. Rolke

LOVE

By the time you swear you're his,
Shivering and sighing,
And he vows his passion is
Infinite, undying—
Lady, make a note of this:
One of you is lying.

—Dorothy Parker

~

I love her for what she is. Wealthy.

~

Many a man in love with a dimple makes the mistake of marrying the whole girl.
—Ring Lardner

~

Two Laws of Love:

1. You will always fall in love and marry someone with the opposite body temperature.

2. If you can't stand his mother and he can't stand yours then you're bound to get married.

❧

Love conquers all thing except poverty and a toothache.   —Mae West

❧

Love is like hash. You have to have confidence in it to enjoy it.   —Bob Hope

❧

Love is insanity with a collaborator.

❧

A woman should marry for love and she should get married until she finds it.   —Elizabeth Taylor

❧

It's easier to love humanity as a whole than to love one's neighbor.   —Eric Hoffer

❧

Love is the triumph of imagination over intelligence.   —H. L. Mencken

❧

Love is staying awake all night with a sick child—or a healthy adult.
                                                              —David Frost

❧

Folks today are in love with love. One fellow bought up every book he saw on the physical art of love. One day he was in an airport and in a little shop he saw a book with the intriguing title, *How to Hug*. He was in such a hurry to catch his plane, he didn't have time to examine it before he paid for it. It wasn't until he was in the air, that he had a chance to see what he had bought— the fifth volume of an encyclopedia.

❧

Love is a fire. But whether it is going to warm your heart or burn down your house, you can never tell.   —Joan Crawford

❧

Love is like a soft mattress: It's easy to fall into, but not so easy to get out of.
                                        —Gladiola Montana and Texas Bix Bender

❧

Love is a word consisting of two vowels, two consonants, and two fools.
                                                              —Jeff Rovin

Love is what happens to men and women who don't know each other.
—W. Somerset Maugham

Love is the only disease that makes you feel better. —Sam Shepard

If you're looking for a man who's attractive, funny, smart, self-confident, sensitive, sexy, affectionate, and romantic, go to the movies. —Bruce Lansky

Love is much nicer to be in than an automobile accident, a tight girdle, a higher tax bracket, or a holding pattern over Philadelphia. —Judith Viorst

I can see from your utter misery, from your eagerness to misunderstand each other, and from your thoroughly bad temper that this is the real thing.
—Peter Ustinov

Be wary of puppy love; it can lead to a dog's life. —Gladiola Montana

The only place you're sure to find love is at the end of a letter from your mother. —Bruce Lansky

Many a man has fallen in love with a girl in a light so dim he would not have chosen a suit by it. —Maurice Chevalier

Love starts when you sink into his arms and ends with your arms in his sink.

In love, you pay as you leave. —Mark Twain

My true love brought me flowers tonight, and I'm all smiles and song. I guess I'm doing something right—or he's done something wrong!
—Maureen Cannon

I Love You Only Valentine cards: Now available in multipacks.
—Sign on a drug store display

Friendship is love minus sex and plus reason. Love is friendship plus sex and minus reason.   —Mason Cooley

❧

Erotic love begins with separateness, and ends in oneness. Motherly love begins with oneness, and leads to separateness.   —Erich Fromm

❧

I never liked the men I loved, and I never loved the men I liked.
                                                                              —Fanny Brice

❧

We always believe our first love is our last, and our last love is our first.
                                                                    —George Whyte-Melville

❧

Nothing takes the taste out of peanut butter like unrequited love.
                                                                            —Charlie Brown

❧

There is no sincerer love than the love of food.   —George Bernard Shaw

❧

When I fall in love . . . Falling in love is awfully simple. Falling out of love is simply awful.

❧

On Sunday, Pastor Harold delivered a fine sermon about love, forgiveness and tempering anger. During the week he spent long, hard hours building a wooden frame to hold cement for a driveway. On Saturday he poured the cement, went to the shed for a tool, and on his return found a neighbor boy walking in the new cement. As he sternly lectured the boy, a parishioner watched with interest before asking, "What happened to your advice on Sunday—love, forgiveness, understanding?" After a few moments the minister answered, "You know, it's far easier to love in the abstract than in the concrete."

LUCK

In 1910 Olav Olavson, a Swedish citizen, fell upon hard times and decided to sell his body for medical research after his death to the Karolinska Institute in Stockholm. The following year he inherited a fortune and resolved to buy himself back. The institute refused to sell its rights to his body, went to court, and won possession of it. Moreover, the institute obtained damages, since Olav had had two teeth pulled out without asking their permission as ultimate owner of his body.　　—David Frost, *Book Of The World's Worst Decisions*

Man to friend: "With my luck, by the time I build a better mousetrap, mice will be declared an endangered species."　　—Al Bernstein

I find that the harder I work, the more luck I seem to have.

—Thomas Jefferson

--- **M** ---

MADNESS

Madness takes its toll. Please have exact change.

A friend of mine told me this story: One day an acquaintance of his family mentioned to his mother: "Does everybody in your family suffer from insanity?" "Not at all, not at all," she smiled, "in fact we all enjoy it."

—Father Mike Malone

MAE WEST

She's the kind of woman who climbed the ladder of success—wrong by wrong.

—Mae West

MAGIC

So there's this magician working on a small cruise ship. He's been doing his routines every night for a year or two now. The audiences appreciate him, and they change over often enough that he doesn't have to worry too much about new tricks. However, there's this parrot who sits in the back row and watches him night after night, year after year. Finally, the parrot figures out how the tricks work and starts giving it away for the audience. For example, when the magician makes a bouquet of flowers disappear, the parrot squawks , "Behind his back! Behind his back!" Well, the magician get really annoyed at this, but he doesn't know what to do. The parrot belongs to the Captain, so he can't just kill it. One day, the ship springs a leak and sinks. The magician manages to swim to a plank of wood floating by and grabs on. The parrot is sitting on the other end of the plank. The just stare at each other and drift. They drift for 3 days and still don't speak. On the morning of the fourth day, the parrot looks over at the magician and says: "OK, I give up. Where did you hide the ship?"

MANAGED HEALTH CARE

For ten years, my wife worked for an HMO (Health Maintenance Organization). In her circles, the following story is making the rounds: The scene is heaven, just outside the Pearly Gates, and three distinguished looking men are waiting to request admittance. Finally, St. Peter arrives and asks each man to identify himself and state his greatest contribution to the human race. The first man says, "I am Christian Barnard and I performed the first successful heart transplant. Because of my work, thousands of lives have been saved." St. Peter seems duly impressed and says, "You may enter into your eternal rest." The gates open, celestial music is heard, and Dr. Barnard disappears. The second man states, "I am Jonas Salk and I discovered the polio vaccine which has saved millions of lives." Once again, St. Peters seems impressed and says, "You may enter into your eternal rest." The gates open, celestial music is heard, and Dr. Salk disappears. The third man says, "I am John Nelson and I invented the notion of managed health care. Because of me millions of dollars have been saved." St. Peter strokes his beard and says, "You, too, may enter into your eternal rest—but only for three days."

M

SIGNS YOU'VE JOINED A CHEAP HMO:

- Directions to your doctor's office include, "Take a left when you enter the trailer park."
- Tongue depressors taste faintly of Fudgesicle.
- Only item listed under Preventive Care feature of coverage is "an apple a day."
- Your "primary care physician" is wearing the pants you gave to Goodwill last month.
- "Patient responsible for 200% of out-of-network charges" is not a typo.
- The only expense covered 100% is embalming.
- With your last HMO, your arthritis pills didn't come in different colors with little "M"'s on them.

MANNERS

Clark Clifford was White House counsel in the administration of Harry Truman, and Secretary of Defense in 1968 and 1969. Clifford was once a guest at a Washington dinner party. He politely turned to a woman seated next to him. "Did I get your name correctly?" he asked. "Are you Emily Post?" "Yes," she replied. He said, ". . . the world-renowned authority on manners?" She said, "Yes, why do you ask?" "Because," he said, "you have just eaten my salad."

At the reference desk of a public library, a young man asked for a book on marriage. The librarian brought him one. When he saw the title, he seemed flustered, and said it was not what he wanted. Did we have anything else on marriage? The second book she brought, more explicit than the first, caused him to blush. It still was not quite what he wanted. The librarian then brought him a very detailed marriage manual. Before delivering it, however, she said to another staff member, "If he can't handle this, he better give up the whole thing." He looked through it, turned deep red and blurted, "All I want to know is—am I supposed to wear a white tie!"

MARK TWAIN

One of Mark Twain's bad habits was calling on neighbors without his collar or necktie. One afternoon upon his return from a neighborhood visit in the usual degree of undress, his wife scolded him for his negligence. Clemens

"My vow of silence has lasted twenty-six years—but now you're standing on my foot!"

departed to his study and in a few moments sent a small package back to the neighbor's house. An accompanying note read somewhat as follows: "Just a while ago I visited you minus my collar and tie. The missing articles are enclosed. Will you kindly gaze at them for 30 minutes and then return them to me?"   —Msgr. Arthur Tonne, *Jokes Priests Can Tell*, Vol. 4

MARRIAGE

A man may be a fool and not know it, but not if he is married.

—H. L. Mencken

~

After five years of marriage, Amber and Ed began having problems. They argued so bitterly that Ed decided he wanted a divorce. Ed went to see a lawyer. At their first session, the lawyer asked Ed, "What first attracted you to this woman?" Ed replied, "Her forthrightness, straightforwardness and frankness." The counselor then asked, "Why then are you now telling me you want to end the relationship?" Ed answered, "Her forthrightness, straightforwardness and frankness."

~

All of a sudden I noticed she was saying my daughter, my son, my silver, my furniture, my house, and your friends, your troubles, your worries, your problems, and your fault.   —H. Martin

~

Henrietta Watson and her husband Wallace had a notoriously troubled marriage. Wally was the owner of the only bank in town but he also the town's most tight-fisted miser. His constant bargain hunting and his insistence that Henrietta curtail her spending was driving the woman crazy. One day she found a note addresed to her in her mail box, which read: "Leave ten thousand dollars under the roots of the dogwood tree in the town square tonight, or we'll kidnap your husband and you'll never see him again." Henrietta left a reply at the dogwood tree, which stated: "I haven't got a hundred dollars, let alone ten thousand, and I'm counting on you boys to keep your promise."

~

In the old days, men rode chargers. Now they marry them.   —Philip Whlie

~

It is more blessed to give than to receive—for example, wedding presents.

—H. L. Mencken

Tommy Lee asked Pastor Parkes, "Reverend, am I right in assuming that the Bible says it's wrong to profit from other people's mistakes?" Pastor Parkes replied, "That is substantially correct." Tommy Lee demanded, "In that case, how about refunding the twenty dollars I paid you for marrying us last year?"

~

My friend Harry was complaining to me recently. His lament: "My wife, a registered nurse, once fussed over every pain or mishap that came my way. Recently, however, I got an indication that the honeymoon is over. I was about to fix the attic fan, and as I lifted myself from the ladder into the attic, I scratched my forehead on a crossbeam. Crawling along, I picked up splinters in both hands, and I cut one hand replacing the fan belt. On the way down the ladder, I missed the last two rungs and turned my ankle. When I limped into the kitchen, my wife took one look and said, 'Are those your good pants?'"

~

Cousin Roberta recalls: "One evening I drove my husband's car to the shopping mall. On my return, I noticed how dusty the outside of his car was and cleaned it up a bit. When I finally entered the house, I called out, 'The woman who loves you the most in the world just cleaned your headlights and windshield.' My husband looked up and said, 'Mom's here?'"

~

Greg Ladego said to his unmarried daughter's boyfriend, "The man who marries my daughter will get a prize." "Okay," said the young man, "but let me see the prize first."

"See any garage sales in that town down there?"

My father's Aunt Ida was at a charity ball and was boasting to a friend about her new diamond ring. "It's the third most valuable diamond in the world!" she boasted. "The first is the Hope Diamond, the second is the Kohinoor Diamond, and then comes this—the Streiker Diamond!" "Unfortunately," she continued, "the owner of the famous Streiker Diamond must also accept the famous Streiker Curse." "What's the Streiker Curse?" her friend asked. "Mr. Streiker," Ida sighed.

~

There is something magical about the fact that success almost always comes faster to the guy your wife almost married.

~

My parents want me to get married. They don't care who any more, as long as he doesn't have a pierced ear, that's all they think about. I think men who have pierced ears are better prepared for marriage. They've experienced pain and bought jewelry.   —Rita Rudner

~

Marriage means commitment. Of course, so does insanity.

~

M

A smart husband buys his wife fine china so she won't trust him to wash it.

~

I married Miss Right. I just didn't know her first name was Always.

~

First friend: "You are wearing your wedding ring on the wrong finger."
Second friend: "I married the wrong man."

~

I haven't spoken to my mother-in-law for eighteen months—I don't like to interrupt her.   —Ken Dodd

~

An elderly man and his wife decide to separate. Before being allowed to do so legally, the Family Court insisted they undergo some marriage counseling to see if their union could be saved. The therapist did her best, but to no avail. The old folks were absolutely determined to go through with separation leading to divorce. Finally, in some desperation, the therapist said to the husband, "But you're ninety-five and your wife is ninety-three. You've been married for seventy-two years! Why do you want to separate now?" To which the wife replied, "We haven't been able to stand each other for the last forty-six years. But we thought we should wait until all the children died before we split up."

~

The only thing my wife and I have in common is that we got married on the same day.   —Ron Dentinger

~

The neighbors seem to have the perfect marriage. He'd rather play golf than eat, and she'd rather go to auctions than cook. They are really addicted. In his sleep he often hollers out, "Fore," and she answers, "Four-fifty."

—Ron Dentinger

~

Only two things are necessary to keep one's wife happy. The first is to let her think she's having her own way. The second is to let her have it.

—Lyndon B. Johnson

~

After issuing driver's licenses for 20 years, my uncle Hank was transferred to the marriage-license bureau. Almost at once, he was in trouble. Young couples were leaving his desk red-faced and angry. His supervisor asked what was wrong. "I can't seem to help it," sputtered Hank. "I just can't get over the habit of asking whether they want the license for business or for pleasure!"

~

Uncle Marty explains: "My wife of twenty years and I have very little in common. I'm a big city boy; she's a small town girl. I like spicy food; she doesn't. I dig action and suspense movies. She goes for romance and comedy. Nothing in common. Yet we are deeply in love. It just goes to show: You don't get harmony when everybody sings the same note."

~

My father's Aunt Frieda married into a wealthy, prominent family in Long Island. She and her husband have only one daughter, whom they named Marjorie. After her graduation from an expensive finishing school and Sarah Lawrence, Marjorie went to Tanzania as a Peace Corps volunteer. Frieda was proud of her daughter's sense of noblesse oblige but was concerned that her daughter had not been fully prepared by her education to occupy a place in her parents' strata. When Marjorie's term with the Peace Corps was nearly complete, the young woman sent her parents a message announcing that she would be bringing her new husband home with her. Her mother and father waited with excited anticipation at the airport gate. Their daughter emerged from the plane on the arm of a man about seven feet tall, who was adorned in feathers, beads, skulls, tigers' teeth, and assorted pouches of magical potions around his neck. He even had a bone through his nose and rings in his ears. The mother fainted. As the father held his now unconscious wife, he shouted to his daughter, "No, no, dear. We said we wanted you to marry a RICH doctor."

~

I married her for her looks, but not the ones she's been giving me lately!

~

My dad says, "The cooing stops with the honeymoon; the billing goes on forever!"

~

My wife and I have an agreement that works . . . she is responsible for the small decisions, and I am responsible for the big ones. This means that she decides things like where to take our next vacation, the color of our next car, and the construction budget for adding on the new family room. I decide whether or not the President should extend most favored nation trading status to China, how high the Federal Reserve should go with short-term interest rates, and the timetable for the elimination of CFCs from automobile air conditioners.

M

~

Aunt Marlene had a troubled marriage. She sought the advice of one of those phone-in psychics. The psychic told her, "Prepare yourself for widowhood. Your husband is about to die a violent death." Marlene sighed deeply and asked, "Will I be acquitted?"

~

A pessimist defines both bigamy and marriage as having one wife too many.

~

Do you know what it means to come home at night to a woman who'll give you a little understanding, a little love, a little affection? It means you've wandered into the wrong home!

~

Actress Shelley Winters advises: "Before you marry a guy, have lunch with his ex-wife."

I have been married so long I'm on my third bottle of Tabasco sauce.

—Susan Vass

Marriage is the only adventure open to the cowardly. —Voltaire

Marriage was the first union to defy management. —Martin A. Ragaway

Today, if a man's wife looks like a new woman, chances are she is.

—Jeff Rovin

Marriage is the alliance of two people, one of whom never remembers birthdays and the other who never forgets them. —Ogden Nash

Being a husband is just like any other job—it's much easier if you like your boss.

The
BORDERLINE ™

By Gabe Martin
borderln@cts.com

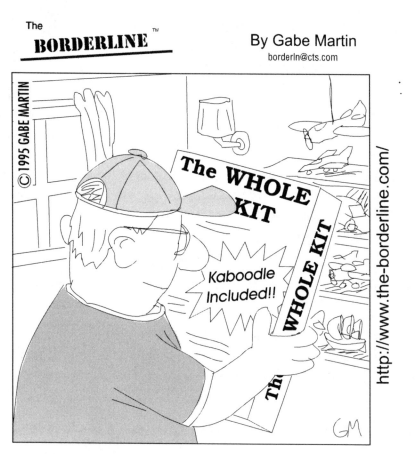

© 1995 GABE MARTIN

http://www.the-borderline.com/

A college freshman was expounding on her idea of the perfect mate. "The man I marry," she said, "must shine among company, be musical, tell jokes, sing, dance, and stay at home." Her boyfriend replied, "It sounds to me like you don't want a husband. What you want is a television set!"

My old uncle Les says, "Somebody told my wife that I had been chasing women." She said, "So what? I've got a dog that chases cars, but he wouldn't know what to do with one if he caught it."

The formula for a happy marriage? It's the same as the one for living in California: when you find a fault, don't dwell on it.

—Jay Trachman, *One to One*

"Do you know what today is?" asked the wife of her husband who was hurrying off to work. Hesitating only a moment and flashing a smile he replied, "Sure, I remember." He didn't propose being caught again . . . forgetting the date of his wedding anniversary . . . so that night he returned home with some candy, flowers and a gift. His wife was overjoyed! "You see," he said smugly, "I did remember what day this is." She laughed and giggled: "Honey, this is the happiest Groundhog Day of my life."

An angry young woman rushed into the clerk's office. In her hand she bore a license. To the clerk she said: "Did you or did you not, issue the license to Albert Briggs for marrying me?" "Yes," I believe I did. "Why?" "Well, what are you going to do about it?" she demanded. "He's escaped."

—*Catholic Workman*

My mother was the old-fashioned kind who was firmly committed to the sanctity of marriage. Just before I got married, she took me aside and said, "I'm not going to give you a long sermon. Just remember one thing: in every marriage, there are grounds for divorce. What you have to do is to keep finding grounds for marriage."

—Lillian Woods

A middle-aged man was sitting on his porch as falling snow swirled all around him. A passing neighbor called out: "Why in the world are you sitting out there in the snow and cold?" The porch-sitter called back: "I have to." "What do you mean . . . I have to?" "Well," declared the man on the porch, "my wife is taking singing lessons, and I don't want the neighbors to think I'm beating her."   —Msgr. Arthur Tonne, *Jokes Priests Can Tell*, vol. 6

❧

The concept of two people living together for twenty-five years without a serious dispute suggests a lack of spirit only to be admired in sheep.

—A. P. Herbert

❧

A woman is getting a sentimental feeling while watching a beautiful love scene in a movie. Her husband leans over and whispers those three little words that are on his mind: "Pass the popcorn."   —Cindy Garner

❧

Mr. and Mrs. Ivers were pushing their cart down the aisle at the supermarket when they spotted an elderly pair walking hand in hand. Said Mrs. Ivers:

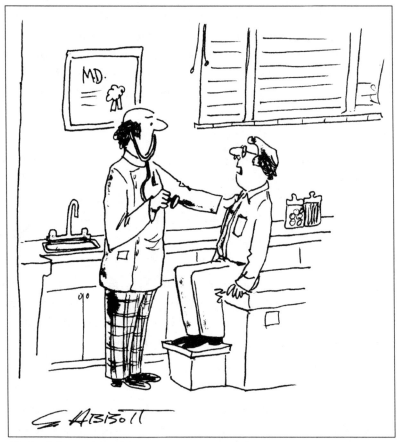

"I don't have a health problem—I just need some advice on hitting out of a sand trap."

"Now, that looks like a happy married couple." "Don't be too sure, dear," replied Mr. Ivers. "They're probably saying the same thing about us."

~

A pastor was called to a local nursing home to perform a wedding. An anxious old man met him at the door. The pastor sat down to counsel the old man and asked several questions. "Do you love her?" The old man replied, "Nope." "Is she a good Christian woman?" "I don't know for sure," the old man answered. "Does she have lots of money?" asked the pastor. "I doubt it." "Then why are you marrying her?" the preacher asked. "'Cause she can drive at night," the old man said.   —George Goldtrap

~

A woman complained to her marriage counselor, "When my husband won a trip for two to Hawaii, he went twice!"   —Martha J. Beckman

~

One of the oldest human needs is having someone to wonder where you are when you don't come home at night.   —Margaret Mead

~

Marriage is like a 7-Eleven. Not much variety, but at 3 A.M., it's always there.

M

~

Woman to marriage counselor: "It was a dating computer that was responsible for our marriage. I'll never understand what the machine saw in him!"
                              —Lichty, North America Syndicate

~

Man confiding to friend: "My wife and I argued so much that we finally saw a marriage counselor. We still argue, but now we call it sharing."
                              —Ivern Ball

~

Man to colleague: "Few things upset my wife. It makes me feel rather special to be one of them."   —*Napa Parts Pups 1992 Joke Book*

~

Marriage is like twirling a baton, turning handsprings or eating with chopsticks. It looks easy until you try it.   —Helen Rowland

~

Just remember: Every man needs a wife. Because you can't blame everything that goes wrong on the government!

Husband to Wife: "Why do you keep reading our marriage license?"
Wife to Husband: "I'm looking for a loophole!"

~

Husband to wife: "I've put up with that intefering old hag for 10 years—your mother will have to go!"
Wife to Husband: "My mother? But I thought she was your mother!"

~

Friend to Wife: "Do you think your husband is hard to please?"
Wife: "I really don't know—I've never tried."

~

Actress Anne Bancroft, who is married to Mel Brooks, maintains: "The best way to get most husbands to do something is to suggest they are too old for it."

~

John bought his new colleague, Peter, home for dinner. As they arrived at the door his wife rushed up, threw her arms around John and kissed him passionately. "My goodness," said Peter, "and how long have you been married?" "Twenty-two years," replied John. "You must have a fantastic marriage if your wife greets you like that after all those years." "Don't be fooled! She only does it to make the dog jealous."

~

Often the difference between a successful marriage and a mediocre one consists of leaving about three things a day unsaid.

~

A happy marriage is the world's best bargain.   —O. A. Batista

~

Love is blind—marriage is the eye-opener.   —Pauline Thomason

~

One wedding guest to another: "It will never last. He's campfire, she's microwave."   —Grindall, King Features

~

A lecturer was giving a talk before a woman's club on life in Egypt, past and present. He stressed how indifferent Egyptians were toward their wives.

"Why," he said, "it's no novelty at all to see a woman and a donkey hitched together over there." "Come to think of it," said a voice from the rear, "it's no novelty in America either."   —*Ottawa Journal*

~

The dear old couple who has been married sixty years were paying a sentimental visit to their home town and paused at one of the street corners. "Isn't it wonderful to remember that we used to meet at this very spot every evening during the first few months we were courting?" the old lady asked, sighing. "I certainly remember, my dear," replied her husband, "but that sign wasn't here then." And he pointed to the notice which read: "DANGEROUS CORNER: Go Slow."   —*Tid-Bits,* London

~

When the late Mr. and Mrs. Henry Ford celebrated their golden wedding anniversary, a reporter asked them, "To what do you attribute your 50 years of successful married life?" "The formula," said Ford, "is the same formula I have always used in making cars—just stick to one model."

—*Nebraska Smoke Eater*

MARRIAGE COUNSELING

Overheard in a marriage counselor's office: "When I don't praise him, he thinks I don't love him and when I do praise him, he thinks he's too good for me."   —Ron Dentinger

M

MATH

Just how much is a billion, anyway?
The number of people who claim they were at Woodstock;
New food products made with oat bran;
How many people have seen Elvis at K-Mart;
Total number of doughnuts eaten by police officers in one year;
Lobbyists in Washington, D.C. (at restaurants alone).   —Ron Rich

~

Back in ancient times a brilliant mathematician came up with the concept of zero. Prior to that there were positive and negative numbers but zero hadn't been used. Knowing that the zero was an important new concept, a dinner was given in honor of the scholar. A banner behind the head table read: "Thanks for nothing."   —Ron Dentinger

~

The first grade teacher was trying to interest her class in arithmetic. "Jimmy," she asked. "If I had two sandwiches and you had two sandwiches, what would we have?" Jimmy answered without hesitation. "A picnic!"   —*Liguorian*

Not everything that can be counted counts, and not everything that counts can be counted. —Albert Einstein

MAXIMS

In my opinion, the only time it's better to give than to receive is if the commodity that's being given is advice. —Ron Dentinger

LAWS TO LIVE BY

- Trust everybody . . . then cut the cards.
- Two wrongs are only the beginning.
- If at first you don't succeed, destroy all evidence that you tried.
- To succeed in politics, it is often necessary to rise above your principles.
- Exceptions prove the rule . . . and wreck the budget.
- Success always occurs in private, and failure in full view.
- Quality assurance doesn't.
- Exceptions always outnumber rules.
- To steal ideas from one person is plagiarism; to steal from many is research.
- No one is listening until you make a mistake.
- He who hesitates is probably right.
- The ideal resume will turn up one day after the position is filled.
- If something is confidential, it will be left in the copier machine.
- One child is not enough, but two children are far too many.
- A clean tie attracts the soup of the day.
- The hardness of the butter is in direct proportion to the softness of the bread. The bag that breaks is the one with the eggs.
- When there are sufficient funds in the checking account, checks take two weeks to clear. When there are insufficient funds, checks clear overnight.
- The book you spent $20.95 for today will come out in paperback tomorrow.
- The more an item costs, the farther you have to send it for repairs.
- You never want the one you can afford.
- Never ask the barber if you need a haircut or a salesman if his is a good price.
- If it says "one size fits all," it doesn't fit anyone.
- You never really learn to swear until you learn to drive.
- The colder the X-ray table, the more of your body is required on it.
- Love letters, business contracts and money due you always arrive three weeks late, whereas junk mail arrives the day it was sent.
- When you drop change at a vending machine, the pennies will fall nearby, while all other coins will roll out of sight.
- The severity of the itch is inversely proportional to the reach.
- Experience is something you don't get until just after you need it.
- Life can be only understood backwards, but it must be lived forwards.
- Interchangeable parts won't.
- No matter which way you go, it's uphill and against the wind.

- If enough data is collected, anything may be proven by statistical methods.
- Work is accomplished by those employees who have not reached their level of incompetence.
- Progress is made on alternative Fridays.
- No man's life, liberty, or property is safe while the legislature is in session.
- The hidden flaw never remains hidden.
- For every action, there is an equal and opposite criticism.
- People who love sausage and respect the law should never watch either of them being made.
- A conclusion is the place where you got tired of thinking.
- When reviewing your notes for a test, the most important ones will be illegible.
- A free agent is anything but.
- The least experienced fisherman always catches the biggest fish.
- Never do card tricks for the group you play poker with.
- The one item you want is never the one on sale.
- The telephone will ring when you are outside the door, fumbling for your keys.
- If only one price can be obtained for a quotation, the price will be unreasonable.

MIXED MAXIMS:

- Don't count your chickens before they cross they road.
- He who laughs first shall be last.
- Mind your own business before pleasure.
- Beauty is only skin deep in the eye of the beholder.—Diane Crosby

M

MEALS

A sign at our hotel gave the hours that meals were served. It read: "Breakfast is served from six to ten. Lunch is served from ten to four. Dinner is served from four to eight." My initial response to this was: "That sure doesn't leave much time for anything else."   —Ron Dentinger

MEANNESS

He is so mean, he won't let his little baby have more than one measle at a time.   —Eugene Field

MEDIA

The hero reveals the possibilities of human nature; the celebrity reveals the possibilities of the media.   —Daniel J. Boorstin, *The Image*

MEDICAL INSURANCE

Insurance is a lot like wearing a hospital gown. You're never covered as much as you think you are.   —Robert Orben, *2500 Jokes To Start 'Em Laughing*

MEDICINE (*See also* DOCTORS)

A lady in the waiting room was complaining bitterly about having to wait so long for the doctor. Seems he took so much time with some patients that he was always behind schedule. "Why don't you change doctors?" another patient asked. "Because," the complainer admitted, "I'm one of the patients he takes so much time with."

~

When Felix, the hypochondriac, died at the age of 96, his tombstone read, "I told you I was sick."

~

Brad went to his doctor for a physical checkup. As he put his shirt back on, he asked, "Well, Doc, do I have to give up wine, women, and song?" "Not exactly, Brad," said the doctor. "You can sing all you want to."

~

He had had much experience of physicians, and said, "The only way to keep your health is to eat what you don't want, drink what you don't like, and do what you'd druther not."   —Mark Twain

~

If you treat a sick child like an adult and a sick adult like a child, everything usually works out pretty well.   —Ruth Carlisle

MEDIOCRITY

Some men are born mediocre, some men achieve mediocrity, and some men have mediocrity thrust upon them.   —Joseph Heller, *Catch-22*

MEETINGS

Belgium's Paul-Henri Spaak was presiding over the first United Nations General Assembly. When it ended, he told his colleagues, "The agenda is exhausted. The secretary-general is exhausted. I am exhausted. At last we have achieved unanimity!"

~

The next time you're in a meeting, look around and identify the yes-butters, the not-nowers and the why-notters. Why-notters move the world.

—Louise Pierson

MEMORY

I'm starting to worry more about getting Alzheimer's than dying . . . but for the life of me I can't remember why.   —Anita Milner

It's sweet to be remembered, but often cheaper to be forgotten.

—Kin Hubbard

A group of French Foreign Legionnaires are marching through the desert. One says to another: "I'm trying to forget about a girl, but it's hard! Her name is 'Sandy.'"

—S. Gross

What's the best thing about losing your memory as you get older? You never have to watch reruns on television.

Aunt Aggie says, "My memory is starting to go. I locked the keys in my car the other day. Fortunately, I had forgotten to get out first."

"We got our new dental benefits!"

My brother Scott's memory is just as bad as mine. We're both convinced we're an only child.

~

Aunt Aggie went to see her physician. She complained, "Doctor, I don't know what to do. You've got to help me. I just can't remember a thing. I've no memory at all. I hear something one minute, and the next minute I forget it." Tell me, what should I do?" Her doctor replied, "Pay in advance!"

~

Aunt Aggie was on an Amtrak train a few months ago. She searched through her purse and pockets for her ticket while the conductor waited patiently. Finally she said, "This is terrible. I know I had a ticket, but for the life of me I can't remember what I did with it." The conductor said, "All is not lost, ma'am. You can pay me directly. Then when you find the ticket you can return it and get your money back." "But that's not the point," said Aunt Aggie in bewilderment. "I don't remember where it is I'm going."

~

Pastor Roger Matthews tells the following story: "We were traveling one summer in the Pocono Mountains and, like a good Presbyterian family, attended church while we were on vacation. One lazy Sunday we found our way to a little Methodist Church. It was a hot day and the folks were nearly out in the pews. The preacher was preaching on and on until, all of a sudden, he said, 'The best years of my life have been spent in the arms of another man's wife.' The congregation let out a gasp, came to immediate attention, and the dozing deacon in the back row dropped his hymnbook. Then the preacher said, 'It was my mother.' The congregation tittered a little and managed to follow along as the sermon concluded. I filed this trick away in my memory, a great way to get the congregation's attention back when it has been lost. Sure enough, the next summer, on a lazy Sunday, I was preaching and the flies were buzzing around and the ushers were sinking lower and lower in their seats in the back row until I could hardly see them. Then I remembered our experience in the Pocono Mountains, and I said in a booming voice, 'The best years of my life have been spent in the arms of another man's wife.' Sure enough, I had their attention. One of the ushers in the back row sat up so fast he hit his head on the back of the pew in front of him. I had them. But you know something, I forgot what came next. All I could think to say was, 'And for the life of me, I can't remember her name!'"

~

If you can look back on your life with contentment, you have one of man's most precious gifts—a selective memory.
                                                                                            —Jim Fiebig

MEN

I'm at the point where I want a man in my life—but not in my house. Just come in, attach the VCR, and get out.   —Joy Behar

Life isn't fair to us men. When we are born, our mothers get all the compliments and the flowers. When we are married, our brides get the presents and the publicity. When we die, our widows get the insurance and the winters in Florida.

—*Viking Vacuum*

If you want to get rid of a man whom you have not been seeing very long, I suggest this: Say, "I love you . . . I want to marry you . . . I want to have your children." Sometimes they leave skid marks.   —Rita Rudner

ELEVEN-STEP GUIDE TO BEING HANDY AROUND THE HOUSE

M

1. If you can't find a screwdriver, use a knife. If you break off the tip, it's an improved screwdriver.
2. Try to work alone. An audience is rarely any help.
3. Despite what you may have been told by your mother, praying and cursing are both helpful in home repair . . . but only if you are working alone.
4. Work in the kitchen whenever you can . . . many fine tools are there, it's warm and dry, and you are close to the refrigerator.
5. If it's electronic, get a new one . . . or consult a twelve-year-old.
6. Stay simple minded: Get a new battery; replace the bulb or fuse; see if the tank is empty; try turning it to the "on" switch; or just paint over it.
7. Always take credit for miracles. If you dropped the alarm clock while taking it apart and it suddenly starts working, you have healed it.
8. Regardless of what people say, kicking, pounding, and throwing sometimes DOES help.
9. If something looks level, it is level.
10. If at first you don't succeed, redefine success.
11. Above all, if what you've done is stupid, but it works, then it isn't stupid.

Because men are simple, they are not physically capable of handling more than one task at a time. Women can easily cook dinner, feed the baby, and talk on the phone all at once. Were a man to try this, he would probably explode.   —Roseanne

Writing in 1941, Professor Marjorie Nicholson said, "The fundamental reason that women do not achieve so greatly as men do is that women have no wives."

~

Anyone who believes that men and women have the same mindset hasn't lived on earth. A man thinks that everything he does is wonderful; a woman has doubts. —Margo Kaufman

~

Take care of him. Make him feel important. If you can do that, you'll have a happy and wonderful marriage—like two out of every ten couples.

—Neil Simons, *Barefoot in the Park*

~

Nellie B. Stull, in *Reader's Digest,* 1935: "A man admires the woman who makes him think, but he keeps away from her. He likes the woman who makes

The Curse of Being George Washington.

him laugh. He loves the girl who hurts him. But he marries the woman who flatters him."

~

When he said we were trying to make a fool of him, I could only murmur that the Creator had beat us to it.   —Ilka Chase

~

A good many men still like to think of their wives as they do of their religion: neglected but always there.   —Freya Stark, *The Journey's Echo*

~

Very few men care to have the obvious pointed out to them by a woman.
                        —Margaret Baillie Saunders, *A Shepherd of Kensington*

~

Question: How do you get a man to exercise?
Answer: Put the remote control between his feet.
Question: Why is it good that there are female astronauts?
Answer: Because when the crew gets lost in space, at least a woman will ask
   for directions.

~

It's been my experience that men who say they believe in 50/50 relationships are prone to telling half-truths.

~

Women see differently than men. If you doubt this, I would merely remind you of the last time a male walked into a room that looked as though it had been ransacked by hostile—and profoundly sloppy—foreign agents and innocently uttered the words: "What mess?"   —Dorian Yeager

~

You can talk to a man about any subject. He won't understand, but you can talk to him.

~

Whatever women do they must do twice as well as men to be thought half as good. Luckily, this is not difficult.   —Charlotte Whitton

~

The softer a man's head, the louder his socks.   —Helen Rowland

~

Blessed is the man who, having nothing to say, abstains from giving in words evidence of the fact.   —George Eliot (Mary Ann Evans)

The average man takes all the natural taste out of his food by covering it with ready-made sauces, and all the personality out of a woman by covering her with his ready-made ideals. —Helen Rowland, *A Guide to Men*

~

We were walking down the street. He looked into another girl's eyes, and just fell madly in love. She was wearing mirrored sunglasses. —Rita Rudner

~

Question: What's the difference between a man and E.T.?
Answer: E.T. phoned home.

~

A man finds out what is meant by a spitting image when he tries to feed cereal to his infant. —Imogene Fey

~

Men have a much better time of it than women. For one thing, they marry later. For another thing, they die earlier. —H. L. Mencken

~

No man is a man until his father tells him he is—I was forty-eight.
—Burt Reynolds

~

Unless your mate goes by the name of John-Boy, chances are he spent his entire childhood mastering the fine art of chore avoidance. This is the essential male pastime, on which all of those lesser avocations—fishing, Monday Night Football, global imperialism—are founded. —Aaron Gell

~

Said a wife at Tottenham police court: "My husband is a jolly good sort, one of those very hearty men. He wears plus fours, smokes a long pipe, and talks about nothing but beer and rugby football. My nerves won't stand much more of it."

~

A modern-day example comes from a longtime female resident of Alaska, asked by a new arrival: "What are the chances of finding a good man around here?" There was a pause. Alaska was full of men. But would she recommend any of them? The old-timer replied: "Well, the odds are good, but the goods are odd." —Dr. Mardy Grothe

~

I never liked a man I didn't meet. —Dorothy Parker

If men can run the world, why can't they stop wearing neckties? How intelligent is it to start the day by tying a little noose around your neck?

—Linda Ellerbee

- Because I'm a guy, I must hold the television remote control in my hand while I watch TV. If the thing has been misplaced, I'll miss a whole show looking for it, though one time I was able to survive by holding a calculator.
- Because I'm a guy, when I lock my keys in the car I will fiddle with a wire clothes hanger and ignore your suggestions that we call a road service until long after hypothermia has set in. Oh, and when the car isn't running very well, I will pop the hood and stare at the engine as if I know what I'm looking at. If another guy shows up, one of us will say to the other, "I used to be able to fix these things, but now with all these computers and everything, I wouldn't know where to start." We will then drink beer.
- Because I'm a guy, when I catch a cold I need someone to bring me soup and take care of me while I lie in bed and moan. You never get as sick as I do, so for you this isn't an issue.
- Because I'm a guy, I can be relied upon to purchase basic groceries at the store, like milk, or bread. I cannot be expected to find exotic items like "Cumin" or "Tofu." For all I know these are the same thing. And never, under any circumstances, expect me to pick up anything for which "feminine hygiene product" is a euphemism.
- Because I'm a guy, when one of our appliances stops working I will insist on taking it apart, despite evidence that this will just cost me twice as much once the repair person gets here and has to put it back together.
- Because I'm a guy, I don't think we're all that lost, and no, I don't think we should stop and ask someone. Why would you listen to a complete stranger—how the heck could HE know where we're going?
- Because I'm a guy, there is no need to ask me what I'm thinking about. The answer is always either sex or football, though I have to make up something else when you ask, so don't.
- Because I'm a guy, I do not want to visit your mother, or have your mother come visit us, or talk to her when she calls, or think about her any more than I have to. Whatever you got her for mother's day is OK, I don't need to see it. Did you remember to pick up something for my mom, too?
- Because I'm a guy, I am capable of announcing, "one more beer and I really have to go," and mean it every single time I say it, even when it gets to the point that the one bar closes and my buddies and I have to go hunt down another. I will find it increasingly hilarious to have my pals call you to tell you I'll be home soon, and no, I don't understand why you threw all my clothes into the front yard. What's the connection?
- Because I'm a guy, you don't have to ask me if I liked the movie. Chances are, if you're crying at the end of it, I didn't.
- Because I'm a guy, yes, I have to turn up the radio when Bruce Springsteen or The Doors comes on, and then, yes, I have to tell you every single time about how Bruce had his picture on the cover of *Time* and *Newsweek* the same day, or how Jim Morrison

M

is buried in Paris and everyone visits his grave. Please do not behave as if you do not find this fascinating.
- Because I'm a guy, I think what you're wearing is fine. I thought what you were wearing five minutes ago was fine, too. Either pair of shoes is fine. With the belt or without it looks fine. Your hair is fine. You look fine. Can we just go now?
- Because I'm a guy and this is, after all, the 90's, I will share equally in the housework. You do the laundry, the cooking, the cleaning, and the dishes, and I'll do the rest.

Bruce Cameron, www.wbrucecameron.com, copyright 1999

Men build bridges and throw railroads across deserts, and yet they contend successfully that the job of sewing on a button is beyond them.

—Heywood Broun

Some time ago a respected national publication reported that you can judge the seven ages of man by his reaction to members of the opposite sex. See if you can guess which age goes with each response.
1. Whaaaa! I want my mama.
2. G'wan, beat it. We don't want any ol' girls around here.
3. Gee, Jennie, you're really pretty.
4. If you don't marry me, I'll kill myself.
5. Go ahead, go home to your mother. See if I care.
6. I know she's younger than I am, but she understands me.
7. Kitchy-koo! Did you hear her call me Grandpa?

MEN AND WOMEN

I think—therefore I'm single.

—Liz Winstead

Women are never disarmed by compliments. Men always are.

—Oscar Wilde

Women with pasts interest men because they hope history will repeat itself.

—Mae West

A man is a person who will pay two dollars for a one-dollar item he wants. A woman will pay one dollar for a two-dollar item she doesn't want.

—William Binger

When a man gets up to speak, people listen, then look. When a woman gets up, people look; then if they like what they see, they listen.

—Pauline Frederick

❧

A man has his clothes made to fit him; a woman makes herself fit her clothes.

—Edgar Watson Howe

❧

Males seek power to compensate for loss of connection; females seek connection to compensate for loss of power.   —Gary Malmon

❧

After a quarrel between a man and a woman the man suffers chiefly from the thought that he has wounded the woman; the woman suffers from the thought that she has not wounded the man enough.   —Friedrich W. Nietzsche

❧

A woman worries about the future until she has a husband, but a man never worries about the future until he has a wife.   —Liselotte Pulver

❧

To a woman the first kiss is the end of the beginning; to a man it is the beginning of the end.   —Helen Rowland

M

You see an awful lot of smart guys with dumb women, but you hardly ever see a smart woman with a dumb guy. —Clint Eastwood

Ann Landers notes: "When a man says, 'Honey, there are only two minutes left in the football game,' it is the same amount of time as when his wife says, 'Honey, I'll be ready in two minutes.'"

When women are depressed they either eat or go shopping. Men invade another country. —Elayne Boosler

The difference between men and women . . . men won't wear stuff that hurts.

Over the years statistics revealed that women are safer drivers than men. Now we know why. The reason is: Men drivers constantly place themselves in unsafe situations—by trying to get a better look at the women drivers.

It was true for Cleopatra, and it is true today. Men are at their weakest when some female is telling them how strong they are.

A college English professor wrote the words "woman without her man is a savage" on the board and asked the students to punctuate it correctly. The males wrote: "Woman, without her man, is a savage." The females wrote: "Woman! Without her, man is a savage." —*Daily Mining Gazette*

METAPHORS

Carolyn Tinker, public affairs director at the University of New Mexico Medical Center, is also a collector of mixed and mangled metaphors. Some of her gems:

- What finally broke the straw.
- You can't go out there cold turkey with egg on your face.
- Run it up the flagpole and see if it sticks.
- We took the thunder out of his sails.

- He sank to new heights.
- She hitched her star to his wagon.
- He's really rubbing it in our noses.
- I'm still green behind the ears.

Jim Arnholz in Albuquerque, N.M., Journal

MIDDLE AGE

I'm at that age where if I go all out, I end up all in.   —Ron Dentinger

Middle-age is when work is a lot less fun, and fun is a lot more work.
                                                      —Milton Berle

My Aunt Flo explains: "Middle age is when broadness of the mind and narrowness of the waist change places."

Middle age begins with the first mortgage and ends when you drop dead.
                                                      —Herb Caen

M

Middle age is . . . when your mind retains nothing, and your waist retains everything.   —Joe Hickman

REVEREND FUN WWW.REVERENDFUN.COM

The really frightening thing about middle age is the knowledge you'll outgrow it.
—Lauren Bacall

~

A man has reached middle age when he's warned to slow down by the doctor instead of the police. The good news is that a university survey indicates that college girls find middle-aged men most attractive. The bad news is that they regard middle age as 24.

~

Middle age is when you want to see how long the car will last instead of how fast it will go. Middle age is when you get out of the shower and you're glad the mirror is fogged up.

~

Middle age is when you're faced with two temptations and you choose the one that will get you home by 9 o'clock.
—Ronald Reagan

~

You know you are middle-aged when your children tell you that you're driving too slow and your parents tell you that you're driving too fast.

~

Midlife crisis is that moment when you realize your children and your clothes are about the same age.
—Bill Tammeus

~

A mid-life crisis is when your daughter's old baby-sitter calls to see if your daughter can baby-sit for her baby.
—William D. Tammeus

~

Middle age is when you wish you could have some of the naps you refused to take as a kid.

MILITARY

Recruit: "If we do happen to step on a mine, sir, what do we do?"
Drill Sergeant: "The normal procedure, son, is to jump 200 feet in the air and scatter oneself over a wide area."

~

"Well," snarled the tough old sergeant to the bewildered private. "I suppose after you get discharged from the army you'll be waiting for me to die so you can come and spit on my grave." "Not me, Sarge!" the private replied. "After I get out of the army, I ain't never going to stand in line again!"

Observing a light across the water, the captain had his signalman instruct the other vessel to change her course ten degrees south. The response was prompt: "Change your course ten degrees north." "I am a captain," he responded testily. "Change your course ten degrees south." The reply: "I'm a seaman first class—change your course north." The captain was furious. "Change your course now. I'm on a battleship." "Change your course ten degrees north, sir—I'm in a lighthouse."

After fighting only 24 hours, the British RAF released the following communique. "TODAY WE DOWNED 90 PLANES; 60 DEFINITE, 30 PLEDGED."

At an afternoon tea for officers and their wives, the commanding general of the base delivered a seemingly endless oration. A young second lieutenant, listening with obvious disfavor, grumbled to the woman at his side, "What a pompous and unbearable old windbag that slob is." The woman turned to him, her face red with rage and said, "Lieutenant, do you know who I am?" "No, ma'am." "I am the wife of the man you just called 'an unbearable old windbag.'" "Indeed," said the young lieutenant, looking steadfast and unruffled, "and do you know who I am?" "No, I don't," said the general's wife. "Thank God," said the lieutenant as he disappeared into the crowd.

The sergeant, explaining the routine to the new recruits, said, "There will always be a choice in your meals: You can take them . . . or leave them."
—*The Rotarian*

A U.S. Army company had gathered to listen to their new commanding officer. "I want you to respect me as your leader," he said, "but if you've got any problems, feel free to talk with me as if I were your father." A voice boomed from the rear: "Hey, pop, can I use the jeep tonight?"   —Richard Armour

MINDS

Some minds are like concrete, thoroughly mixed up and permanently set.
—Rev. Denny J. Brake

MINISTERS (*See also* CLERGY)

The 27-year-old minister had been assigned to his first post only a short time when he noticed that one of his parishioners, an old lady, had missed several Sundays in a row. He decided to see her and find out the reason. "Young man," she answered him firmly, "you aren't old enough, to have sinned enough, to have repented enough, to be able to preach about it!" —*Funny Funny World*

A disconcerted minister to his congregation: "Crying babies and disruptive children, like good intentions, should be carried out immediately."

Marlin Hopkins, the pastor of Holy Apostles Covenant Church, was so proud of his new loose-leaf Bible and decided to use it as he began preaching a series from Genesis. The second week of his series he was on the story of the fall of man and as he was reading his text he read, "And Adam said to Eve . . ." Then he turned the page to complete the verse, but the rest of the text was missing. He was puzzled for a few seconds. Then, finally realizing what had happened, he looked up rather embarrassed and said, ". . . it looks like a leaf is missing!"

One of the toughest tasks a church faces is choosing a good minister. A member of an official board undergoing this painful process finally lost patience. He'd watched the pastoral relations committee reject applicant after applicant for some fault, alleged or otherwise. It was time for a bit of soul-searching on the part of the committee. So he stood up and read a letter purporting to be from another applicant.

"Gentlemen: Understanding your pulpit is vacant, I should like to apply for the position. I have many qualifications. I've been a preacher with much success and also have had some success as a writer. Some say I'm a good organizer. I've been a leader most places I've been. I'm over 50 years of age. I have never preached in one place for more than three years. In some places, I have left town after my work caused riots and disturbances. I must admit I have been in jail three or four times, but not because of any real wrongdoing. My health is not too good, though I still get a great deal done. The churches I have preached in have been small, though located in several large cities. I've not gotten along well with religious leaders in towns where I have preached. In fact, some have threatened me and even attacked me physically. I am not too good at keeping records. I have been known to forget whom I baptized. However, if you can use me, I shall do my best for you."

The board member looked over at the committee. "Well, what do you think? Shall we call him?"

The good church folk were aghast. Call an unhealthy, trouble-making, absentminded, ex-jailbird? Was the board member crazy? Who signed the application? Who has such colossal nerve?

The board member eyed them all keenly before he answered, "It's signed, the Apostle Paul."

Todd Roberts, a Pentecostal pastor who is very popular with his congregation, explains his success as the result of a silent prayer that he offers each time he takes to the pulpit. It goes thus: "Lord, fill my mouth with worthwhile stuff, And nudge me when I've said enough."

As dessert was served to the visiting pastor, the hostess apologized for not having any cheese to go with the apple pie. Hearing this, her little son slipped down from his chair and left the room for a moment. He returned shortly with a small piece of cheese and shyly placed it on the pastor's plate. "Well, thank you, son," said the guest. "You must have sharp eyes to have seen that piece of cheese when your mother didn't. Where did you find it?" Flushing with pride, the little boy said, "Oh, it was in the mousetrap."

Our pastor was preaching on Proverbs 16:24: "Pleasant words are as a honeycomb, sweet to the soul, and health to the bones." The minister then added, "You can catch more flies with honey than with vinegar." My wife leaned over, put her head on my shoulder and whispered in my ear, "I just love to watch your muscles ripple when you take out the garbage."

A country church had just acquired a brand-new pastor. He drove around the local area one day, calling on homes to get acquainted with the parishioners. He had been up a narrow lane to the house on top of a hill, not far from the highway. Finding no one home, he proceeded back down the hill to where the lane opened onto the highway. Not at all familiar with the roads in the area, he came upon the intersection more suddenly than he expected and almost crashed into another car entering the narrow lane. The woman driving the other car grumbled to herself, "Reckless driver—I should've gotten your license number and reported you." Reaching her home on the top of the hill, the woman parked the car and was nervously trying to unlock the front door when she noticed a note attached to the door. "Sorry I missed you this time," it said. "Will try again soon.—The new pastor."   —Daniel Scott

A preacher was making his rounds to his parishioners on a bicycle, when he came upon a little boy trying to sell a lawn mower. "How much do you want for the mower?" asked the preacher. "I just want enough money to go out and buy me a bicycle," said the little boy. After a moment of consideration, the preacher asked, "Will you take my bike in trade for it?" The little boy asked if he could try it out first, and after riding the bike around a little while said, "Mister, you've got yourself a deal." The preacher took the mower and began to try to crank it. He pulled on the string a few times with no response from the mower. The preacher called the little boy over and said, "I can't get this mower to start." The little boy said, "That's because you have to cuss at it to get it started." The preacher said, "I am a minister, and I cannot cuss. It has been so long since I have been saved that I do not even remember how to cuss." The little boy looked at him happily and said, "Just keep pulling on that string. It'll come back to ya!"

GOOD NEWS AND BAD NEWS FOR A PASTOR

Good News: You baptized seven people today in the river. Bad News: You lost two of them in the swift current.

Good News: The Women's Guild voted to send you a get-well card. Bad News: The vote passed by 31-30.

Good News: The Elder Board accepted your job description the way you wrote it. Bad News: They were so inspired by it, they also formed a search committee to find somebody capable of filling the position.

Good News: You finally found a choir director who approaches things exactly the same way you do. Bad News: The choir mutinied.

Good News: Mrs. Jones is wild about your sermons. Bad News: Mrs. Jones is also wild about the "Gong Show," "Beavis and Butthead" and "Texas Chain Saw Massacre."

Good News: The trustees finally voted to add more church parking. Bad News: They are going to blacktop the front lawn of your parsonage.

Good News: Church attendance rose dramatically the last three weeks. Bad News: You were on vacation.

Good News: Your biggest critic just left your church. Bad News: He has been appointed the Head Bishop of your denomination.

Good News: The youth in your church come to your house for a surprise visit. Bad News: It's in the middle of the night and they are armed with toilet paper and shaving cream to "decorate" your house.

Cindy: "I can be sick for nothing because my father's a doctor."

Mindy: "That's nothing. I can be good for nothing because my father's a minister."

—Irish Grit

To his horror, the pastor discovered during the service that he had forgotten his sermon notes, so he said to the congregation, by way of apology, that this morning he should have to depend upon the Lord for what he might say, but next Sunday he would come better prepared.

Henry Ward Beecher, the famous New England minister, was entering his pulpit one Sunday morning. Awaiting him was an unmarked envelope. Opening it, he found a single sheet of paper on which was written the single word, "FOOL." After chuckling to himself, he held the paper up to the congregation and said: "I have known many an in- stance of a man writing letters and for- getting to sign his name. But this is the only instance I've ever known of a man signing his name and forgetting to write his letter."

Pastors, of course, are not supposed to curse. Instead of cursing, one pastor I know, when he's alone, calls out the names of several members of his congregations—with feeling.

—Rev. Dennis R. Fakes

James Huskins recalls: "While I was the new pastor of a church in rural east Tennessee, I assisted a family of parishioners who owned a feed store. It was their busy season, and they needed someone to help fill 100-pound sacks of corn. As I pulled my first bag off the scale and started to close it, I noticed a look of concern on the face of the store owner. 'When we tie sacks, we use a miller's knot,' he said. 'I don't suppose you can do that.' He didn't know that I had spent ten years farming before entering the ministry. When I easily tied the knot, he was visibly impressed. 'You're the first preacher I ever saw,' he told me, 'who knew anything at all about working.'"

When I received my first call, to be pastor of the St. John's Congregational Church in Philadelphia, I found the first few months at my new job very interesting. One day I'd have ink up to my elbows from repairing a mimeo- graph machine. The next day, I'd be arranging a rummage sale or a pancake breakfast. The next, I'd be hanging from a tree trying to trim the limbs without getting into the power lines. Then, I'd try to hunt down a carburetor for the church's antique bus. Next, I'd repaint the church nursery. Roofing, plumbing and wiring were also included in my work. One thing's for sure: my instructors were right on target when they said, "The seminary won't teach you all you need to know about being a pastor."

Rev. Mel, a local Baptist minister, liked to slip old proverbs into his sermons, but had trouble getting them right. For example, he would remind the congregation not to "kick a gift horse in the mouth" or that "a stitch in line saves time" or "a fool and his money are soon started" or "you can lead a horse to water, but that's a horse of a different color." One Sunday, he was describing how easy some task was to perform and said, "It's just like falling off a log." We all thought he had finally mastered one. Then he added, "Once you learn how, you never forget."

I was attending a conference out-of-town with two deacons from my congregation. The first evening's meeting did not finish until rather late. So we decided to have something to eat before going to bed. Unfortunately, the only place still open was a seedy bar-and-grill with a questionable reputation. After being served, one of the deacons asked me to say grace. "I'd rather not," I replied. "I don't want Him to know I'm here."

REAL LETTERS TO MINISTERS:

Dear Pastor, I know God loves everybody but He never met my sister. Yours sincerely, Arnold. Age 8, Nashville

Dear Pastor, Please say in your sermon that Peter Peterson has been a good boy all week. I am Peter Peterson. Sincerely, Pete. Age 9, Phoenix

Dear Pastor, My father should be a minister. Every day he gives us a sermon about something. Robert, Age 11, Anderson

Dear Pastor, I'm sorry I can't leave more money in the plate, but my father didn't give me a raise in my allowance. Could you have a sermon about a raise in my allowance? Love, Patty. Age 10, New Haven

Dear Pastor, My mother is very religious. She goes to play bingo at church every week even if she has a cold. Yours truly, Annette. Age 9, Albany

Dear Pastor, I would like to go to heaven someday because I know my brother won't be there. Stephen. Age 8, Chicago

Dear Pastor, I think a lot more people would come to your church if you moved it to Disneyland. Loreen. Age 9. Tacoma

Dear Pastor, I liked your sermon where you said that good health is more important than money but I still want a raise in my allowance. Sincerely, Eleanor, Age 12, Sarasota

Dear Pastor, Please pray for all the airline pilots. I am flying to California tomorrow. Laurie. Age 10, New York City

Dear Pastor, I hope to go to heaven some day but later than sooner. Love, Ellen, Age 9. Athens

Dear Pastor, Please say a prayer for our Little League team. We need God's help or a new pitcher. Thank you. Alexander. Age 10, Raleigh

Dear Pastor, My father says I should learn the Ten Commandments. But I don't think I want to because we have enough rules already in my house. Joshua. Age 10, South Pasadena

Dear Pastor, Are there any devils on earth? I think there may be one in my class. Carla. Age 10, Salina

Dear Pastor, I liked your sermon on Sunday. Especially when it was finished. Ralph, Age 11, Akron

Dear Pastor, How does God know the good people from the bad people? Do you tell Him or does He read about it in the newspapers? Sincerely, Marie. Age 9, Lewiston

---

One of the members of our pastors' study group may have hit on an excellent idea for church-state relations in these difficult economic times. "The greatest thing the federal government could do for the church," he quipped, "is to stop printing $1 bills." —Rev. Julie A. Hart

M

REVEREND FUN WWW.REVERENDFUN.COM

©COPYRIGHT 1999 GOSPEL FILMS, INC.

"Wow!! . . . That was the best sermon on tithing that I've ever been to."

The minister was invited to dinner. During the meal he was amazed to hear little eight-year-old Ann, the daughter of the house, say that a person had to be mighty brave to go to church these days. "Why do you say that, my dear?" "Well, last Sunday I heard Daddy tell Mother that there was a big gun in the pulpit and the choir murdered the anthem and the organist drowned the choir!"

~

The parishioners were gathered at the hall to honor their pastor, who was celebrating his twenty-fifth anniversary in the ministry. He was called on to say a few words and his opening remark went something like this: "I feel like the boy who got F in spelling: words fail me."

~

A circuit rider asked for a room at a wayside inn. The proprietor said he could accommodate him. "Sir," continued the proprietor, "I perceive you are a clergyman—please let me know whether you are a Presbyterian or a Methodist." "Why do you inquire?" the preacher asked. "Because I wish to please my guests. I have observed that a Presbyterian is very particular about his own food and bed and a Methodist is particular about the feed and care of his horse." "Very well," the preacher replied. "I'm a Presbyterian but my horse is a Methodist."

—*Grit*

MISERS

Not all Scotsmen are penny pinchers—despite their reputation. But one was as frugal as frugal can be. His name is Duffy McDuff. On a visit to New York, he caught a taxi and as it sped along, it was hit by another car. The door flew open and Duffy was thrown to the pavement, bleeding and in great pain. The cab driver jumped out, ran to Duffy, and asked if there was anything he could do for him. "There sure is," Duffy moaned. "Shut off the meter."

~

A pastor approached Duffy McDuff, one of the wealthiest members of his congregation, about making a pledge to the church. McDuff asked if the pastor knew that the man's father was about to have his farm foreclosed, and that his mother needed surgery. The pastor said that he had not known about these things. The wealthy man then asked if the pastor knew that his brother had been badly injured in an automobile accident and needed reconstructive surgery . . . and that his brother-in-law was going to prison unless he was able to come up with the money to make up a shortage in his account by next Tuesday. The embarrassed pastor admitted that he had not known of any of these tragic circumstances in the life of this man. The pastor apologized for taking up the time of McDuff and started to leave. But the wealthy man was not finished with his tirade against the pastor: "Well, Pastor, if I'm not going to give a single dime to my family in their times of need, what makes you think I'm going to give any to the church?"

~

There is an old saying: "Misers may not be very much fun to live with, but they make extremely good ancestors." —Ron Dentinger

~

McDuffy was standing outside the church after his fifth daughter's wedding ceremony when a reporter came up to him and asked, "McDuffy, this is your fifth daughter's wedding. You must be a very proud man." "Och aye, I'm proud, but the confetti is just getting a wee bit gritty."

"You and your 'Let's buy the half-priced circus seats.'"

My uncle Irv was notoriously thrifty. He and my aunt had always wanted a ride in an old-fashioned biplane. On a visit to California they noticed an air taxi service that took passengers for rides in Gypsy Moths for $50 a passenger. Uncle Irv tried negotiating the fare to a more affordable level. The conversation went back and forth for forty minutes. Finally the frustrated pilot said, "I will make you a proposition, Mr. Streiker. You and your wife get in and I will give you a ride for half an hour. If you don't say single word while we are up, I will only charge you $5." Irv thought this was a fair proposal and he and his wife climbed into the plane. The pilot thereupon took them on the wildest half hour's ride that could possibly be imagined, looping the loop, riding upside down, and going through dizzying dives and tailspins. Finally, he set his craft down on the ground. "I've got to hand it to you, Mr. Streiker," said the pilot. "It took guts to go through all that without uttering a sound." "Indeed," said Irv, mopping his brow with his handkerchief. "But you'll never know how close I came to talkin' when the wife fell out."

❧

My uncle Irv, the family tightwad, expressed himself as highly sympathetic to the viewpoint and aims of the National Anti-Tipping Society, but his enthusiasm waned perceptibly when he heard the annual dues were two dollars a year. "Two dollars," he moaned. "I can save money at that figure by going on tipping, right through the year."

❧

My Uncle Irv is so cheap he sends one Christmas card out each year—in the form of a chain letter.

❧

My tightwad Uncle Irv joined an organization that fights inflation but he was very disappointed. An hour after he joined, they raised the dues.

❧

Duffy McDuff sent an indignant letter to the editor of the newspaper. He said that if any more stories about stingy Scotchmen appeared in the columns, he was going to stop borrowing the paper.

❧

A penny-pinching patron stopped in a garage and asked for a pint of anti-freeze. The man on duty asked: "What kind of car is it for?" "It's not for a car," replied the patron, "I'm going to drink it and save buying myself an overcoat this winter."

—Brian O'Hara

MISTAKES

I made a deal with my wife. I will stop calling her the little woman if she will stop calling me the big mistake.   —Ron Dentinger

~

You can profit from your mistakes. Have a garage sale.   —Ron Dentinger

~

During World War II, my uncle Ed, a naval aviator, went into a barber shop to get a shave, and since the manicurist was really beautiful, he asked for a manicure at the same time. He kept looking at her, really taken with her, and finally said, "How about going out with me tonight?" She said, "No, I'm married." He said, "Well, just tell your husband you're busy tonight." "Tell him yourself," she said. "He's shaving you."

~

We usually call our blunders mistakes, and our friends call our mistakes blunders.   —Henry Wheatley

~

Half of our mistakes in life arise from feeling where we ought to think, and thinking where we ought to feel.   —John Churton Collins

~

Victory goes to the player who makes the next-to-last mistake.
               —Chessmaster Savielly Grigorievitch Tartakower (1887–1956)

MODERATION

Flora Lewis, columnist for the New York *Times,* criticizing simplistic, cure-all "solutions" to complex political, economic, national and world problems:" "I am a rock-ribbed, hard-nosed, knee-jerk, bleeding-heart moderate."

MODERN LIFE

Data is flying around, across, and through your systems at speeds the Jetsons could appreciate, but has any of this technology let you go home one minute early? I doubt it.   —Richard Santalesa

~

I never expected to see the day when girls would get sunburned in the places they now do.   —Will Rogers

~

They say that people are healthier, they have more money, and better sex lives today. I have no joke about this but, it's important that I remind myself of that fact.   —Bill Maher

We live in an age when pizza gets to your home before the police.

—Jeff Marder

~

Marianne Peters, a newly minted Ph.D. sociologist on an African jungle expedition, held up her camera to take pictures of the native children at play. Suddenly the youngsters began to yell in protest. Turning red, the sociologist apologized to the chief for her insensitivity and told him she had forgotten that certain tribes believed a person lost his soul if his picture was taken. She explained to him, in long-winded detail, the operation of the camera. Several times the chief tried to get a word in, but to no avail. Certain she had put all the chief's fears to rest, the sociologist then allowed him to speak. Smiling, he said, "The children were trying to tell you that you forgot to take off the lens cap."

~

These days the marriages just do not last very long. In fact, any more, if I write a check for a wedding gift, I postdate it.   —Ron Dentinger

~

"In the wilderness, we need to keep learning," Boy Scout leader Bud Wilcox said to his troop as they took off on a long hike. "Remember, fellows, if you become lost in the woods at night, get your bearings from the sky." "How do we do that, especially if it's cloudy?" asked one scout. "Just look," said Wilcox. "A glow will indicate the nearest shopping center."

~

Census-takers have found that one third of all married couples aren't.

~

You have to question any period in history in which people are saying that God is dead and Elvis is alive.   —Robert Orben

~

An elderly doctor listened to the wails of a woman who bemoaned the disappearance of the family physician, the good old-fashioned doctor. Finally he lost patience and replied, "Madam, if you will show me an old-fashioned family, I will produce a doctor for it."   —*Today's Health*

~

The U.S. is the only country where a housewife hires a woman to do her cleaning so she can do volunteer work at the nursery where the cleaning woman leaves her child.   —Helen Bender

"Why did you have to let your maid go?" a woman asked her neighbor. The neighbor replied, "Well, I started thinking about our house and I decided that with my completely automatic kitchen and laundry, and all the other gadgets around the place I didn't really need a maid . . . So, I hired a mechanic."

—*Capper's Weekly*

The woman who remembers her first kiss now has a daughter who can't even remember her first husband.

Message on a church answering machine: "For a church service schedule, press one. For office hours, press two. For the forgiveness of sins, press three. If you want to pray alone, hang up."

—M. Larry Zanen

It is the old story again: once we had wooden chalices and golden priests, now we have golden chalices and wooden priests. —Ralph Waldo Emerson

"On cable TV, they have a weather channel—24 hours of weather," says comedian Dan Spencer. "We had something like that where I grew up. We called it a window."

M

REVEREND FUN WWW.REVERENDFUN.COM

©COPYRIGHT 1999 GOSPEL FILMS, INK.

"If you don't mind . . . I was talking to that bush!"

The Psychiatric Hotline: "Hello, Welcome to the Psychiatric Hotline. If you are obsessive-compulsive, please press 1 repeatedly. If you are co-dependent, please ask someone to press 2. If you have multiple personalities, please press 3, 4, 5 and 6. If you are paranoid-delusional, we know who you are and what you want. Just stay on the line so we can trace the call. If you are schizophrenic, listen carefully and a little voice will tell you which number to press. If you are manic-depressive, it doesn't matter which number you press. No one will answer."

❧

Man to friend: "Exactly when was 'Have a nice day' replaced with 'Please visit our web site'?" —Mike Shapiro

❧

One sign that we are no longer a rural nation is that hailstones, which used to be classified as the size of hen's eggs, are now compared to golf balls and baseballs. —Bill Vaughan

❧

Driving Tip: If you rear-end a car on the freeway, your first move should be to hang up the phone. —Tom Adams

❧

Dan Schow, a resident of San Francisco's Nob Hill, spent a semi-sleepless night last summer listening to what he calls "the ridiculously self-important sound of a car alarm." Next morning, as he tottered bleary-eyed to work, he was gratified to find this scrawled note on the windshield of the offending BMW: "Thieves! Please break into this car. Disconnect the car alarm and you can have the stereo as a thank-you gift from the neighborhood." —Herb Caen

❧

The phrase "melting pot" used to mean the United States of America. Now it means you put the wrong container in the microwave. —Robert Orben

❧

A New Yorker came across a variation on the basic "No Radio" sign in the window of a parked car: "I'm not going to lie to you. I do have a radio, but it's broken. Actually, it's stuck on one station? WQXR. So unless you like classical music, it doesn't make sense for you to break into my car. I am planning to get the radio fixed, maybe even add a tape player. I'll keep you posted." —Jim Witkin

❧

What this country needs is a scale that takes off five pounds for good intentions. —Bill Walton

What this country needs is something that outlasts the box it came in.

What this country needs is self-destructing campaign and yard sale posters.

The shipwrecked mariner had spent several years on a deserted island. Then one morning he was thrilled to see a ship offshore and a smaller vessel pulling out toward him. When the boat grounded on the beach, the officer in charge handed the marooned sailor a bundle of newspapers and told him, "With the captain's compliments. He said to read through these and let us know if you still want to be rescued." —Bill Leverette, *On Edgar Bergen's Lap*

About the only thing you can do on a shoestring these days is trip.
—Los Angeles Times Syndicate

One newborn baby in the hospital nursery to another: "You know what's cool? We're all born with an automatic $5000 credit limit."
—Mick Stevens in *USA Weekend*

M

MONDAYS

If it is bright and sunny after two cold and rainy days, it is probably Monday.   —Hugh B. Brous, Jr.

❧

Mondays are the potholes in the road of life.

—Tom Wilson

MONEY

A billion here, a billion there, sooner or later you're talking real money.

—Senator Everett Dirksen

❧

Zorba Dukakis, a wealthy art dealer, discovers he has a terminal illness. Zorba calls his three best friends, a doctor, a priest and a lawyer, and gives them $500,000 apiece. He tells them, "I know I can't take it with me, but I want to try. I want your assurances that you will put this $500,000 cash into my casket at my funeral and have it buried with me." A month later, Zorba died and following the funeral, the three friends got together. The doctor said, "I've got to confess, I didn't put the money in the casket. I gave it to the hospital's foundation to build a new children's wing." The priest said, "I've got to confess too. I didn't put that $500,000 in the casket either. I gave it to the Little Sisters of the Poor to build a new treatment center at the nursing home." The lawyer said, "Well, I'm aghast. I just want you to know that he was buried with my personal check for $500,000 in his casket!"

❧

A study of economics usually reveals that the best time to buy anything is last year.   —Marty Allen

❧

Uncle Sid was a notorious tightwad, and alleviated his few twinges of conscience by giving a quarter to the miserable-looking woman who sold bagels from a pushcart on the corner near his office. He never bought a bagel, having already breakfasted, but he always put a quarter into her grimy palm and felt himself a virtuous man. This went on for months, until one day the bagel-seller tugged at his immaculate cuff. "Mister, Mister, I gotta tell ya somethin'." "Ah," acknowledged Sid with a gracious smile, "I suppose you wish to know why I give you a quarter every day but never take the bagel?" "Nah, that's yer business," she snorted. "My business is tellin' ya the price's gone up to thirty-five cents."

A man of some wealth overheard a lady remarking, "Oh, if I only had fifty dollars I would be perfectly content." He thought about that for a few moments. "If the lady only had fifty dollars she would be content." He thought to himself, "Well, I can help her out." So he walked up to her and handed her a fifty dollar bill with his best wishes. She was very overt in her show of gratitude. She really appreciated his gift. As she walked away he heard her mumble under her breath, "Why on earth didn't I say one hundred dollars?"

～

A wife came to the living room one day after having answered the front door. "There's a man at the door who wants to see you about a bill you owe," she told her husband. "What does he look like?" the husband inquired. "He looks like you'd better pay him," the wife declared.

～

Some persons are concerned about money almost to the point of desperation. A mail carrier tells of greeting a four-year-old boy who had planted himself

The
BORDERLINE™   By Gabe Martin
                                    borderln@cts.com

© 1995 GABE MARTIN

http://www.the-borderline.com/

"So—how's the opportunity for advancement in this place?"

firmly in front of his family's mailbox and would not budge. With his feet spread wide and his arms folded, he told the mail carrier firmly, "My mom says she can't TAKE any more bills."

~

As somebody said: "A nickel goes a long way nowadays. You can carry it around for days and not find anything you can buy with it."

~

Inflation is creeping up, a young man said to his friend. "Yesterday I ordered a $25 steak in a restaurant and told them to put it on my Visa . . . and it fit."

~

Things aren't always what they seem. A million dollar house in Beverly Hills could be a $600,000 house with a $400,000 burglar alarm.

—*Funny Funny World*

~

An American history teacher, lecturing the class on the Puritans, asked: "What sort of people were punished in the stocks?" To which a small voice from the back of the room responded: "The small investor."

~

The young couples' Sunday school class was studying the story of Abraham and Sarah, who in their 90s were blessed with a child, Isaac. "What lesson," the teacher asked, "do we learn from this story?" A young mother blurted out, "They waited until they could afford it."

~

I like the story about Ralph the cab driver who had accumulated $100,000 and was going to retire. As was customary, the company gave him a farewell dinner. At the toast, Ralph said a few words." I owe my retirement in part to my thrifty habits," said Ralph. "Even more, I owe it to the good judgment of my wife. But still more, I owe it to my aunt who died and left me $95,000."

~

Cecil Rhodes was an enormously wealthy man. One day a newspaperman said to him, "You must be very happy." Rhodes replied, "Happy?! No! I spent my life amassing a fortune only to find I have spent half of it on doctors to keep me out of the grave, and the other half on lawyers to keep me out of jail!"

~

Billionaire Jean Paul Getty was once asked the secret of his success. Said Getty, "Some people find oil. Others don't."

A terrible thing happened to me last week. I tried to live within my means and was picked up for vagrancy.   —Bob Orben

❧

I saw a new book just this week entitled *How To Be Happy Without Money.* I would have bought it, but it cost $29.95.

❧

Uncle Sid says he buys things on the "lay awake plan." He lays awake each evening trying to figure out how he will pay for it.

❧

I like the sign I saw on the front of one church: "You can't take it with you, but you can send it on ahead."

❧

Money still talks. Usually it says good-bye.

❧

One man was asked, "What would you do if you had all the money in the world?" He replied, "I'd apply it to all my debts as far as it would go."

❧

As Adlai Stevenson once put it, "There was a time when a fool and his money were soon parted, but now it happens to everybody."

❧

A pollster taking a survey of how much of people's income goes to different kinds of spending? The person being interviewed said, "I spend 40 percent of my income on housing, 20 percent on clothing, 40 percent on food, and 20 percent on transportation and amusement." The amazed pollster said, "But sir, that adds up to 120 percent." The reply was, "I know it!"

❧

The fortune-teller peering into his crystal ball, said: "You will be poor and unhappy until you are 30." The client asked: "And then?" The fortune-teller answered: "Then you'll get used to it."

❧

"Pastor," said Mr. Paulson, "I am a spendthrift. I spend money like a drunken sailor. I throw my money around right and left. In this morning's service I want you to pray that I may be cured of this habit." "Yes, my friend," said the pastor, "I'll be happy to pray for you—right after the offering."

"A millionaire's money is," to quote Mark Twain, "twice tainted—tain't yours and tain't mine."

Trying to sell a housewife a home freezer a salesman pointed out, "You can save enough on your food bills to pay for the freezer." "Yes, I know," the woman agreed, "but you see we're paying for our car on the carfare we save. Then we're paying off our washing machine on the laundry bills we save, and we're paying for the house on the rent we're saving. We just can't afford to save any more right now."   —*Irish Grit*

Money sometimes makes fools of important persons, but it may also make important persons of fools.   —Walter Winchell

Woman paying bills, to husband: "Our financial situation definitely is fluid. We're going straight down the drain."

—Hoest and Reiner, King Features Syndicate

An American tourist in Tel Aviv was about to enter the impressive Mann Auditorium to take in a concert by the Israel Philharmonic. He was admiring the unique architecture, the sweeping lines of the entrance, and the modern decor throughout the building. Finally he turned to his escort and asked if the building was named for Thomas Mann, the world-famous author. "No," his friend said, "It's named for Fredric Mann, from Philadelphia." "Really? I never heard of him. What did he write?" "A check."

No one can earn a million dollars honestly.   —William Jennings Bryan

It is better to have a permanent income than to be fascinating.

—Oscar Wilde

Behind every great fortune there is a crime.   —Honore de Balzac

These days if somebody pays you in cash you get suspicious—you think maybe his credit is no good.   —Joey Adams

To be sure your cash is safe, hide it in an empty beer bottle on your lawn. No one will pick it up there.   —Noel Wical

❧

If someone says, "It's not the money, it's the principle," it's the money.
                    —Angelo Valenti, consulting psychologist, Nashville, Tenn.

❧

People say money is not the key to happiness, but I have always figured if you have enough money, you can have a key made.   —Joan Rivers

❧

As was grandma's custom, when Ann, her 5-year-old granddaughter, was about to head for home following an afternoon visit, she handed the child about $1 in change. "Thank you, grandma," Ann said. "But this time I think I'll spend the money instead of putting it into my piggy bank." "Why?" grandma asked. "Well," replied Ann. "It's turning ma and pa into bank robbers."
                                                            —*Catholic Digest*

❧

My Uncle Les only carries $50 and $100 bills—for health reasons: Lucre can **M** be filthy literally as well as figuratively, according to a study by two doctors at the University of Louisville. They found that 13% of the coins and 42% of the bills they examined contained potentially disease-producing bacteria. Their advice? Carry only less-handled $50 or $100 bills.   —*Today's Health*

MORALITY

The newspaper editor grew weary of the abusive letters he received. Finally, instead of an editorial he simply printed a copy of the Ten Commandments. A few days later he received a letter which said, "Cancel my subscription. You're getting too personal."

❧

A news announcer on a radio show found himself with a few minutes to spare. Slowly, in the sincerest and deepest tones he was capable of, he said, "It is not often that such a glorious opportunity is presented to me. Ladies and gentlemen, I ask for a moment or two of your silence and attention." He then went on to read the Ten Commandments. When he finished, there were tears in his eyes, which dried very quickly when the station-break announcer broke in with, "The opinions just expressed aren't necessarily those of the sponsor."
                                                            —Sam Levenson

MOSQUITOES

No sound concentrates so much spitefulness and malice into a very small volume as the pinging of mosquitoes.

—Elspeth Huxley, *The Flame Trees of Thika*

MOTHERS

A young man said to the psychiatrist, "I had a strange dream last night. I dreamed you were my mother. I woke up and couldn't understand it. Why should I dream you were my mother?" The psychiatrist said, "Well, what did you do after having the dream?" "I had this appointment with you first thing in the morning, so I grabbed a cookie and a diet soda for breakfast and rushed out here." The psychiatrist frowned, "A cookie and a diet soda? You call that a breakfast?"

∼

I idolized my mother. I didn't realize she was a lousy cook until I went into the Army.

—Jackie Gayle

∼

John Whitehall, a wealthy Texan, wanted to send his mother an unusual, expensive gift for Mother's Day. The owner of a pet shop told him of a mynah bird worth well over twenty thousand dollars. "What makes this bird so valuable?" asked Whitehall. The owner responded, "This mynah bird is the only one in the world that can recite the Lord's Prayer, the twenty-third Psalm, and 1 Corinthians 13." "I'll take it," said the Texan. "I don't care how much it costs. Mother is worth it and will get so much comfort hearing it recite Scripture." So he wrote a check and had it shipped off to his mother. The Monday after Mother's Day he called her long distance. "Did you get my present?" "I certainly did, and thank you." "And how did you like the bird?" "Oh son, it was delicious!"

∼

Mother's Day perfume is kind of an all-purpose gift. It pleases mothers one day a year—and kills mosquitoes the rest.

∼

Motherhood is full of frustrations and challenges. Eventually, though, they move out.

Mothers all want their sons to grow up to be president, but they don't want them to become politicians in the process.   —John F. Kennedy

Lawyer's mother: "My son is a brilliant attorney. He can look at a contract and instantly tell you whether it's verbal or written. My son is so intelligent that talking with him is equivalent to passing the bar exam."

Two friends who hadn't seen each other in years met in a supermarket. One woman asked, "Tell me, Ruth, how is your son George?" "He's getting along fine," Ruth replied. "He's a poet. He just received his master's degree in literature from the university." "And what about Mary?" "She's just as smart as George," Ruth replied. "She graduated from college with a degree in modern art." "Wonderful!" "And how is little Freddy? What is he doing?" "Well, Ruth," she said, "Freddy is still Freddy." "He wouldn't go to college—he became a plumber instead. If it weren't for him, we'd all be starving."

Doctor to new mother: "It appears you're not getting enough sleep. If the baby starts to cry in the middle of the night, who gets up?" She says, "The whole neighborhood."   —Ron Dentinger

M

Mother: "Every time you're naughty I get another gray hair."
Son: "Gee, Mom, you must have been a terror when you were young . . .
    just look at Grandma."   —King Duncan

A super-cautious mother always wore a gauze mask when coming near her baby and insisted that all visitors do likewise. Several older and wiser women tried to tell her tactfully that she was carrying things too far, but the young mother insisted that most parents were absolutely criminal in their carelessness about a child's health. Then the mother mentioned that she thought the baby was beginning to cut a tooth and she wished she could find out about it in some way. A friend with more experience said, "Why, just put your finger in his mouth and . . ." There was such a horrified expression on the mother's face that the friend quickly added, "Of course, boil your finger first."

—King Duncan

I heard about one poor man who had a very difficult mother, but he felt obligated to take care of her. He had a basement apartment built in his home just for her. One day a friend of his paid a visit. They were chatting in the living room. "I remember," said his friend, "what a difficult time your mother gave you. Where is the old girl now?" Fearing that the conversation would be overheard, the poor man simply pointed downward in the direction of the basement apartment. "Oh, I'm sorry," said his friend, "I didn't even know she had died."

—King Duncan

When his pager went off during a council meeting in Knoxville, Tenn., police chief Phil Keith was startled to see that the call was from his mother. Concerned, he rushed to the press table and phoned her. "Phil Keith, are you chewing gum?" asked his mom, who had been watching the council meeting on cable TV. "Yes, ma'am." "Well, it looks awful. Spit it out." Keith dutifully removed the gum and went back to his meeting.

—Knoxville, Tenn., *News Sentinel.*

In 1995 my wife and I bought a new home near the Pacific ocean. When my father learned the price, he asked me how I had come up with the down payment. My reply: "I owe my success to keen investments in the stock market, my wife's thrift, and my mother's failure to throw away my comic book collection."

The harried housewife sprang to the telephone when it rang and listened with relief to the kindly voice in her ear. "How are you, darling?" it said. "What kind of a day are you having?" "Oh, mother," said the housewife, breaking into bitter tears, "I've had such a bad day. The baby won't eat and the washing machine broke down. I haven't had a chance to go shopping, and besides, I've just sprained my ankle and I have to hobble around. On top of that, the house is a mess and I'm supposed to have two couples to dinner tonight." The mother was shocked and was at once all sympathy. "Oh, darling," she said, "sit down, relax, and close your eyes. I'll be over in half an hour. I'll do your shopping, clean up the house, and cook your dinner for you. I'll feed the baby, and I'll call a repairman I know who'll be at your house to fix the washing machine promptly. Now stop crying. I'll do everything. In fact, I'll even call George at the office and tell him he ought to come home and help out for once." "George?" said the housewife. "Who's George?" "Why, George! Your husband! . . . If this 555-1373?" "No, it's 555-1375." "Oh, I'm sorry. I guess I have the wrong number." There was a short pause and the housewife said, "Does this mean you're not coming over?"

—Isaac Asimov, *Asimov Laughs Again*

Isaac Asimov recalled: When my mother was in her nursing home during the last year of her life, I called her frequently and she was always delighted to hear from me and seized the opportunity of telling me the latest news. She said to me: "Yesterday, I was speaking to an old woman of ninety-four"—my mother was seventy-seven at the time—"and in the middle of the conversation, she just dropped dead. Oh, Isaac, everything happens to your mother."

—Isaac Asimov, *Asimov Laughs Again*

M

When my grandson Jonathan was five, he was looking at his parents' wedding pictures in the family album. Matt, his father, described the ceremony and tried to explain its meaning. In a flash, Jonathan understood (or thought he did). He exclaimed, "I think I've got it. That's when Mom came to work for us, right?"

MY MOTHER TAUGHT ME . . .

- My Mother taught me . . . LOGIC . . . If you fall off that swing and break your neck, you can't go to the store with me.
- My Mother taught me MEDICINE . . . If you don't stop crossing your eyes, they're going to freeze that way.
- My Mother taught me TO THINK AHEAD . . . If you don't pass your spelling test, you'll never get a good job!
- My Mother taught me ESP . . . Put your sweater on; don't you think that I know when you're cold?
- My Mother taught me TO MEET A CHALLENGE . . . What were you thinking? Answer me when I talk to you . . . Don't talk back to me!
- My Mother taught me HUMOR . . . When that lawn mower cuts off your toes, don't come running to me.

- My Mother taught me how to BECOME AN ADULT . . . If you don't eat your vegetables, you'll never grow up.
- My mother taught me about GENETICS . . . You are just like your father!
- My mother taught me about my ROOTS . . . Do you think you were born in a barn?
- My mother taught me about the WISDOM of AGE . . . When you get to be my age, you will understand.
- My mother taught me about ANTICIPATION . . . Just wait until your father gets home.
- My mother taught me about RECEIVING . . . You are going to get it when we get home.
- And my all time favorite thing—JUSTICE one day you will have kids, and I hope they turn out just like YOU . . . then you'll see what it's like.

Moms Really Are Special

Mom and Dad were watching TV when Mom said, "I'm tired, and it's getting late. I think I'll go to bed." She went to the kitchen to make sandwiches for the next day's lunches, rinsed out the popcorn bowls, took meat out of the freezer for supper the following evening, checked the cereal box levels, filled the sugar container, put spoons and bowls on the table and started the coffee pot for brewing the next morning. She then put some wet clothes into the dryer, put a load of clothes into the wash, ironed a shirt and secured a loose button. She picked up the newspapers strewn on the floor, picked up the game pieces left on the table and put the telephone book back into the drawer. She watered the plants, emptied a wastebasket and hung up a towel to dry. She yawned and stretched and headed for the bedroom. She stopped by the desk and wrote a note to the teacher, counted out some cash for the field trip, and pulled a textbook out from hiding under the chair. She signed a birthday card for a friend, addressed and stamped the envelope and wrote a quick note for the grocery store. She put both near her purse. Mom then creamed her face, put on moisturizer, brushed and flossed her teeth and trimmed her nails. Hubby called, "I thought you were going to bed." "I'm on my way," she said. She put some water in the dog's dish and put the cat outside, then made sure the doors were locked. She looked in on each of the kids and turned out a bedside lamp, hung up a shirt, threw some dirty socks in the hamper, and had a brief conversation with the one up still doing homework. In her own room, she set the alarm, laid out clothing for the next day, straightened up the shoe rack. She added three things to her list of things to do for tomorrow. About that time, the hubby turned off the TV and announced to no one in particular, "I'm going to bed," and he did.   —*The Good, Clean Funnies List*

September is when millions of shining, happy faces turn toward school. They belong to mothers.

❧

When my mother moved from Manhattan to a rural area in Connecticut, she missed the Yiddish newspaper, *The Forward,* she had been reading for many years. So my sisters and I decided to give her a subscription as a gift. I phoned *The Forward* and explained to the woman who answered that I wanted to buy a gift subscription for my mother. "We don't do gift subscriptions," she replied crisply. "We'll set up an ordinary subscription for your mother and then you write her a nice letter and tell her it's a gift. She'll love to hear from you."
                                                                    —Sophie Glazer

❧

One day a man comes home from work to find total mayhem at home. The kids were outside still in their pajamas playing in the mud and muck. There were empty food boxes and wrappers all around. As he proceeded into the house, he found an even bigger mess. Dishes on the counter, dog food spilled on the floor, a broken glass under the table, and a small pile of sand by the back door. The family room was strewn with toys and various items of clothing, and a lamp had been knocked over. He headed up the stairs, stepping over toys, to look for his wife. He was becoming worried that she may be ill, or that something had happened to her. He found her in the bedroom, still in bed with her pajamas on, reading a book. She looked up at him, smiled, and asked how his day went. He looked at her bewildered and asked, "What happened here today?" She again smiled and answered, "You know everyday when you come home from work and ask me what I did today?" "Yes," was his reply. She answered, "Well, today I didn't do it!"

❧

I still hadn't recorded a greeting on my new answering machine. My mother was visiting, so I asked her to tape one. "This is Marcia's mother," my machine announced. "Marcia is an only child; she never writes, she never calls. So why not give me a buzz? I'd be happy to talk to you. My number is . . ." Everyone called my mother. She loved the attention.

❧

The teen-ager lost a contact lens while playing basketball in his driveway. After a fruitless search, he told his mother the lens was nowhere to be found. Undaunted, she went outside and in a few minutes returned with the lens in her hand. "I really looked hard for that, Mom," said the youth. "How'd you manage to find it?" "We weren't looking for the same thing," she replied. "You were looking for a small piece of plastic. I was looking for $150."

—*Ohio Motorist (AAA)*

My mother said, "You won't amount to anything because you procrastinate." I said, "Just wait." —Judy Tenuta

A mother need only step into the shower to be instantly reassured she is indispensable to every member of her family." —Lynn M. Williams

A mother was very much annoyed because a written excuse explaining her little son's absence from school following a heavy snowfall was demanded by his teacher. Whereupon she wrote: "Dear Teacher: My little Eddie's legs are fourteen inches long. The snow was eighteen inches deep. Now maybe you understand why he didn't get to school yesterday." —*Nuggets*

Lunching with friends, a young mother listened to the older women in the group discuss elaborate burglar alarms at great length. They weighed the pros and cons of systems that connect directly to the police station and those that produce shrill electronic sounds. During a lull in the conversation, one of the women asked the silent mother what she would do if a thief broke into her home. She shrugged and replied, "Well, you know, I have four small children. If some burglar came into my bedroom, I'm sure I'd just get up, take him by the hand, and lead him to the bathroom."

Entering the supermarket with her five bouncing, exuberant children, a harassed mother asked the manager, "Isn't there a cereal that will sap their energy?"

The mother was bravely gulping down some of the cake her young daughter had so thoughtfully baked as a "surprise" for her birthday. After somehow managing to convey the idea, between laborious swallows, that she was enjoying herself, the little girl beamed, "I'm so glad you like it, Mommy. There should have been 32 candles on the cake but they were all gone when I took it out of the oven."   —*Family Digest*

A woman who wanted to show off her son's scientific knowledge to members of her bridge club called the youngster in and asked: "Bobby, what does it mean when steam comes out of the spout of the kettle?" "It means," said Bobby, "that you are going to open one of Daddy's letters."
                                                           —*Woodside Chain News*

The psychiatrist turned to the child's mother and said, "I will see Buddy next month, but you need help yourself. You are upset and worried about the child, so I suggest you take one of these tranquilizers each day until I see you again." A month later the mother brought the child back. "How is Buddy getting along?" asked the doctor. "Who cares?" replied the mother.
                                                           —*Woodmen of the World*

MOTHERS-IN-LAW

Behind every successful man stands an absolutely astounded mother-in-law.

The man who claims that his mother-in-law can't take a joke forgets himself.
                                                           —Jeff Rovin

I said to my mother-in-law, "Mi casa, su casa" and last week she sold it.

The cop stopped the speeding motorist and asked, "Where's the fire, buddy?" Replied the anguished man behind the wheel, "In the place my wife's going to give me if I miss the plane her mother's coming in on."
                                                           —*Wall Street Journal*

MOVIES

A few years ago, I read that the movie, *Forrest Gump,* had taken in well over 300 million dollars. But the studio insists that it has actually lost 62 million. Maybe Forrest Gump was doing their accounting.   —*Screen Gem*

In Hollywood, there are just three ages for women: babe, district attorney, and *Driving Miss Daisy.*   —Olivia Goldsmith, *The First Wives Club*

My three grandsons were on their way to the movies to see a cowboy picture, but one objected to it because he'd heard it had too many kissing scenes. His younger brother said, "That's okay—when the kissing starts, we can close our eyes and pretend he's choking her."

Actor James Garner, when asked if he would ever do a nude scene, replied, "No. I don't do horror films."

Some of my best leading men have been dogs and horses.

—Elizabeth Taylor

They say the movies should be more like life. I think life should be more like the movies.   —Myrna Loy

Hollywood: It's a great place to live, but I wouldn't want to visit there.

—Will Rogers,

Some of my best leading men have been dogs and horses.

—Elizabeth Taylor

A young man, returning a library book about movie stars of the silent-film era, opened it to a photograph of vamp queen Theda Bara. "Was she really a sex symbol in the '20s?" he asked. "Yes, she was," the librarian answered. The teen-ager studied the photograph. "Boy," he said finally, "no wonder you people had a depression.

MULES

Only a fool argues with a skunk, a mule or the cook.   —Harry Oliver

MURDER

If the desire to kill and the opportunity to kill came always together, who would escape hanging?   —Mark Twain

MURPHY'S FAMOUS LAW

If anything can go wrong, it will—is said to have entered history in 1949 at Edwards Air Force Base, when a malfunctioning strap transducer moved a Captain Murphy to his highest eloquence. Other truths attributed to Murphy are:

- Nothing is ever as simple as it seems.
- Everything takes longer than you expect, and, left to themselves, things always go from bad to worse.

Since Murphy's extraordinary leap into immortality, many imitators have sought in similar manner to plumb the human condition. Perhaps the most successful was British historian C. Northcote Parkinson, who found that work expands to fill the time allotted to it. Next in notoriety is the (Lawrence) Peter Principle, that in every hierarchy each employee tends to rise to his level of incompetence.

Lesser known, but just as penetrating, are all the slippery laws of money. For example, there's Parkinson's Second Law, which states that expenditures rise to meet income. Further refined by Dunn's Discovery—that the shortest measurable interval of time is the time between the moment you put a little extra aside for a sudden emergency and the arrival of that emergency. This state of affairs is summed up in Gumperson's Law: that after a rise in salary you will have less money at the end of each month than you had before. With regard to products, Graditor's Laws: (1) If it can break it will, but only after the warranty expires, and (2) A necessary item only goes on sale after you have purchased it at the regular price. To which you can add Dyer's Discovery: it's easy to tell when you've got a bargain—it doesn't fit. And Herblock's Law: If it's good, they'll stop making it.

Car owners are well acquainted with Hartman Automotive Laws: (1) Nothing minor ever happens to a car on the weekend. (2) Nothing minor ever happens to a car on a trip. (3) Nothing minor ever happens to a car. Which brings me to Goldwyn's Law of Contracts: A verbal contract isn't worth the paper it's written on.

Such "law"-giving actually precedes Murphy by a good many centuries. Samuel Butler knew that all progress is based on the innate desire for every organism to live beyond its income. Josh Billings similarly admonished: Live within your income, even if you have to borrow to do it.

Another great name in the field is Finagle. His unique contributions came in the area of science, but Finagle's Laws on Information apply equally to understanding financial transactions: (1) The information you have is not what you want. (2) The information you want is not what you need. (3) The information you need is not what you can obtain. (4) The information you can obtain costs more than you want to pay.

The difference between rich and poor is sharply caught by Getty's Reminder, that the meek shall inherit the earth but not its mineral rights. Followed by the Golden Rule of Arts and Sciences: Whoever has the gold makes the rules. Donohue's Law says that what's worth doing is worth doing for money. And Goldfarber's Law, that under any system a few sharpies will beat the rest of us.

On pocketbook matters, everyone has to keep his eyes open. It's Gross's Law that when two people meet to decide how to spend a third person's money, fraud will result. As in O'Doyle's Corollary: No matter how many reporters share a cab, and no matter who pays, each puts the full fare on his own expense account.

Woody Allen said that the lion shall lay down with the lamb, but the lamb won't get much sleep. To which add Clopton's Law: For every credibility gap there's a gullibility fill. The Checkbook Balancer's Law holds that in matters of dispute, the bank's balance is always smaller than yours. But if you think the problem is bad now, Epstein adds, just wait until we've solved it. Then there is Quinn's Law: The reader interest generated by any newspaper column is inversely proportional to the importance of its subject.

In his book, *The Official Rules at Home,* Paul Dickson adds a few new corollaries. Here is a sample of Dickson's laws, rules, observations and maxims:

Ballweg's Discovery: Whenever there is a flat surface, someone will find something to put on it. Rabbe's Rule of the Bedroom: The spouse who snores louder always falls asleep first. Rosenbaum's Rule: The easiest way to find something lost around the house is to buy a replacement. Smith's Fourth Law of Inertia: A body at rest tends to watch television.

Last, but not least, are the new creations:

MURPHY'S LAWS OF TECHNOLOGY

- Murphy's Technology Law #1: You can never tell which way the train went by looking at the track.
- Murphy's Technology Law #2: Logic is a systematic method of coming to the wrong conclusion with confidence.
- Murphy's Technology Law #3: Technology is dominated by those who manage what they do not understand.
- Murphy's Technology Law #4: If builders built buildings the way programmers wrote programs, then the first woodpecker that came along would destroy civilization.
- Murphy's Technology Law #5: An expert is one who knows more and more about less and less until he/she knows absolutely everything about nothing.
- Murphy's Technology Law #6: Tell a man there are 300 billion stars in the universe, and he'll believe you. Tell him a bench has wet paint on it, and he'll have to touch to be sure.
- Murphy's Technology Law #7: All great discoveries are made by mistake.
- Murphy's Technology Law #8: Nothing ever gets built on schedule or within budget.
- Murphy's Technology Law #9: All's well that ends . . . period.
- Murphy's Technology Law #10: A meeting is an event at which minutes are kept and hours are lost.
- Murphy's Technology Law #11: The first myth of management is that it exists.
- Murphy's Technology Law #12: A failure will not appear until a unit has passed final inspection.
- Murphy's Technology Law #13: New systems generate new problems.
- Murphy's Technology Law #14: To err is human, but to really foul things up requires a computer.
- Murphy's Technology Law #15: We don't know one-millionth of one percent about anything.
- Murphy's Technology Law #16: Any given program, when running, is obsolete.
- Murphy's Technology Law #17: A computer makes as many mistakes in two seconds as 20 men working 20 years make.

MUSIC

I've never heard such corny lyrics, such simpering sentimentality, such repetitious, uninspired melody. Man, we've got a hit on our hands!

—Brad Anderson

The Beatles said, "All you need is love." And then they broke up.

—Larry Norman

Russian pianist and composer Anton Rubinstein was notoriously difficult to rouse in the mornings. The story goes that his wife figured out a way to get him out of bed. She would play an incomplete chord on the piano. This would so annoy the maestro's ear that he'd leap out of bed, go to the piano and complete the chord. While he was doing this, his wife would remove the bedclothes.

From a British schoolboy's essay: "Johann Sebastian Bach was a most prolific composer. He was the father of twenty children. In his spare time he practiced in the attic on a spinster."

Too many pieces of music finish too long after the end.   —Igor Stravinsky

Anything that is too stupid to be spoken is sung.   —Voltaire

M

I don't know anything about music. In my line you don't have to.
                                                           —Elvis Presley

There are some experiences in life which should not be demanded twice from any man, and one of them is listening to the Brahms Requiem.
                                                   —George Bernard Shaw

Wagner's music is better than it sounds.   —Mark Twain

These are stories and test question answers accumulated by music teachers in the state of Missouri.

- Agnus Dei was a woman composer famous for her church music.
- Refrain means don't do it. A refrain in music is the part you better not try to sing.
- A virtuoso is a musician with real high morals.
- John Sebastian Bach died from 1750 to the present.
- Beethoven wrote music even though he was deaf. He was so deaf he wrote loud music. He took long walks in the forest even when everyone was calling him. I guess he could not hear so good.
- Beethoven expired in 1827 and later died from this.

- Henry Purcell is a well known composer few people have ever heard of.
- Aaron Copland is one of your most famous contemporary composers. It is unusual to be contemporary. Most composers do not live until they are dead.
- An opera is a song of bigly size.
- In the last scene of Pagliacci, Canio stabs Nedda who is the one he really loves. Pretty soon Silvio also gets stabbed, and they all live happily ever after.
- Music sung by two people at the same time is called a duel.
- Caruso was at first an Italian. Then someone heard his voice and said he would go a long way. And so he came to America.
- Most authorities agree that music of antiquity was written long ago.
- Probably the most marvelous fugue was the one between the Hatfields and Mc-Coys.
- My very best liked piece of music is the Bronze Lullaby.
- My favorite composer is Opus.
- A harp is a nude piano.
- A trumpet is an instrument when it is not an elephant sound.
- While trombones have tubes, trumpets prefer to wear valves.
- The double bass is also called the bass viol, string bass, and bass fiddle. It has so many names because it is so huge.
- When electric currents go through them, guitars start making sounds. So would anybody.
- Question: What are kettle drums called? Answer: Kettle drums.
- A bassoon looks like nothing I have ever heard.
- Last month I found out how a clarinet works by taking it apart. I both found out and got in trouble.
- For some reason, they always put a treble clef in front of every line of flute music. You just watch.
- I can't reach the brakes on this piano!
- Anyone who can read all the instrument notes at the same time gets to be the conductor.
- The flute is a skinny-high shape-sounded instrument.
- Music instrument has a plural known as orchestra.
- I would like for you to teach me to play the cello. Would tomorrow or Friday be best?
- It is easy to teach anyone to play the maracas. Just grip the neck and shake him in rhythm.
- Just about any animal skin can be stretched over a frame to make a pleasant sound once the animal is removed.

Missouri School Music Newsletter, collected by Harold Dunn

═══════════════════════════════════╪═══════════════════════════════════

At a party to celebrate the success of the musical *Showboat,* the wife of the composer Jerome Kern was approached by a gushing fan. "And to think your husband wrote that fabulous song 'Old Man River'! It's absolutely my favorite—" "No, you've got it wrong," interrupted the wife of Oscar Hammerstein.

"My husband wrote 'Old Man River.' Her husband wrote, 'Dum dum dum-dum, da dum dum dum-dum . . .'"

~

Q: What happens when you play country music backwards?
A: Your wife comes back, you get your truck back, your boss gives you back your job, your momma gets out of jail, the man you shot in Reno survives and drops all charges . . .

~

The local symphony orchestra in a small midwestern town was rehearsing for a concert at a Marriott hotel. After the last strains of Handel's Largo floated out, the mother of one of the violinists went up to the conductor and said, "Won't you please play Handel's Largo?" "But we've just finished playing it," the conductor replied. The woman sank back in her chair. "Oh, I wish I'd known it," she sighed. "It's my favorite piece."

~

Q: What do you get when you play New Age music backward?
A: New Age music.

~

Explaining why the keys of his piano were so yellow, Victor Borge insisted that it was not because the piano was old, but because the elephant smoked too much.

~

During rehearsals and performances of the opera *Thais,* baritone Sherrill Milnes was required to lift leading lady Beverly Sills an aggregate of 30 times and carry her across the stage. At one point she apologized for those weighty artistic duties, but a cheerful Milnes assured her they didn't really bother him. "After all," he said, "I was a farm boy and accustomed to hoisting five-hundred-pound bales of hay." "Somehow," she says, "our love scene that night lacked its usual ardor."
                                        —Beverly Sills, *Bubbles, An Encore*

~

Periodically, the comment is heard that "The Star-Spangled Banner" is too hard to sing. But much of the charm of public gatherings In the United States is the suspense over whether the soloist is going to make it.

NAMES

Professional golfer Karen Permezel hails from Yackandandah, Australia. Finding that name to be a mouthful, writers sometimes ask Permezel where the town is located. Permezel is happy to be of assistance. "It's near Mount Murramurrabong, not far from Tangambalanga," she replies. —*Sports Illustrated*

～

Heintz Loeffler, a successful businessman, was a Rear Admiral during World War II, and he is so listed in various directories. One day he received a letter from a respected charity that began, "Dear Rear . . ."

NATIVE AMERICANS

When NASA was preparing for the Apollo project, they did some astronaut training on a Navajo reservation. One day, a Navajo elder and his son were herding sheep and came across the space crew. The old man, who spoke only Navajo, asked a question which his son translated. "What are these guys in the big suits doing?" A member of the crew said they were practicing for their trip to the moon. The old man got all excited and asked if he could send a message to the moon with the astronauts. Recognizing a promotional opportunity for the spin-doctors, the NASA folks found a tape recorder. After the old man recorded his message, they asked the son to translate it. He refused. So the NASA reps brought the tape to the reservation where the rest of the tribe listened and laughed but refused to translate the elder's message to the moon. Finally, the NASA crew called in an official government translator. He reported that the moon message said, "Watch out for these guys; they have come to steal your land."

～

When asked by an anthropologist what the Native Americans called America before the white man came, one of them said simply, "Ours."

～

A Native American petitioned a judge in a New Mexico court for permission to change his name to a shorter one. "What is your name now?" asked the judge. "Chief Screeching Train Whistle." "And what do you wish to change it to?" The Indian folded his arms and grunted, "Toots."
—*How the Platform Professionals Keep 'em Laughin'*

NATURE

One day recently our five-year-old daughter, Roberta, was sitting very quietly in the kitchen, staring out the window. I thought she was wrestling with a very serious problem, so I asked her what was on her mind. "Dad," she replied, "is Mother Nature God's wife?"   —*Irish Grit*

NEIGHBORHOODS

My neighborhood is so dangerous, AOL can't even deliver e-mail here.
—Bill Jones

NEIGHBORS

Don't buy the house; buy the neighbor.   —Russian proverb

The Bible tells us to love our neighbors, and also to love our enemies; probably because they are generally the same people.   —G. K. Chesterton

Nothing makes you more tolerant of a neighbor's noisy party than being there.
—Franklin P. Jones

The only thing more disturbing than a neighbor with a noisy old car is a neighbor with a quiet new one. Don't be jealous if your neighbor has a nicer house than you do; it may help when you go to sell.   —Richard C. Miller

NEW YEAR

May all your troubles last as long as your New Year's resolutions.

Paw was getting a little boisterous at the New Year's Eve party. Maw: "Remind me to put some steak on your black eye when we get home." Paw: "But I haven't got a black eye." Maw: "You're not home yet." —*Catholic Workmen*

NEW YORK

Question: How many polite, considerate New Yorkers does it take to screw in a light bulb?
Answer: Both of them.

THE RULES FOR DRIVING IN NEW YORK CITY

- When on a one-way street, stay to the right to allow oncoming traffic to pass.
- Never, ever, stop for a pedestrian unless he flings himself under the wheels of your car.
- The first parking space you see will be the last parking space you see. Grab it.
- Never get in the way of a car that needs extensive body work.

- Always look both ways when running a red light.
- Never use directional signals when changing lanes. They only warn other drivers to speed up and not let you in.
- Making eye contact revokes your right of way.
- Whenever possible, stop in the middle of a crosswalk to ensure inconveniencing as many pedestrians as possible. And if a pedestrian ahead of you steps into the road, speed up, honk or yell obscenities loudly and chase him back upon the curb. Pedestrians have no rights.

"Night Heat," a CBS detective series, is filmed in Toronto, Canada, and the city's much-vaunted cleanliness sometimes presents a problem for co-producers Sonny Grosso and Larry Jacobson. Being New Yorkers, "we thought an alley we were shooting in was too clean," says Jacobson. "So we sprayed some graffiti on it. We took a lunch break, and when we got back it was all cleaned up."
—Ben Yagoda in *TV Guide*

A man who was interested in joining New York City's Citizen Pruner Corps—a group that prunes street trees—decided that the job was "too dangerous." It seems an acquaintance had taken it upon himself to clip a dead limb from a tree in front of his apartment building. He cut his hand, fell out of the tree and landed on a passerby, who thought he was being attacked. The passerby slugged the pruner, who staggered into the street and was almost hit by a taxi before he fled, only to be brought down by a neighborhood dog that bit him and tore his pants.
—William E. Geist

New York City's former mayor David N. Dinkins, when urged by Manhattan officials to buy some property thought to be an "extraordinary opportunity for the city," said: "If they're selling elephants two for a quarter, that's a great bargain. But only if you have a quarter—and only if you need elephants."

NEWLYWEDS

My niece Charlotte after ten months of marriage exclaimed: "I have my husband eating out of my hand." My reply: "Beats washing dishes, doesn't it?"

When Connie and I were first married, my parents visited us in our new home. Dad was impressed with the various safety precautions I had taken. He noted the smoke detectors, the first-aid kit and a list of emergency phone numbers. Dad also saw that I had four fire extinguishers—one in the kitchen, one in the garage; one in the family room next to the woodstove; and one in the master bedroom. With a sly look on his face, Dad elbowed Mom in the ribs and said, "Gee, Alice, it's been years since we needed a fire extinguisher in our bedroom!"

~

A word to new brides: if you want to be remembered forever, don't write a thank-you note for a wedding gift.   —Edward L. Rankin, Jr.

NEWSPAPERS

News article: "A hole has been found in the fence surrounding the Happydale Nudist Colony. Police are looking into it."

~

In my opinion the nightly news on television is a big waste of time. It's the same news every night. It just happens to different people.   —Ron Dentinger

~

John Franklin, a noted evangelist, was speaking at two different churches in a large city in the same week. A reporter was present at the first service. After the sermon the evangelist pleaded with the reporter not to publish in the local paper any of the jokes he had used that night, since he was going to use the same stories the following night at the other church. The next morning the reporter published an excellent review of the evangelist's message and concluded with these words: "The Rev. Mr. Franklin also told many stories that cannot be published."

N

~

Headline on a Utica, N.Y., *Observer-Dispatch* report of a docking accident: "Staten Island Ferry Hits Pie, 18 Injured."

~

In a North Platte, Neb., *Telegraph* story about Croatia: "The restaurants serve fresh Adriatic octopus and bars serve just about any alcoholic drunk you can think of."

~

Item from the Cincinnati *Post:* "Representatives of teachers' organizations appeared before the board to ask for a further cost-of-loving adjustment in wages."

~

The Wooster, Ohio, *Daily Record* printed a coupon for a local car wash with this claim: "Absolutely nothing touches your car except soup and water."

The widow phoned the newspaper and asked how much they charged for running obituaries. "A dollar an inch," she was told. "Oh dear," she said, "It will be far too expensive. My husband was six feet tall."

Fred Abernathy was a devoted reader of the obituary column of his local paper. All of Fred's friends knew of this habit, so one day they decided to play a trick on him by placing his name and picture in the obituaries. The following morning Fred picked up his newspaper, turned to the obituary page, and there he saw his name, his biography and his photo. Startled, he went to the telephone and rang up his pal, George. "Listen," he said. "Do you have the morning paper? You do? Please turn to the obituary page. You have? What do you see in the second column?" There was a pause, then George said, "Holy smoke! It's you, Fred! It's you all right! Listen, where are you calling from?"

The fact that a man is a newspaper reporter is evidence of some flaw of character.

—Lyndon Johnson

ACTUAL HEADLINES:
Lawyer Says Client Is Not That Guilty
Alzheimer's Center Prepares for an Affair to Remember
Include Your Children When Baking Cookies
Something Went Wrong in Jet Crash, Experts Say
Police Begin Campaign to Run Down Jaywalkers
Gas Cloud Clears Out Taco Bell
Harrisburg Postal Employees Gun Club Members Meet
Drunks Get Nine Months in Violin Case
Iraqi Head Seeks Arms
British Left Waffles on Falkland Islands
Clinton Wins Budget; More Lies Ahead
Plane Too Close to Ground, Crash Probe Told
Miners Refuse to Work After Death
Juvenile Court to Try Shooting Defendant
Stolen Painting Found by Tree
Legislator Wants Tougher Death Penalty
Man Jumps Off 2nd Street Bridge. Neither Jumper Nor Body Found
After Detour to California Shuttle Returns to Earth
Man Found Dead in Cemetery
Gunfire in Sarajevo Threatens Cease-fire

War Dims Hope for Peace
If Strike Isn't Settled Quickly, It May Last a While
Couple Slain; Police Suspect Homicide
Man Struck by Lightning Faces Battery Charge
New Study of Obesity Looks for Larger Test Group
Properly Drafted Will Reduces Anxiety After Death
Study Reveals Those Without Insurance Die More Often
Experts Increase Probability of Big Quake in California
Kids Make Nutritious Snacks
Local High School Dropouts Cut in Half
Fried Chicken Cooked in Microwave Wins Trip
Woman Improving After Fatal Crash
Typhoon Rips Through Cemetery; Hundreds Dead
Red Tape Holds Up New Bridge
Deer Kill 17,000
Chef Throws His Heart into Helping Feed Needy
Arson Suspect Is Held in Massachusetts Fire
British Union Finds Dwarfs in Short Supply
Lansing Residents Can Drop Off Trees
New Vaccine May Contain Rabies
Man Minus Ear Waives Hearing
Deaf College Opens Doors to Hearing
Prosecutor Releases Probe into Undersheriff
Old School Pillars Are Replaced by Alumni
Hospitals Are Sued by 7 Foot Doctors
Marijuana Issue Sent to a Joint Committee
Publicize Your Business Absolutely Free! Send $6.

The Boston Globe ran a story on the Ford/Volvo deal. The headline was "Have You Driven a Fjord Lately?"

~

In an item about a pet tattoo clinic, the West Bend, Wisconsin Daily News reported: "The fee for the tattooing is $5 per dog and is $3 for senior citizens age 55 and over."

NOISE

The worst wheel of the cart makes the most noise.   —Benjamin Franklin

~

Noise proves nothing. Often a hen who has merely laid an egg cackles as if she has laid an asteroid.   —Mark Twain

NOTHING

When you have nothing to say, say nothing. —Charles Caleb Colton

❦

The trouble with doing nothing is that you never know when you are finished.
—Edna Wolf

❦

Nothing's as good as . . .
A good yawn, with a good stretch.
Knowing the answer to a quiz-show question (and having somebody around
to hear us answer it).
Being a pound lighter on the bathroom scale.
Hearing oneself quoted.
A parking meter with ten minutes left on it.
Hearing laughter in the house in the morning.
A reachable itch. —James Alexander Thom

NOVEMBER

November is nature's way of giving you time to eat up the leftover Halloween candy before you have to start eating up the leftover turkey. — Bill Tammeus

------------------------------ O ------------------------------

OLD AGE

"What are you so happy about?" I asked my 101-year old great-aunt one day. "I broke a mirror," she replied. "But that means seven years of bad luck." "I know," she said, beaming. "Isn't it wonderful?"

❦

The doctor asked the weather-beaten mountaineer how he was feeling. "It's like this," drawled the man from the hills after a few seconds of silence, "I'm still kickin', but I ain't raising any dust." —Ed Steiner

❦

Why can't we build orphanages next to homes for the aged? If someone's sitting in a rocker, it won't be long before a kid will be in his lap.
—Cloris Leachman

❦

You know you're getting older when in the morning you hear snap, crackle, pop, and it isn't your breakfast cereal.

An elderly couple came back from a wedding one afternoon and were in a pretty romantic mood. While sitting on their loveseat, the elderly woman looked at her companion and said, "I remember when you used to kiss me every chance you had." The old man feeling a bit obliged leaned over and gave her a peck on the cheek. Then she said, "I also remember when you used to hold my hand at every opportunity." The old man again feeling obligated reached over and gently placed his hand on hers. The elderly woman then stated, "I also remember when you used to nibble on my neck and send chills down my spine." This time the old man had a blank stare on his face and started to get up off the couch. As he began to walk out of the living room his wife asked, "Was it something I said? Where are you going?" The old man looked at her and replied, "I'm going in the other room to get my teeth!"

In Cape Coral, Florida, two elderly women were out driving in a large car, both could barely see over the dashboard. As they were cruising along they came to an intersection. The stoplight was red but they just went on through the red light. The woman in the passenger seat thought to herself, "I must be losing my mind, I swear we just went through a red light." After a few more minutes they came to another intersection and the light was red again, and again they went right through. This time Bessie in the passenger seat was almost sure that the light had been red, but was really concerned that she was mistaken. She was getting nervous and decided to pay very close attention to the road and the next intersection to see what was going on. At the next intersection, sure enough, the light was definitely red and they went right through. She turned to the woman driving and said, "Shirley! Did you know we just ran through three red lights in a row! You could have killed us!" Shirley turned to her and said, "Oh, am I driving?"

A man once counseled his son that if he wanted to live a long life, the secret was to sprinkle a little gunpowder on his cornflakes every morning. The son did this religiously, and he lived to the age of 93. When he died, he left 14 children, 28 grandchildren, 35 great-grandchildren, and a 15-foot hole in the wall of the crematorium.

Why do so many retirees move south into the sun and then do everything they can to stay out of it? —Ed Fischer and Jane Thomas Noland,
What's So Funny About Getting Old?

In the village post office a stranger saw the local patriarch sitting on a flour barrel, whistling. A by-stander informed him that the old fellow already had passed his hundredth birthday. Impressed, the man exclaimed, "That's amazing!" "We don't see nothing amazing about it around here," was the laconic reply. "All he's done is grow old—and he took longer to do that than most people would!"

—Jim Kelly

William Mann tells about the old-timer talking with his grandson. "If you were 16 years old, Granddaddy, what would you wish for most of all?" the lad questioned. The elderly gentleman thought only a moment before answering, "I reckon nothin' else, son."

OOPS!

Herb Uttley walked into the Cottonwood Drugstore and asked the pharmacist if he had a cure for hiccups. The pharmacist walked around the corner and approached Herb. He reached out and slapped Herb soundly in the back. The pharmacist then hopefully asked, "Do you have the hiccups now?" As Herb composed himself after such a sudden blow, he answered the pharmacist, "No, I do not! But I'll just bet you that my wife out in the car still does."

The following was written on the program of the New Mexico Arts and Crafts Fair: "Graduating with a B.F.A. from Northern Arizona University in 1976, Ernest Wilmeth turned to clay in 1982."

A family spent the night in a motel and the wife had awakened early. She packed the bags and carried them to the car. Returning after one load she accidentally went into the wrong room. Seeing a sleeping man and assuming it was her husband, she shook the headboard and shouted as loud as she could, "Get out of that bed!" Suddenly she realized her mistake, and she turned and ran out. As she ran she heard the man exclaim, "Boy, that sure is some wake-up service."

An elderly lady did her shopping and, upon return, found four males in her car. She dropped her shopping bags and drew her handgun, proceeding to scream at them at the top of her voice that she knows how to use her gun and that she will if required: so get out of the car. The four men didn't wait around for a second invitation but got out and ran like mad, whereupon the lady proceeded to load her shopping bags into the back of the car and get into the driver's seat. Small problem: Her key wouldn't fit the ignition. Her car was identical and parked four or five spaces farther down. She loaded her bags into her car and drove to the police station. The sergeant to whom she told the story nearly tore himself in two with laughter and pointed to the other end of the counter, where four pale white males were reporting a carjacking by a mad elderly white woman; no charges were filed.

From Illinois State University's *Daily Vidette:* "Correction: It was incorrectly reported that today is T-shirt Appreciation Day. In fact, it is Teacher Appreciation Day."

From the Prescott, Ariz., *Daily Courier:* "Arizona's fifth-largest bank is seeking experienced bankers to stuff a downtown office."

The Peoria, Ill., *Journal Star* reported that after an accident a man was ticketed for driving while expired.

From a card in a Moroccan hotel room: "Males and snacks may be served in your room at any time. Please call room service."

From the Haverford, Pa., Main Line Art Center class-registration booklet: "Advanced Life Painting Studio. This group grows out of a need for professional artists to have an opportunity to paint from the model. Tuition includes model feel."

A wedding announcement in the Norwich, Conn., *Bulletin* described the bride-to-be: "She is employed as an athletic strainer by the University of New Haven."

The dosage on a doctor's prescription for a congested Bremerton, Wash., four-year-old: "Give half teaspoon four times daily for funny nose."

From a hospital cafeteria menu, printed in the Moscow Pullman, Idaho, *Daily News:* "Wednesday lunch—Grilled Pastrami and Swill on Dark Rye."

In the Houston, Texas, *Chronicle* classified-ad section for farms and ranches: "Deer, turkey, wild wife."

Classified ad in St. Peters, Mo., *Journal,* listing job benefits: "Advancement Opportunities. Professional Training. $350 per week plus bones."

~

In the police-report section of the Valdosta, Ga., *Daily Times:* "A man was arrested and charged with felony terroristic threats and possession of a forearm by a convicted felon."

~

In the Sterling, Kan., *Bulletin:* "Promotion exercises will be held Thursday for 53 eighth-graders. The choir will sing 'I Am But a Small Vice.'"

~

From a wedding announcement: "Following a trip to Mexico, the couple, who met on a blind date set up by a fiend, will live in Waco."

~

In a restaurant review: "If prime rib is your thing, they have a dull dinner with salad, potato, dessert and beverage."

~

Classified ad in the Edina, Minn., *Star Tribune:* "String of perils, 30 years old, with box."

~

Help-wanted ad in *The Blowing Rocket,* Blowing Rock, N.C.: "Part-time youth director wanted. Salary confiscated with experience."

~

In the *San Diego Union-Tribune:* "San Marcos Mayor Lee Thibadeau was quoted incorrectly in an article about his candidacy for county supervisor. Thibadeau compared the country to 'a ship in a storm with a bunch of holes in it,' not 'a ship in a storm with a bunch of fools in it,' The *San Diego Union-Tribune* regrets the error."

~

Elisabeth Shoemaker Linscott, one of the first women to enlist in the Marine Corps in 1918, tells about the dispersal of her unit when the war ended: "The Secretary of the Navy dismissed us at a big press-covered ceremony. He said the Corps would miss us, and finished, in ringing tones, with, 'We will not forget you. As we embraced you in uniform yesterday, we will embrace you without uniforms tomorrow.'"
                                                        —*Modern Maturity*

~

Spotted in the *Sacramento Bee:* "In some editions of today's Food Section, an incorrect number of jalapeño peppers was given for Elaine Corn's Southwestern chicken-salad recipe. The recipe should call for two, not 21, jalapeño peppers."

～

From an engagement announcement in the Springfield, Mass., *Union-News:* "The future bride graduated with a master's degree in English and she is pursuing a Ph.D. and an English instructor."

～

Realty ad in Ishpeming, Mich., *Action Shopper:* "Starter home, large kitchen with mice eating area."

～

Classified ad for drivers in the Harrisburg, Pa., *Sunday Patriot News:* "Taking applications for experienced dumb truck drivers."

～

From a Lenexa, Kan., church bulletin's Order of Service: "We present our thighs and offerings."

～

An Associated Press report described Fresno State University basketball coach Jerry Tarkanian: "During the scrimmage, Tarkanian paced the sideline with his hands in his pockets while biting his nails."

～

O

In a Pittsburgh *Post-Gazette* brief about the Pittsburgh Zoo seeking historical items: "The zoo will use the material for marketing and public relations porpoises."

～

The Columbus, Ohio, *Dispatch* reported that country singer Garth Brooks was worried whether his new album would sell: "Perhaps he's trying to lower expectations in case it doesn't go plutonium."

～

In the 1993 school calendar published by Sherman Union High School in Moro, Ore., the list of rules for students riding school buses included this one: "Pupils will remain sedated while the bus is in motion."

～

Notice published in the Elizabethtown, Ky., *News Enterprise:* "Two-year-old family pet, male, chocolate-covered Lab retriever, lost Sept. 18 on Hill Street."

Mother to daughter: "Did your girlfriends admire your engagement ring?" The daughter says, "More than that. Two of them recognized it."

~

A correction in the Yuma, Arizona, *Daily Sun* still needs work. It reads: "Terri K is not a Marine sergeant, as reported in Thursday's 'Yuma Roundup.' He is the wife of one."

~

From an article in the Beech Grove, Indiana, *Perry Weekly:* "For 33 years, Elton H. Geshwiler has presided over the Beech Grove city-council meetings.

His last one was Monday night. The council honored the mayor by resenting him with an official resolution."

~

Notice in *This Month in Waco,* a bulletin published in Waco, Texas: "Zoo Trackers: If you are working in the Cameron Park Zoological Society office or at the zoo, please sign in and out on the sheep provided for volunteers."

~

The first mistake that Scott Reyst made was breaking into the home of James Bannon, Detroit's executive deputy police Chief. The 18-year-old's second mistake was showing up at the preliminary hearing wearing the deputy chief's boots. —*Punch*

~

From a department-store ad in the Elmira, N.Y., *Star-Gazette:* "Whatever type your father is, we know we can help you choose a gift to make him grim all over." —Antony B. Lake, *A Pleasury of Witticisms and Word Play*

~

From a classified ad in the Fairmont, W. Va., *Times West Virginian:* "Siding and roofing crews needed. Must have own fools and trucks."

~

From the Madison County, Ky., *Post-Advertiser:* "For her daughter's wedding Mrs. C wore a floor-length melon grown with white accessories."

~

In a TV program guide in the Chicago *Tribune:* "10 P.M.: 'Dick Cavett.' Isaac Bashevis, singer."

From an ad in Western *Angling:* "A complete line of fishing gear. Fishing lies and information available."

~

From an engagement announcement in the Jonesboro, Ark., *Sun:* "He will receive a B.S. degree in Wildwife Management."

~

From a California bar association's newsletter: "Correction—the following typo appeared in our last bulletin: 'Lunch will be gin at 12:15.' Please correct to read '12 noon.'"

~

In the Bellingham, Wash., *Herald:* "The recipe for Chewy Oatmeal Surprise Cookies in yesterday's food section omitted the three cups of oatmeal. The rest of the ingredients are correct."

~

From the Webster, Mass., *Times:* "The letter to the editor that objected to a dog in Dudley should have read 'the owner should be fined and warned,' not 'fixed and wormed.'"

Before you send out your next résumé, weed out the goofs, cautions recruiting executive Robert Half, who has been collecting examples of "resumania" for years. Some of his favorites:

1. "Please call after 5:30 P.M. because I am self-employed and my employer does not know I am looking for another job."
2. "I am very conscientious and accurite."
3. "I am also a notary republic."
4. "The firm currently employs 20 odd people."
5. "My consideration will be given to relocation anywhere in the English-speaking world and/or Washington, D.C."
6. Under physical disabilities: "Minor allergies to house cats and Mongolian sheep."
7. Reasons given for leaving the last job: "The company made me a scapegoat—just like my previous three employers did."

Business Times

From the Placerville, California, *Mountain Democrat:* "Actor Jimmy Stewart's name was incorrectly spelled in Wednesday's 'Beyond the Beat' column as H-e-n-r-y F-o-n-d-a."

From *Focus,* an AT&T employee magazine: "Our Feb. 9 issue reported our 1987 earnings per share as $1.88 billion. The addition of 'billion' was a typesetter's error, and we apologize for any ecstasy the error may have caused."

In the Oxford, Ohio, *Press:* "Gourmets of any religious persuasion can register to attend the class entitled 'Fundamental Gourmet Cooking Methods and Techniques.' A typographical error in last week's paper was not intended to limit the class to Methodists only."

OPERATORS

The following are real conversations Directory Enquiries operators had with callers, as revealed in interviews with staff at the Cardiff DE Centre.

Caller: I'd like the number of the Argoed Fish Bar in Cardiff, please.
Operator: I'm sorry, there's no listing. Is the spelling correct?
Caller: Well, it used to be called the Bargoed Fish Bar but the B fell off.

Then there was the caller who asked for a knitwear company in Woven.

Operator: Woven? Are you sure?
Caller: Yes. That's what it says on the label—Woven in Scotland.

Caller: I'd like the RSPCA please.
Operator: Where are you calling from?
Caller: The living room

Caller: The water board please.
Operator: Which department?
Caller: Tap water.

Operator: How are you spelling that?
Caller: With letters.

Caller: I'd like the number for a reverend in Cardiff, please.
Operator: Do you have his name?
Caller: No, but he has a dog named Ben.

Caller: The Union of Shopkeepers and Alligators please.
Operator: You mean the Amalgamated Union of Shopkeepers?

On another occasion, a man making heavy breathing sounds from a phone box told the worried operator: "I haven't got a pen so I'm steaming up the window to write the number on."

OPPORTUNITY

The wolves were decimating the farmers' sheep. So the farmers' association raised the bounty on them to a hundred dollars a pelt. Two hunters, Sam and

Ed, decided they could use the money. So they got their gear together and headed out to the wide open spaces to shoot some wolves and make themselves rich. They had just fallen asleep out under the stars when a noise woke Ed. By the light of the campfire he saw the eyes of a hundred wolves—teeth gleaming. He shook his friend and whispered hoarsely, "Sam! Sam! Wake up! We're rich!"

I was seldom able to see an opportunity until it had ceased to be one.

—Mark Twain

Lots of people know a good thing the minute the other fellow sees it first.

—Job E. Hedges

You miss 100 percent of the shots you never take.   —Wayne Gretzky

The
BORDERLINE ™
By Gabe Martin
borderln@cts.com

People who live in glass houses have trouble getting good maids.

Dig where the gold is . . . unless you just need some exercise.

—John M. Capozzi, *Why Climb the Corporate Ladder When You can Take the Elevator?*

OPTIMISM

The sports reporter asked the football coach, "How do you keep your spirits up when your team is losing?" He shrugged and replied, "I'm the kind of guy who, if I fell in a mud puddle, would get up and feel in my pockets for fish."

❧

Charlie Pell, Clemson football coach, said it best. "I expect my players to think as positively as the eighty-five-year-old man who married a twenty-five-year-old woman and ordered a five-bedroom house near an elementary school."

ORGANIZATIONS

All organizations were set up to extinguish the principles for which they were founded.

P

PACIFICISM

No man can tame a tiger into a kitten by stroking it.   —Franklin D. Roosevelt

PARENTS

Before I got married I had six theories about bringing up children. Now I have six children and no theories.   —Lord Rochester

❧

Miss Swenson's fifth grade class was assigned to write a short essay on parents. Samantha Peters' essay read: "The trouble with parents is that when we get them they are so old it is very hard to change their habits."

❧

Setting a good example for children takes all the fun out of middle age.

—William Feather

❧

Wrinkles are hereditary. Parents get them from their children.   —Doris Day

Parenthood remains the greatest single preserve of the amateur.

—Alvin Toffler

~

If parents would only realize how they bore their children.

—George Bernard Shaw

~

My Aunt Marie was standing at our front door after Thanksgiving dinner, ready to go home. Her four little children stood at her side and her arms were full of coats. Her husband, coming down the stairs asked why she was standing there. She replied, handing him the coats, "This time you put the children's coats on and I'll go honk the horn."

~

After the kids leave home, some parents suffer from the empty-nest syndrome; others change the locks.

~

The way I look at it, if the kids are still alive when my husband comes homes from work, then I've done my job.

—Roseanne

~

Parent: Something so simple even a child can operate it.

~

One of the college grad's first big discoveries is that jobs are handed out by some person who thinks and acts a lot like his or her parents.

—Bob Talbert

~

As a little boy in a baseball uniform was walking disconsolately down the street, a sympathetic neighbor called out: "What's the matter? Didn't the game go well?" "It was a cool game," the boy replied, "but we had to call it in the third inning because the parents were rioting."

PARKING

A distinguished-looking man entered a Geneva bank and inquired about taking out a loan for 1000 Swiss francs. "What security can you offer?" the banker asked. "My Rolls-Royce is parked out front," he said. "I will be away for a few weeks. Here are the keys." A month later, the man returned to the bank and paid off the loan, 1017 francs with interest. "Pardon me for asking," the banker said, "but why a one-thousand franc loan for a man of your obvious means?" "Very simple," he replied. "Where else can you store a Rolls for a month for seventeen francs?"

~

Don't park a mobile home on top of a hill. It can leave you if it is so inclined.

—Frank Tyger

~

One of life's simple pleasures is parking on someone else's dime.

~

The parking situation was getting worse and worse and when he got a $100 parking ticket, he decided to see a lawyer. 'I've heard of a $4 ticket for parking, an $8 ticket for double parking, a $15 ticket for parking by the pump," said the lawyer. "But how were you parked to get a $100 ticket?" "On top of another car," he answered.

—*Ohio Motorist*

PEACE

Ramsay MacDonald, one-time Prime Minister of England, was discussing with another government official the possibility of lasting peace. The latter, an expert on foreign affairs, was unimpressed by the Prime Minister's idealistic viewpoint. He remarked cynically, "The desire for peace does not necessarily ensure it." This MacDonald admitted, saying, "Quite true. But neither does the desire for food satisfy your hunger. However it at least gets you started towards a restaurant."

PERFECTION

If it wasn't for my faults, I'd be perfect.

PERSISTENCE

If your ship doesn't come in, swim out to it.   —Jonathan Winters

Don't worry if your job is small
And your rewards are few,
Remember that the mighty oak
Was once a nut like you!

PERSPECTIVE

During a hard period in Soviet history, the government showed the film version of Steinbeck's *The Grapes of Wrath,* on the state-run television network. The government wanted to show how much worse off people were in the United States. All that the Soviet citizens noticed was that even the poorest Americans owned cars!

P

Thomas was an entrepreneur with a reputation for dishonesty. One day, he went to Smythe, a new but talented attorney. He told Smythe that he would not pay any fees unless there seemed a clear cause of legal action. Smythe agreed to evaluate the case. After a lengthy discussion, Smythe told Thomas, "Your case is absolutely airtight. The other party is dead wrong, and cannot hope to win the case. I will be happy to represent you for a retainer of $10,000." Thomas then got up to leave. The attorney protested, "But I told you that your case was good, and you agreed to pay me if you had a claim! You have to pay me my fee!" Thomas replied, "Absolutely not. I'm leaving town. I told you the other guy's side."

Former Undersecretary of the Interior John C. Whitaker is reminded of how easy it is to get an out-of-perspective feeling about one's importance in government whenever he thinks of an 85-year-old woman who has lived her life in one spot in Nova Scotia. The population there swells to nine in summer and stays steady at two during the winter. Whitaker, who has been fishing there every year since he was 12, flew in one day. Miss Mildred welcomed him into her kitchen and said, "Johnny, I hate to admit I don't know, but where is Washington? " When Whitaker realized that she wasn't kidding, he explained: "That's where the President is. That's like where you have the Prime Minister in Ottawa." Then she asked how many people lived there, and Whitaker said there were about two million. She said, "Think of that, two million people living so far away from everything."

~

Never mistake motion for action. —Ernest Hemingway

~

The average person thinks he isn't. —Father Larry Lorenzoni

PESSIMISM

A young man entered a jewelry store and purchased an expensive engagement ring. The jeweler asked, "What names do you wish it engraved in it?" he asked. "From Lance to Cindy," the young man whispered, red-faced. The jeweler looked from the ring to the young man and smiled. "Take my advice, young fellow," he said. "Have it engraved simply, 'From Lance.'"

~

The pessimist sees the difficulty in every opportunity; the optimist, the opportunity in every difficulty. —L. P. Jacks

PETS

I have fish for pets. That's what I have. Goldfish. It was originally for the stress thing. They say if you watch fish, it helps you relax, to fall asleep, which explains why I always doze off while I'm snorkeling. —Ellen DeGeneres

~

I've got a sheep dog. He doesn't have fleas—he's got moths. —Joey Adams

~

I bought an ant farm. I don't know where I'm gonna find a tractor that small. —Steven Wright

~

Dogs have so many friends because they wag their tails, not their tongues.

Dogs come when they're called; cats take a message and get back to you.

—Mary Bly

A dog doesn't want much and is happy to get it. A cat doesn't know what it wants and wants more of it.   —Richard Hexem

What do you call a parrot wearing a raincoat? Polly unsaturated.

PHILOSOPHY

Being a philosopher, I have a problem for every solution.

—Robert Zend

Tonight we're going to consider one of the great questions of our time: Why the people who forget to turn off their car headlights always remember to lock the doors.

—Robert Orben, *2500 Jokes To Start 'Em Laughing*

PLACES

On the flat terrain of Winnipeg: "It's the only town where you can watch your dog run away for three days."   —Pat Burns

Green Bay, a city with fewer residents than L.A. has rioters.

—Mike Royko in *Chicago Tribune*

P

PLASTIC

Nowadays, when you get right down to brass tacks, they're plastic.

—Gil Stern

PLAY

As Plato remarked, "You can discover more about a person in an hour of play than in a year of conversation."

PLUMBERS

A man, toolbox in hand, rang the doorbell. A woman answered. "Good morning, I've come to fix the pipe. I'm the plumber." "But I didn't call a plumber." "What? Aren't you Mrs. Foster?" "No. She moved away a year ago." "How do you like that? They ask for a plumber, claiming it's an emergency, and then they move."   —Hugh Harrison

POETS

After a dinner party, poet Robert Frost and the other guests went out onto the veranda to watch the sunset. "Oh, Mr. Frost, isn't it a lovely sunset?" exclaimed a young guest. "I never discuss business after dinner," Frost replied.

—Little, Brown Book of Anecdotes

POLICE

A rookie police officer was asked in an examination what he would do to break up a crowd. His answer indicated a deep knowledge of human nature. He replied, "I would take up a collection."

A women went to the police station with her next door neighbor to report that her husband was missing. The police officer asked for a description. She said, "He's 35 years old, 6 foot 2, has dark eyes, dark wavy hair, an athletic build, weighs 185 pounds, is soft-spoken, and is good to the children." The next-door neighbor protested, "Wait a minute! Your husband is 5 foot 4, chubby, bald, has a big mouth, and is mean to your children." The wife replied, "Sure, but who wants him back?"

Deputy Todd pulled alongside a speeding car on the freeway. Glancing at the car, he was astounded to see that the woman at the wheel was knitting! Todd cranked down his window and yelled, "PULL OVER!" "NO," the woman yelled back, "IT'S A SCARF!"

My stepson Todd, who is a sheriff's deputy, pulled over a speeding motorist and asked, "Do you have any ID?" The motorist replied, "About what?"

Officer Mark Blank stopped George Goodman driving the wrong way on a one-way street. At the court hearing, the traffic judge asked Goodman, "Didn't you see the arrow?" "Arrow? Honest, your honor, I didn't even see the Indians."

One night a guy was driving home from a party and he was stopped by the Highway Patrol. The cop said, "Sir, you were driving 77." The guy said, "No, I wasn't. I had it on Cruise-a-matic. I was driving 55." Cop: "Sorry, sir. My radar said 77." The guy said, "Officer, I'm going to have your job, your badge, and then, I'm going to punch you in the nose." The cop turned to the man's wife and said, "Is he always like this?" The wife replied, "Only when he's drunk."

Roger Adams was cruising along in his BMW, doing about 90 on the freeway. Suddenly, a highway patrol car, siren wailing, appeared behind him. He pulled over and when the officer approached, Roger rolled down his window and began to speak even before the officer did. "I know you're going to ask me why I was driving so fast. You see, just last week my wife of ten years ran off with a handsome highway patrolman." "I'm sorry to hear it," said the officer, "but that still doesn't explain why you were speeding." "Well, it's simple," Roger explained. "When I saw your patrol car behind me, I was afraid you might be trying to bring her back!"

The police in Worcester, Massachusetts, were able to put out unusually specific information about a robbery suspect. The suspect had decided to rob a tailor, Philip Smith, only after the tailor had measured him completely for a new suit.

When Sheriff Jacobs arrived at the scene of a car accident, he saw a horrible sight smashed against the inside of the windshield. Immediately he radioed for an ambulance on his walkie-talkie as he ran over to the car. Earnestly, he addressed the man in the front seat: "Are you badly hurt?" The driver quickly replied: "Naw, but this pizza sure is a terrible mess."

My cousin Sandy is a highway patrol officer. Recently she pulled over a driver for speeding. The irate speeder confronted Officer Sandy and said: "Why don't you people get organized? First you take away my driver's license and the next day you ask to see it."

Policeman: "Why didn't you report the robbery right away? Didn't you suspect something when you came home and discovered all the drawers opened and the contents scattered about?"

Woman: "No, I didn't suspect a thing. I just thought my husband was looking for a clean shirt."   —*Quote*

When our son Todd was a police officer in training, he and his trainer found three hand grenades in an abandoned cabin and decided to take them to the police station. "What if one of them explodes?" asked Todd. "It doesn't matter," reassured the experienced officer. "We'll say we only found two."

A man was driving along in his beat up old Dodge, when suddenly it broke down. He was parked on the side of the road trying to fix it, when a Jaguar pulled up in front of him and offered to help. After a few minutes the two men obviously weren't going to get the old car going again, so the Jaguar driver offered to tow the Dodge to the nearest garage. A few minutes later the two had hitched up the old Dodge to the Jaguar, and they agreed that if the Jaguar driver was going too fast, the man should blow his horn and flash his lights to get him to slow down. With that the two men got into their cars and the Jaguar driver started to pull away with the Dodge behind it. At the first traffic light, a Ferrari pulled up beside the Jaguar and started to rev his engine. As soon as the light turned green the Ferrari and the Jaguar hit their accelerators and took off. Before long the cars were racing at over 120 mph. As the cars sped along, they passed through a police speed trap. The officer couldn't believe his eyes when he saw the three cars go by, and he decided that he couldn't catch them all by himself, so he decided to radio for help: "You won't believe what I just saw! I saw a Ferrari and a Jaguar doing 120 mph side by side, and a beat up old Dodge behind them flashing his lights and blowing his horn trying to get by!"

～

Police in Los Angeles had good luck with a robbery suspect who just couldn't control himself during a lineup. When detectives asked each man in the lineup to repeat the words, "Give me all your money or I'll shoot," the man shouted, "That's not what I said!"

～

A bank robber in Virginia Beach got a nasty surprise when a dye pack designed to mark stolen money exploded in his Fruit-of-the-Looms. The robber apparently stuffed the loot down the front of his pants as he was running out the door. "He was seen hopping and jumping around," said police spokesman Mike Carey, "with an explosion taking place inside his pants." Police have the man's charred trousers in custody.

～

If you're stopped by the police, shut off your engine and put your mouth in neutral.   —Newspaper Enterprise Assn.

～

A speeding driver was signaled to the side of the highway by a motorcycle officer. "I'm a good friend of the mayor," the speeder told him. "Great," said the officer as he wrote the ticket. "Now he'll know I'm on the job."

The police sent out mug shots of an escaped convict in six different poses. A constable from a town nearby sent the following telegram two days later: "Have captured five of them and am on the trail of the sixth."

POLITICS

A bishop advised a politician to go out into the rain and lift his head toward heaven. It will bring a revelation to you, he said. The next day the politician reported: "I followed your advice and no revelation came. The water poured down my neck and I felt like a fool." "Well," replied the bishop, "isn't that quite a revelation for the first try?"

A candidate for office can have no greater advantage than muddled syntax; no greater liability than a command of the language.   —Marya Mannes

A Congressman is awakened in the middle of the night by his wife who whispers, "I think there's a burglar in the house." "Not in the House," her husband says. "Perhaps in the Senate, my dear, but not in the House."

—Walter Belson

A politician is a guy who shakes your hand before an election and your confidence afterwards.

A politician's willingness to listen to advice rises in inverse proportion to how badly he thinks he is doing.   —Pat Caddell

Adlai Stevenson was one of the wittiest men in American politics. A supporter said to him on one occasion, "Governor, you will have the support of every thinking American." Stevenson replied, "Madam, unfortunately, that is not enough. I need a majority."

Former Senator Eugene McCarthy once said, "Being in politics is like being a football coach. You have to be smart enough to understand the game and dumb enough to think it's important."

He is the kind of politician who would cut down a redwood tree, then mount the stump and make a speech for conservation.   —Adlai Stevenson

Henry Fallow was talking with a new acquaintance who was thinking of running for political office. "I used to be in politics myself," Henry said. "I was dog catcher in my town for two years but finally lost my job." "What happened?" asked his new friend. "A change of mayors?" "Nope," he replied. "I finally caught the dog."

I am not a member of any organized party. I am a Democrat.   —Will Rogers

I heard Bill Clinton was Grand Marshal of a stock car race during the Labor Day weekend. A politician strikes me as an excellent choice to preside over an event where people drive around and around in circles at high speed.

I know a politician who believes that there are two sides to every question—and takes them both.
—Ken Murray

I like political jokes, unless they get elected.

I once said cynically of a politician, "He'll double-cross that bridge when he comes to it."
—Oscar Levant

I think the next four years we should try it with no President.
—Dana Fradon

I voted for the Democrats because I didn't like the way the Republicans were running the country, which is turning out to be like shooting yourself in the head to stop your headache.   —Jack Mayberry

I would like to nominate a man who is honest and courageous. I'd like to, but this party doesn't have one of them kind of people.

My candidate does not know the meaning of the word compromise, does not know the meaning of the word appeasement, does not know the meaning of the word cowardice—and has done quite well despite his lousy vocabulary.
—Vaughn Meader

"I wouldn't vote for you if you were St. Peter himself," I told one candidate with whom I was in particular disagreement. "Don't worry," he replied. "If I were St. Peter, you wouldn't be in my district."

〜

If you can't convince them, confuse them.   —Harry S Truman

〜

In politics, it's a good rule to follow the first law of holes. If you are in one, stop digging.
—Denis Healey

〜

It is dangerous for a national candidate to say things that people might remember.
—Eugene McCarthy

〜

The politician began his speech like this. "Ladies and gentlemen, please let me tax your memories for a moment." Someone in the crowd immediately spoke up, "Well, you've tried to tax everything else."

〜

Henry Cabot Lodge, Jr.'s, advice to then novice political campaigner, Dwight D. Eisenhower: "Meet the sun every day as if it could cast a ballot."

〜

A fellow in Vermont said to his mother one day, "Mother, I don't believe you'd vote for God Himself if He ran on the Democratic ticket!" To which she replied: "Of course not. If He switched parties at this late date, he wouldn't be very reliable, now would He?"

〜

Ninety-eight percent of the adults in this country are decent, hardworking, honest Americans. It's the other lousy two percent that get all the publicity. But then, we elected them.   —Lily Tomlin

〜

Perhaps the greatest compliment ever paid President Grover Cleveland was when he was put in nomination before the Democratic Convention. The orator who presented his name said, "We love him for the enemies he has made."

〜

Political success is the ability, when the inevitable occurs, to get credit for it.
—Laurence J. Peter

Politicians are like bananas. They're green when you pick 'em, and then they hang around in bunches and get rotten.

～

Politicians have stopped passing the buck. Now it stays with them.

～

Politics has reached the level where we're goin' some if we can even get good, efficient people to vote, to say nothin' of runnin' for office.   —Kin Hubbard

～

Politics is the ability to foretell what is going to happen tomorrow, next week, next month and next year. And to have the ability afterwards to explain why it didn't happen.   —Winston Churchill

～

Politics is the gentle art of getting votes from the poor and campaign funds from the rich by promising to protect each from the other.

—Oscar Ameringer

～

Politics is the art of the possible.   —Otto von Bismarck (1815–1898)

～

Several years ago, during a debate in the British Parliament, a minister from the Labor Party got up to speak about socialism. "Under our Socialist government, more housing units have been built than ever before," he said. "Under Socialism, more hospitals have been built than ever before. And under Socialism, we have witnessed the greatest population increase in the history of this island." At that point, the great Winston Churchill had heard enough. He rose and said, "Would the Honorable Minster perhaps concede that the baby boom is due to private enterprise?"

～

When you're leading, don't talk.   —Thomas E. Dewey

～

Winston Churchill once noted that the nation will find it hard to look up to leaders who keep their ears to the ground.

～

You campaign in poetry. You govern in prose.   —Mario Cuomo

～

You really have to be careful of politicians who have no further ambitions. They may run for president.   —Harry S Truman

The 1980 Presidential campaign contained a heavy emphasis on economic issues. Candidate Ronald Reagan warned of the coming of another depression if America continued in its present path. President Jimmy Carter responded, "That shows how much he knows. Mr. Reagan clearly does not know the difference between a depression and a recession." That reaction gave Reagan, the communicator, a platform comment to build his campaign on. Reagan responded, "If Mr. Carter wants a definition, I'll give him one. Recession is when your neighbor loses his job, depression is when you lose yours, and recovery will be when Jimmy Carter loses his."

～

In an article on Northern Ireland, the political party Sinn Fein was described as the political wing of the IRA. I guess that makes the U.S. Democratic Party the political wing of the IRS.

～

Some months after his defeat in the Presidential race of 1984, former Vice President Walter Mondale was giving a talk about terrorism at the American Bar Association convention in London. Suddenly there was an explosion. Security men jumped to their feet and the audience stiffened. It quickly became apparent that the noise had come from an exploding TV camera light. Unfortunately, this was immediately followed by fire sprinklers going into action, drenching all the occupants of the room. Mondale looked around and then said, "Once you're out of office, you find that there's very little dignity in this world."

P

～

State legislators are merely politicians whose darkest secrets prohibit them from running for higher office.   —Dennis Miller

～

The only ones who know all the answers are politicians out of a job.
                                                           —Charles E. Wilson

～

The only people who say worse things about politicians than reporters do, are other politicians.   —Andy Rooney

～

The only way to combat criminals is by not voting for them.
                                                              —Dayton Allen

There are three types of politicians: those that cannot lie, those that cannot tell the truth, and those that cannot tell the difference.

There is a story about a gubernatorial candidate in Texas who got an urgent call from the manager of his campaign in Houston. "Jim, you should get over here right away," the manager said. "The opposition is telling a lot of lies about you around the city." "Can't come today," the candidate told him. "I've got to go to Dallas." "But, Jim, this is important. They're telling lies about you in Houston," the manager protested. "Dallas is even more important," said Jim. "They're telling the truth about me there."

There were so many candidates on the platform that there were not enough promises to go around.
—Ronald Reagan

Two elderly women were walking around a typical overcrowded English country churchyard and came upon a tombstone on which was the inscription, "Here lies John Smith, a politician and an honest man." "Good heavens," said one woman to the other, "isn't it awful that they had to put two people in the same grave!"

Vote for the man who promises least. He'll be the least disappointing.
—Bernard Baruch

Voting in this election is like trying to decide which street mime to stop and watch.
—A. Whitney Brown

Watching the Democratic party in a presidential contest is like watching a washing machine with a defective bearing. It starts up smoothly enough, but soon it begins to wobble and shake, jumping violently from place to place, until it tears itself to pieces, spewing dirty laundry all over the room.

Question asked of actor Jimmy Stewart: "Why did you never think of running for President?" Answer: "I can't talk fast enough to be a politician."

I used to say that politics was the second oldest profession. I have come to know that it bears a gross similarity to the first.
—Ronald Reagan

Uncle Irv ran for alderman in Chicago. He came home late on election night and gave his wife the glorious news., "Darling, I've been elected!" "Honestly?" she replied heartily. "Hey," he said, "why bring that up?"

〜

During his stint as governor of Georgia, Lester Maddox explained why his state should not create a consumer protection agency as follows: "Honest businessmen should be protected from the unscrupulous consumer."

〜

I think that the undecideds could go one way or the other.   —George Bush in 1988

〜

I believe we are on an irreversible trend toward more freedom and democracy. But that could change.   —Vice-President Dan Quayle

〜

The trouble with politicians is they always put our money where their mouths are.   —Baloo in *Forbes*

〜

Jim Miles, South Carolina's secretary of state, admitted that campaigning for public office can be a humbling experience. He was in a small town waiting to be interviewed on radio. "When I got to the station," said Miles, "the newsman was running out the door. 'You'll have to come back later,' he said. 'There's an alligator crossing Highway 278.'"   —Aiken, S.C., *Standard*

P

〜

Political debates are sort of like stock-car races—no one really cares who wins; they just want to see the crashes.   —Molly Ivins

〜

Any man who is under 30, and is not a liberal, has no heart; and any man who is over 30, and is not a conservative, has no brains.
                    —Winston Churchill

〜

You have all the characteristics of a popular politician: a horrible voice, bad breeding, and a vulgar manner.   —Aristophanes

〜

Have you heard about the latest dance craze? It's called the Politician's Polka. You take one step forward, two steps back and sidestep the issue.
                    —Jack Rosenbaum

Any politician who starts shouting election-year demagoguery about the rich and the poor should be asked, "What about the other 90 percent of the people?"

—Thomas Sowell

"Can you believe a candidate dropped out of the race because of a lack of campaign funds?" asks comedian Kevin Nealon. "Any politician who stops spending just because he's out of money doesn't belong in Washington anyway!"

Politicians, are people who, when they see light at the end of the tunnel, go out and buy some more tunnel.

—John Quinton

Terry Sanford writes about the effort he made in one of his gubernatorial campaigns to persuade North Carolinians to improve public education: In a fairly remote county one evening, a woman stood up and demanded, "Where are you going to get the money for all this stuff?" I decided to give her a blunt answer. "Where do you think we will get the money?" I said. "From taxes." The audience broke out in the best applause I had heard. Later I turned to an aide. "Do you realize what we experience tonight?" I said. "Voters applauded when I said we would get new money from taxes. That's remarkable!" "I wouldn't be too sure," he replied, laughing. "They thought you said Texas."

—*But What About the People?*

Politics is perhaps the only profession for which no preparation is thought necessary.

—Robert Louis Stevenson

A group of politicians, shortly before an oncoming election, were busily engaged in a Texas cemetery, copying names from gravestones, in order to vote for them, fraudulently. They came to one stone that was overgrown with moss, the name hard to decipher, so they decided to skip that one, and go on to the next. At this, the leader of the group registered a vehement protest: "No! No! No! Go right back and get that name! That fellow has just as much right to vote as anybody in this cemetery!"

—Hugh Harrison

A banker, an electrician, and a politician were taking an IQ test. One of the questions was "What term best describes the problem when outflow exceeds inflow?" The banker wrote, "Overdraft." The electrician answered, "Overload." The politician scratched his head and wrote, "What problem?"

Grandma Jones disagrees with the view that someday there may be a woman President. "I'll tell you why," she says. "If the woman who runs for that high office is homely, the men won't vote for her. And if she's good looking, the women won't." —*Ozarks Mountaineer*

POSITIVE THINKING

I was going to buy a copy of *The Power of Positive Thinking,* and then I thought: What good would that do? —Ronnie Shakes

POST OFFICE

In 1984, 500 postal workers received their paychecks three days late—because their original checks were lost in the mail. —AP

~

In the post office: "I don't want to say the mail is slow, but last week my flower seeds arrived as a bouquet." —Joey Adams

~

Morris Udall, U.S. Congressman from Arizona, has suggested that the Post Office be put in charge of the inflation problem: "They wouldn't solve it, but they'd certainly slow it down." —*Time*

~

The increased rates will make it possible for the Post Office to use highly sophisticated electronic equipment. Instead of a $300-a-week clerk your letters will be lost by a $20 million computer!
—Robert Orben, *2500 Jokes To Start 'Em Laughing*

PRAISE

Praise does wonders for the sense of hearing. —*Bits & Pieces*

PRAYER

My brother Scott says the country is in far worse shape than most people suspect. His evidence: "Every time I call Dial-a-Prayer I get a busy signal."

~

My next door neighbor, Mrs. Pulaski, was telling me: "My 2½-year-old niece, Kelli, went with her neighbor girl to church for First Communion practice. The pastor has the children cup their hands, and when he gives them the Host—in this case, a piece of bread—he says: God be with you. Apparently this made quite an impression on my niece. She came home and told her mother to cup her hands and bend down. Kelli took a piece of bread from her sandwich, placed it in her mother's hands, and whispered, in her most angelic voice: 'God will get you.'"

~

Little Darlene surprised her mother with the postscript to her bedtime prayer: "And, dear Lord, please send the beautiful snow to keep the little flowers warm through the winter." Climbing into her bed, she confided to her mother: "That time I fooled him. I want the snow so I can go sledding with my new sled."

—Capper's Weekly

~

The object of most prayers is to wangle an advance on good intentions.

—Robert Brault

~

Helen Simonson, the mother of a religious family, was listening to her daughter Susanna saying a rather lengthy bedtime prayer. "Dear God," prayed the child,

"let me do well in my test tomorrow. Make my friends be nice to me. Tell my brother not to mess up my room. And please get my father to raise my allowance. And . . ." The mother interrupted, "Don't bother to give God instructions. Just report for duty."

~

Susanna, age eight, was reprimanded by her mother for laughing while saying her bedtime prayers. "It's okay, Mom," she replied, "I was just sharing a joke with God."

~

May those that love, love universities and those that don't love us, may God turn their hearts; and if He doesn't turn their hearts, may He turn their ankles so we'll know them by their limping. —An Irish Prayer

~

Jean had been troublesome and had been sent into the den to think things over. After a while she came out all smiles and said, "I thought and I prayed." "Fine," said her mother. "That will help you to be good." "Oh, I didn't ask God to help me to be good, I just told him to help you put up with me," she said.

—Grit

~

One time when Cardinal Spellman was visiting Boston, and was chatting with Joe Cronin and Tom Yawkey of the Boston Red Sox ball club, the baseball men asked the cardinal if he wouldn't like to attend a game. "Thanks, but I don't think I will," the cardinal answered. "Last time I saw a ball game, I got hit on the knee with a foul ball." The cardinal's eyes twinkled as he added, "and you know, I have to keep my knees in good condition."

—Boston Globe

The 8-year-old didn't exactly dislike going to church; it was the excruciatingly long pastoral prayer which seemed especially tiresome to him. So he was naturally a little apprehensive when his father asked the visiting minister to say grace at dinner. Surprisingly, the prayer was brief and to the point. Pleased, the child looked up and observed: "You don't pray so long when you're hungry, do you?"

—Grit

PREACHERS/PREACHING

Pastor Betsy Sessions finished a forceful sermon on the Ten Commandments. One parishioner, David Getz, was crushed momentarily, but soon perked up. "Anyway," Getz told himself, "I've never made a graven image."

Prison Chaplain Larry Swenson said to a soon-to-be ex-convict, "As you make your way in the world, son, remember the sermons you heard while you were

REVEREND FUN WWW.REVERENDFUN.COM

©COPYRIGHT 1999 GOSPEL FILMS, INC.

"Maybe you should tell me a little more about this God of yours before we go on."

here." Replied the about-to-be-released prisoner: "Chaplain, no one who's heard you preach would ever want to come back here."

~

This has happened to every minister. You spend hours poring over the biblical text and every relevant book in your library. You write and write, polish and polish. You practice your delivery in front of your wife, your dog, the mirror, and on Saturday night in the empty sanctuary. You toss and turn Saturday night, get up before dawn on Sunday morning to read over and revise your text. You pray for an hour, get dressed, eat breakfast, go to church and preach your heart out. Then someone comes up to you and gushes, "Reverend, every sermon you preach is better than the next one!"

~

What I meant to say was, "Let us bind ourselves with willing bonds to our covenant with God. The way it came out was, Let us bind ourselves with willing blondes . . ."

~

The average man's idea of a good sermon is one that goes over his head and hits a neighbor.

~

The preacher was wired for sound with a lapel mike, and as he preached, he moved briskly about the platform, jerking the mike cord as he went. Then he moved to one side, getting wound up in the cord and nearly tripping before jerking it again. After several circles and jerks, a little girl in the third pew leaned toward her mother and whispered, "If he gets loose, will he hurt us?"

~

As a visiting preacher, D. L. Moody was warned that some of the congregation usually left before the end of the sermon. When he rose to begin his sermon, he announced, "I am going to speak to two classes of people this morning; first to the sinners, then to the saints." He proceeded to address the "sinners" for awhile, and then said they could leave. For once, every member of the congregation stayed to the end of the sermon.   —Viola Walden

~

Pastor Reynolds at First Presbyterian Church tended to make his sermons much too long, and members of the congregation were looking for a way to tell him this in a tactful way. One Sunday, after the preacher came in with a bandaged finger, a parishioner asked him, "Pastor, what happened? Did you cut your finger?" The pastor replied, "I was thinking about my sermon, and I cut my finger." "Oh, I see," said the member. "Well, next time I suggest that you think about your finger and cut your sermon."

~

Our pastor delivered a compelling sermon describing the plight of the poor, reminding everyone in strong terms that it is a charitable duty of the rich to share their wealth. After Mass a friend asked our pastor if he thought he had persuaded the parishioners. "Well, I'm sure it was at least a partial success," he answered with a smile. "I'm sure I convinced the poor!"

~

Two brothers, one a famous baseball pitcher, the other a minister, met after a long separation. Some time was spent in exchange of reminiscences of bygone days. Finally, the minister said, "How is it, Bill—I spent four years in college and three years in seminary, and you've never done anything but play ball. Now you're getting a salary of $30,000, and I'm getting $3,000. I can't understand." Bill thought a minute, then said, "I'll tell you how it is, Jim, it's all in the delivery!"

—Grit

PREDICTIONS

We all make mistakes. Consider the following judgments:

- There is no reason anyone would want a computer in their home.—Ken Olson, president, chairman and founder of Digital Equipment Corp., 1977
- 640K ought to be enough for anybody.—Bill Gates in 1981
- The concept is interesting and well-formed, but in order to earn better than a 'C,' the idea must be feasible.—A Yale University management professor in response to student Fred Smith's paper proposing reliable overnight delivery service (Smith went on to found Federal Express Corp.)
- Who the heck wants to hear actors talk?—H. M. Warner (1881–1958), founder of Warner Brothers, in 1927
- We don't like their sound, and guitar music is on the way out.—Decca Recording Co. rejecting the Beatles, 1962
- Everything that can be invented has been invented.—Charles H. Duell, Commissioner, U.S. Office of Patents, 1899

PREGNANT

A friend who was eight months pregnant went to visit a sick relative in Memphis and took a wrong turn. Stopping at a filling station for directions, she said, "I don't know where I went wrong, but I'm trying to get to Baptist

Hospital." The attendant, who couldn't help but notice her condition, smiled and replied, "I don't know where you went wrong either, but if you drive four blocks straight ahead you'll get there."   —Jessye Lee Alexander

PREJUDICE

Thinking is what a great many people think they are doing when they are merely rearranging their prejudices.   —William James

PRESIDENTS

Jimmy Carter's promise of amnesty to the Haitian generals had the White House very upset. "We don't care what Carter promised. If President Clinton wanted to grant pardons, he would have sent Gerald Ford."

Mr. Coolidge is the best Democrat we ever had in the White House. He didn't do nothin', but that's what we wanted done.   —Will Rogers

President Wilson's mind, as has been the custom, will be closed all day Sunday.
                    —George S. Kaufman

President Woodrow Wilson had a lively sense of humor. Early James, Director of the Wilson House Museum in Washington, D. C., says the following story fits the Wilson personality and is very likely true. A New Jersey man telephoned the White House at three o'clock in the morning and asked to speak to the President on a matter of national importance. The operator rang and woke Wilson. When the man got through to the President he told him, "The collector of customs here in New Jersey has died." The President replied, "I'm sorry to hear that, but why are you calling at this hour?" The reply came back, "Because I want to replace him." President Wilson responded, "Well, if the undertaker has no objection, neither do I."

Two birds were perched on the high fence on the perimeter of the White House. One bird said, "Are you for the President?" The other bird said, "Why not? He's for us!"

Former President Jimmy Carter spoke at the Economic Club luncheon and told the joke about three envelopes that each incoming president should have for guidance. "If the going gets tough during the first year, the president should open the first envelope that says: 'Blame the past president!' After the second year, if there is no improvement, he should open the second envelope that declares: 'Blame Congress!' If things continue to get progressively worse, the President should open the third envelope. This one advises: 'Prepare three envelopes.'" —*How the Platform Professionals Keep 'em Laughin'*

~

When Franklin D. Roosevelt was President, the pastor of the church he attended in Washington was asked over the phone, "Is the President expected to attend church this Sunday?" "I don't know," replied the minister. "But I can assure you that God will be there, which should be incentive enough."

~

As playwright Gore Vidal tells it, when his play *The Best Man* was being cast back in 1959 Ronald Reagan was proposed for the lead role of the distinguished front-running Presidential candidate. He was rejected. It was decided that he lacked the "Presidential look." —*Fifty Plus*

~

When asked what his favorite song was, John F. Kennedy replied, "I think 'Hail to the Chief' has a nice ring to it."

~

Preparing for a citizenship test, a lady was shown a photo of Abraham Lincoln by her son and asked to identify it. "That's Abe Lincoln," she said confidently. The he showed her a picture of bewigged George Washington. She looked at the picture perplexedly and then answered, "That's his wife." —*R & R Magazine*

PRESS

Wooing the press is an exercise roughly akin to picnicking with a tiger. You might enjoy the meal, but the tiger always eats last. —Maureen Dowd

PRICES

After eating a meal in a first-class restaurant nowadays, you need an after-dinner mint—such as the one in Denver. —Irving Lazar

PRIDE

During World War II, industrialist Henry J. Kaiser came to Washington, D.C., to testify concerning his ship-building activities. He had claimed to be able to build a ship a day. A somewhat hostile young lawyer was cross-examining Kaiser. The lawyer said, "So you think you can build a ship a day. You know, Rome wasn't built in a day." Henry J. Kaiser looked the young lawyer squarely in the eye and answered, "I wasn't there."

Early to bed and early to rise makes a man healthy, wealthy, and hell-bent to talk about it.   —Franklin P. Jones

To hide the shameful fact that his father had been hanged for cattle stealing, a lawyer rewrote his own family history thus: Father died while taking part in a public ceremony when the platform gave way.

—Msgr. Arthur Tonne, *Jokes Priests Can Tell,* vol. 6

He was as shy as a newspaper is when referring to its own merits.

—Mark Twain

Did you ever have one of those nights where you didn't want to go out . . . but your hair looked too good to stay home?   —Jack Simmons

PRIESTS

Father O'Brien, the new parish priest was making a visit to my nephew's home. He knocked on the door, and Tad, their little 4-year-old boy went to the door and saw the priest. He called to his father, "Hey, Dad! That guy that works for God is here!"

I was visiting my friend Father Miles at his office in the city. As I entered, he instructed his secretary, "Unless it's the archbishop or the pope, don't put any calls through." In the middle of our meeting, the phone rang. Annoyed, Father Miles answered it. Then his eyes widened. "Yes," he said, "that's right. I told her not to let any calls through unless they came from the archbishop, the pope or you, Mom."

While I was visiting Father Miles, the UPS guy came by with a large package. He had a very strange look on his face. "I have a package for the Father," he explained and had Miles sign for it. I clearly understood the delivery man's chagrin when I saw what was stamped on the box: Contents: FULL COLOR MADONNA CALENDARS.

When I first met Father Miles, he had just come from the Catholic church across from his office, where he had been celebrating mass. He looked odd to me in his cassock and to cover my discomfort I quipped,, "I didn't know you wore dresses!" Without losing a beat, Father Miles replied, "Oh, this old thing?"

PRIORITIES

One Sunday, my then eight-year-old daughter Susie was given two quarters as she left for church, one for the collection plate and one for herself to spend as she wished. As she walked to Sunday school she was playing with the quarters in her hand, and one dropped on the street and rolled through the grates of a sewer. Susie looked down into the watery depths and said sadly, "There goes God's quarter."

PRISON

In his youth, my friend Ralph was a prison chaplain. His first day on the job, he visited a man on death row. Ralph established a good rapport with the condemned felon, visited him daily for several weeks, and when it came time for the criminal to be executed by the electric chair, Ralph was asked to be there and console the man on the way to his death. When the day arrived, Ralph walked the last mile with the convict, but was very anxious about what to say. "Good-bye" seemed trite, "See you later" seemed inappropriate, and he became desperate for the right words. Just as they got to the electric chair, Ralph blurted out, "More power to you!!"

—

The warden was very upset that his daughter married one of the convicts. Partially because the guy was a lifer, but mostly because they eloped.

—Ron Dentinger

P

PROBLEMS

I don't have a solution, but I admire your problem.

PROCRASTINATION

She said procrastination was the cause of all my sorrow.
I don't know what that big word means . . . I'll look it up tomorrow.

—Mary Alice Sherman

—

I think I can, I think I could,
I think I may, I think I should,
I think I might, I think I will,
I think I better think more still.

—Susan Hambor

Procrastinators suffer from hardening of the oughteries.
> —*The Pundit,* The International Save the Pun Foundation.

PROFESSIONS

All professions are conspiracies against the laity.   —George Bernard Shaw

A doctor can bury his mistakes, but an architect can only advise his clients to plant vines.   —Frank Lloyd Wright

A sea captain and his chief engineer argued about who was more important to the ship, and decided they'd swap places to find out. After a couple of hours,

the captain emerged from the engine room completely covered with oil and soot, and confronted the chief on the bridge. "Chief!" he yelled, wildly waving a monkey wrench, "you'll have to come down! I can't make 'er go!" "Of course you can't," replied the chief. "She's aground."
> —Colville, Washington, *Statesman-Examiner*

PROGRESS

Progress is man's ability to complicate simplicity.
> —Thor Heyerdahl

PROJECTS

They say there are six phases to any project:
1. Enthusiasm
2. Disillusionment
3. Panic
4. Search for the guilty.
5. Punishment of the innocent.
6. Praise and honors for the nonparticipants.

PROMISES

And all of my free programs come with a money-back guarantee.
> —Jim Butterfield, early Commodore software superstar, 1983

PROVERBS

Rolling Stones gather an audience   —Ray Przybysz

A stitch in time saves embarrassment.   —Al Frisbie in *Omaha World-Herald*

Where there's life there's cope. —Lane Olinghouse

PRUDENCE

I believe in practicing prudence at least once every two or three years.

—Molly Ivins

PSYCHIATRISTS

Psychiatrists tell us that most women tend to marry men who are like their fathers. My brother-in-law's wife adds: "That's why the mothers always cry at weddings." —Ron Dentinger

I ran into my psychiatrist yesterday. She was pushing a sofa down the street. "Why the couch?" I asked. "House call," she replied.

Julia Winton explained to a psychiatrist that her husband Fred thought he was the Lone Ranger. The psychiatrist asked, "How long has this been going on?" "About twenty years." "Bring him in. I'll cure him." The woman nodded and said, "I guess it's the right thing to do. But Tonto is so good with the children!"

A man walks into a psychiatrist's office and says, "Doc, I'm going crazy. I keep imagining I'm a zebra. I look at myself in the mirror, and I see my entire body covered with black stripes." The doctor says, "You are not a zebra. Calm down, go home, take these pills, and get a good night's sleep. I'm sure the black stripes will disappear." The man goes home

and takes the pills. Next day, he's back. "Doc," he says, "the black stripes disappeared! I feel great! Now, got anything for the white stripes?"

—Robert Menchin, *101 Classic Jewish Jokes*

You know how everyone wants a second opinion these days? Well, this lady had been going to a psychiatrist for years and finally she decided she'd had enough of it. "Doctor," she announced, walking into his office, "I've been seeing you every week for five years now. I don't feel any better, I don't feel any worse. What's the story? I want you to level with me. What's wrong with me?" "All right," said the doctor, "I'll tell you. You're crazy." "Now wait just a minute," she protested. "I think I'm entitled to a second opinion." "Fine," he responded. "You're ugly, too." —Mel Calman

Two women were comparing notes on their psychotherapists. "Frankly, mine drives me crazy," said Eileen. "Three years I've been going to her now and she never says a single word to me. Just sits there and nods." "That's nothing," responded Ruthie. "After six years I finally get three words out of mine." "Oh, yeah? What'd he say?" "No hablo Ingles."

～

And then there was the psychiatrist who showed very poor taste when he equipped his waiting room with a cuckoo clock.   —Ron Dentinger

～

"I can't imagine," Betty James said indignantly to Harvey Nuxall, the prominent psychiatrist, "why my family has insisted upon dragging me to see you. What's wrong with loving pancakes?" "Nothing at all," agreed the psychiatrist in a tone of obvious surprised. "I like pancakes myself." "Wonderful," said the Mrs. James. "You must come to my house and let me show you my collection. I've got display case after display case full of them."

～

My cousin Ed is a psychiatrist. He firmly believes in shock treatment. He gives his clients their bills in advance.

～

I told my psychiatrist, "I sometimes feel so inferior that I don't think anyone notices me at all." He said, "Next."

～

A doctor was making his rounds in a mental hospital and stopped in a room with two patients. He asked the fellow near the door: "What is your name?" "Napoleon," replied the fellow briskly. "Who said you were Napoleon?" demanded the doctor. "God," replied the patient. From the patient in the other bed came the shouted denial: "I did not!"   —Brian O'Hara

～

Our guide on a tour bus pointed to a mansion as we drove by. "This place was built by a psychiatrist. You'll notice the porch is done completely in over-wrought iron."   —*Ohio Motorist*

～

In Russia, three patients in a mental institution prepare for an examination given by the chief psychiatrist. If the patients pass the exam, they will be free to leave the hospital. However, if they fail, the institution will detain them for five years. The doctor takes the three patients to the top of a diving board looking over an empty swimming pool, and asks each patient in turn to jump. The first patient jumps head first into the pool and breaks both arms. The second patient jumps and breaks both legs. The third patient looks over the side and refuses to jump. "Congratulations! You're a free man. Just tell me why didn't you jump?" asked the doctor. "Well, Doc," replied the patient, "I can't swim!"

A guy wearing a beret, a smock, and a goatee, goes to see a psychiatrist. The psychiatrist says, "You fantasize you're an artist." The guy says, "No." The psychiatrist says, "Then you really are an artist?" The guy says, "No." The psychiatrist says, "Then why are you wearing a beret and that smock?" The guy says, "That's what I came here to find out."

Shakey went to a psychiatrist. "Doc," he said, "I've got trouble. Every time I get into bed, I think there's somebody under it. I get under the bed, I think there's somebody on top of it. Top, under, top, under . . . you gotta help me, I'm going crazy!" "Just put yourself in my hands for two years," said the shrink. "Come to me three times a week, and I'll cure your fears." "How much do you charge?" "A hundred dollars per visit." "I'll sleep on it," said Shakey. Six months later the doctor met Shakey on the street. "Why didn't you ever come to see me again?" asked the psychiatrist. "For a hundred bucks a visit? A carpenter cured me for ten dollars." "Is that so! How?" "He told me to cut the legs off the bed!"

PSYCHOLOGY

The psychology instructor had just finished a lecture on mental health and was giving an oral test. Speaking specifically about manic depression, she asked, "How would you diagnose a patient who walks back and forth screaming at the top of his lungs one minute, then sits in a chair weeping uncontrollably the next?" A young man in the rear raised his hand and answered, "A basketball coach?"

PUNCTUALITY

Duncan prided himself on his punctuality. He followed a very precise routine every morning. His alarm went off at 5:30 A.M. He rose, shaved, showered, dressed, ate his breakfast, brushed his teeth, picked up his briefcase, got into his car, drove to a nearby ferry landing, parked his car, rode the ferry across to the downtown business area, got off the ferry, walked to his building, rode the elevator to the seventeenth floor, hung up his coat, opened his briefcase, spread his papers out on his desk, and sat down in his chair at precisely 8:00 A.M. Not 8:01, not 7:59. Always at 8:00 A.M. He followed this same routine without variation for eighteen years. Until one morning his alarm did not go off and he slept fifteen minutes late. He woke in a panic. He rushed through his shower, nicked himself when he shaved, threw his clothes on, gulped down his breakfast, only half-way brushed his teeth, grabbed up his briefcase, jumped into his car, sped to the ferry landing, jumped out of his car and looked for the ferry. There it was, out in the water, approximately 15 feet from the shore. "I think I can make it," he said to himself, running toward the dock at full speed. Reaching the edge of the water he gave an enormous leap out into the water and miraculously landed with a loud thud on the deck of the ferry. The captain rushed down to make sure he was all right. "Son, that was a tremendous leap, the captain said, but if you would have waited just another minute, we would have been to the shore."

❧

The trouble with being punctual is that nobody's there to appreciate it.

—Franklin P. Jones

PUNISHMENT

An old-fashioned, hell-and damnation preacher was scolding his congregation for their terrible misdeeds. "Remember what it says in the Bible," he thundered. "Jesus told us that for those who do evil there shall be weeping and gnashing of teeth." [Matthew 22:13] At this point the preacher saw a very old parishioner grinning up at him, unconcerned, toothless. He accepted the challenge and pointed at the grinning gums, "Don't worry, James Lippincott. Teeth will be provided!"

PUNS

Three animals were having a huge argument over who was the best: The first, a hawk, claimed that because of his ability to fly, he could attack anything repeatedly from above, and his prey had nary a chance. The second, a lion, based his claim on his strength—none in the forest dared to challenge him. The third, a skunk, insisted he needed neither flight nor strength to frighten off any creature. As the trio debated the issue, a grizzly bear came along and swallowed them all: hawk, lion and stinker!

❧

A frog goes into a bank and approaches the teller. He can see from her name-plate that the teller's name is Patricia Whack. So he says, "Ms. Whack, I'd like to get a loan to buy a boat and go on a long vacation." Patti looks at the frog in disbelief and asks how much he wants to borrow. The frog says $50,000. The teller asks his name and the frog says that his name is Kermitt Jagger and that it's OK, he knows the bank manager. Patti explains that $50,000 is a substantial amount of money and that he will need to secure some collateral against the loan. She asks if he has anything he can use as collateral. The frog says, "Sure, I have this," and produces a tiny pink porcelain elephant, about half an inch tall. It is bright pink and perfectly formed. Very confused, Patti explains that she'll have to consult with the manager and disappears into a back office. She finds the manager and says, "There's a frog called Kermitt Jagger out there who claims to know you and wants to borrow $50,000. And he wants to use this as collateral." She holds up the tiny pink elephant. "I mean, what the heck is this?" So the bank manager looks back at her and says, "It's a knick knack, Patti Whack. Give the frog a loan. His old man's a Rolling Stone."

Fifty years ago, my Uncle Marty, then a photographer for *National Geographic,* gained considerable notoriety when he made a two-week trek, completely alone, through some of the most forbidding and unmapped wilds of the Gobi Desert, and did it without a compass! "Nothing to it!" he airily told reporters. "You've just got to mark every jog in the route, so you can go back the way you came. Every time I changed direction, I just built a little cairn of rocks, so I'd know one way from another. It's a snap if you just leave no turn unstoned."

Presidio Little League's Sefton Field in Mission Valley, Calif., has been devastated by floods for years. When the water receded last year, attorney Terry Lehr, a reclamation volunteer, reported that they found exposed electrical wiring, several hundred golf balls from the Stardust course next door, and a 15-pound carp. This led, ineluctably, to Lehr's pun: "For a while, we were the only Little League in the country with its own electric golf carp."   —Tom Blair

John Scott tells of the Indian chief who could not decide which of his two sons, Straight Arrow or Falling Rocks, should succeed him as leader of the tribe. As a test he sent them into the woods armed with only a knife, for three moons. At the end of the period, Straight Arrow returned sound and healthy, loaded down with a fine assortment of pelts. Falling Rocks failed to return that day or any other. "To this day the tribe still hunts for him," Scott declares, "Because anywhere you drive in this great nation of ours you will see their signs, 'Watch out for Falling Rocks.'"

~

Among the runners finishing last in a marathon was an older man wearing a T-shirt that proclaimed: "Abominably Slow Man."

~

Because his trip to North America took so long, Leif Ericson returned home only to learn that his name had been crossed from the list of village inhabitants. He complained to the village chief, who relayed the adventurer's displeasure to the village statistician. "I'm so sorry," said the census keeper. "I must have taken Leif off my census."

~

The game show contestant was only 200 points behind the leader and about to answer the final question—worth 500 points! "To be today's champion," the show's smiling host intoned, "name two of Santa's reindeer." The contestant, a man in his early thirties, gave a sigh of relief, gratified that he had drawn such an easy question. "Rudolph!" he said confidently, "and, . . . Olive!" The studio audience started to applaud (like the little sign above their heads said to do,) but the clapping quickly faded into mumbling, and the confused host replied, "Yes, we'll accept Rudolph, but could you please explain . . . 'Olive?!?'" "You know," the man circled his hand forward impatiently and began to sing, "Rudolph the Red Nosed Reindeer—had a very shiny nose. And if you ever saw it, you would even say it glows. Olive, the other reindeer. . . ."

~

I was complaining the other day to my friend Harry about the knot in my tie. He asked, "Do you know how to do a Windsor knot?" I replied, "It doesn't matter if you Windsor knot, it's how you play the game!"

~

I was driving down a lonely country road one cold winter day when it began to sleet pretty heavily. My windows were getting icy and my wiper blades were badly worn and quickly fell apart under the strain. Unable to drive any further because of the ice building up on my front window I suddenly had a great idea. I stopped and began to overturn large rocks until I located two very lethargic hibernating rattle snakes. I grabbed them up, straightened them out flat and installed them on my blades and they worked just fine. What! You've never heard of . . . wind chilled vipers?

Recently a guy in Paris nearly got away with stealing several paintings from the Louvre. However, after planning the crime, breaking in, evading security, getting out and escaping with the goods, he was captured only two blocks away when his Econoline van ran out of gas. When asked how he could mastermind such a crime and then make such an obvious error, he replied: "I had no Monet to buy Degas to make the Van Gogh."

Many years ago, in the South Pacific, there was a small island kingdom that was ruled by a kind and benevolent King. Each year, on the King's birthday, the residents of the island gave the King a new throne as token of their love and respect for him. And each year, the King would put last year's gift up in the attic of his small house. After many years of ruling the island, the weight of the large number of birthday presents stored up in the attic became too heavy and caused the house to fall down. The moral of the story is: People in grass houses shouldn't stow thrones.

Sonia Flynn was bagging groceries at a supermarket. One day the store installed a machine for squeezing fresh orange juice. Intrigued, the young lady asked if she could be allowed to work the machine, but her request was denied. Said the store manager, "Sorry, kid, but baggers can't be juicers."

The bad and ugly king had a beautiful girl as a captive. Though her beauty shone like a thousand moons, the dress she was forced to wear was very unbecoming. She waited day and night, looking with hope out the dungeon window, searching for the knight who would free her. However, every knight was scared away by her dress, which, as I've said before, was very ugly. She was crying in hopelessness when the evil king jeered, . . . "See, I told you no knight would rescue a damsel in this dress!!!"

The other day I decided to bake a cake and so, with my wife's permission, I got set to work in the kitchen. Then I discovered that we didn't have any butter, so I sent my dog to buy some. On the way, he passed a bookstore and, being intrigued by a display in the window, he went in and came home with a dog-eared book of poems. The point of my story is: Never send a literary dog to the grocery store because . . . he'll get verse before he gets butter!

—Carl Hess

QUOTATIONS

It is better to be quotable than to be honest.   —Tom Stoppard

～

She had a pretty gift for quotation, which is a serviceable substitute for wit.

—W. Somerset Maugham

～

Fine words! I wonder where you stole them.   —Jonathan Swift

─────────── **R** ───────────

RACE

Isaac Asimov loved the following, possibly apocryphal, story about Thurgood Marshall, the first black member of the Supreme Court: He was mowing the lawn at his posh residence in a Washington suburb when a car stopped in the street. The woman driving the car noted a black man mowing a lawn and called out, "How much do you charge for mowing a lawn, my good man?" Marshall hesitated, and the woman said, "Well, what does the lady of the house pay you?" And Marshall said, "She doesn't pay me anything ma'am. She just lets me sleep with her every night."

—Isaac Asimov, *Asimov Laughs Again*

RADIO

Then coming through Iowa I heard a Des Moines radio announcer warn: "Drivers, if you are going north or south on I-80, be extremely cautious because I-80 runs east and west."   —Ron Dentinger

～

Jack Benny and Fred Allen staged a running feud on their radio programs. When Jack was appointed honorary chairman of the March of Dimes campaign, Fred Allen quipped, "The dime hasn't been minted that could march past Jack Benny." The feud ran a year and a half and America loved every bit of it.

～

Sportscaster Vin Scully once received a letter from a Los Angeles woman whose spouse was a dedicated Scully listener. "My husband falls asleep at night listening to the Dodgers game. The radio is on his side of the bed, and to turn it off, I have to crawl across him. I want you to be the first to know that we're expecting a baby in about six months."

RAILROADS

People may complain about the railroads but I never spent three hours on one circling the station.　　—Robert Orben, *2500 Jokes To Start 'Em Laughing*

RAIN

Question: What normally follows two days of rain?
Answer: Monday.　　　　　　　　　　　　　　　—Ron Dentinger

~

Rain was trouble enough when it contained only water.

READING

The man who does not read good books has no advantage over the man who cannot read them.　　　　　　　　　　　　—Mark Twain

REAL ESTATE

Real-estate agent to prospective home buyers: "Yes, we have a house in your price range. Its present owner is a German Shepherd named Prince."

~

At a neighborhood cocktail party, a new Coronado, California, resident who'd just paid $300,000 for a tiny house on a little lot on an alley was seeking reassurance. "Do you think I paid too much?" she asked her host. "Nah, you can't lose in Coronado," the neighbor replied. "But $300,000, and it's so small," she persisted. "If you don't trust me, ask this guy," the neighbor said. "He's one of our top brokers." "I just bought a house near here, and I'm worried," she blurted out to the real-estate salesman. "You can't lose in Coronado," he interrupted. "Look, some idiot just paid $300,000 for a tiny house on a little lot fronting on an alley."　　　　　—Tom Blair in *San Diego Union*

~

Whoever uses the term "dirt cheap" probably hasn't bought any real estate lately.　　　　　　　　　　　　　　—D. O. Flynn in *On the Upbeat*

~

The realtor had spent her entire day showing one couple through homes for sale. "And this," she said in the ninth house they'd toured, "is the hobby room.

R

Do you folks have any hobbies?" "Yes, indeed," replied the man enthusiastically. "Our hobby is looking at homes for sale!" —Hugh Harrison

RECOGNITION

See that fellow over there? Well—he's gotten so bald and so fat he didn't even recognize me!

~

I don't recognize you—I've changed a lot. —Oscar Wilde

REFORMS

Every abuse ought to be reformed unless the reform is more dangerous than the abuse itself. —Voltaire

REJECTION

It was hard for me to leave my hometown . . . covered in tar and feathers as I was. —Gene Perret

~

I was so ugly when I was a kid, my imaginary playmate was ashamed to hang around with me.

~

An elaborate example of a euphemism recently appeared in Herb Caen's column in the San Francisco *Chronicle:* A rejection slip sent to a writer by a Chinese economic journal was delicately phrased as follows: "We have read your manuscript with boundless delight. If we were to publish your paper, it would be impossible for us to publish any work of a lower standard. And as it is unthinkable that, in the next 1,000 years, we shall see it equal, we are, to our regret, compelled to return your divine composition and beg you a thousand times to overlook our short sight and timidity." Caen's translation: "Don't ever send us this kind of garbage again."

~

You have to know how to accept rejection and reject acceptance.
—Ray Bradbury, advice to writers.

~

It is better to be looked over than overlooked.
—Mae West, in *Belle of the Nineties* (1934)

REJOINDER

He came up to my table. "Hey darling," he goes, "you're OK in my book." He wouldn't let up either. He took my glasses off and said, "Without your glasses, why, you're beautiful." "Without my glasses," I said, "you're not half bad either." —Kit Hollerbach

RELATIVES

Wanda and Millard Prufrock's happy married life almost went on the rocks because of the presence in the household of old Aunt Flora. For eighteen long years she lived with the Prufrocks. Aunt Flora was always crotchety, always demanding, never satisfied, always the first one at the table at mealtimes even though she complained about every meal set before her. Finally, the old woman caught double pneumonia and died. On the way back from the cemetery, Mr. Prufrock told his wife that he had a confession to make. "Darling," he said, "if I didn't love you so much, I don't think I ever could have stood having your Aunt Flora in the house all that time." His wife looked at him, aghast. "My Aunt Flora!" she cried. "I thought she was your Aunt Flora!"

My Aunt Beverly is famous for her green thumb. The last time I visited her, my Uncle Dick warned me as I drove up to their house: "Keep your car doors locked! This is zucchini season!"

One of Deion Sanders' nephews was a little short of cash, so he wrote to his rich and famous uncle and asked for a short-term loan. The usually generous Sanders was annoyed that the young man would ask him for money considering that they had not seen one another for years. The multi-talented athlete wrote a chilly note to his nephew suggesting that he earn the money through his own diligence. The young man promptly sold the letter for a thousand dollars.

My wife's Aunt Aggie is looking for an older man with a strong will—made out to her.

My Uncle Will was an angry man. In his will, he instructed my Aunt Celia to put on his tombstone: "What are you lookin' at?"

Uncle Sid says, "My brother-in-law works at the same company I do—he's our anchor man. We call him that because he keeps us from moving forward."

RELATIVITY

Asked to explain this theory of relativity in layman's terms, Albert Einstein replied: "When a man sits with a pretty girl for an hour, it seems like a minute. But let him sit on a hot stove for a minute—and it's longer than any hour."

RELAXATION

The time to relax is when you don't have time for it.   —Sydney J. Harris

RELIGION

If you want to be a holy man, you have to be committed. When you make a decision you cannot waver in any way. You'd never see Gandhi during a hunger strike sneaking into the kitchen in the middle of the night. "Gandhi—what are you doing down there?" "I ummmm I thought I heard a prowler . . . and was going to hit him over the head with this giant bowl of potato salad."

—Jim Carrey

~

Most people have some sort of religion; at least they know which church they're staying away from.   —John Erskine

~

While we were discussing religious sects one day, I asked my lawyer, Ralph Getz, if he would like to become a Jehovah's Witness. He declined, as he hadn't seen the accident, but allowed as to how he'd still be interested in taking the case.

~

Following the Vatican declaration that women cannot become priests because they do not resemble Christ, sources reported that Colonel Sanders declared that he would not employ anyone who didn't resemble a chicken.

—Jane Curtin

~

A man going into church was stopped cold by a huge sign the janitor had placed in front of the area of the floor that he just washed. It read: "PLEASE DON'T WALK ON THE WATER."

~

Somebody put it rightly: Almost everybody believes in tithing—a few even practice it.

~

A rabbi and a soap maker went for a walk together. The soap maker said, "What good is religion? Look at all the trouble and misery of the world! Still there, even after years—thousands of years—of teaching about goodness and truth and peace. Still there, after all the prayers and sermons and teachings. If religion is good and true, why should this be?" The rabbi said nothing. They continued walking until he noticed a child playing in the gutter. Then the rabbi said, "Look at that child. You say that soap makes people clean, but see the dirt on that youngster. Of what good is soap? With all the soap in the world, over all these years, the child is still filthy. I wonder how effective soap is, after all!" The soap maker protested. "But, Rabbi, soap cannot do any good unless it is used!" "Exactly," replied the Rabbi. "Exactly!"

—Norm Lawson

Did you hear the story about Adam who began staying out late and sneaking back into the Garden of Eden in the wee hours? Eve watched these goings on suspiciously for a while and then one morning, after Adam had crept in and fallen into a heavy sleep, Eve stole silently to his side and carefully counted his ribs.

—How the Platform Professionals Keep 'em Laughin'

A preacher saw a group of little boys sitting in a circle with a dog in the middle. He asked them what they were doing with the dog. One little fellow said, "We ain't doin' nuthin to the dog. We're just tellin' lies, and the one that tells the biggest one gets to keep the dog." The preacher told them that he was very shocked, that when he was a little boy, he would never have even thought of telling a lie. The little boy said, "Give him the dog, fellas."

R

An aging church custodian once said: "I've seen 12 preachers come and go and I STILL believe in God." —Larry Eisenberg

Notice on a church bulletin board: "Work for the Lord. The pay is not much but the retirement plan is out of this world."

Two fellows are talking religion. One says to the other, "Sometimes I'd like to ask God why he allows poverty, famine and injustice when he could do something about it." "What's stopping you?" asks the second. And the first replies, "I'm afraid God might ask me the same question."

～

Sister Serafina was on a much desired mission assignment to the Apache Indians. She was so excited that she drove past the last gas station without noticing that she needed gas. She ran out of gas about a mile down the road, and had to walk back to the station. The attendant told her that he would like to help her, but he had no container to hold the gas. Sympathetic to her plight, he agreed to search through an old shed in the back for something that might suffice. The only container that would hold fuel was an old bedpan. He was doubtful, but the grateful nun told him that the bedpan would work just fine. She carried the gasoline back to her car, taking care not to drop an ounce. When she got to her car, she carefully poured the contents of the bed pan into the tank. A truck driver pulled alongside the car as the nun was emptying the container into the tank. He rolled down his window and yelled to her, "I wish I had your faith, Sister!"

～

Many folks want to serve God, but only as advisers.   —Sr. Monique Rysavy

～

It is easier to preach ten sermons than it is to live one.
                                           —Rev. Robert E. Harris

～

There are ten church members by inheritance for one by conviction.
                                           —Eugene O'Neill

～

If your religion does not change you, then you should change your religion.
                                           —Elbert Hubbard

～

It is a test of a good religion whether you can make a joke about it.
                                           —G. K. Chesterton

～

In a rural, quite religious farm community, there was a disastrous drought and the crops were dying. In desperation, the local preacher announced that the whole community would assemble at the edge of one of the fields and pray for rain. A large crowd gathered, and the preacher climbed on a bale of hay and surveyed the flock. He said, "Brothers and sisters, you have come here to pray for rain." "Amen!" responded the crowd. "Well," said the preacher, "do you have sufficient faith?" "Amen! Amen!" shouted the crowd. "All right, all right," said the preacher, "but I have one question to ask you." The crowd stood silent, puzzled, expectant. "Brothers and sisters," shouted the preacher, "where are your umbrellas?"   —Eric W. Johnson, *A Treasury of Humor*

When a rural Kansas preacher returned after visiting New England, a parishioner met him at the train station. "How are things out our way, Hiram?" the preacher asked. "Sad, sir. A cyclone came and wiped out my house." "Dear, dear," cried the parson. "Well, I'm not surprised, Hiram. You remember I warned you about the way you had been living. Punishment for sin is inevitable." "It also destroyed your house, sir," said Hiram. "It did?" The pastor was horrified. "Ah me, the ways of the Lord are past human understanding."
          —Oren Arnold, *Snappy Steeple Stories*

A Jew and a Christian were indulging in a friendly argument about their respective faiths. "Most of the good things you Christians have, you've taken from us," the Jew said. "The Ten Commandments, for instance." "I'll admit we took the Ten Commandments from you," answered the Christian, "but you can't say that we've kept them."   —*Fraternal Monitor*

REPAIRS

No one can make you feel more humble than the repairman who discovers you've been trying to fix it yourself.   —Savannah, Ga., *Pennysaver*

REPUTATION

Reputation is character minus what you've been caught doing.

RESEARCH

LAWS OF RESEARCH:
1st Law of Research: If you think of something new, it's been done.
2nd Law of Research: If you think something is important, no one else will.
3rd Law of Research: If you throw it away, someone else will publish it, obtain a grant, write a book, and get on the Oprah Winfrey show.

Research is what I'm doing when I don't know what I'm doing.
          —Wernher Von Braun

Bacteriologist Robert Koch discovered the causes for Cholera, TB and Bubonic Plague, but not one of his peers, not even his wife, shook his hand to congratulate him. In fact, every night before she'd let him get into bed she sprayed him with Lysol.

RESPECT

Boris Yeltsin is being driven from his dacha to Moscow and is in a hurry. He is getting irritated with the slowness of his driver. "Can't you go any faster?" he says angrily. "I have to obey the speed limits," says the driver. Finally Yeltsin orders the driver into the back and takes the wheel. Sure enough a patrol car soon pulls them over. The senior officer orders the junior to go write up the ticket. But the junior officer comes back and says he can't give them a ticket, the person in the car is too important. "Well, who is it?" the senior officer asks. "I didn't recognize him," says the junior officer, "but Boris Yeltsin is his chauffeur."

RESPONSIBILITY

Alec McKeon, a traveling preacher, finds himself caught in a tremendous rainstorm. Within a few hours, the motel he's staying in is flooded. As the water rises, the preacher climbs to the roof and starts praying. Just then, a Coast Guard rescue party floats by in a rowboat. "Let's go, mister, into the boat." "I'll stay here," says the preacher. "The Lord will save me." An hour later, a second boat reaches the motel. "Sir, you better get in. The water is still rising." "No thanks," says the preacher. "The Lord is my salvation." Toward evening, the motel is almost completely under water, and the preacher is clinging to the satellite dish on the roof. "Hey buddy, get in the boat! This is your last chance!" "I'm all right," says the preacher, looking toward heaven. "I know the Lord will provide." As the boat departs, the satellite dish is hit by lightning, and the preacher is killed. When he arrives at the Pearly Gates he is furious. "What happened?" he shouts. "I thought the Lord would provide!" Within seconds, a thunderous reply is heard: "Gimme a break, pal. I sent three boats!"

Donna, the minister's eight-year-old daughter, ran into the house, crying as though her heart would break. "What's wrong, dear?" asked the pastor. "My doll! Jeffrey broke it!" she sobbed. "How did he break it, Donna?" "I hit him over the head with it."

REST

Nothing wilts faster than laurels that have been rested on.

RESTAURANTS

Connie Wilson, a successful real estate broker, stopped at a coffee shop and ordered a cup of coffee. The waitress grudgingly delivered it and asked, "Anything else?" "Yes," said the businesswoman, "I'd like some sugar, cream, a spoon, a napkin, and a saucer for the cup." "Well, aren't you the demanding one?" snapped the waitress. "Look at it from my point of view," said Connie. "You served a cup of coffee and made five mistakes."

～

I went into an authentic Mexican restaurant. The waiter poured the water and warned me not to drink it.
—Brad Garrett

～

Last night my father ordered a whole meal in French and even the waiter was surprised. It was a Chinese restaurant.

～

My dad is allergic to onions so whenever he eats out, he always inquires as to the presence of onions in the food. When we were at a restaurant during a recent visit my parents made to the West Coast, he asked the waitress if there were any onions in the crab salad and told her of his allergy. She reassured him, "There's nothing to worry about. There are onions in the salad but they are very finely chopped!"

～

A mountaineer happened to get to Boston where he entered a seafood restaurant. "Bring me the best meal you have," he told the waiter. "I want to find out what you Bostonians eat." The waiter brought a bowl of clam chowder. The hillbilly eyed it suspiciously but ate it. He also ate a shredded cabbage salad. Finally, the waiter brought in the main course, a fine broiled lobster. The man stared at it for a moment, then jumped to his feet and cried:" I drunk your dishwater and I et your weeds, but I'm not touching your big red bug!"
—Msgr. Arthur Tonne, *Jokes Priests Can Tell,* vol. 6

R

～

Going out to eat is expensive. I was out at one restaurant and they didn't have prices on the menu. Just faces with different expressions of horror.
—Rita Rudner

～

After my car skidded on wet pavement and struck a light pole, I was bruised and disheveled. When I got out of the car, I slipped and fell in some mud. The police officer who had come to the scene, pointed to an exclusive restaurant across the road and suggested that I could clean up there. As I entered, the maitre de recoiled in disgust. "Excuse me," I said. "Where's the bathroom?" "Go down the hall and turn left," replied the maitre de. "When you see the sign marked 'Gentlemen,' pay no attention to it and go right inside."

~

Ever notice . . . that the disparity between a restaurant's price and food quality rises in direct proportion to the size of its pepper mill?   —Bryan Miller

~

At a small coffee shop, a counterman was pouring a cup of coffee for a customer. After he added milk, the customer shouted, "Say, could you make that a little lighter?" The counterman poured the milk generously. "Hold it! Hold it!" cried the customer. "That's far too light." With a shrug of his shoulders, the counterman responded, "Next time bring a swatch."

—Ross Gaffney

~

When a group of us entered a delicatessen that I frequent in Minneapolis, the owner came up to take our order. A friend of mine, in a playful mood, ordered the following: "Ron, I want 140 knockwursts on pumpernickel buns, 100 with the works and 40 with just hot mustard. Then give me 27 pints of coleslaw,

"I'm sorry, Sir, but our catch-of-the-day got away."

about 40 of baked beans. And could you toss in about six dozen kosher dills and 37 pieces of cheesecake and hold the cherries on seven of them?" Ron looked at my friend, cupped his hand to his mouth, turned toward the kitchen and hollered: "Number 3."   —Dave Wood

The difference between eating out and dining out is about twenty dollars per person.

Buffet. A French word that means "Get up and get it yourself!"

Once I was in a French restaurant that had enough stars to qualify as a minor constellation. The wine came cradled in the tuxedoed arms of a waiter who looked down his considerable nose and presented the bottle with a condescending, "Monsieur?" My host, a cosmopolitanite who was immune to the hauteur of waiters with accents, ignored the proffered dollop and requested the cork. I half-expected him to sniff it, but with a bold look at the wine steward, he raised the cork and put it in his ear. "Sounds good," he said, nodding sagely. "Pour it."   —Ben Blackburn

"What does this mean?" howled the customer in a greasy spoon cafe. "There's an insect at the bottom of my cup." "Listen, Bud," the proprietor said. "If you want your fortune told, go see a Gypsy."   —*Male*

RESUMES

How bad a mistake can you make on your resume? Here are some real-life examples:

- "My intensity and focus are at inordinately high levels, and my ability to complete projects on time is unspeakable."
- "Education: Curses in liberal arts, curses in computer science, curses in accounting."
- "Instrumental in ruining entire operation for a Midwest chain store."
- "Personal: Married, 1992 Chevrolet."
- "I have an excellent track record, although I am not a horse."
- "I am a rabid typist."
- "Created a new market for pigs by processing, advertising and selling a gourmet pig mail order service on the side."
- "Exposure to German for two years, but many words are not appropriate for business."
- "Proven ability to track down and correct erors."

- "Personal interests: Donating blood. 15 gallons so far."
- "I have become completely paranoid, trusting completely nothing and no one."
- "References: None, I've left a path of destruction behind me."
- "Strengths: Ability to meet deadlines while maintaining composer."
- "Don't take the comments of my former employer too seriously, they were unappreciative beggars and slave drivers."
- "My goal is to be a meteorologist. But since I possess no training in meteorology, I suppose I should try stock brokerage."
- "I procrastinate—especially when the task is unpleasant."
- "I am loyal to my employer at all costs. Please feel free to respond to my resume on my office voice-mail."
- "Qualifications: No education or experience."
- "Disposed of $2.5 billion in assets."
- "Accomplishments: Oversight of entire department."
- "Extensive background in accounting. I can also stand on my head!"
- Cover letter: "Thank you for your consideration. Hope to hear from you shorty!"

RETIREMENT

A recently retired man came into the house after a morning of gardening and said, "One of the greatest joys of retirement is using my neckties to tie up tomato plants."   —*Capper's Weekly*

It is time I stepped aside for a less experienced and less able man.
—Professor Scott Elledge on his retirement from Cornell

But you have noticed that retired couples have reached a level of maturity where they never have any of those piddling little quarrels that other people do? They have one big argument that starts at seven in the morning and goes

"Pastor isn't taking kindly to retirement."

right through till bedtime . . . Retirement is when the husband comes up with all kinds of theories on how to do the cooking, housework, and shopping better. And retirement is also when his wife comes up with a theory—that all pills don't come in bottles!

—Robert Orben, *2500 Jokes To Start 'Em Laughing*

REUNIONS

Two women overheard at a class reunion:

"Did you ever look at a guy and kind of wish you were single again?"

"Yes."

"Who was it?"

"My husband."

—Ron Dentinger

RICH

My rich Aunt Minnie is worried about going to heaven. The other day she asked me, "When St. Peter opens up the Pearly Gates, how much should I tip him?"

RIGHT

It is better to be approximately right than precisely wrong. —Warren Buffett

Being right half the time beats being half-right all the time.

—Macolm S. Forbes

ROCK MUSIC

The reason guitars are so popular is they're easy to learn. For instance, my kid knows two chords. One is C major—and the other isn't.

—Robert Orben, *2500 Jokes To Start 'Em Laughing*

Show me an adult who can smile through a rock and roll concert, and I'll show you a hearing aid with weak batteries!

—Robert Orben, *2500 Jokes To Start 'Em Laughing*

RONALD REAGAN

Our family didn't exactly come from the wrong sides of the tracks, but we were certainly always within the sound of the train whistles.

—Ronald Reagan

Ronald Reagan has held the two most demeaning jobs in the country—President of the United States and radio broadcaster for the Chicago Cubs.

—George Will

~

Ronald Reagan is not a typical politician because he doesn't know how to lie, cheat, and steal. He's always had an agent for that. —Bob Hope

~

Speaking at the 1992 Republican National Convention, former president Ronald Reagan observed, "When we see all that rhetorical smoke billowing out from the Democrats, ladies and gentlemen, I'd follow the example of their nominee. Don't inhale."

~

When Soviet leader Mikhail Gorbachev called President Ronald Reagan, a White House official rushed to the President and said, "The good news, Mr. President, is that General Secretary Gorbachev is calling to say he is in favor of free speech. The bad news is, he's calling collect."

~

Ronald Reagan was beyond the age at which most Americans retire when he ran for the presidency in 1980. At age 69, he conducted a vigorous campaign, never passing up the chance to defuse the issue of his age with humor. On one occasion, he remarked, "I want to say that I don't mind at all any of the jokes or remarks about my age. Thomas Jefferson made a comment about the Presidency and age. He said that one should not worry about one's exact chronological age in reference to his ability to perform one's task. And ever since he told me that, I stopped worrying."

~

Probably his best such moment came during his second presidential election campaign, during his televised debate in 1984. A reporter asked Reagan if he was too old to serve another term. Reagan was more than ready for the question. He said, "I'm not going to inject the issue of age into this campaign," he began. "I am not going to exploit for political gain my opponent's youth and inexperience."

RUDENESS

Rudeness is a weak man's imitation of strength. —Eric Hoffer

RUSSIA

A Russian man loses his pet parrot. He looks everywhere, all around the neighborhood, in the park, everywhere. He just can't find the parrot. Finally, he goes around to the local KGB office, and tells the desk officer his problem. The desk officer is a little puzzled. " Look comrade, I'm sorry you lost your pet, but this is the KGB. We don't handle missing animal reports." "Oh, I know that," says the man. "I just wanted you to know, if you do happen to find my parrot—I don't know where he could have picked up his political ideas."

Two Russians are standing in a very long line for vodka. The first one says, "This line is too long! We must always wait for everything! I am going to go to the Kremlin and shoot Yeltsin!" After about an hour, he returns. The second Russian asks him, "Well, did you shoot him?" "No, the line was too long!"

In a Moscow café, a man asks the waiter for a cup of coffee and a copy of *Pravda*. "Here is your coffee, sir," says the waiter, "but *Pravda* is not available anymore." "Waiter," says the man, "I asked for a cup of coffee and *Pravda*." "I'm sorry but *Pravda* is no longer published." "Bring me coffee and *Pravda!*" the man insists. "I told you, sir, there is no *Pravda!*" says the waiter, losing patience. "Why do you persist in asking for it?" "Because," smiles the man, "I like to hear it again, and again, and again."   —Vladimir Bukovsky

S

SAFETY

SAFETY TIP: Wait one hour before going into the water after eating. Three days if you had sponge cake.   —Ron Dentinger

There is a story about a monastery in Europe perched high on a cliff several hundred feet in the air. The only way to reach the monastery was to be suspended in a basket which was pulled to the top by several monks who pulled and tugged with all their strength. Obviously the ride up the steep cliff in that basket was terrifying. One tourist got exceedingly nervous about half-way up as he noticed that the rope by which he was suspended was old and frayed. With a trembling voice he asked the monk who was riding with him in the basket how often they changed the rope. The monk thought for a moment and answered brusquely, "Whenever it breaks."

When Billy was in kindergarten his class visited the local fire station to watch a film on fire safety. In the film, children were told that if their clothes ever caught fire they should "Stop, drop, and roll" on the ground to extinguish the flames. After the film ended a fireman quizzed the children about what they had learned. "What would you do if your clothes were on fire?" he asked Billy, who answered matter-of-factly, "I wouldn't put them on."

—Catholic Workman

A brakeman on a midnight local freight was passing lantern signals from the top of a boxcar when his lantern slipped from his hand and fell to the ground. A yard clerk, walking past, picked it up and tossed it up to the brakeman. The engineer stopped the string of cars with a jerk and came running up, shouting as he came, "Don't you know anything about safety? Don't ever do that again!" "Do what again?" asked the brakeman. "Jump from the ground to the top of a boxcar."

—Train Dispatcher

SALES

A businessman was having trouble with his sales. So he called in a consultant to give him an objective view and some good advice. After he had explained all of his plans and problems, he showed the consultant a map into which he had stuck brightly colored pins wherever he had a salesman. Then he said, "O.K., for a starter, what is the first thing we should do?" "Well," said the consultant, "the first thing is to take those pins out of the map and stick them in the salesmen."

—Eric W. Johnson, *A Treasury of Humor* II

REVEREND FUN WWW.REVERENDFUN.COM

YARD SALE EVERYTHING MUST GO!

Scrolls 2 for 1

My father's cousin Josh was a fantastic salesman. He actually made a handsome living going door to door selling signs that read, "No salespeople allowed."

❧

The salesman was showing his prospect through a house. Everything was fine until the prospect glanced up at the ceiling and found unmistakably obvious signs of water damage. "It's a bit damp, isn't it?" he asked. "Damp!" the salesman enthused. "Of course it's damp. Just think what an advantage that would be in case of fire!"   —*Good Reading*

SANITY

Show me a sane man and I will cure him for you.   —Carl Gustav Jung

❧

Sanity is a madness put to good uses.   —George Santayana

The
BORDERLINE™   By Gabe Martin
                                    borderln@cts.com

© 1996 GABE MARTIN

http://www.the-borderline.com/

S

". . . And in addition to all that, this little baby here also comes equipped with 100 cup-holders."

SCHOOL

I will never forget my first day of school. My mom woke me up, got me dressed, made my bed, and fed me. Man, did the guys in the dorm tease me.

—Michael Aronin

~

Mrs. Hildrick, the third grade teacher was quizzing her pupils on natural history. "Now, Jason, tell me where the elephant is found." Jason struggled for the answer. Finally a look of pride lit up his face as he replied, "The elephant is so big that he's never lost."

~

Teacher: Give me a sentence with antidotes in it.
Pupil: My uncle kinda likes me, but auntie dotes on me.

~

Mrs. Hilton, the kindergarten teacher, was suddenly taken ill and a replacement was hastily found. The substitute teacher had a degree in computer science

and was at a loss as to what to do with the children. She decided to tell them stories. And always, at the end of each story, she would say, "And the moral of that story is. . . ." Hearing dozens of stories, the children had sat through dozens of morals. In a few days, Mrs. Hilton recovered from her illness and returned to her class. One of her students greeted her with a smile and said, "Teacher, I'm glad you're back. I like you better than that other teacher." Mrs. Hilton was flattered by the child, but was curious. "Why do you like me better than the other teacher?" The child looked into the teacher's eyes and said, "Because you don't have any morals."

~

School is never the same after you get your driver's license. A teenager got back home from his first day at school as a driver. His mother asked him what he learned at school today. "I learned," said the son, "that if I don't get to school early, I don't get a good parking place."

~

When the power failed at the elementary school, the cook couldn't serve a hot meal in the cafeteria, so at the last minute she whipped up great stacks of peanut-butter-and jelly sandwiches. As one little boy filled his plate, he said, "It's about time. At last—a home-cooked meal."

Gregory, a second-grader came home from school and asked his mother for a dollar. His explanation: "Our principal's leaving, so we're all chipping in to give her a little momentum."

A teacher was asking her class: "What is the difference between 'unlawful' and 'illegal'"? Only one hand shot up. "OK, answer, Joan," said the teacher. "'Unlawful' is when you do something the law doesn't allow and 'Illegal' is a sick eagle."

SCHOOL BLOOPERS

Probably the most pirated, photocopied, e-mailed, and otherwise reproduced humor material of the past few decades is Richard Lederer's compilation of bloopers and blunders found in student history exams. Extensive excerpts from Lederer's book, *Anguished English,* are found throughout the Internet under such titles as "History of the World" and "The World According to Student Bloopers." Rarely is Lederer given credit. I contacted him directly and asked him for an authorized selection. His reply follows:

> Dear Lowell: Here's my approximately 329-word version of "The World According to Student Bloopers"—as much humor per square syllable as I can possibly muster.
>
> All Good Luck With Your Humor Projects,
> Rich Lederer

Excerpted and adapted from Richard Lederer, *Anguished English* (Wyrick, Dell), this condensed version of the opening is composed entirely of genuine, certified, authentic student fluffs and flubs and goofs and gaffes.

- Ancient Egypt was inhabited by mummies, and they all wrote in hydraulics. They lived in the Sarah Dessert, which they cultivated by irritation.
- Ancient Egyptian women wore a loose-fitting garment which began just below the breasts which hung to the floor.
- The Bible is full of many interesting caricatures.
- Noah's wife was called Joan of Ark.
- Lot's wife was a pillar of salt by day and a ball of fire by night.
- Moses went up on Mt. Cyanide to get the ten commandments, but he died before he ever reached Canada.
- Solomon had 300 wives and 700 porcupines.
- Jesus was born because Mary had an immaculate contraption.
- An epistle is the wife of an apostle.
- The Greeks were a highly sculptured people, and without them we wouldn't have history.

- The Greeks invented three kinds of columns: corinthian, ironic, and dorc. They also invented myths.
- A myth is a female moth. One myth tells us that the mother of Achilles dipped him in the river Stinks until he became intolerable.
- The Romans conquered the Geeks. Their leader, Julius Caesar, extinguished himself on the battlefields of Gaul and when the Ides of March murdered him, he expired with these immortal words upon his dying lips: "Tee hee, Brutus"! Then came the Middle Ages, when everyone was middle aged. King Arthur lived in the Age of Shivery, with brave knights on prancing horses and beautiful women. Magna Carta ensured that no free man should be hanged twice for the same offense. Joan of Arc was burnt to a steak. People contracted the blue-bonnet plague, which caused them to grow boobs on their necks. They also put on morality plays about ghosts, goblins, virgins, and other mythical creatures.
- Then came the Renaissance, a time of a great many discoveries and inventions. Gutenberg invented the Bible and removable type. Sir Walter Raleigh discovered cigarettes and started smoking. And Sir Francis Drake circumcised the world with a 100-foot clipper.

A heavy snowstorm closed the schools in one town. When the children returned to school a few days later, one grade-school teacher asked her students whether they had used the time away from school constructively. "I sure did, teacher," one little girl replied. "I just prayed for more snow."

—Catherine Hall

The old pastor made it a practice to visit the parish school one day a week. He walked into the fourth-grade class, where the children were studying the states, and asked them how many states they could name. They came up with

about 40 names. He jokingly told them that in his day students knew the names of all the states. One lad raised his hand and said, "Yes, but in those days there were only 13."

—Msgr. Charles Dollen

It's Elementary! A first-grader had just been given an introduction to vowels. "Which is correct," his teacher asked, "an egg or a egg?" "An egg," he replied, "because egg starts with a fowl."

—NEA Journal

The teacher had asked her pupils to list, in their opinions, the 11 greatest Americans. As they were writing, she stopped at one desk. "Have you finished

your list, Bobby?" she asked. "Not quite," answered the boy. "I can't decide on the fullback."
                                                                    —Dan Bennett

~

Dad tells his fourth grader, "If your grades are B+ or better, I'll give you twenty dollars." It starts the kid thinking. The next day the kid walks up to his teacher and says, "How'd you like to make yourself an easy ten bucks?"

~

"Just to establish some parameters," said the professor, "Mr. Nichols, what is the opposite of joy?" "Sadness," said the student. "And the opposite of depression, Ms. Biggs?" "Elation." "And you Mr. Johnson, how about the opposite of woe?" "I believe that would be 'giddy up.'"

~

The teacher was giving her class of seven-year-olds a natural-history lesson. "Worker ants," she told them, "can carry pieces of food five times their own weight. What do you conclude from that?" One child was ready with the answer: "They don't have a union."
                                    —Peterborough in *Daily Telegraph,* London

~

As long as there are tests, there will be prayer in public schools.
                    —*Evenstar's Extensive Collection of One-Liners* website

~

Upon seeing the same pupil again, the annoyed principal said, "This is the fifth time this week you've been sent to my office. What do you have to say for yourself?" Small boy: "Thank heaven it's Friday."   —*Carolina Country*

SCIENCE

From Lloyd Smith, MD, during his address at the graduation ceremony for the University of Texas Medical School at Galveston: "Then there was the man who was so imbued with the scientific method that he sent two of his children to Sunday school and kept the other two at home as controls."

~

This isn't right. It isn't even wrong.
                —Wolfgang Pauli, on a paper submitted by a physicist colleague

~

My uncle Leo once crossed a chicken with a silkworm. He got a hen that lays eggs with a pantyhose in them!

FOUND IN STUDENT SCIENCE TEST ANSWERS:

- One horsepower is the amount of energy it takes to drag a horse 500 feet in one second.
- You can listen to thunder after lightening and tell how close you came to getting hit. If you don't hear it, you got hit, so never mind.
- Talc is found on rocks and on babies.
- The law of gravity says no fair jumping up without coming back down.
- When they broke open molecules, they found they were only stuffed with atoms. But when they broke open atoms, they found them stuffed with explosions.
- When people run around and around in circles we say they are crazy. When planets do it we say they are orbiting.
- Rainbows are just to look at, not to really understand.
- While the earth seems to be knowingly keeping its distance from the sun, it is really only centrificating.
- Someday we may discover how to make magnets that can point in any direction.
- South America has cold summers and hot winters, but somehow they still manage.
- Most books now say our sun is a star. But it still knows how to change back into a sun in the daytime.
- Water freezes at 32 degrees and boils at 212 degrees. There are 180 degrees between freezing and boiling because there are 180 degrees between north and south.
- A vibration is a motion that cannot make up its mind which way it wants to go.
- There are 26 vitamins in all, but some of the letters are yet to be discovered. Finding them all means living forever.
- There is a tremendous weight pushing down on the center of the Earth because of so much population stomping around up there these days.
- Lime is a green-tasting rock.
- Many dead animals in the past changed to fossils while others preferred to be oil.
- Genetics explain why you look like your father and if you don't why you should.
- Vacuums are nothings. We only mention them to let them know we know they're there.
- Some oxygen molecules help fires burn while others help make water, so sometimes it's brother against brother.
- Some people can tell what time it is by looking at the sun. But I have never been able to make out the numbers.
- We say the cause of perfume disappearing is evaporation. Evaporation gets blamed for a lot of things people forget to put the top on.
- To most people solutions mean finding the answers. But to chemists solutions are things that are still all mixed up.
- In looking at a drop of water under a microscope, we find there are twice as many H's as O's.
- Clouds are high flying fogs. I am not sure how clouds get formed. But the clouds know how to do it, and that is the important thing. Clouds just keep circling the earth around and around. And around. There is not much else to do. Water vapor gets together in a cloud. When it is big enough to be called a drop, it does.

- Humidity is the experience of looking for air and finding water. We keep track of the humidity in the air so we won't drown when we breathe.
- Rain is often known as soft water, oppositely known as hail. Rain is saved up in cloud banks.
- In some rocks you can find the fossil footprints of fishes.
- Cyanide is so poisonous that one drop of it on a dogs tongue will kill the strongest man.
- A blizzard is when it snows sideways.
- A hurricane is a breeze of a bigly size.
- A monsoon is a French gentleman.
- Thunder is a rich source of loudness.
- Isotherms and isobars are even more important than their names sound.
- It is so hot in some places that the people there have to live in other places.
- The wind is like the air, only pushier.

Why do scientists call it research when they're looking for something new that's never been searched?

Scientist to Colleague: "I'm not afraid of the unknown. The stuff we already know is what scares us!"   —Bob Goddard in *St. Louis Globe-Democrat*

SCREAM

Sometimes a scream is better than a thesis.   —Ralph Waldo Emerson

SECRETARIES

If you really want a job done, give it to a busy, important man. He'll have his secretary do it.
    —Calvin Coolidge

SELF

Know thyself? If I knew myself, I'd run away.
    —Johann Wolfgang von Goethe

SELF-CENTERED

If you are all wrapped up in yourself, you are overdressed.

SELF-DEFENSE

Aunt Aggie reports: "My 9-year-old grandson Donny, who had taken several judo lessons, was very impressed with Billy, a boy in his class at public school, who held a blue belt in judo. Donny came home from school one day and excitedly told his mother that Billy had given the class bully a bloody nose.

When asked which judo technique Billy had used, Donny replied, 'He stuck out his foot and tripped him!' "

SENSITIVITY

At a parent-teacher conference, a mother told the teacher, "My son Paul is a very sensitive boy." "Yes," said the teacher, "I've noticed that. Is there anything we should do about it?" "Well," said the mother, "if Paul misbehaves, please spank the boy next to him."   —Eric W. Johnson, *A Treasury of Humor*

SERIOUS

They that are serious in ridiculous things will be ridiculous in serious affairs.
                —Cato the Elder (234–149 B.C., AKA Marcus Porcius Cato)

SERVICE

A man dropped into a bank on business and found the customer-service clerk chatting on the phone, discussing new restaurants with her friend. After three minutes of exchanging dark glances with the man, she told her caller, "Hold on a minute? I'm being interrupted by a customer."   —Jim Allen

SEX

Seventeen-year-old Tony and his grandfather Al went fishing one day. Al began expostulating about how times have changed. The teenager added a few thoughts of his own about lax sexual mores and the dangerous diseases that had emerged. The following conversation ensued:

Tony: "Grandpa, they didn't have a whole lot of problems with herpes and AIDS when you were young did they?"
Grandpa: "Nope."
Tony: "Well, what did you guys use for safe sex?"
Grandpa: "A wedding ring."

~

Nine-year-old Heather quizzed her mother as to her origin, and was given the traditional answer, "God sent you." "And how did you get here, Mother? Did God send you, too?" "Yes, dear." "And grandma?" "Yes, dear." "And great-grandma?" "Yes, dear." "Do you mean to say, Mother, that there have been no normal births in this family for over a hundred years?"

~

Literature is mostly about having sex and not much about having children. Life is the other way round.   —David Lodge

The wonderful thing about celibacy is that you don't have to bother reading the manual.   —Sheldon Keller

Men reach their sexual peak at eighteen. Women reach their sexual peak at thirty-five. Do you get the feeling God is into practical jokes? We're reaching out sexual peak right around the same time they're discovering they have a favorite chair.   —Rita Rudner

SHOPPING

Heard at the mall: "I'd like a pair of stockings for my wife." "Sheer?" "No, she's at home."

A lot of antique dealers charge you extra if they have to stand there and listen to you tell them about what your mother used to have.   —Ron Dentinger

My aunt loves to watch the Home Shopping Channel and QVC. She says that television used to exhibit bad taste. Now, thanks to home shopping, you can have it delivered.

My favorite contact sports—football and Christmas shopping.

My wife will buy anything marked down. Yesterday, she tried to buy an escalator.   —Joey Bishop

Pat Schwab notes, "For the past few years, my watch word has been: I came, I saw, I bought! Or, as they say in Latin, 'Veni, Vidi, VISA'!"

S

Recent studies claim there are millions of adults who can't read or count—and if you don't believe it, take a look at the folks in front of you at the express checkout.   —Jay Trachman

Spend each day as if it were your last . . . and you'll be broke by sunset.
                                           —Los Angeles Times Syndicate

Supermarket carts carry a lot of wait.   —Steve Keuchel

A middle-aged couple were shopping . . . that is, she was shopping and he was questioning the need for each item she selected. When she chose an expensive brand of hair color, he asked plaintively, "When are you going to let your hair go gray like Barbara Bush's?" "On your Inauguration Day, dear," she sweetly replied. —Joni Cagle

SHYNESS

The following letter is self-explanatory:

Mrs. Ladybird Johnson

The White House, Washington

Dear Mrs. Johnson: I like the idea of beautifying American cities and I want to help you in your project, so I am enclosing my check for $8. You'll pardon me for not signing it, but I want to remain anonymous.

Scientists have found the gene for shyness. They would have found it years ago, but it was hiding behind a couple of other genes. —Jonathan Katz

SIGNS OF THE TIMES

In a supermarket in Westchester, a sign informs the shopper: "THIS IS THE EXPRESS LANE. YOU ARE LIMITED TO FIFTEEN ITEMS OR LESS. THE NUMBER FIFTEEN IS NOT SUBJECT TO NEGOTIATION."

The sign on the desk of an airline executive in Chicago reads: "Don't bother to agree with me, I've already changed my mind."

In a store this anti-shoplifting message: "God helps those who help themselves. We prosecute them."

SIGNS CURRENTLY ON DISPLAY:

- On a real estate agent's car: Site-seeing bus
- On the sales lot for mobile homes: Wheel Estate
- In a public utilities office: We're Pleased to Meter You!
- In a TV repair shop: Do it yourself—then call us.
- In a doctor's office: The doctor is very busy—please have your symptoms ready.
- Sign on a college bulletin board: "Books for sale. Like new. Hardly used."
- Sign seen by the entrance to a maternity shop: "Clothes for the wait conscious."
- Sign seen in an obstetrician's office: "Pay as You Grow."
- Sign in a Minneapolis toy store: "No eating, drinking, or whining."
- Sign in front of a Colonie, N.Y., church: "We have a prophet-sharing plan for you."
- Sign in a science-fiction bookstore: "Warning—shoplifters will be disintegrated."
- Notice posted for the All Seasons Resorts in Lake Delton, Wisconsin: "Closed for the winter."
- Sign in a veterinarian's office: "The doctor is in. Sit. Stay."
- A bumper sticker on a Rabbit convertible: "I'm not a brat. Am not, am not, am not!"

On the desk of a plumbing supply manufacturer: "Don't tell me what I mean. Let me figure it out myself."

Sign in a cemetery: "Persons are prohibited from picking flowers from any but their own graves."

Signspotter Sheila Gould caught this in the cafe of Borders Books at Union Square: "Do not leave tables unattended. We are not responsible for articles left while browsing and we must keep tables available for eating customers." Forget the table, I'll have mine to go.   —Herb Caen

On the door at the U.S. Patent Office: "This patent office is a government agency. Should you decide to patent your invention, copies of all documentation must be stored in triplicate for a minimum of 20 years, costing hundreds, if not thousands of dollars. Should a commercial interest decide to implement your invention on a commercial scale, tens of millions of dollars could be required in tooling and production costs. Should your invention have military applications, it could be responsible for hundreds if not thousands of deaths. Should your invention turn out to be a new destructive force far in excess of anything known and potentially deadly in the wrong hands, it could be responsible for the end of life as we know it on this planet. Are you sure that you want to do this?"

~

Sign in the hallway of a railroad division office, above a row of hooks: "For supervisory personnel only." Underneath someone had added: "May also be used for coats and hats." *—Capper's Weekly*

~

On an outdoor sign at Northway Christian Church (Disciples of Christ) in Dallas, Texas: "Premarital Workshop 8 hours May 17 and 18. Grief Recovery Starts Tuesday May 21."

~

Sign outside a Philadelphia business: "Open most days about 9 or 10, occasionally as early as 7, but some days as late as 12 or 1. We close about 4 or 5, but sometimes as late as 11 or 12. Some days we aren't here at all, and lately I've been here just about all the time, except when I'm someplace else."

SIGNS AND BLUNDERS

On October 13, 1944, the Durham N.C. *Sun* reported that a local resident had been brought before a Judge Wison in traffic court for having parked his car on a restricted street right in front of a sign that read "No Stoping." Rather than pleading guilty, the defendant argued that the missing letter in the sign meant that he had not violated the letter of the law. Brandishing a Webster's dictionary, he noted that stoping means: "extracting ore from a stope or, loosely, underground." "Your Honor," said the man, "I am a law-abiding citizen and I didn't extract any ore from the area of the sign. I move that the case be dismissed." Acknowledging that the defendant hadn't done any illegal mining, the judge declared the man not guilty and commented, "since this is Friday, the 13th, anything can happen, so I'll turn you loose."

"No Stoping" is a blunderful example of the suspect signs and botched billboards that dot the American landscape. Here are some others that need to be re-signed:
• At restaurant-gas stations throughout the nation: "Eat here and get gas."
• At a Sante Fe gas station: "We will sell gasoline to anyone in a glass container."

- In a New Hampshire jewelry store: "Ears pierced while you wait."
- In an New York restaurant: "Customers who consider our waitresses uncivil ought to see the manager."
- In a Michigan restaurant: "The early bird gets the worm! Special shoppers' luncheon before 11:00 A.M."
- On a delicatessen wall: "Our best is none too good."
- On the wall of a Baltimore estate: "Trespassers will be prosecuted to the full extent of the law."—Sisters of Mercy
- On a long-established New Mexico dry cleaning store: "Thirty-eight years on the same spot."
- In a Los Angeles dance hall: "Good clean dancing every night but Sunday."
- On a movie theater: "Children's matinee today. Adults not admitted unless with child."
- In a Florida maternity ward: "No children allowed!"
- In a New York drugstore: "We dispense with accuracy."
- On a New York loft building: "Wanted: Woman to sew buttons on the fourth floor."
- In the office of a loan company: "Ask about our plans for owning your home."
- In a New York medical building: "Mental health prevention center."
- In a toy department: "Five Santa Clauses—no waiting."
- On a New York convalescent home: "For the sick and tired of the Episcopal Church."
- On a Maine shop: "Our motto is to give our customers the lowest possible prices and workmanship."
- At a number of military bases: "Restricted to unauthorized personnel."
- In a number of parking areas: "Violators will be enforced and Trespassers will be violated."
- On a display of "I Love You Only" Valentine cards: "Now available in multi-packs."
- In the window of a Kentucky appliance store: "Don't kill your wife. Let our washing machines do the dirty work."
- In a funeral parlor: "Ask about our layaway plan."
- On a window of a New Hampshire hamburger restaurant: "Yes, we are open. Sorry for the inconvenience."
- In a clothing store: "Wonderful bargains for men with 16 and 17 necks."
- In a Tacoma, Washington men's clothing store: "15 men's wool suits—$10.00—They won't last an hour!"
- On an Indiana shopping mall marquee: "Archery tournament. Ears pierced."
- Outside a country shop: "We buy junk and sell antiques."
- On a North Carolina highway: "EAT 300 FEET."
- On an Ohio highway: "Drive Slower When Wet."
- On a New Hampshire highway: "You are speeding when flashing."
- On a Pennsylvania highway: "Drive carefully: Auto accidents kill most people from 15 to 19."
- In downtown Boston: "Calahan Tunnel/No. End."
- In a Massachusetts parking area reserved for birdwatchers: "Parking for birds only."
- In a New Jersey restaurant: "Open 11:00 A.M. to 11:00 P.M. Midnight."
- In front of a New Hampshire restaurant: "Now serving live lobsters."

S

- In front of a New Hampshire store: "Endurable floors."
- On a radiator repair garage: "Best place to take a leak."
- On a movie marquee: "Now Playing: Adam and Eve with a cast of thousands!"
- In the vestry of a New England church: "Will the last person to leave please see that the perpetual light is extinguished."
- On a roller coaster: "Watch your head."
- On a New Hampshire road: "Will build to suit Emory A. Tuttle"
- On the grounds of a private school: "No trespassing without permission."
- In a library: "Blotter paper will no longer be available until the public stops taking it away."
- On a Tennessee highway: "Take Notice: When this sign is under water the road is impassable."
- Similarly in a New Hampshire car wash: "If you can't read this, it's time to wash your car."

Posted at an Arizona church at the beginning of August every year: "You think it's hot here?"   —Thomas LaMance

In a German hotel room: "If you wish for breakfast in your bedroom, just lift your telephone and speak to the receptionist. This will be enough to bring your food up."   —San Francisco Examiner

At a watch-repair shop in Providence, R.I.: "Come in and see us when you haven't got the time."   —Ludlow Mahan

At a reducing salon: "Thinner Sanctum."   —Thomas LaMance

At a credit union in New Brunswick, Canada: "A Loan Again? See Us."
                                                    —Susan Osborne

On the top of a mountain in Idaho: "Skiing Beyond This Point May Result in Death And/Or Loss Of Skiing Privileges."   —*St. Paul Pioneer Press*

At a repair shop: "Cuckoo Clocks Psychoanalyzed."   —Thomas La Mance

In front of a Cleveland restaurant: "T-Bones 85 cents. With meat $5.95."
                                                    —Ed Szalkowski

In a plant nursery: "We will sell no vine before its time." —Shelby Friedman

In the office of a marriage counselor: "Lead us not into tempertation."

—Jacqueline Schiff

In Highland Park, Ill.: "Parks will not issue parking permits to fish."

—Jack Eppolito

At a tax office: "It is more deductible to give than to receive."   —Hal Evans

From the Costa Mesa, Calif., *Orange Coast Pilot:* "Free: One owner, low-mileage used cat. Answers to Tabitha or electric can opener."

Sign in Dillard's department store in Omaha, Neb.: "For your convenience the elevator is located in China."

Ben and Carol Stowell live beside a dirt road in New Hampshire that becomes practically impassible during mud season. For eight years, people came knocking at their door at all hours, asking to be towed out. Stowell finally posted a sign: "Mud! Pass at your own risk! If you pass, the following charges will apply: To use the phone—$5; to be towed out—$25; to have me come out and say, 'I TOLD YOU SO'—free of charge!" The end of mud season came, and not one person had stopped for help.   —*Yankee*

A Phoenix, Ariz., hardware store that sells propane had this sign out front: "Tank heaven for little grills."

A dentist in Southern Pines, N.C., posted this sign in his office: "Floss that bridge when you come to it."

Sign on a newspaper reporter's desk: "The strongest desire is neither love nor hate. It is one person's need to change another person's copy."

—Gilbert Cranberg

MORE SIGNS

- Posted outside a furniture refinishing shop in Lawrenceville, Ga.: "Male stripper on duty."
- At a plumber's: "We repair what your husband fixed."
- On the trucks of a local plumbing company in Pennsylvania: "Don't sleep with a drip; call your plumber."
- At a tire shop in Milwaukee: "Invite us to your next blowout."
- Door of a plastic surgeon's office: "Hello, can we pick your nose?"
- At a dry cleaner's: "How about we refund your money, send you a new one at no charge, close the store and have the manager shot. Would that be satisfactory?"
- At a towing company: "We don't charge an arm and a leg. We want tows."
- Billboard on the side of the road: "Keep your eyes on the road and stop reading these signs."
- On an electrician's truck: "Let us remove your shorts."
- In a nonsmoking area: "If we see smoking we will assume you are on fire and take appropriate action."
- At an optometrist's office "If you don't see what you're looking for you've come to the right place."
- On a taxidermist's window: "We really know our stuff."
- In a podiatrist's office: "Time wounds all heels."
- On a butcher's window: "Let me meat your needs."
- On a fence: "Salesman Welcome. Dog food is expensive."
- At a car dealership : "The best way to get back on your feet—miss a car payment."
- Outside a muffler shop: "No appointment Necessary, we hear you coming."
- Outside a hotel: "Help! We need inn-experienced people."
- On a desk in a reception room: "We shoot every 3rd salesman, and the 2nd one just left."
- At the electric company: "We would be de-lighted if you send in your bill. However, if you don't you will be."
- On the door of a computer store: "Out for a quick byte."
- In a restaurant window: "Don't stand there and be hungry, come on in and get fed up."
- Sign in a gas station: "Coke—49 cents. Two for a dollar."

Billboard promoting Boston's Charles Hayden Planetarium at the Museum of Science: "Visit Our Planetarium, You Tiny, Insignificant Speck in the Universe."

—Herm Albright

Cheese shop: "Our Swiss has 22-percent fewer cavities."

Delicatessen: "Some people come in just for the smell of it."   —Norma Levi

Health-food store: "Our hamburger is something else." —Marge Bernsen

～

Hot-dog stand: "Franks for the memory." —Irene Hannigan

～

Bakery: "Our ryes have seen the glory."

～

Sign in store window: "Any faulty merchandise will be cheerfully replaced with merchandise of equal quality."

～

Art museum: "Come In and Browse to Your Art's Content." —Shelby Friedman

～

Allergist's office: "Wheeze Be Seated."

～

Poultry farm: "Quiet! May They Roost in Peace." —Jane Hunt Clark

～

Diet salon: "No Amnesty for Desserters." —Lois Lindauer

～

Building-supply store: "Planks to You, We're Lumber One."

～

Sign in the window of a florist shop: "End-of-season clearance sale! Catch us with our plants down."

～

On a community bulletin board: "Wanted—a set of golf clubs that shoot in the low 80s." —Rudy Joe Mano

～

In a Greek tailor shop window, recommending that customers order summer suits early: "In big rush we will execute customers in strict rotation."
—*Wall Street Journal*

～

On a billboard for the Niagara Falls Aquarium in Niagara Falls, Ontario: "Everyone welcome—except Mrs. Paul!" —Mary Ann Janda

～

On Marks & Spencer Bread Pudding: "Product will be hot after heating."
—Good Clean Fun Web site

On Nytol (a sleep aid): "Warning: may cause drowsiness."

—Good Clean Fun Web site

On Sainsbury's Peanuts: "Warning: contains nuts."

—Good Clean Fun Web site

On a bag of Fritos: "You could be a winner! No purchase necessary. Details inside."

—Good Clean Fun Web site

On a hotel-provided shower cap: "Fits one head."

—Good Clean Fun Web site

For a sale on hammocks: "We can support you the rest of your life."

—Pauline C. Bartel

BUMPER SNICKERS

- I've taken a vow of poverty. To annoy me, send money.
- A waist is a terrible thing to mind.
- Support Your Local Lawyer. Send Your Kid To Medical School.
- Energizer bunny arrested, charged with battery.
- Santa's elves are just a bunch of subordinate clauses.
- Editing is a rewording activity.
- My life has a superb cast, but I can't figure out the plot.
- Out of my mind. Back in five minutes.
- Gene Police: YOU!! Out of the pool!
- I used to be indecisive; now I'm not sure.
- My reality check just bounced.
- What if there were no hypothetical questions?
- No sense being pessimistic. It wouldn't work anyway.
- 43.3% of statistics are meaningless!
- I used to have a handle on life, but it broke.
- You're just jealous because the voices only talk to me.
- I'm not a complete idiot, some parts are missing.
- The more you complain, the longer God lets you live.
- Help wanted, telepathy: you know where to apply.
- Hang up and drive.
- I took an IQ test and the results were negative.
- Always remember you're unique, just like everyone else.
- Consciousness: that annoying time between naps.
- Ever stop to think, and forget to start again?

- If you try to fail, and succeed, which have you done?
- Be nice to your kids. They'll choose your nursing home.
- Stupidity does not qualify as a handicap, park elsewhere!
- Very funny, Scotty. Now beam down my clothes.
- The gene pool could use a little chlorine.
- I don't suffer from insanity. I enjoy every minute of it.
- Okay, who put a "stop payment" on my reality check?
- Air Pollution is a mist-demeaner.
- Anything free is worth what you pay for it
- Everyone is entitled to my opinion.
- Don't take life too seriously, you won't get out alive.
- Hard work has a future payoff, laziness pays off now.
- Warning: Dates in Calendar are closer than they appear.
- Lottery: A tax on people who are bad at math.
- Age is a very high price to pay for maturity.
- I doubt, therefore I might be.
- Procrastination is the art of keeping up with yesterday.
- If all the world is a stage, where is the audience sitting?
- Where are we going, and what am I doing in this handbasket?

In a real-estate office: "For rent. Four-story beach house—five stories when the tide is out." *—California Highway Patrolman*

At a bank promoting vacation loans: "Bye now, pay later." —James Alexander Thom in *Nuggets*

At the entrance to a one-lane bridge in Sonoma, California: "When this sign is underwater, this road is impassable." —Jeffrey Freiberg

Sign on the road from an Arkansas farm: For Sale. 1962 Ford Smokes, but is old enough. $135

Sign at church parking lot: We forgive those who trespass against us, but they'll be towed just the same. —St. Olaf Catholic Church, Minneapolis

SILENCE

Drawing on my fine command of language, I said nothing.   —D. E. Knuth

It's better to remain silent and be thought stupid than to open your mouth and forever remove all doubt.

He didn't utter a word, but he exuded mute blasphemy from every pore.

—Mark Twain

Few slanders can stand the wear of silence. —Mark Twain

Folks who think they must always speak the truth overlook another good choice—silence. —C. L. Null

To keep your marriage brimming
With love in the loving cup
Whenever you're wrong, admit it
Whenever you're right, shut up! —Ogden Nash

Silence is argument carried out by other means. —Ernesto "Che" Guevara

SIMPLICITY

Simple pleasures . . . are the last refuge of the complex. —Oscar Wilde

SIN

Once Margaret Denton, an elderly church member, was discussing with me an uncle of hers who had repented of his sins and joined a Southern Baptist church after a lifetime of riotous living. "Will my converted uncle's sins be forgiven, Pastor?" she asked. "Oh, certainly, yes!" I replied. "Remember, the greater the sins, the greater the saint." Margaret thought silently for a time. Then she said, "Oh, Pastor, I wish I'd known this fifty years ago."

Poverty is reflected in many places, even in the hearts of men, according to a Maryknoll missionary in Bolivia. The missionary, hearing confessions at a badly run-down ranch here, asked the penitent: "Do you have any sins?" The penitent replied: "Padre, we are so poor in our house that we don't even have sins." —*Maryknoll News*

Most of us spend the first six days of each week sowing wild oats, then we go to church on Sunday and pray for a crop failure. —Fred Allen

SINCERITY

It is dangerous to be sincere unless you are also stupid.

—George Bernard Shaw

SINGING

One pastor was trying to encourage better participation in singing the new hymns. "Remember," he said, "if the Lord gave you a good singing voice, this is the way to thank Him. If He didn't, this is also a good way to get even."

—Catholic Digest

A Milwaukee couple called a neighbor to extend birthday greetings. They dialed his number and then sang Happy Birthday into the telephone. But when they had finished their off-key rendition, they discovered they had the wrong number. "Don't let that bother you," said the stranger. "You folks sure can use the practice!"   *—Milwaukee Journal*

Son: "Dad, why do you always make me sing every time Mrs. Burmally comes?"
Dad: "It's not as rude as telling her to leave."   *—Irish Grit*

SINGLE

I'm 33, single . . . Don't you think it's a generalization you should be married at 33? That's like looking at somebody who's 70 and saying, hey, when are you gonna break your hip? All your friends are breaking their hip—what are you waiting for?   —Sue Kolinsky

I don't think of myself as single. I'm romantically challenged.

—Stephanie Piro

SLEEP

Overheard: "My insomnia is worse. Now I can't even sleep when it's time to get up."   —Ron Dentinger

SMALL TOWNS

Small Town: Where people go to church on Sunday to see who didn't.

I moved recently to Cottonwood, California, a town so small it only has two streets in it—Main Street and Non-Main Street.

I live in a town so dull that our local newspaper doesn't even have a front page.

Nothing ever happens in our town. Our town gossip had to hire a writing staff.

~

Tourist: "What's the speed limit through this one-horse town of yours?"
Native: "Ain't any. You folks cain't go through here fast enough to suit us."
—*Modern Maturity*

~

You can't walk for exercise in a little town. It takes too long to explain what you're doing to all the neighbors who honk, stop, and offer you a ride.
—*The Milwaukee Journal*

~

A public-relations man on assignment in tiny Beatty, Nev., stopped at a local store for high-speed film. "I need two rolls of 35-millimeter, 1000 ASA film," he told the shopkeeper. "Honey," she drawled, "nobody needs 1000 ASA film in Beatty, Nevada. There's nothin' here moves that fast." —Dick Licciardi

~

The manager of a touring theatrical company wired to the proprietor of the theater in a small town where his company was due to appear. "Would like to hold rehearsal next Monday afternoon at three. Have your stage manager, property man, carpenter, electrician, and all stage hands present at that hour." Four hours later he received the following reply: "All right. He'll be there."
—C. Kennedy

SMILING

She would smile, and all her wrinkles would rearrange themselves into pleasure. —Irene Mortenson Burnside

SMOKING

A friend said, "I quit smoking cold turkey." I said, "What do you smoke now? Ham?" —Yakov Smirnoff

~

Pipe smokers are almost always model citizens. They're so busy cleaning, filling, and relighting their pipes, they just haven't time to get into trouble.
—William Vaughan

~

The FCC came along and it said no more cigarette commercials on television . . . I'd much rather watch a pretty girl offer me a cigarette than an old lady ask if I'm constipated. —Mark Russell

A rebel leader was finally apprehended by the military police and summarily sentenced to death. The generallissimo watched as the blindfolded man was led before the firing squad, then magnanimously came over to offer him a last cigarette. "No, thanks," was the condemned man's answer. "I'm trying to quit."

My Uncle Irv smoked unfiltered cigarettes for forty years. He would take one puff from a cigarette, throw it down and step on it. He did this hour after hour, day in day out. Last week he came down with cancer of the shoe.

It's easy to give up smoking. All you need are willpower, determination, and wet matches.   —*Funny Funny World*

SNOBBERY

The stuffy but elegant matriarch of a prominent family asked the dog breeder, "Is this a dog of which my family and I can be proud? Does he have a good pedigree?" "Indeed, he does," declared the breeder. "If he could talk, he wouldn't speak to either of us!"

Aunt Laura is such a snob that her automobile sports the following sign: "Private bumper sticker. Do not read."

Snobs talk as if they had begotten their own ancestors.   —Herbert Agar

He's so snobbish he has an unlisted zip-code.   —Earl Wilson

SNORING

Dinner was over and Grandpa retreated to his easy chair to relax. Pretty soon the rafters were shaking with his resounding snores. Mother came in just in time to see Junior twisting one of Grandpa's vest buttons. "Don't disturb Grandpa," she said. "I'm not," protested Junior. "I'm just trying to get another station."   —*Capper's Weekly*

SNOW

This should be an interesting winter. My neighbor and I have parallel driveways—and we both bought snow blowers.
                    —Robert Orben, *2500 Jokes To Start 'Em Laughing*

SOLITUDE

In Genesis it says that it is not good for a man to be alone, but sometimes it is a great relief.   —John Barrymore

SONS

Somewhat skeptical of his son's newfound determination to become Charles Atlas, the father nevertheless followed the teenager over to the weight-lifting department. "Please, Dad," wheedled the boy, "I promise I'll use 'em every day . . ." "I dunno. It's really a commitment on your part," the father pointed out. "Please, Dad?" "They're not cheap either." "I'll use 'em Dad, I promise. You'll see." Finally won over, the father paid for the equipment and headed for the door. From the corner of the store he heard his son yelp, "What! You mean I have to carry them to the car?"

～

I still vividly remember the little talks I had with my son. One time I said, "When I was your age, I never thought of doing any of the things you do." To which he replied, "And that's the only reason you didn't do them."

SPACE

Black holes are where God divided by zero.   —Steven Wright

SPEAKING

Back in 1955, Uncle Jack made the following speech to a large conference of sales representatives: "I dictated my talk to my secretary and told her to cross out anything she thought was dull and uninteresting. 'And so, in conclusion'—"

～

The banquet speaker droned on and on, apparently hypnotized by the sound of his own voice. Finally, one trapped listener who could tolerate no more without falling asleep, put his napkin over his left arm, picked up a pitcher of water, and slipped out—as one more waiter.

—Msgr. Arthur Tonne, *Jokes Priests Can Tell,* vol. 6

～

Douglas Fairbanks, Jr., began a speech with one of the all-time best opening lines: "I feel like a mosquito in a nudist colony. I look around and I know it's wonderful to be here, but I don't know where to begin."

～

In a talk to the Louisiana Trial Lawyers Association, speech professor Waldo Braden began by noting that all the other speakers had highly technical backgrounds related to the practice of law. Then he analogized his position to William Howard Taft's great granddaughter. "When she was asked to write her autobiography in the third grade, the young lady responded: 'My great grandfather was president of the United States, my grandfather was a United

States senator, my father was an ambassador, and I am a Brownie.' On this morning, at this elegant hotel here in the French Quarter in this distinguished company, I feel like a Brownie."

Commencement speakers have a good deal in common with grandfather clocks: standing usually some six feet tall, typically ponderous in construction, more traditional than functional, their distinction is largely their noisy communication of essential commonplace information.   —Willard Wirtz

Gen. John W. Vessey, Jr., Chairman of the Joint Chiefs of Staff, was telling an audience about the best speech he had ever heard. It was delivered by Gen. Curtis LeMay, then Chief of Staff of the Air Force. "'I have a speech,' he quoted General LeMay as saying. 'It's a good speech. It was written by a smart lieutenant colonel who works for me, and I read it on the way here. Now I'm going to put it in the library, and you can read it, too.'"

SPEEDING

"What am I supposed to do with this?" inquired the motorist when the clerk handed him a receipt for his traffic fine. "Keep it," advised the clerk. "When you get four of them, you get a bicycle."   —*Catholic Digest*

SPELLING

It is a poor mind indeed that can't think of at least two ways of spelling any word.   —Andrew Jackson

SPILLS

A spilled drink flows in the direction of the most expensive object.
—Judye Briggs

SPORTS

Question asked of Bob Uecker, actor, sportscaster, and former major leaguer: "How did you handle pressure as a player?" Answer: "It was easy. I'd strike out and put the pressure on the guy behind me."

Whoever invented bungee jumping must have watched a lot of Road Runner cartoons.   —Nick Arnette

Chicago Bulls rookie forward Stacy King scored one point in a basketball game in which Michael Jordan scored sixty-nine points. His analysis of the game was: "I'll always remember this as the night that Michael Jordan and I combined to score seventy points."

~

One night at a basketball banquet the president of our local junior college was congratulating the coach and the team profusely. The beaming coach asked the president, "Would you still like me as much if we didn't win?" "I'd like you as much," the president replied. "I'd just miss having you around."

~

The difference between soccer and baseball is that in baseball you have a father taking his son and explaining the strategy, and in soccer you have the son taking his father and explaining it to him.　　　—Danny Villanueva

~

If sports are supposed to be good for you, how come athletes are over the hill at 31?
　　　—Bill Vaughan

~

Do you know why mountain climbers rope themselves together? To prevent the sensible ones from going home.

~

A Hampshire, England, cricketer who had his hand injured in a match had to complete an accident insurance claim form. Under "Witnesses" he put: "2891 spectators, 21 players, two reserves, two umpires, two groundsmen, three gatekeepers and one schoolboy up a tree."
　　　—Reginald Mitchell, *Amusing Tales From Hampshire and Dorset*

~

ESPN sportscaster Dave Campbell on the quickness of Toronto Blue Jays second baseman Roberto Alomar: "He gets to the ball quicker than Cinderella's sisters."

~

Dan Shaughnessy in the *Boston Globe:* "Defensively the Red Sox are a lot like Stonehenge. They are old, they don't move, and no one is certain why they are positioned the way they are."

In-line skating provides thrills, cardiovascular conditioning and muscle tone. It can also introduce you to a whole new set of friends—ambulance drivers, emergency room technicians and physical therapists, as well as those nice neighbors on the next block who called the rescue squad.   —Chuck Moss

We're going to turn this team around 360 degrees.
                              —Jason Kidd, upon his drafting
                              to the Dallas Mavericks

Sports historians pretty much agree that we may never know what made Babe Ruth, Ty Cobb and Lou Gehrig so great. There's absolutely no record of what brand of shoes they wore.

Remember sports fans, if you can't control your emotions, it can be costly. It cost my neighbor $300 because he threw a full can of beer at the umpire. And it could have cost more, but he was watching on their old television.

Pro Bowler Mark Williams was once asked, "Why do you travel the PBA tour in a van instead of flying?" "I'd sure like to fly," Williams replied. "But did you ever try to check 20 bowling balls?"   —*Sports Illustrated*

Basketball coach Bill Jones of Alabama's Jacksonville State University was asked if his team's 37-point win over Kentucky Wesleyan in the NCAA Division II tournament was beyond his wildest dreams. "My wildest dreams," Jones replied, "don't include basketball."   —*Sports Illustrated*

S

When the TV movie "A Love Affair: The Eleanor and Lou Gehrig Story" premiered on Greek TV last year, the film lost its subtitle but gained a racy subplot. Next to a scene from the film showing the Yankees' legendary Lou Gehrig and Babe Ruth locked in warm embrace, the blurb in Greece's TV magazine reported: "'A Love Affair' is the title of a dramatic adventure that really happened. The film is about the love link between baseball player Lou Gehrig and the beautiful 'Babe' Ruth. The idyll of the two young people ended up in marriage. But their happiness didn't last long. Mrs. Babe became very ill and . . ."   —*Sports Illustrated*

A college swimming coach was summarizing his team's achievements at the annual athletic banquet. "Well, we didn't win any meets," he conceded, "but we all had a good time, and nobody drowned." —*Washington Post*

STEALING

Finishing their shopping at the mall, a couple discovers that their brand-new car has been stolen. They file a report at the police station, and a detective drives them back to the parking lot to look for evidence. To their amazement, the car has been returned and there's a note in it that says, "I apologize for taking your car. My wife was having a baby and I had to hot-wire your ignition to rush her to the hospital. Please forgive the inconvenience. Here are two tickets for tonight's Shania Twain concert." Their faith in humanity restored, the couple attends the concert. But when they return home, they find their house has been ransacked. On the bathroom mirror is another note: "I have to put my kid through college somehow, don't I?" —*Playboy*

STOCK MARKET

A broker is a man who takes your fortune and runs it into a shoestring.

—Alexander Woollcott

❧

The Bible says that we came into this world without riches and that we shall take no riches with us into the next. So, in a sense, stockbrokers are just doing the Lord's work. —Florence Berglund

STORIES

During my graduate school days, Meyer Peller, my maternal grandfather, had a massive heart attack and was not expected to live. I sent him a letter telling him that my son often asked me what I did when I was his age. I told Grampa that I would tell him about the many days I spent with him and about the time when I was helping him in the garden. Grampa couldn't figure out why the onions which I had planted took so long to emerge. When he finally harvested them he said that they were the longest onions he had ever seen. I had planted all the bulbs upside-down! My letter was read to the old man, the resignation that had gripped his spirits lifted, and he rallied. Never doubt the power of a good family story!

❧

To make a long story short, don't tell it. —Tal Bonham

STRESS

Not long ago a prominent lawyer called upon his doctor for an annual check-up. The examination indicated signs of hypertension and stress. The doctor warned him to slow down, to take up a hobby—perhaps painting—to relax. He readily agreed and left his physician's office. The next day, the doctor phoned to check on his patient's progress. "Doc," the lawyer responded enthusiastically, "this painting stuff is wonderful. I've already finished ten of them!"

Talk about stress. I'll tell you how much stress there is in my life. You know those coin changers that hang on your belt? I got one that dispenses Rolaids.

—Ron Dentinger

STUDENTS

Student answers to test questions:

- Matrimony is a place where souls suffer for a time on account of their sins.
- Where was the Declaration of Independence signed? At the bottom.
- Where is Cincinnati? First place in the American Football League.
- Denver is located just below the O in Colorado.
- The soil of Prussia was so poor, the people had to work hard just to stay on top of it.
- The climate of Bombay is such that its inhabitants have to live elsewhere.

STUPIDITY

Only two things are infinite, the universe and human stupidity, and I'm not sure about the former.   —Albert Einstein

There is more stupidity than hydrogen in the universe, and it has a longer shelf life.   —Frank Zappa

If stupidity got us into this mess, then why can't it get us out?

—Will Rogers

He was born stupid, and greatly increased his birthright.   —Samuel Butler

He was distinguished for ignorance; for he had only one idea and that was wrong.   —Benjamin Disraeli

His mind is so open—so open that ideas simply pass through it.

—F. H. Bradley

~

No more sense of direction than a bunch of firecrackers. —Rob Wagner

~

They never open their mouths without subtracting from the sum of human knowledge. —Thomas Brackett Reed

~

While he was not dumber than an ox he was not any smarter either. —James Thurber

~

Ordinarily he is insane. But he has lucid moments when he is only stupid. —Heinrich Heine

~

She never lets ideas interrupt the easy flow of her conversation.

—Jean Webster

STYLE

A new convict is sitting in his cell at the state prison. Suddenly someone yells out, "419." The whole cellblock starts laughing. Someone yells, "78." Everyone laughs. "642." Hysteria. And this goes on every afternoon between two and three o'clock. The new guy can't figure it out. He asks his cell mate. "What's so funny?" "There's only one book in the prison library," the cell mate explains. "It's a joke book. We've all heard it so many times we memorized all the jokes. All we have to hear are the numbers." So the new guy goes to the library and studies the book. A few weeks later he's ready. Two o'clock arrives. Someone yells, "316." Everyone's howling. "56." Gales of laughter. The new guy yells, "237." There's dead silence. He asks his cell mate what happened. The cell mate says, "Some people can tell a joke and some people can't."

SUCCESS

Jim Fixx, author of a best-selling book on running, was asked if fame and fortune had changed his life. He said yes, and explained, "One day I took a check for $100,000 to deposit in the bank, and the female teller said to me, 'Are you married?'" —"Good Morning America" (ABC)

~

The only thing that ever sat its way to success was a hen. —Sarah Brown

SUMMER

A perfect summer day is when the sun is shining, the breeze is blowing, the birds are singing, and the lawn mower is broken. —James Dent

SUNDAY SCHOOL

The Sunday before Christmas, Melissa James asked her Sunday school students at Holy Trinity Lutheran Church to draw a picture of the Holy Family. When the pictures were handed in, she saw that some of the youngsters had drawn the conventional pictures—the Holy Family in the manger, the Holy Family riding on the mule, and so forth. But she was confused by the drawing made by little Joshua, so she called him up and asked him to explain his picture, which showed an airplane with four heads sticking out of the plane windows. She said, "I can understand why you drew three of the heads to show Joseph, Mary, and Jesus. But who's the fourth head?" "Oh," answered Joshua, "that's Pontius the Pilot!"

Ruth Troutman, the Sunday school teacher, was very keen on religious ceremonies and had spent an entire session talking to the class about the correct way to pray. "Now," she said finally, "suppose we want to pray to God for forgiveness. What must we do first of all?" "Sin?" suggested one little boy.

Austin Markle, the Sunday School teacher, asked his class: "What are sins of omission?" After some thought one little fellow said: "They're the sins we should have committed but didn't get around to."

A Sunday School teacher asked a group of children in her class. "Why do you believe in God?" In reporting some of the answers the teacher confessed that the one she liked best came from a boy who said, "I don't know, unless it's something that runs in the family." —King Duncan

Little Johnny came home from Sunday School and told his mother that if he missed three Sundays in a row, the teacher would throw him into the furnace. The horrified mother telephoned the teacher at once. "What I said was," the calm teacher explained, "that if any child missed three Sundays in a row, he would be dropped from the register." —*Presbyterian Life*

The children were invited to participate in the groundbreaking ceremony for the new Sunday school building. Each child turned over a small shovelful of dirt. Later in the day, Granddad asked his little granddaughter what they did at church that morning. "Well," she said sadly, "we dug for a new Sunday school, but we didn't find it."   —*Liguorian*

One Sunday late in Lent a Sunday School teacher decided to ask her class what they remembered about Easter. The first little fellow suggested that Easter was when "all the family comes to the house and they eat a big turkey and watch football." The teacher suggested that perhaps he was thinking of Thanksgiving, not Easter, so she let a pretty young girl answer. She said Easter was the day "when as you come down the stairs in the morning you see all the beautiful presents under the tree." At this point, the teacher was really feeling discouraged. But after explaining that the girl was probably thinking about Christmas, she called on a lad with his hand tentatively raised in the air. Her spirits immediately perk up as the boy says that Easter is the time "when Jesus was crucified and buried." She felt she had gotten through to at least one child until he added, "And then He comes out of the grave and if He sees His shadow we have six more weeks of winter."

A little boy in Sunday School gave the explanation as to why Mary and Joseph took baby Jesus to Egypt. He claimed: "They couldn't get a sitter."

At Sunday school the topic was Elijah and the prophets of Baal. The teacher explained that Elijah built an altar, placed wood upon it, cut the sacrificial bullock in pieces and laid them on the wood. He then commanded that the people fill four jars with water and pour the water over the sacrifice. "Why do you think they did that?" asked the teacher. A little girl raised her hand and said, "To make gravy."   —Bill Dana

Nine-year-old Joey, was asked by his mother what he had learned in Sunday school. "Well, Mom, our teacher told us how God sent Moses behind enemy lines on a rescue mission to lead the Israelites out of Egypt. When he got to the Red Sea, he had his engineers build a pontoon bridge and all the people walked across safely. Then he used his walkie—talkie to radio headquarters for reinforcements. They sent bombers to blow up the bridge and all the Israelites were saved." "Now, Joey, is that really what your teacher taught you?" his mother asked. "Well, no, Mom. But if I told it the way the teacher did, you'd never believe it!"

～

A Sunday school teacher asked her little children as they were on the way to church service, "And why is it necessary to be quiet in church?" One bright little girl replied, "Because people are sleeping."

SWISS

Swiss Army Knives got their names because it takes the entire Swiss army just to carry one.
　　　　　　　　　　　　　　　　　　　　　　　　　　　　—Nick Arnette

T

TACT

Tact is the art of making guest's feel at home when that's really where you wish they were.
　　　　　　　　　　　　　　　　　　　　　　　　　　—George E. Bergman

TATTOOS

Tattoo: Permanent proof of temporary insanity.　　　　　　　—Wise & Aldrich

TAXES

A sportswriter once asked Joe Louis, "Who hit you the hardest during your ring career?" His reply was, "Uncle Sam."

～

Arthur Godfrey once said, "I feel honored to pay taxes in America. The thing is, I could probably feel just as honored for about half the price."

～

Of the two classic certainties, death and taxes, death is preferable. At least you're not called in six months later for an audit.　　　—Bill Vaughan

～

They say that everybody should pay their taxes with a smile. Well, I tried it, but they wanted cash.

～

I'm not sure what I should do about my taxes this year. The way I've got it figured . . . if I use the short form, the government gets my money. And if I use the long form, the accountant gets my money.　　　　—Ron Dentinger

Internal Revenue service auditor to nervous taxpayer: "Let's begin with where you claim depreciation on your wife."

~

Around April 15 we discover that America is the land of untold wealth.

~

INCOME TAX FORMS are a test of the power of deduction.

~

Interesting Tax Facts: The Gettysburg address is 269 words, the Declaration of Independence is 1,337 words, and the Holy Bible is only 773,000 words. However, the tax law has grown from 11,400 words in 1913, to 7 million words today. There are at least 480 different tax forms, each with many pages of instructions. Even the easiest form, the 1040E has 33 pages in instructions, and all in fine print. The IRS sends out 8 billion pages of forms and instructions each year. Laid end to end, they would stretch 28 times around the earth. Nearly 300,000 trees are cut down yearly to produce the paper for all the IRS forms and instructions. American taxpayers spend $200 billion and 5.4 billion hours working to comply with federal taxes each year, more than it takes to produce every car, truck, and van in the United States. The IRS employs 114,000 people—that's twice as many as the CIA and five times more than the FBI. Sixty percent of taxpayers must hire a professional to get through their own return. Taxes eat up 38.2% of the average family's income; that's more than for food, clothing and shelter combined.

~

Last April, Stephen Sprenger, who owns the H&R Block on Denny Way in Seattle, commented, "It's that time of year: the time for ceiling deductions." "Ceiling deductions?" I asked. Sprenger explains, "You ask how many miles the client drove and he looks at the ceiling and says, 'About 8,000.'"

~

Speaking on United States tax law, evasion, and tax shelters, Calvin Trillin explained: "The laws providing tax shelters reflect the strong philosophical commitment of the Founding Fathers, particularly Alexander Hamilton, to the principle that the public good would be served if dentists owned cattle ranches."

~

A decade ago, Tom Lehrer remarked: "On my income tax form 1040 it says 'Check this box if you are blind.' I wanted to put a check mark about three inches away."

The botanical name for the American yew tree, used extensively for shrubbery around Washington government buildings, is *Taxus taxus*.   —David Gordon

~

IRS agent to taxpayer: "Just because your mother-in-law lives in the suburbs and you have two teen-agers at home, you cannot list the telephone company as a dependent."
—George E. Bergman

~

A government bureau is where they keep the taxpayer's shirt.   —Graffiti

~

Noel Coward, on leaving England to take up residence in Switzerland for the obvious purpose of avoiding taxes, was met by the press at the airport. Why, asked a reporter, was he moving to Switzerland? "Devoted to chocolates," was Coward's reply.   —William F. Buckley, Jr., *Four Reforms*

~

IRS Auditor to taxpayer: "The trick is to stop thinking of it as your money."
—Serrano

TEACHERS

A teacher, asked why she preferred working in an elementary school, explained: "Well, I love children of all ages, but at the grade school I'm always sure of finding a parking space."   —*Capper's Weekly*

~

When a teacher calls a boy by his entire name it means trouble.
—Mark Twain

~

When he was in junior high school, my son Stephen was asked by his English teacher to give her a sentence with an object. "You are very pretty," he answered. "What's the object?" the teacher asked. Stephen replied, "To get an A in English."

~

A rather stout schoolmistress was talking about birds and their habits. "Now," she said, "at home I have a canary, and it can do something that I cannot do. I wonder if any of you know just what that thing is?" Little Eric raised his hand, "I know, teacher. Take a bath in a saucer."   —*Kablegram*

An elderly woman strolled calmly out into the street after a policeman had flagged her to stay on the sidewalk. "Lady," he bellowed, "don't you know what it means when I holdup my hand?" "I ought to," she snapped, "I was a schoolteacher for 40 years."

TEACHING

Good teaching is one-fourth preparation and three-fourths theater. —Gail Godwin

TEAMWORK

On his way to give a talk at a rural high school a speaker slipped into the ditch. He walked to the nearest house to find that the farmer's tractor wouldn't work. The only power was an old, blind mule. They hitched the mule to the car and the farmer shouted: "Giddap, Frankie; Giddap, Bessie." The mule didn't move. "Giddap, Ben; Giddap, Mabel: shouted the farmer. The mule didn't budge. Then the farmer shouted: "Giddap, Mike!" The mule leaned into the harness and pulled the car out. "How come?" asked the traveler, "he didn't move until you called him 'Mike?'" "Well," explained the farmer, "Mike's his name. Blind Mike, cuz he can't see. When I call out those other names, he things there are a lot of other mules pulling too. But he won't start until I call his name. If he thought he was the only one he would never even try." —Ed Steiner

TECHNOLOGY

At their Thursday evening card game, Manfred Oogle and Tetzell Edwards were discussing the marvels of technology. Oogle asked Edwards to identify an invention that he would classify as miraculous. Edwards answered, "The thermos bottle." "Why the thermos bottle?" asks Oogle. Edwards responded, "When you put hot things in it, it keeps them hot, and when you put cold things in it, it keeps them cold." "So what's the miracle?" asks Oogle. Edwards' answer: "How does it know?"

❧

These days it's absolutely in to know how to use word processors and computers. But the manager of an aerospace company was a cyberphobic (one who is afraid of electronic devices). One day he entered his office and found a computer terminal set up next to his desk. "What's this?" asked the manager.

An engineer replied vigorously, "It's your new terminal, and it's just waiting for you to give it a command." The manager glared at the computer and said, "Go away!"

~

A hot trend these days is computers, word processors, and all sorts of cybernetic devices. Perhaps we should have a sense of perspective about this. Consider a rod of graphite encased in wood, first used in the 16th century. It's called a pencil. Here are some of the marvels about it: It can write underwater. It can write in outer space. A standard 7¼-inch pencil can draw a line 35 miles long. It can write 45,000 words. It can scratch your back. It can lubricate a stuck zipper. It can pin up long hair. Pencils can be bought for three dollars a dozen.

TEENAGERS

Telling a teenager the facts of life is like giving a fish a bath.
—Arnold H. Glasow.

~

Remember that as a teenager you are at the last stage in your life when you will be happy to hear that the phone is for you.   —Fran Lebowitz

~

My neighbor Marie told me of a recent experience: Late one Saturday evening, I was awakened by the ringing of my phone. In a sleepy, grumpy voice, I said, "Hello." The party on the other end of the line paused for a moment before rushing breathlessly into a lengthy speech. "Mom, this is Susanna and I'm sorry I woke you up, but I had to call because I'm going to be a little late getting home. See, Dad's car has a flat, but it's not my fault. Honest! I don't know what happened. The tire just went flat while we were inside the theater. Please don't be mad, okay?" Since I don't have any daughters, I knew the person had misdialed. "I'm sorry, dear," I replied, "but I have to tell you you've reached the wrong number. I don't have a daughter named Susanna. In fact, I don't have any daughter at all." A pause. "Gosh, Mom," came the young woman's quavering voice, "I didn't think you'd be this mad."

~

After listening to a lengthy lecture from his father about his sloppy appearance, shaved head, Van Dyke beard, numerous body piercing, earrings, and general attitude, the teenager blurted out: "But, Dad, I gotta be a nonconformist . . . How else can I be like the other kids?"

Four men at the office were discussing what they hoped to get out of their new cars. "Economy," said one man. "Dependability," said another. "Styling," added the third. They all turned to the fourth fellow, who was standing there with a grim expression on his face. "What I'd most like to get out of my new car," he said, "is my teenage son." —*Liguorian*

On their way to church the other Sunday, my friend's teenage daughter, who had just gotten her driving permit, asked her dad, "Can I drive, dad? I'm old enough." He thought about it and then, looking at his new car, told his daughter, "Yes, you are old enough, dear. But the car isn't." —*Family Digest*

I asked my neighbor how much gas mileage he was getting from his new, sporty car. He thought it over and answered, "As near as I can figure, I get about five miles to the gallon. My teenage son gets the other 20."

—*Ford Times*

Dennis Miller's definition of body piercing: "A powerful compelling visual statement that says, 'Gee, in today's competitive job market, what can I do to make myself less employable?'"

There's nothing wrong with teenagers that reasoning with them won't aggravate.

"What do you MEAN you're thirsty?"

Commuter to seatmate: "We're equipped three ways to have all the answers—we've got an encyclopedia, a home computer, and a teenager."

—Laurence J. Peter, *Peter's Almanac*

⌇

My teenage son Dave and his heavy-metal rock band had lined up a few concerts and had asked me to make their stage costumes. But because of the time involved, I told them I couldn't do it. As we drove home from church one day, we passed a secondhand furniture store. Dave did a double take and quickly made a U-turn back to the store. Posted in the shop's window was a sign: "Heavy-metal wardrobes for sale."

—Thelma Baddorf in *The Christian Reader*

⌇

Adolescence is not so much a period as it is an exclamation point.   —*Chicago Tribune*

⌇

A 14-year-old girl got her own phone for her room. Her father ventured into no man's land one day and found his daughter sobbing amid the sea of debris. "The telephone just rang," she cried. "I heard it, but I couldn't find it."

⌇

It isn't what a teenager knows that worries his parents. It's how he found out.

—Ann Landers

⌇

They say teenagers are smarter than ever so I asked mine to do something about the snow on the front walk. Well, sir—that vacuum cleaner will never be the same!   —Robert Orben, *2500 Jokes To Start 'Em Laughing*

⌇

The minister's son was about 16 years old, still a year and a half from finishing high school but he wanted his father to promise him his own car on graduation. His father thought for a moment and then agreed, on three conditions: "First, you must do better in your Bible study. You are doing fairly well now, but you could do much better. Second, you can also do better in your class work, even better than you are doing now. Third, you will have to cut off some of your long hair." The lad agreed and really tried. He read his Bible more often and more devoutly. He hit the books at school and at home. His father expressed pleasure. But then the boy had a question: "Dad, about this long hair bit. The Bible says that Jesus and His apostles all wore long hair." To which his father retorted: "You're right, son, but did you notice that the Bible says they walked everywhere they went."   —Douglas Siebert

~

Following dialogue was overheard between teenage son and parent: "I'm off to the party." "Well, have a good time." "Look, Pop, don't tell me what to do."
—*The Railway Clerk*

~

Smart Son: "Dad, I just siphoned a couple of gallons of gas out of your car for my old bus. It's okay, isn't it?"
Smarter Father: "Sure, it's okay, son. I bought the gas with your allowance for next week. So run along and have a good time." —*Sunshine Magazine*

~

The mother of a teenage boy was going on holiday, leaving him alone for the first time. Concerned about his eating habits, she wanted to make sure he ate balanced, nutritious meals in her absence. She phoned him a few days after her departure and thinking of vegetables, asked anxiously: "Have you been eating anything green?" "Only the bread," he replied.   —*Rosary*

TELEVISION

Husband to wife: "I'll say this for television. The more unsuitable the program, the quieter it keeps the children!"

~

Imitation is the sincerest form of television.   —Fred Allen

~

When the politicians complain that TV turns the proceedings into a circus, it should be made clear that the circus was already there, and that TV has merely demonstrated that not all the performers are well trained.
—Edward R. Murrow

~

There's so much comedy on television. Does that cause comedy in the streets?
—Dick Cavett

~

Do you know what happens to little boys who keep interrupting? They grow up and make a fortune doing commercials on television.

~

Educational television should be absolutely forbidden. It can only lead to unreasonable expectations and eventual disappointment when your child discovers that the letters of the alphabet do not leap up out of books and dance around the room with royal-blue chickens.   —Fran Lebowitz

It is difficult to produce a television documentary that is both incisive and probing when every twelve minutes one is interrupted by dancing rabbits singing about toilet paper.   —Rod Serling

Television—a medium. So called because it is neither rare nor well-done.
                                                                —Ernie Kovacs

Television remote controls encourage couch potatoes to exercise their options while broadening their base.   —William Arthur Ward

Why do they report power outages on TV?

A small public relations company is engaged by a major television network to conduct a phone survey to determine the popularity of a new TV series. To avoid offending their lucrative new client the PR firm words the results: "98% of the people really loved it, but we kept running into the other 2%."

During intermission at the Metropolitan Opera in New York, I saw a familiar face. Thinking it was someone I knew, I said, "Hi, where have we met before?" He shook my hand, smiled and said, "I'm Edwin Newman, and you've been watching too much television."   —Lea K. Bleyman

Television news is like a lightning flash. It makes a loud noise, lights up everything around it, leaves everything else in darkness and then is suddenly gone.
                                                               —Hodding Carter

Little Heather's grandmother told her that they didn't have television when she was a little girl. The four-year-old was silent for a moment, and then asked. "What did your mother turn off when you were bad?"

TEMPER
Ever notice, it's easier to control your temper if the other guy is bigger?

TEMPTATION

Lately it seems like I don't have to worry about avoiding temptation. At my age temptation is avoiding me. —Ron Dentinger

~

Those who flee temptation generally leave a forwarding address.

—Lane Olinghouse

TENSION

Americans are so tense and keyed up that it's impossible even to put them to sleep with a sermon. —Norman Vincent Peale

TEXANS

Did you hear about the wealthy Dallas oil man who went on vacation to Hawaii? He went out to the beach one afternoon to discover that his wife had just been rescued from the surf, and was being revived by the lifeguards. "What are you doing?" he asked. The lifeguards replied, "We are giving her artificial respiration." "Artificial nothing," the oil man shouted, "Give her the real thing. We can afford it."

~

A Texan in New York City needed to call a nearby community from a pay phone. "Deposit $1.85 please," instructed the operator. Pulling himself up to full height and dropping into his thickest Texas drawl, he objected, "Ma'am, I'm from Texas, and in Texas we can place a call to Hell and back for $1.85!"

"I understand, sir," retorted the operator, "but in Texas, that's a local call."

~

An Easterner was riding with a rancher across a blistering hot stretch of Texas. Equally warm was the glowing praise of the rancher for the glories of his home state. Suddenly a beautiful plumed bird dashed across the road. "What kind of bird is that?" asked the easterner. "Bird of Paradise," said the Texan. The easterner rode in silence for a few more bumps, then remarked, "Long way from home, isn't he?"

—*Woodchuckles*

THEORY

In theory, there is no difference between theory and practice. But, in practice, there is. —Jan L. A. van de Snepscheut

THIEVES

As through this world I've traveled, I've seen lots of funny men. Some will rob you with a six-gun. And some with a fountain pen.   —Woody Guthrie

Ludlow Bean was arrested the other day for stealing a woman's change purse. He told the judge that he hadn't been feeling well, and he thought the change would do him good.   —Charley Weaver (Cliff Arquette)

Some people like stories about winners. It gives them something to aspire to. Some of us prefer stories about losers. Losers help us feel better about our own lives. Like Mrs. Dora Wilson, an English housewife. On February 18, 1981, Mrs. Wilson looked out her window in Harlow, Essex, and saw a group of men loading her neighbors' priceless collection of Persian carpets into a moving van. "What are you doing?" she called, knowing her neighbors were on vacation. "We're taking them to be cleaned, madam," the men replied. Quick as a flash Mrs. Wilson decided to take advantage of the service they offered. "Will you please take mine, too?" she asked. The men obliged. They, of course, were burglars.

—David Frost, *Book Of World's Worst Decisions*

REVEREND FUN

"Tenets anyone?"

©Gospel Films • Used By Permission • http://www.gospelcom.net/rev-fun

My grandfather invented the burglar alarm but someone stole it from him.

—Victor Borge

~

There's one good thing about kleptomania—you can always take something for it.

~

This guy was a terrible burglar. He didn't even take our TV. He just took our remote control. Now he drives by once in a while and changes channels on us.

—Brian Kile

~

She could carry off anything; and some people said that she did.

—Ada Leverson

~

In Modesto, CA, Steven Richard King was arrested for trying to hold up a Bank of America branch without a weapon. King used a thumb and a finger to simulate a gun, but unfortunately, he failed to keep his hand in his pocket.

~

Fire investigators on Maui have determined the cause of a blaze that destroyed a $127,000 home last month—a short in the homeowner's newly installed fire prevention alarm system. "This is even worse than last year," said the distraught homeowner, "when someone broke in and stole my new security system."

TIME

An Air Force lieutenant with a terrible cough went to see a doctor. "This cough is serious," diagnosed the doctor. "Do you smoke?" "No," answered the lieutenant, "I gave up smoking." The physician was not convinced. "When did you give it up?" The lieutenant's response was immediate: "Nineteen fifty-nine." "That long ago?" questioned the surprised doctor, "I don't think that is possible." "What's the big deal," asked the annoyed lieutenant as he looked at his watch. "It's only twenty-one sixteen now."

~

Last year, when daylight savings time ended, I realized that you cannot turn a digital watch backwards one hour to get back to standard time. My wife said, "All you have to do is turn it ahead twenty-three hours. I did . . . and for six months I was a day early for all my appointments."   —Ron Dentinger

There is no distance on this earth as far away as yesterday.

—Robert Nathan, *So Love Returns*

~

While proudly showing off his new apartment to friends, a college student led the way into the den. "What is the big brass gong and hammer for?" one of his friends asked. "That is the talking clock," the man replied. "How's it work?" the friend asked. "Watch," the man said, then proceeded to give the gong an ear shattering pound with the hammer. Suddenly, someone screamed from the other side of the wall "KNOCK IT OFF, YOU IDIOT! It's two o'clock in the morning!

~

Three o'clock is always too late or too early for anything you want to do.

—Jean-Paul Sartre

~

My Uncle Jack, the traveling salesman, drove all night long to meet a client in a small town in Alabama. He arrived two hours early, so he decided to stop in the local park and catch some shuteye. Just as he dozed off, there was a knock on the window. Outside the car, the man saw a jogger. "Excuse me, can you give me the time?" "Yeah, it's 6:27." The man settled back and was almost asleep when there was another knock on the window. Another jogger. "I'm sorry to disturb you. Do you have the time?" "Yeah. It's 6:34." The man rolled up the window and realized this could go on indefinitely. So he took paper and pen and made a sign which read: "I DO NOT KNOW THE TIME." He stuck the sign in the window and again nestled himself back in the seat. Then . . . yet another tap on the window. The man looked and sure enough, another jogger. He disgustedly rolled down the window and said, "Yeah, what is it?" The jogger replied, "It's 6:42."

~

Unaware that Indianapolis is on Eastern Standard Time and Chicago on Central Standard Time, a man inquired at the Indianapolis airport about a plane to Chicago. "One leaves at 1 P.M.," a ticket agent said, "and arrives in Chicago at 1:01 P.M." "Would you repeat that, please?" the man asked. The agent did so and then inquired, "Do you want a reservation?" "No," said the man. "But I think I'll hang around and watch that thing take off."

—*United Methodists Today*

TRAFFIC

The first one to see the light turn green is the driver of the second car back.

—Terry Marchal

One time a cop pulled me over for running a stop sign. "Didn't you see the stop sign?" the officer asked. "Yeah," I said. "But I don't believe everything I read." —Steven Wright

TRAGEDY

"In this world there are only two tragedies. One is not getting what one wants, and the other is getting it." —Oscar Wilde

TRAINS

Then there was the guy who was applying for a job as a flagman/switch operator on the railroad. The engineer was conducting the interview. "What would you do if the Northern Express was heading north on Track 1 and the Southern Central was heading south on Track 1?" The guy thought. "Well, I'd call my brother." The engineer just sat there for a second. "Why would you call your brother?" "He's never seen a train wreck before."

TRANSLATIONS

English translation printed on a sign inside a ferry in San Juan Harbor: "In case of emergency, the lifeguards are under the seats in the center of the vessels."

TRAVEL

A long sea-voyage not only brings out all the mean traits one has, and exaggerates them, but raises up others which he never suspected he possessed, and even creates new ones. —Mark Twain

～

In the Dominican Republic, a tour guide pointed out the tomb of Christopher Columbus. "That's interesting," said a tourist. "In Spain, a few years ago, I was shown the tomb of Columbus in Seville." "Ah," replied the Dominican guide, "the one in Seville is the tomb of the old Christopher Columbus. This is the tomb of the young Christopher Columbus."

～

A journey of 1000 miles begins with a single delay of two hours before takeoff.

～

Jet lag is nature's way of making you look like your passport photo. —Linda Perret

～

The journey of a thousand miles must begin with wondering if you turned off the iron. —William Rotsler

REVEREND FUN

Thanks to the interstate highway system, it is now possible to travel across the country from coast to coast without seeing anything.   —Charles Kuralt

The following are actual stories provided by travel agents:

- I had someone ask for an aisle seat so that his hair wouldn't get messed up by being near the window.
- A client called in inquiring about a package to Hawaii. After going over all the cost info, she asked, "Would it be cheaper to fly to California and then take the train to Hawaii?"
- A man called, furious about a Florida package we did. I asked what was wrong with the vacation in Orlando. He said he was expecting an ocean-view room. I tried to explain that is not possible, since Orlando is in the middle of the state. He replied, "Don't lie to me. I looked on the map and Florida is a very thin state."
- I got a call from a man who asked, "Is it possible to see England from Canada?" I said, "No." He said, "But they look so close on the map."
- A nice lady just called. She needed to know how it was possible that her flight from Detroit left at 8:20 A.M. and got into Chicago at 8:33 A.M. I tried to explain that Michigan was an hour ahead of Illinois, but she could not understand the concept of time zones. Finally I told her that the plane went very fast, and she bought that!
- I just got off the phone with a man who asked, "How do I know which plane to get on?" I asked him what exactly he meant, which he replied, "I was told my flight number is 823, but none of these darn planes have numbers on them."

T

- A businessman called and had a question about the documents he needed in order to fly to China. After a lengthy discussion about passports, I reminded him he needed a visa. "Oh no I don't, I've been to China many times and never had to have one of those." I double checked and sure enough, his stay required a visa. When I told him this he said, "Look, I've been to China four times and every time they have accepted my American Express."

Three guys and a woman are driving cross-country together—one from Idaho, one from Iowa, the woman is from Florida, and the last man is from New York. A bit down the road the man from Idaho starts to pull potatoes from his bag and throws them out the window. The man from Iowa turns to him and asks, "What the heck are you doing?" The man from Idaho says, "Man, we have so many of these darned things in Idaho they're laying around on the ground, I'm sick of looking at them!" A few miles down the road, the man from Iowa begins pulling husks of corn from his bag and throwing them out the window. The woman from Florida asks, "What the heck are you doing that for?" The man from Iowa replies, "We have so many of these things in Iowa I'm sick of looking at them!" Inspired by the others, the woman from Florida opens the car door and pushes the New Yorker out.

"Oh, well . . . in THAT price range, I can offer you one of our LOVELY travel posters."

Columbus headed for India and wound up in Santo Domingo. Today, if you head for India, you get to India. It's your baggage that winds up in Santo Domingo.

When Executive Travel invited readers to relate their worst flying experience of the year, the winner was a businessman who described the following: "Officials, after discovering a domestic West African flight had been grossly overbooked, asked all passengers with boarding cards to run twice around the plane. The fastest ones got the seats."   —AP

A traveler was stopped by an airport customs officer and asked if he had anything to declare. "No, I don't," he answered. "Are you sure?" "Of course I'm sure." "What about that elephant standing behind you with bread in his ears?" the agent persisted. "Sire, what I put in my sandwiches in my own business!"   —Seymour Rosenberg

Woman to travel agents: "We've already seen the world. What else do you have?"   —E. A. Harris

TROUBLE

Borrow trouble for yourself if that's your nature, but don't lend it to your neighbors.   —Rudyard Kipling, *Rewards and Fairies*

If a husband has troubles, he should tell his wife, and if he hasn't he should tell the world how he does it.

T-SHIRTS

SUGGESTED SAYINGS FOR T-SHIRTS:

- Well, this day was a total waste of makeup.
- Make yourself at home! Clean my kitchen.
- Who are these kids and why are they calling me Mom?
- I thought I wanted a career, turns out I just wanted paychecks.
- Don't bother me. I'm living happily ever after.
- Do I look like a people person?
- Is it time for your medication or mine?

- I started out with nothing and still have most of it left.
- I pretend to work. They pretend to pay me.
- If I throw a stick, will you leave?
- Therapy is expensive, poppin' bubble wrap is cheap! You choose.
- I like cats, too. Let's exchange recipes.
- Everyone thinks I'm psychotic, except for my friends deep inside the earth.
- Ambivalent? Well, yes and no.
- If only you'd use your powers for good instead of evil . . .
- Allow me to introduce my selves.
- Sarcasm is just one more service we offer.
- Whatever kind of look you were going for, you missed.
- Suburbia: where they tear out the trees and then name streets after them.
- Do they ever shut up on your planet?
- I'm just working here till a good fast-food job opens up.
- A woman's favorite position is CEO.
- Chaos, panic, and disorder—my work here is done.
- I'm trying to imagine you with a personality.
- A cubicle is just a padded cell without a door.
- Stress is when you wake up screaming and you realize you haven't fallen asleep yet.
- Here I am! Now what are your other two wishes?
- Don't worry. I forgot your name, too!
- Adults are just kids who owe money.
- I have a computer, an ice cream maker, and pizza delivery. Why should I leave the house?
- Nice perfume. Must you marinate in it?
- I'm not tense, just terribly, terribly alert.
- Can I trade this job for what's behind door #2?

At the coin laundry, a little gray-haired woman was wearing a T-shirt that read: "I finally got it all together and now I forgot where I put it."

—Contributed by Nadine Saunders Saundwes

TWINS

I grew up with Jonathan and Gene Katz, who were twin brothers. One became a minister and the other a physician. It was almost impossible to tell the twins apart. A man approached one of them on the street and asked, "Are you the twin who preaches?" "No," came the answer, "I'm the one who practices."

Know why the Siamese twins moved to London? So the other one could drive.

My neighbor told me his girlfriend is a twin. I asked him if he ever kissed the wrong twin. He said, "No, her brother won't even come near me."

—Ron Dentinger

A woman has twins. Unfortunately due to her financial situation, she gives them up for adoption. One of them goes to a family in Egypt and is named "Amal." The other goes to a family in Spain they name him "Juan." Years later, Juan sends a picture of himself to his birth mom. Upon receiving the picture, she tells her husband that she wishes she also had a picture of Amal. Her husband responds, "But they are twins—if you've seen Juan, you've seen Amal."

TYPOS

LOVE THOSE TYPOS . . .

- For sale—one executive desk, one secretarial desk with chains.—Classified ad in Jefferson, *Wisconsin Advertiser*
- Personal Coping Machine With Paper Supply—Montrose, Pennsylvania, *Shopping Guide*
- Hall of Fame To Indict Nine New Members.—Headline in Pleasanton, California, *Tri-Valley Herald*
- Hot tub, seats eight, rearly used.—Classified ad spotted in Pittsburgh Pennysaver
- Appalling two-story home in quiet neighborhood.—Classified ad in Ionia County, Michigan, *Shopper's Guide*
- Do's and Don'ts for Hormonious Honeymoon.—Headline on advice article for brides in Cedar Park, Texas, *Hill Country News*
- 1981 Citation, goof transportation.—In Bay City, Michigan, *Times*

U

UNFULFILLED PROPHECIES

U

"The place will be crawling with great-looking girls."
"When it says empty, there are always a couple of gallons left."
"Counting drinks and tip, you'll pay thirty dollars tops."
"They'll feel wonderful once you break them in."
"We're bringing it in right under budget."
"You can assemble it yourself in minutes."
"It won't feel cold once you dive in."
"You'll housebreak him in no time."

VACATIONS

Talk about your unbelievable coincidences: Every year I go on vacation at the very same time the fish do.　　　　　　　　　　　　　　—Ron Dentinger

A family vacation is one where you arrive with five bags, four kids and seven I-thought-you packed-its.　　　　　　　　　　　　　　—Ivern Ball

Wife to husband: "Our vacation isn't a total loss, dear. Most people go a lifetime without ever seeing icicles on palm trees."　　　　—Franklin Folger

This summer one third of the nation will be ill-housed, ill-nourished and ill-clad. Only they call it a vacation.　　　　　　　　　—Joseph Salak

The family that travels together often unravels together.　—*New York Times*

Take a vacation to get away from it all, and you run into a lot of people who want to get it all away from you.　　　　　　　　—Lane Olinghouse

Real charity is the ability to hope that the guy whose work you are doing while he vacations in the sun is having a wonderful time.　—Bill Vaughan

REVEREND FUN

Dear Moses,
The promised land is really cool. Wish you were here.
- Israelites

You know that summer camp is going to be expensive when it lists the weenie roast as a "frankfurter flambé"   —Arch Napier

~

Woman to friend: "Our neighbor's vacation was over three months ago, and would you believe were still suffering from slide effects?"   —Ivern Ball

VEGETARIANS

I was a vegetarian until I started leaning toward sunlight.   —Rita Rudner

VICE PRESIDENTS

Women are being considered as candidates for Vice President of the United States because it is the worst job in America. It's amazing that anyone will take it. A job with real power is first lady. I'd be willing to run for that. As far as the men who are running for President are concerned, they aren't even people I would date.   —Nora Ephron

~

The man with the best job in the country is the Vice President. All he has to do is get up every morning and say, "How is the President?"   —Will Rogers

~

The Vice-Presidency is sort of like the last cookie on the plate. Everybody insists he won't take it, but somebody always does.   —Bill Vaughan

~

When Calvin Coolidge was Vice President, he and his wife lived in the Willard Hotel in Washington. A fire alarm in the middle of the night brought every guest into the lobby, in a variety of nightgowns, negligees, robes, and fancy pajamas. Mr. Coolidge glanced about, surmised that there was no danger, and started to trudge back to his room. "Nothing doing," said the fire marshal, "get back in that lobby." You are speaking to the Vice President," said Coolidge with obvious self-regard. "OK," then, said the marshal. "Go ahead." A moment later he called suspiciously, "What are you Vice President of?" "The United States," said Coolidge. "Come back down here," ordered the marshal. "I thought you were Vice President of the hotel."

VIRTUE

An unprincipled businessman who liked to appear full of virtue, told Mark Twain, "Before I die, I'm going to make a pilgrimage to the Holy Land. I shall climb to the top of Mount Sinai and read the Ten Commandments aloud." "I have a better idea," said Mark Twain. "You do?" said the businessman. "I'd like to hear it." "About the Ten Commandments," Twain replied, "why don't you stay right at home in Boston and keep them."

VISITING

Santa Claus has the right idea. Visit people once a year.   —Victor Borge

---

W

WAITERS/WAITRESSES

Waiter to diner: "I'm sorry. My lawyer suggested that I don't make any more recommendations."

I stopped for lunch at a tiny diner in New Mexico. After I had eaten my lunch, I asked for a cup of coffee with cream and sugar. I was rather annoyed that the waitress forgot to bring me a spoon with my coffee. After trying unsuccessfully to get the waitress' attention, I announced in a voice loud enough to be heard from one end of the establishment to the other, "This coffee is going to be pretty hot to stir with my fingers." Within seconds, the waitress appeared with another cup of coffee. "This one isn't so hot, sir," she beamed.

The worst new dining trend is hearing the waiter exclaim, "Good choice!" immediately after a person at your table selects a dish. It was bad enough in the old days, when waiters introduced themselves to us. Now they're reviewing us.   —Alan Richman

WAITING

Being on the tightrope is living; everything else is waiting.   —Karl Wallenda

The man who goes alone can start today; but he who travels with another must wait till that other is ready.   —Henry David Thoreau

WASHING

The three-year-old boy was ordered by his mother to carry all those cloth animals in his room to the washing machine in the basement so that she could give them the cleaning they badly needed. While she was busy in the laundry room, the telephone rang and her son ran back upstairs to answer it. A man's voice inquired, "Is your mother home?" "Yes, she is," the youngster said, "but she can't come to the phone right now. She's busy putting an elephant into the washing machine." There was a long silence on the other end of the line. "I guess I have the wrong number," the man stammered and quickly hung up.

—*American Weekly*

WASHINGTON

A Princeton graduate applied for a job with the State Department in Washington. The personnel director called one of the fellow's references to ask about him, and received a lengthy response detailing the applicant's fine social standing and family background from Pilgrim stock. "Sir," the personnel director responded, "I think you misunderstood. We want to employ the young man for diplomatic purposes, not breeding purposes."

President Clinton learned that a biologist had perfected a way to rid Washington, D.C., of rats. The procedure would cost the city a million dollars, but there would be no charge if a single rat survived. The President agreed, whereupon the biologist opened a velvet-lined mahogany box. Out jumped a large purple rat, which began to run through the city. Soon there was a horde of rats following the purple leader. He ran to the Potomac and dove into the river. All the other rats followed. A few hours later, all the rats had drowned except the purple one, who swam back to shore and was put back in his box. Assured that no other rats remained in the city, the President ordered the biologist to be paid. As the scientist turned to leave, the President pulled him aside. "You wouldn't happen to have a purple Republican, would you?"

Where but in Washington could you get 500 Congressmen, 400 lobbyists, 300 economists and 200 computers working on a plan to simplify taxes?

Turkeys will be more expensive this Thanksgiving, except in Washington— where there is always a surplus.

How on earth did we expect to know who the good guys were in Kosovo when we can't even figure out who the good guys are in Washington?

W

WEALTH

Every day I get up and look through the Forbes list of the richest people in America. If I'm not there, I go to work.

—Robert Orben

WEATHER

Heard on National Weather Service radio in Memphis: "The weather warning alarm system will be activated today for test purposes between 11 and 11:30 A.M., weather permitting."

TEMPERATURE (DEGREES FAHRENHEIT):

- +60 Californians put on sweaters.
- +50 Miami residents turn on the heat.
- +45 Vermont residents go to outdoor concert.
- +40 You can see your breath. Californians shiver uncontrollably. Minnesotans go swimming.
- +35 Italians cars don't start.
- +32 Water freezes.
- +30 You plan your vacation in Australia.
- +25 Ohio water freezes. Californians weep pitiably. Minnesotans eat ice cream. Canadians go swimming.
- +20 Politicians begin to talk about the homeless. New York City water freezes. Miami residents plan vacation further south.
- +15 French cars don't start. Cat insists on sleeping with you.
- +10 You need jumper cables to get the car going.
- −5 American cars don't start.
- −10 Alaskans put on T-shirts.
- −10 German cars don't start. Eyes freeze shut when you blink.
- −5 You can cut your breath and use it to build an igloo. Arkansans stick tongues on metal objects. Miami residents cease to exist.
- −20 Cat insists on sleeping in pajamas with you. Politicians actually do something about the homeless. Minnesotans shovel snow off roof. Japanese cars don't start.
- −25 Too cold to think. You need jumper cables to get the driver going.
- −30 You plan a two week hot bath. Swedish cars don't start.
- −40 Californians disappear. Minnesotans button top button. Canadians put on sweater. Your car helps you plan your trip south.
- −50 Congressional hot air freezes. Alaskans close the bathroom window.
- −80 Hell freezes over. Polar bears move south. Green Bay Packer fans order hot cocoa at the game.
- −90 Lawyers put their hands in their own pockets.
- −100 Canadian buildings turn off air conditioning.

When temperatures plunged to 26 degrees below zero Fahrenheit, the Rockford, Ill., *Register Star* asked its readers to finish the sentence, "It was so cold that . . ." Here are some of the responses: . . . you could freeze an egg on the sidewalk. . . . I had to go up and break the smoke off my chimney. . . . we opened the refrigerator to heat the house. . . . when police saw a bank-robbery suspect and said, "Freeze!" he did. . . . I saw a 32nd-degree Mason, and he was down to 15. . . . when I called home to Arizona, the message caused the cactus to frost over. . . . I let my dog out, and I had to break him loose from the tree.

—*Quote*

WEDDINGS

Late one Saturday afternoon, Pastor Harold returned home. "How did the wedding go?" his wife asked. "Fine, my dear, until I asked the bride if she would obey," and she said, 'Do you think I'm crazy?' and the bridegroom, who was in sort of a stupor, mumbled, 'I do,'—then things began to happen!"

Some couples can't even agree before they get married. I heard one couple talking in the shopping mall. They couldn't agree on two rather picky little details for a wedding. She wanted the bridesmaids to wear long blue gowns, and he didn't want to get married.

—Ron Dentinger

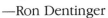

A Midwest preacher received this thank you note from a bridegroom he had married: "Dear Reverend, I want to thank you for the beautiful way you brought my happiness to a conclusion."

At a wedding reception attended by four pairs of the divorced and remarried parents and stepparents of the bride and groom, one father rose and gave the following toast to the newlyweds: "I wish you the joy and humor of Jesus, good health, longevity, and only one Christmas every year."

Elmo Stites became the groom of Miss Bonnie Rooney in a lovely ceremony at the United Brethren church Saturday evening. The groom wore a two-piece tan suit. The trousers were gathered at the waist, fell in a straight line to the floor. A cuff of about an inch and a half extended around the bottom of each trouser leg. The groom's coat hung loosely from the shoulders. The left lapel overlapped the right in a daring deep V neckline held in place at the waist by

W

a charming button. His tie was arranged in a full windsor knot, hung daintily to a point just above the waistline. His shoes were secured by a dark cord interwoven through ten eyelets. The bride was attended by Miss Floy Mulkey of Philomath, Oregon.   —Actual report in a Kansas weekly

WHY DID THE CHICKEN CROSS THE ROAD?

Stay tuned as a panel of chickens reveals the shocking truth!

—Gerald Rivera

Whether the chicken crossed the road or the road crossed the chicken depends upon your frame of reference.   —Albert Einstein

To boldly go where no chicken has gone before.

—Gene Roddenberry

Give me ten minutes with the chicken and I'll find out.   —Tomas de Torquemada, Grand Inquisitor of the Spanish Inquisition

You tell me.   —The Sphinx

Whaddaya want, it should just stand there?   —Jackie Mason

To die. In the rain.   —Ernest Hemingway

It may very well have been one of the most astonishing events to grace the annals of history. An avian biped's attempt at such a herculean achievement, formerly relegated to Homo sapien pedestrians, is truly a remarkable occurrence.   —Howard Cosell

To prove to the 'possum it could be done.

What? I missed one?   —Colonel Sanders

And the No. 1 reason? Fricassee!   —David Letterman

WHY IS IT

That the same guy who has a $1000 treadmill has a $2000 riding mower?

WILLS

Where there's a will there's a wail.   —Arnold H. Glasow

❧

The old man on his deathbed made the final adjustments to his will. "And to each employee who has been with me 20 years or more," he said to the attorney, "I bequeath $10,000." "Very generous of you," said the lawyer. "I wouldn't say so," said the dying man. "None of them has been with me that long. But it will look pretty good in the papers, don't you think?"

—The Malabar Herald

WINNING

An older gentleman won millions in the state lottery. Since he had a weak heart, his wife enlisted the pastor's help to gently break the good news. The priest did a fine job, and the winner was jubilant indeed. "Father," he exclaimed, "I want to give half of it to our parish!" And the pastor dropped dead.   *—The Priest*

WISDOM

Wisdom is the ability to keep your mouth shut while your mind continues to talk to itself.

❧

Conrad Hilton, the hotel mogul, had a droll sense of humor. Once he was on the Johnny Carson show, and he was asked if he had a message for the American people. He looked straight into the camera and said, slowly and distinctly to about 30 million listeners. "Please put the shower curtain inside the tub."

❧

The difference between a smart man and a wise man is that a smart man knows what to say, and a wise man knows whether or not to say it.

—Frank M. Garafola

❧

Some folks are wise and some are otherwise.   —Tobias George Smolett

W

WISHES

Wife: "You're always wishing for something you haven't got."
Husband: "What else is there to wish for?"

~

When you reach for the stars, you may not quite get one, but you won't come up with a handful of mud either. —Leo Burnett

WIT

Wit is educated insolence. —Aristotle

~

You can pretend to be serious; you can't pretend to be witty. —Sacha Guitry

~

Wit ought to be a glorious treat, like caviar. Never spread it about like marmalade. —Noel Coward

WIVES

A bridge table is the only place I've seen where a wife is usually eager to do her husband's bidding. —Charles Goren

~

My father's cousin, the respected Judge Louis Streiker, had a wife, forty years his junior, who was just a bit too fond of the grape. At a party one afternoon at the governor's mansion, he reproved her, "My dear, that's the seventh time you've gone up to the bar and asked for another whiskey sour. Doesn't it embarrass you? Don't you worry about what the people at the bar think?" "Why should it?" she chirped merrily. "I just explain I'm getting them for you."

~

Rob: "My wife is very touchy. The smallest thing will set her off."
Stan: "You're fortunate. Mine is a self-starter."

~

There is no use arguing with the inevitable. Do what your wife says in the first place. —O. Battista

~

My wife thinks I'm too nosy. At least that's what she scribbles in her diary.
—Drake Sather

When a man steals your wife, there is no better revenge than to let him keep her.
                                                                                    —Sacha Guitry

❧

Aunt Roz explains, "Uncle Albert and I have managed to be happy together for forty years. I guess this is because we're both in love with the same man."

❧

When it comes to preaching, my wife is my severest critic. One Sunday after church, she whispered in my ear: "Lowell, dear, I believe Jesus wanted us to CLOTHE the naked, not VISIT them as you said in your sermon today!"

❧

Thomas Wheeler, chief executive officer of the Massachusetts Mutual Life Insurance Company, tells a good story on himself. He says that while he and his wife were out driving he noticed they were low on gas. So he pulled off at the first exit and came to this dumpy little gas station with one pump. There was only one man working the place, so he asked the man to fill it up while he checked the oil. He added a quart of oil, closed the hood, and he saw his wife talking and smiling at the gas station attendant. When they saw him looking at them, the station attendant walked away and pretended as if nothing had happened. Wheeler paid the man and he and his wife pulled out of that seedy little station. As they drove down the road, he asked his wife if she knew the attendant. Well, she admitted she did know him. In fact, she had known him very well. For it seems that they not only had gone to high school together, but they dated seriously for about a year. Well, Wheeler couldn't help bragging a little and said, "Boy, were you lucky I came along. Because if you'd married him you'd be the wife of a gas station attendant instead of the wife of a chief executive officer." His wife replied, "My dear, if I had married him, he'd be the chief executive officer and you'd be the gas station attendant."
                                                                                    —*Vital Speeches*

❧

My wife makes the budget work. We do without a lot of things I don't need.
                                                                                    —Milton Berle

W

❧

My VISA card was stolen two months ago, but I don't want to report it. The guy who took it is using it less than my wife.

While my wife and I were shopping at the mall, a shapely young woman in a short, form-fitting dress strolled by. My eyes followed her. Without looking up from the item she was examining, my wife asked, "Was it worth the trouble you're in?"

❧

The easiest way to get your wife's attention is by looking comfortable.

❧

My Aunt Mindy told her fellow bridge club members: "I have the most marvelous recipe for goulash—all I have to do is mention it to my husband and he says, 'Let's eat out.'"

❧

If you want to be sure you'll always remember your wife's birthday, just try forgetting it once.

❧

The wife of an Episcopalian priest passed away suddenly one Thursday evening. Next morning the grief-stricken husband telephoned his bishop: "My wife passed away last night. Please send a substitute for the weekend."
—Brian O'Hara

❧

I've found that, even if my wife and I have a radical difference of opinion, we can still get along just fine if she doesn't find out about it.

WOMEN

High heels were invented by a woman who has been kissed on the forehead.
—Christopher Morley

❧

In politics, if you want anything said, ask a man. If you want anything done, ask a woman.
—Margaret Thatcher

❧

When women kiss, it always reminds me of prize fighters shaking hands.
—H. L. Mencken

❧

Woman to woman: "Working full-time and trying to do the housework, too, really gets me. After work I came home and I washed the clothes and I washed the dishes. Tomorrow I have to wash the kitchen floor and wash the front windows . . ." "What about your husband?" "Absolutely not! He can wash himself."
—Ron Dentinger

Here's to woman! Would that we could fall into her arms without falling into her hands.
                                                                —Ambrose Bierce

Woman begins by resisting a man's advances and ends by blocking his retreat.
                                                                —Oscar Wilde

Women are like elephants to me. I like to look at them but I wouldn't want to own one.
                                                                —W. C. Fields

Women's styles may change, but their designs remain the same.
                                                                —Oscar Wilde

There are two times when a man doesn't understand a woman—before marriage and after marriage.

The answer to a maiden's prayer sometimes makes you wonder if the Lord was paying much attention. I'm the modern, intelligent, independent-type woman. In other words, a girl who can't get a man.
                                                                —Shelley Winters

There's a difference between beauty and charm. A beautiful woman is one I notice. A charming woman is one who notices me.   —John Erskine

You'd be surprised how much it costs to look this cheap.   —Dolly Parton

Any girl can be glamorous. All you have to do is stand still and look stupid.
                                                                —Hedy Lamarr

If women didn't exist, all the money in the world would have no meaning.
                                                                —Aristotle Onassis

W

A woman's mind is cleaner than a man's. She changes it more often.
                                                                —Oliver Herford

A reader writes: "Who originated the custom of the man giving the woman a diamond engagement ring?" We're not sure, but we think it was a woman.

~

One young woman about another: "She's never really cared for a man's company—unless he owns it." —Quipster, in Odessa, Texas, *American*

~

They keep trying to tell us that women are smarter than men, but did you ever see a man wearing a shirt that buttoned in the back?

WORDS

The difference between the right word and the almost right word is the difference between lightning and the lightning bug. —Mark Twain

~

Recreational wordplayers wonder why we drive on a parkway and park on a driveway. And in what other language do people play at a recital and recite at a play? —Richard Lederer in *Crazy English*

~

At a retirement dinner: "Today we honor a man who doesn't know the meaning of the word dissemble, who doesn't know the meaning of the word fear, who doesn't know the meaning of the word quit. And so, we've all chipped in to get him this dictionary." —*Orben's Current Comedy*

~

Naked and nude mean the same thing—except that naked sounds like a surprise while nude suggests it was done on purpose. —Beryl Pfizer

~

Ever notice that PRICE and WORTH mean the same thing, but priceless and worthless are opposites? —Jay Trachman

~

When ideas fail, words come in very handy. —Goethe

~

Metaphors are apt to do a speaker in unless they are carefully crafted. Columnist William Safire recounted a story about the late Sen. Everett Dirksen, who rose in the Senate to say, "Around the world there is a feeling that there is a firm hand on the rudder of the ship of state." Explains Safire: "As Dirksen's speechwriter, I was chagrined later to learn that the man with the hand on the rudder would be drowning, and nobody would be minding the tiller."

—Jack Valenti, *Speak Up With Confidence*

WORK

When Abraham Lincoln was a young man he took a sack of grain to be ground at the mill. The owner had the reputation for being the slowest and laziest miller in Illinois. After watching him for a while, Lincoln said, "You know, I think I could eat that grain as fast as you are grinding it." "But how long could you keep it up?" the miller replied ungraciously. "Until I starve to death," the future president retorted.

Millions of people in this country aren't working, and that is scary. However, the real problem is that so many of these people are employed.

—Ron Dentinger

The virtues of hard work are extolled most loudly by people without calluses.

John came home flushed with pride. "I've been promoted," he announced. "I have a new job! They've made me an expediter." "What's an expediter?" asked his wife. "Well, it's hard to explain but if you did what I'm supposed to do, it would be called nagging."

Three crews were competing for a contract with the telephone company. In order to select the most qualified, the phone company instructed each crew to go out and see how many telephone poles they could erect in one day. At the end of the day the first crew reported thirty-five poles to the phone company official, who was obviously impressed. "Good, but not good enough," he told the second crew, who had installed thirty-two. "Well?" he asked, turning to the third crew. "Two," said the foreman proudly. "So why are you so proud of yourself? Those guys did thirty-five and those did thirty-two," he said, pointing to the other crews. "Yeah," said the foreman, "but look how much they left sticking out of the ground."

W

Wife: "You look tired dear. Did you have a bad day at the office?"
Husband: "I'll say. I took an aptitude test, and believe me, it's a good thing I own the company!"

Two exasperated company executives were discussing a scatterbrained office boy who had a habit of fouling up important errands. "How long has he been with us, anyway?" asked one of the executives. "He's never been with us," replied the other. "He's been against us from the start." —*Quote*

A business manager, in search of talent within his own organization, passed out a list of questions to his younger workers. One question asked, "What is your chief reason for believing that you possess executive ability?" Many of the answers were duplications, but one stood out unequaled. It read, "I think I would make a very successful executive because I seldom get lonesome, and would not mind working in a private office." —*Quote*

Receptionist to salesman: You can either wait till the boss comes back or I can give you the old runaround myself.

In the words of Robert Frost, the great American poet, "The brain is a wonderful organ. It starts working the moment you get up in the morning and does not stop until you get to the office."

REVEREND FUN

STAFF ENTRANCE

©Gospel Films • Used By Permission • http://www.gospelcom.net/rev-fun

"I'll meet you inside . . . I'm required to use THIS entrance."

I used to work in a fire hydrant factory. You couldn't park anywhere near the place. —Steven Wright

My Uncle Irv always contended: "The trouble with getting to work on time is that it makes the day so long."

Man to co-worker: "I learn more from originals left in the copier than I do from the employee newsletter." —Litzler in *The Wall Street Journal*

Employee: "The stress my boss puts me under is killing me. I have migraines, my blood pressure is going through the roof, I can't sleep at night, I just found out I have an ulcer, and as long as I stay in this job, the only question is whether I'll have a stroke or a heart attack."
Friend: "So why don't you quit?"
Employee: "I have a great health plan." —Richard Jerome

A new employee stood before one of the office machines, looking confused. "Do you need some help?" asked a co-worker. "Yes," the new man answered. "How does this thing work?" "Simple," she said, taking his big report and feeding it into the shredder. "Thanks," the new man replied, "but where do the copies come out?"

Pope John XXIII was a kind man with a marvelous sense of humor. Someone once asked him how many people worked at the Vatican. "Half of them," he said. —Theodore M. Hesburgh, *God, Country, Notre Dame*

- When you take a long time, you're slow. When your boss takes a long time, he's thorough.
- When you don't do it, you're lazy. When your boss doesn't do it, he's too busy.
- When you make a mistake, you're an idiot. When your boss makes a mistake, he's only human.
- When doing something without being told, you're overstepping your authority. When your boss does the same thing, that's initiative.
- When you take a stand, you're being bull-headed. When your boss does it, he's being firm.
- When you overlooked a rule of etiquette, you're being rude. When your boss skips a few rules, he's being original.

W

- When you please your boss, you're apple polishing. When your boss pleases his boss, he's being cooperative.
- When you're out of the office, you're wandering around. When your boss is out of the office, he's on business.
- When you're on a day off sick, you're always sick. When your boss is a day off sick, he must be very ill.
- When you apply for leave, you must be going for an interview. When your boss applies for leave, it's because he's overworked.

At the water cooler: "They gave him a watch when he retired, and in a week it quit working too."
—Clyde Moore

Employee: I have been here 11 years doing three men's work for one man's pay. Now I want a raise.

"I am not lazy. I'm just ambition-challenged."

The trend lately is to find some job where you can work out of your home. A reader writes to say, "This is okay if they are working with a computer, but the guy who lives upstairs from me is a blacksmith."

In an employment office: "Confident? Look at his résumé. It's the first time I've seen 'omnipotence' listed under job skills." —*Orben's Current Comedy*

Nobody is sicker than the man who is sick on his day off.

The owner of a manufacturing plant decided to make a surprise tour of the shop. Walking through the warehouse, he noticed a young man lazily leaning against a packing crate. "Just how much are you being paid a week?" the boss angrily asked him. "A hundred bucks," answered the lounging guy. The boss pulled out his wallet and peeled off five $20 bills. "Here's a week's pay," he shouted. "Now get out and don't come back!" Wordlessly, the young man stuffed the money into his pocket and took off. The warehouse manager, standing nearby, stared in amazement. "Tell me," the boss said, "how long has that guy worked for us?" "He didn't work here," replied his employee. "He was just delivering a package." —P. Reidy in *Boys' Life*

WORRY

Don't sweat the petty things and don't pet the sweaty things.
—Jacquelyn Small

When I don't have anything to worry about, I begin to worry about that.
—Walter Kelly

WORTH

The real worth of a person is determined by what that person does when there is nothing to do.

WRITING

The difference between fiction and reality? Fiction has to make sense.
—Tom Clancy

Said the literary agent to the aspiring novelist, "When did they open up that sidewalk cafe I saw you in last night?" "That wasn't a sidewalk cafe," replied the writer sadly. "That was my furniture."

My father says he can't understand why a person would take a year to write a novel when he can easily buy one for a few dollars.

~

A good novel tells us the truth about its hero; but a bad novel tells us the truth about its author. —G. K. Chesterton

~

A four-year-old was diligently banging away on her daddy's old typewriter. She informed him that she was writing a story. "What is your story about?" he asked. "I don't know," she replied. "I can't read." —*Capper's Weekly*

~

A friend of the George Bernard Shaws tells of an evening he spent with them. While G.B.S. told stories, Mrs. Shaw busied herself knitting. "What are you knitting?" asked the guest in an aside. "Oh, nothing, nothing at all," whispered

Mrs. Shaw. "It's just that I've heard these stories of his two thousand times, and if I didn't do something with my hands, I'd choke him."

~

Better to write for yourself and have no public, than to write for the public and have no self.

—Cyril Connolly

~

Author-historian Shelby Foote, upon completion of the third and final volume of his epic narrative *The Civil War,* noted: "In response to complaints that it took me five times longer to write the war than the participants took to fight it, I would point out that there were a good many more of them than there was of me."

~

Anybody who corrects all his mistakes is probably writing his autobiography.
—*Chicago Tribune*

~

Clare Boothe Luce comments on writing her memoirs: "I'll never do it. All autobiographies are alibiographies." —"Dick Cavett Show," PBS

~

An autobiography usually reveals nothing bad about its writer except his memory. —Franklin P. Jones

These days the wages of sin depend on what kind of deal you make with the publisher.
—Irvern Ball

I heard someone tried the monkeys-on-typewriters bit trying for the plays of W. Shakespeare, but all they got was the collected works of Francis Bacon.
—Bill Hirst

Manuscript: something submitted in haste and returned at leisure.
—Oliver Herford

Everywhere I go I'm asked if I think the university stifles writers. My opinion is that they don't stifle enough of them.
—Flannery O'Connor

Some editors are failed writers, but so are most writers.
—T. S. Eliot

There's many a bestseller that could have been prevented by a good teacher.
—Flannery O'Connor

In America, only the successful writer is important, in France all writers are important, in England no writer is important, and in Australia you have to explain what a writer is.
—Geoffrey Cottrell

A great many people now reading and writing would be better employed keeping rabbits.
—Edith Sitwell

A writer is someone for whom writing is more difficult than is for other people.
—Thomas Merton

A woman writing at a post-office desk was approached by a man whose hand was in a cast. "Pardon me," said the man, "but could you please address this post card for me?" The woman gladly did so, agreeing also to write a short message and sign for him. "There," said the woman, smiling. "Is there anything else I can do for you?" "Yes," the man replied. "At the end could you put, 'P.S.—Please excuse the handwriting?'"
—*Leadership*

W

YOGI BERRA

You got to be careful if you don't know where you're going, because you might not get there. —Yogi Berra

Half this game is ninety percent mental. —Yogi Berra

YOUTH

I'm all for the young taking over and thank God I won't be here when they do. —Arthur Treacher

Youth is a religion from which one always ends up being converted.
—Andre Malraux

There's only one thing wrong with the younger generation: a lot of us don't belong to it any more.
—Bernard Baruch

This month I turned fifty-eight and after all these years I've finally made up my mind what I want to be. I want to be twenty-one. —Ron Dentinger

We knew they were too young to get married when they insisted on going to summer camp for their honeymoon. —Gene Perret

I am not young enough to know everything. —Oscar Wilde

You can only be young once, but you can be immature forever.

Parents often talk about the younger generation as if they didn't have anything to do with it. —*Funny Funny World*

ZOO

In a huff, a woman rushed up to a zoo attendant. "You should see what's going on in the monkey cage!" she exclaimed. "Four chimps are sitting at a table playing cards!" "So what?" answered the attendant, shrugging his shoulders. "They're only playing for peanuts." —*Good Living*